T0397332

Marketing and Gamification

Gamification plays a major role in individual and business decision-making in today's digital era, remarkably changing the way businesses perform basic functions. Gamification techniques can be applied to a variety of marketing activities to help marketers create a more immersive and interactive experience for their customers, by leveraging elements such as points, badges, leaderboards, challenges, quizzes, sweepstakes, and rewards to encourage desired behaviors, foster engagement, and build a sense of community around a brand or product.

In this book, international academicians and researchers will discuss the influence and potential of gamification on marketing management dynamics. This edited collected investigates why the use of gamification in marketing is vital to enhance the customer base and increase revenue, whilst also critically exploring the dark side of gamification and ethical issues. Chapters cover various marketing domains, including tourism marketing, social marketing and sustainable marketing, to provide a comprehensive resource on this emerging area.

This volume will be an essential resource for scholars researching and teaching across marketing, as well as innovation, technology, and business ethics.

Sahil Gupta is Associate Professor at the Jaipuria School of Business, Ghaziabad, Uttar Pradesh, India, and Guest Associate Professor at UCSI University, Kuala Lumpur, Malaysia.

Razia Nagina is Associate Professor at Mittal School of Business, Lovely Professional University, Phagwara, Punjab, India.

Mandakini Paruthi is Assistant Professor at IBS Hyderabad, IFHE University, Hyderabad, Telangana, India.

Gaurav Gupta is Assistant Professor at Amity University, Greater Noida, Uttar Pradesh, India.

Routledge Studies in Marketing

This series welcomes proposals for original research projects that are either single or multi-authored or an edited collection from both established and emerging scholars working on any aspect of marketing theory and practice and provides an outlet for studies dealing with elements of marketing theory, thought, pedagogy and practice.

It aims to reflect the evolving role of marketing and bring together the most innovative work across all aspects of the marketing 'mix' – from product development, consumer behaviour, marketing analysis, branding, and customer relationships, to sustainability, ethics and the new opportunities and challenges presented by digital and online marketing.

9. Storytelling in Marketing and Brand Communications
S M A Moin

10. Marketing and Gamification
Applications, Challenges, and Ethics
Edited by Sahil Gupta, Razia Nagina, Mandakini Paruthi, and Gaurav Gupta

11. Marketing in Developing Nations
Contemporary Developments, Cases and Problems in Africa Asia and the Middle East
Edited by Ayodele C. Oniku

12. Money and Marketing in the Art World
Henrik Hagtvedt

For more information about this series, please visit: www.routledge.com/Routledge-Studies-in-Marketing/book-series/RMKT

Marketing and Gamification

Applications, Challenges, and Ethics

Edited by Sahil Gupta, Razia Nagina, Mandakini Paruthi, and Gaurav Gupta

Routledge
Taylor & Francis Group

LONDON AND NEW YORK

First published 2025
by Routledge
4 Park Square, Milton Park, Abingdon, Oxon OX14 4RN

and by Routledge
605 Third Avenue, New York, NY 10158

Routledge is an imprint of the Taylor & Francis Group, an informa business

British Library Cataloguing-in-Publication Data
A catalogue record for this book is available from
the British Library

Library of Congress Cataloging-in-Publication Data
Names: Gupta, Sahil, editor.
Title: Marketing and gamification : applications, challenges, and
   ethics / edited by Sahil Gupta, Razia Nagina, Mandakini Paruthi,
   and Gaurav Gupta.
Description: Abingdon, Oxon ; New York, NY : Routledge, 2025. |
   Series: Routledge studies in marketing | Includes bibliographical
   references and index.
Identifiers: LCCN 2024027304 (print) | LCCN 2024027305
   (ebook) | ISBN 9781032694177 (hardback) | ISBN 9781032694214
   (paperback) | ISBN 9781032694238 (ebook)
Subjects: LCSH: Marketing. | Gamification.
Classification: LCC HF5415 .M29694 2025 (print) | LCC HF5415
   (ebook) | DDC 658.8—dc23/eng/20240628
LC record available at https://lccn.loc.gov/2024027304
LC ebook record available at https://lccn.loc.gov/2024027305

ISBN: 978-1-032-69417-7 (hbk)
ISBN: 978-1-032-69421-4 (pbk)
ISBN: 978-1-032-69423-8 (ebk)

DOI: 10.4324/9781032694238

Typeset in Sabon
by Apex CoVantage, LLC

Contents

List of Figures and Charts   viii
List of Tables   ix
About the Editors   x
List of Contributors   xi
Foreword   xxii
PRATIK MODI
Preface   xxiv
Acknowledgment   xxix

PART 1
Understanding Gamification from a Marketing
Perspective   1

1 Gamification as a Strategic Move: Redefining Storytelling
   through a Unique Medium   3
   AGUNG PRASETYO WIBOWO, RENI DIAH KUSUMAWATI AND
   VIKAS KUMAR

2 Role of Gamification in Crowdsourcing   24
   GESTY ERNESTIVITA, VIKAS KUMAR AND TIARA NUR ANISAH

PART 2
Gamification as an Influencer for Consumer Behavior
and Engagement   39

3 Gamification as an Influencer for Consumer Behavior
   and Engagement   41
   APARNA TEMBULKAR

4 Effects of Gamification on Brand Engagement of Toy
   Brands: First Cry and Hamleys   57
   SHWETA KATYAL, RUHI LAL AND RAVINDER RENA

5 Gamification and Online Shopping Experience: A Systematic
   Literature Review   81
   RITU YADAV AND CHAND PRAKASH SAINI

PART 3
Gamification and Branding   **101**

6 Impact of Customer Engagement and Brand Love through
   Gamification and Brand Love on Online Travel Agencies (OTAs)   103
   GARIMA MALIK, SUNETRA SAHA AND ARPITA SRIVASTAVA

7 Gamification Stimulates Customer E-Purchase Intention:
   A Conceptual Analysis   121
   JASPREET KAUR AND KAJAL PURI

PART 4
Gamification and Specific Marketing Domains   **141**

8 The Effect of Gamification on Virtual Tourist Experiences in
   the Tourism Industry   143
   ISHANI SHARMA AND ARUN AGGARWAL

9 Role of Gamification in Influencer Marketing: Studying
   the Mediating Role of Utilitarian, Hedonic, and Attitude
   on eWOM   157
   MITHILESH PANDEY, PINNIKA SYAM YADAV AND
   RAJSHEKAR REDDY POTHIREDDY

10 Gamified Communication in Social Media for Brand
    Advocacy of Start-Ups   170
    RADHIKA BAIDYA, DHARMENDRA KUMAR AND DANIEL OMER
    LIVVARCIN

11 Gamification Strategies for Enhancing Sustainability
   Marketing: Engaging Consumers in Eco-Friendly Behaviors   192
   FAIZ AHMAD, MOHD DANISH KIRMANI AND ASADUL HAQUE

12 Ethical Dilemmas in Gamified Marketing Approaches   222
   LIPSA DAS, T.S. POORNACHANDRIKA AND DEEPSHIKHA BHARGAVA

   Index   *246*

Figures and charts

Figures

3.1	Concept map of theoretical models	46
3.2	Word cloud showing higher word frequency for the words "SDT", "TAM", "acceptance", and "Determination"	47
3.3	Word cloud of elements showing badges, points, and leaderboards as words with higher frequency	49
3.4	Word cloud depicting high-frequency words like "Gamification", "Consuming", "Behaviour", and "Engagement"	52
4.1	Conceptual framework	59
5.1	PRISMA technique	83
6.1	Conceptual framework	109
7.1	Theoretical representation of the influence of playfulness on digital shopper behaviour	130
9.1	Conceptual model	161
10.1	Conceptual framework	175
10.2	Theoretical framework	176
11.1	Global gamification market size (in US$ billion)	194
11.2	From market-driven to sustainable marketing – two-dimensional shift	196
11.3	Integration of theories	203
12.1	Positioning diversity in gamification	238

Charts

5.1	Published articles	85
5.2	Country base	85
5.3	Subject area	86

Tables

3.1	Table of Various Game Elements	48
4.1	Research Tool Mapping	62
4.2	Phases of Case Study Analysis	67
4.3	Process of Data Analysis from the Case Study	67
4.4	Framework of Case Study Consideration	68
4.5	Frequency Test Results of the Survey	71
4.6	Comprehensive Results of Correlation Analysis	73
5.1	Citation Base	87
5.2	Relevant Review of Literature	88
6.1	Hypothesis Testing	114
6.2	Structure Model Analysis	114
9.1	Variable Heads' Terminologies	163
9.2	Model Construct	163
9.3	HTMT	164
9.4	Construct Hypothesis	164
10.1	Phases of Case Analysis	177
10.2	Process of Data Analysis from the Case Study	178
10.3	Framework of Case Study Consideration	180
10.4	Gamification Strategies	180
10.5	Social Gratification of Gamified Communication Initiatives	181
10.6	Challenges and Limitations	186

About the Editors

Dr. Sahil Gupta is working as Associate Professor at Jaipuria School of Business, Ghaziabad, Uttar Pradesh, India, and also Guest Associate Professor at UCSI University, Kula Lumpur, Malaysia. He has published his research among top tier journals including A*/A category journals. He has done his doctoral studies in Digital Marketing strategies.

Dr. Razia Nagina is Associate Professor in Mittal School of Business, Lovely Professional University, located in Phagwara, Punjab, India. With over a decade of academic experience, she has exclusively served at Lovely Professional University. She has developed five online courses in Accounting and Business Laws and has published over 20 papers in esteemed indexed journals including Scopus, ABDC, and UGC-CARE. Her research interests span Financial Markets Anomalies, Institutional Investment Behavior, Cointegration of Markets, Financial Reporting, Financial Statement Analysis, and Consumer Behavior.

Mandakini Paruthi, with a PhD in Marketing, is currently serving as Assistant Professor at IBS Hyderabad, IFHE University, Hyderabad, Telangana, India. She is the recipient of Junior Research Fellowship Grant from University Grants Commission and has also cleared National Eligibility Test (NET). Her work-to-date, which has centered on online engagement and consumer brand engagement, has been published in Q1 Journals like *Journal of Internet Commerce*, *Telematics and Informatics*, *Spanish Journal of Marketing*, and many more. Her areas of interest are Consumer Engagement, Social Media-based Brand Communities, and Volatile Consumer Behavior.

Gaurav Gupta is currently Assistant Professor in Marketing at Amity University, Greater Noida, Uttar Pradesh, India. He earned his doctorate and master's in Business Administration degree with a concentration in Marketing from Punjabi University, Patiala, Punjab, India. He also studied marketing at the prestigious Wilkes University, Wilkes-Barre, Pennsylvania, the United States, and is a recipient of Erasmus+, IIM-Bangalore Fellowship(s).

Contributors

Arun Aggarwal
Dr. Arun Aggarwal is Assistant Professor in Chitkara Business School at Chitkara University, Rajpura, Punjab, India. He currently holds prestigious editorial roles, including Senior Editor of Global Business and Organizational Excellence (Wiley) and Editorial Board Member of the *International Journal of Work Innovation*. His prior experience includes a significant tenure as a Senior Research Fellow at the University School of Applied Management, Punjabi University Patiala, Patiala, Punjab, India. Dr. Aggarwal's expertise spans Human Resource Management, Organizational Behavior, Industrial Relations, Labor Laws, and Research Methodology. His guidance in research is noteworthy, having supervised numerous PhD theses. With an impressive publication record, his work is recognized in high-impact journals, cumulating an impact factor over 45. Dr. Aggarwal also contributes significantly to Faculty Development Programs, sharing his knowledge as a resource person across various institutions. His intellectual contributions extend to holding a copyright on the interplay of abusive supervision, organizational commitment, and organizational deviance.

Faiz Ahmad
Dr. Faiz Ahmad is working Assistant Professor in the area of Marketing at Centre for Consumer Research in India, Paari School of Business, SRM University-AP, Andhra Pradesh, India. He is an academician and researcher with a keen focus on digital marketing, social media marketing, and consumer decision-making. He has more than six years of experience in academia and industry. He has qualified UGC-NET in both the subjects of Management and Commerce. He holds a PhD in Management Studies from the University of Hyderabad. His research, particularly on the role of social media in consumer purchase decisions, reflects his commitment to exploring contemporary marketing trends. He has published papers in various renowned journals indexed in ABDC, Scopus, WOS, etc. Driven by a passion for education and research, he continues to make valuable contributions to the academic and business realms.

Radhika Baidya

Radhika Baidya is pursuing PhD in Mass Communication from Amity School of Communication, Amity University, Noida, Uttar Pradesh, India. She received Bachelor of Arts (Economics and Marketing) from University of Delhi, New Delhi. This was followed by Master of Arts (Advertising and Marketing Management) from Amity University, Noida, Uttar Pradesh. She has published research papers and participated in national and international conferences. She has attended a number of seminars, workshops, FDPs, etc. Along with that, she has worked in the industry for more than three years dealing with national and international organizations.

Deepshikha Bhargava

Deepshikha Bhargava is working as Professor in Amity University, Greater Noida, Uttar Pradesh, India. She has also served as Visiting Fellow at Université des Mascareignes (UDM), Ministry of Education and Human Resources, Tertiary Education and Scientific Research, Mauritius. She is also empaneled in PaperVest Press Scientific Advisors, PaperVest University Publisher of Centro Universitário Facvest – UNIFACVEST, Brazil. Recently, she has been included as Reviewer for UGC Fellowship and Research Grant Schemes and NSF Graduate Research Fellowship Program (GRFP) by National Science Foundation (NSF), the United States. Prof. Bhargava also received the awards: "Active Participation Woman Award" and "Best Faculty of the year" under subcategory "Authoring Books on Contemporary Subjects" to name a few. She also awarded by MHRD, Govt. of India in the year 1992 for academic excellence. She is member of UN Online Volunteering; Institute of Engineers (IE); ACM-W; ACM–CSTA; Computer Society of India (CSI); Project Management Institute (PMI), Indian Society of Lightening Engineers (ISLE); and Vigyan Bharti (Vibha) and is Senior Member –IEEE. Overall, four PhDs were completed under her guidance. Her research thrust areas are Artificial Intelligence, Bio-Inspired Computation, and Healthcare Informatics.

Lipsa Das

Lipsa Das is Assistant Professor at the Department of Electronics and Communication Engineering at Amity University with 11 years of teaching experience both online and offline. She has received her B. Tech degree from BPUT, Rourkela, Odisha, India, and received M. Tech degree from IIT Kharagpur, West Bengal, India. Currently, she is pursuing her PhD degree from Amity University, Noida. Her research is situated in the field of Technology and Innovation, with a special focus on VLSI Design, Cloud Services, and the application of IoT, AI, and ML. She has published several research papers in international conferences, has book chapters and copyrights to her credits, and has also published a number of Indian patents. She has reviewed a number of research papers/book chapters for various reputed conferences and edited books. In addition to her teaching experience, she has accomplished many administrative activities.

Gesty Ernestivita

Gesty Ernestivita is Senior Lecturer at Janabadra University, Yogyakarta, Indonesia. She is best known for her work on Marketing and Digital Marketing. She has promoted as the best graduate and received the highest GPA 3.93 out of 4.0 on her doctoral degree in Marketing Management at STIESIA Surabaya, Indonesia. Her teaching passions are in Marketing, Digital Marketing, E-Commerce, International Business, and Investment and Portfolio Management. She has published more than 100 articles/ research papers in a wide range of marketing management journals indexed with Scopus, SINTA, Copernicus and so on. She received the Best Paper Award in some international conferences like CSR, ICOBUSS, and ICPMI. She has already published three ISBN books. She has also organized workshops in the scope of marketing for SMEs. She is on the panels of Scopus and ABDC indexed journals as reviewer.

Asadul Haque

Dr. Asadul Haque is currently working as Assistant Professor at Centre for Consumer Research in India, Paari School of Business, SRM University-AP since October 2021. He has more than seven years of teaching experience having previously worked at Amity University, Lucknow, Uttar Pradesh, India, and AMU Kishanganj Centre. His teaching interests include Integrated Marketing Communication, Marketing Strategies, and Services Marketing. His research interests include Online Consumer Behavior, Young Consumers, and Branding Practices. Dr Asad has completed his PhD in Business Administration from Aligarh Muslim University with a specialization in Marketing. He has research publications in several Scopus and ABDC (1 A, 1 B, and 2 C) listed journals. He also has a corporate experience of about two and a half years. Before joining academics, he has previously worked at State Bank of India (as Deputy Manager) and Bharti Airtel (as Territory Sales Manager) after completing his MBA from Jamia Millia Islamia, New Delhi, India. His hobbies include playing sudoku and watching football.

Shweta Katyal

Shweta Katyal is pursuing her PhD in Mass Communication from Amity School of Communication, Amity University, Noida, Uttar Pradesh. She received Bachelor of Arts (Journalism and Mass Communication) from Guru Jambheshwar University of Science and Technology, Hisar, Haryana, India. This was followed by obtaining Master of Arts (Journalism and Mass Communication) from Amity University, Noida, Uttar Pradesh. She has published research papers and participated in national and international conferences. She has attended a number of seminars, workshops, FDPs, etc.

Jaspreet Kaur

Dr. Jaspreet Kaur is working as Assistant Professor in P.G. Department of Commerce and Management, Hans Raj Mahila Maha Vidyalaya, Jalandhar, Punjab, India. She is known for her work in the field of finance. She has qualified UGC-NET and received her doctoral degree in the area of "Equity Decision Making and Investor Protection: A Study of Punjab" on a JRF basis. She has published more than ten research papers in a wide range of leading management and business journals including *International Journal of Law and Management* and many more renowned journals indexed with Scopus, WOS, etc. She has coauthored two chapters for CRC Press, Taylor & Francis Group, and more than ten papers in edited books. She has been awarded Second Best Research Paper General Management Track for the paper presentation in the International Entrepreneurship Summit "Avlokan 2.0" 2022. She has acted as a resource person in Faculty Enrichment Program on the topic "Online tools for Research Management" held at Hans Raj Mahila Maha Vidyalaya.

Mohd Danish Kirmani

Dr. Mohd Danish Kirmani is working as Assistant Professor in Centre for Consumer Research in India, Paari School of Business, SRM University. He has around seven years of teaching experience. His research interests are Online Consumer Behavior and Sustainable and Responsible Consumption. He has research papers published in various journals ranked by ABDC such as *Journal of Retailing and Consumer Services*, *Food Quality and Preference*, and *Journal of Global Scholars of Marketing Science* among others.

Dharmendra Kumar

Dr. Dharmendra Kumar, Professor and Head Assessment and Examination at Amity School of Communication, Amity University, Noida, Uttar Pradesh, holds an industry experience of more than 2 years in print industry and 18 years of academic experience in teaching. He has received his PhD in Mass Communication from Kurukshetra University, Haryana. He also has Arena Multimedia Specialist Diploma from Arena Multimedia. His areas of specialization are Graphics/Web Design, Animation, Audio/Video Editing, and Visual Effects. He was awarded as best faculty at Arena Multimedia and also won first prize in 3D animation. He presented many research papers in national and international conferences and also has to his credit published research papers in Scopus, UGC Care, and in peer-reviewed national and international journals. He also has organized conferences, workshops, and FDPs.

Vikas Kumar

Dr. Vikas Kumar is serving at the Central University of Haryana, Jant-Pali, Mahendergarh, India, and is Visiting Professor at the Indian Institute of Management, Indore, Madhya Pradesh, India, and University of Northern Iowa, Cedar Falls, Iowa, the United States. Dr. Kumar is also President of "Society For Education and Research Development". Vikas Kumar received his MSc in Electronics from Kurukshetra University, Haryana,

India. This was followed by an MSc in Computer Science and further PhD from the same university. He also did his MBA in the area of Information Systems and Operations Management. His PhD work was in collaboration with CEERI, Pilani, Rajasthan, India, and he has worked in a number of ISRO-sponsored projects. He is a life member of Indian Science Congress Association, Computer Society of India, IETE, ICEIE, IPA, VEDA, IVS, and Magnetic Society of India. Dr. Kumar has designed and conducted a number of training programs for the corporate sector and is a trainer for a number of Govt. of India departments. Along with 15 books, he has more than 100 research papers to his credit in various national and international conferences and journals. Out of which, 93 are with the Scopus-indexed journals. He was the editor of International Quarterly Refereed Journal *Asia-Pacific Business Review* during June 2007 to June 2009. He is a regular reviewer for a number of international journals and is on panel of examiners on a number of government universities for UG/PG and doctoral programs. He has visited Sweden, France, Hungary, Austria, the Netherlands, Germany, China, Japan, Thailand, Indonesia, Malaysia, Algeria, Uganda, the United States, Ethiopia, Slovenia, the UAE, and Jordan on sponsored research projects. The specific areas of his interest include Business Intelligence, e-Business, Social Media Analytics, and Web Analytics.

Reni Diah Kusumawati
Department of Management, Lecturer at Gunadarma University, Indonesia.
Dr. Reni Diah Kusumawati holds the position of Secretary in the Doctoral program of Technology Industry at Universitas Gunadarma. In her role as a lecturer, she imparts knowledge across a spectrum of subjects, including Marketing, Introduction to Information System Accounting Technology, Organizational Behaviour, and Marketing.

Dr. Kusumawati is currently a candidate for the position of Associate Professor in the applied field of Economics Management. She is widely recognized for her significant contributions to the field of Economics Management Science. She has successfully completed her doctoral degree in Economics, focusing particularly on the specialized area of "Consumer Behaviour and Marketing".

Ruhi Lal
Dr. Ruhi Lal is a highly skilled advertising professional, academician, researcher, and author, presently working as Professor at Manav Rachna International Institute of Research and Studies, Haryana, India. She is a D.Litt. from VBU and holds a PhD in Mass Communication. She is a recipient of Best Media Educator of the Year 2021 in Advertising Research by MFI, India. She received the 5th Gyan Shree National Award for promoting talents in Hindi Literature from Savitri Foundations. She received "Vishist Sewa Samman" from BJP Delhi for delivering services

to especially abled people in December 2021. She has 22 years of work experience, with a blend of 8 years of industry and 17 years of teaching and research experience at Amity School of Communication. Dr. Lal has 148 research contributions including 13 books, 4 patents, and 52 research papers published (7 – Scopus, 2 – Web of Science, 35 – UGC-Care listed journals, 8 peer-reviewed journals), 30 case studies, 34 research papers presented in conferences, and 15 book chapters. She also has eight funded research projects – three MHRD projects, two MGNCRE, one Radio Amity with DAVP and SMART NGO, one Amity MOOC Project, and one corporate project.

Daniel Omer Livvarcin

Dr. Daniel Omer Livvarcin is working as part-time Professor in Telfer School of Management, University of Ottawa, Canada; he is also Chief Executive Officer, Vectors Group, Canada. He is a renowned expert in the nonprofit sector, known for developing tools like the ViStA Strategic Management Framework and the Executive Strategic Evaluation Process. He is also Founder of the Nonprofit Management Laboratory. With a PhD and dual master's degrees, he has assisted numerous organizations, including Tim Hortons Foundation, Kagita Mikam, Wequedong Lodge, and Ottawa Food Bank. Dr. Livvarcin is passionate about empowering marginalized groups, advocating for women's rights, and promoting education for underrepresented communities. He actively participates in initiatives aimed at ensuring equitable opportunities and recognition for these groups, demonstrating his dedication to creating a world that values respect and uplifts everyone.

Garima Malik

Dr. Garima Malik is Doctoral Scholar of Marketing at Xavier School of Management, XLRI Jamshedpur, Jharkhand, India. She has more than 18 years of academic experience. She is also associated with BIMTECH, Greater Noida, Uttar Pradesh, India, as Assistant Professor in the Department of Marketing. Her areas of research include Gamification, Marketing Analytics, Customer Engagement, and Customer Relationship Management. Her research papers are published in various leading journals such as *International Journal of Bank Marketing, Tourism Analysis, Journal of Event Management, Information Technology & Tourism, International Journal of Healthcare Management, Journal of Global Marketing, Innovative Marketing, Pacific Asia Journal of the Association for Information Systems, Journal of Science and Technology Policy Management*, among others.

Tiara Nur Anisah

Tiara Nur Anisah is Junior Lecturer at the Faculty of Economics and Business at Janabadra University, Yogyakarta, Indonesia. She earned her master's degree from STIE YKPN, Yogyakarta, Indonesia. As a dedicated academic, Tiara has been active in publishing research articles in national and international journals, as well as presenting her research results in leading conference proceedings in the field of consumer behavior and market trends. Her main focus is on green and sustainable practices. Alongside her academic career, Tiara is also a YouTube content creator, providing beauty tips and sharing her passion for her work with the public through the platform. With a burning passion, Tiara not only seeks new knowledge but also shares inspiration with others through various communication channels available.

Mithilesh Pandey

Dr. Mithilesh Pandey is Assistant Professor at ICFAI Business School, IFHE University, Hyderabad, Telangana, India. He has obtained his MBA (Marketing), MPhil (Management), and PhD (Management) degrees. He has published books, chapters in edited books, and research papers in reputed journals. He is also a reviewer and editor of highly regarded journals. His areas of research interest include Social Marketing, Social Finance, and Technology Intervention. He has also been engaged in case writing and has published cases with "Emerald", "Case Center", and "ET cases". He has received the "Special Mention Case Award" at 7th PAN-IIM conference.

T.S. Poornachandrika

Dr. T.S. Poornachandrika is working as Associate Professor in CBIT-School of Management Studies, CBIT, Hyderabad, Telangana, India. She is a senior academician having an overall experience of 24 years in teaching and 2 years in the industry. She has completed her MBA with dual specializations (HRM and Marketing), has earned MPhil in HRM, and has acquired her doctoral degree in the area of HR Outsourcing. She has been teaching HRM, Marketing, and General Management subjects for over two decades. She has published more than 50 articles/research papers in a wide range of leading management journals. She has also organized Faculty Development Program in (association with AIMS) and Management Development Programs (MDPs) and has facilitated various management workshops. She is acting as a reviewer and is also on the advisory board of a leading digital marketing firm.

Rajshekar Reddy Pothireddy

Dr. Rajshekar Reddy Pothireddy is Assistant Professor at IBS Hyderabad, IFHE University, Hyderabad, Telangana, India. He has obtained his MBA and PhD (Management) from Lovely Professional University, India. Dr Pothireddy's research interests are in Social Media Marketing, and he has published several research papers in reputed journals.

Kajal Puri

Dr. Kajal Puri is working as Assistant Professor at P.G. Department of Commerce and Management, Hans Raj Mahila Maha Vidyalaya, Jalandhar, Punjab, India. She is a meticulous professional possessing affluent teaching experience of over 17 years. As far as her academic excellence is concerned, she has obtained PhD, MCom, MPhil, and PGDBM and is UGC-NET qualified. She has coauthored four books pertaining to the area of Commerce and Management. She has published six research papers in reputed journals and four papers in edited books. Her research papers have been published in reputed journals like *Journal of Critical Reviews*, indexed with Scopus, *International Journal of Management Technology and Engineering*, *Kala Sarovar*, *Vidyabharti International Interdisciplinary Research Journal*, all of which are UGC approved. Her paper has been awarded best paper in management category at KCLIMT in International Conference 2019. She has been certified by MINDLER and Career Development Alliance, the United States, for the completion of International Certified Career Coach Program (foundation and advance level).

Ravinder Rena

Prof. (Dr.) Ravinder Rena is Professor of Economics at DUT Business School, Faculty of Management Sciences, Durban University of Technology (DUT), Durban, South Africa, and Adjunct Professor of Economics for Master's and Doctorate Programs at Monarch Business School, Hagendorn, Switzerland. He holds an experience of 30 years in academics. He was IIU's Honorary Country Director for South Africa and Visiting Professor at Sri Sri University, Cuttack, Odisha, India, and Sparsh Global Business School, Greater Noida, Uttar Pradesh, India. Dr. Rena received the PhD Gold Medal from Hyderabad's Osmania University; his MA, BEd, MPhil, PhD from Osmania University; and BA and LLB from Kakatiya University, Warangal. The 2022 Durban University of Technology Best Researcher Award, the 2011 Namibia University of Science and Technology Best Researcher Award, and the 2012 American Biographic Institute Award – Man of the Year are among his honors. Prof. Rena has written 150 peer-reviewed articles, ten books, and 60 papers at national and international seminars. In South Africa, India, and Brazil, he consults for BRICS research forums/international conferences and visits over 300 colleges and institutions. Prof. Rena founded Inderscience's *International Journal of Education Economics and Development* (IJEED) and is Associate Editor of Emerald's Scopus-indexed *The Bottom Line*. Over 200 national and international conferences in Europe, America, Africa, and Asia have been his keynotes.

Sunetra Saha

Dr. Sunetra Saha is distinguished Assistant Professor, Amity Business School, Noida, specializing in Marketing, bringing a wealth of expertise and experience to the academic arena. With a robust educational foundation including a PhD in Management from Amity University and an MBA in Marketing Management and a BCom (Hons) from Calcutta University,

Dr. Saha has dedicated an impressive 17 years to shaping the minds of future professionals. For the past 14 years, she has been a key member of the faculty at Amity Business School, Noida, where she currently serves as Course Coordinator for Digital Marketing and Marketing Strategies. Dr. Saha's proactive leadership is evident through her roles as Faculty Coordinator of the Marketing Club and Mentoring Program Coordinator at the university level. Her research contributions include several publications in Scopus-indexed journals, ABDC-indexed journals, and in reputable peer-reviewed publications. Beyond academia, she extends her influence as a certified trainer under RASCI, conducting impactful sessions on marketing for TATA Motors employees and the Directorate General of Resettlement. Dr. Saha's dedication to education and research positions her as a respected figure in the field of marketing.

Chand Prakash Saini

Dr. Chand Prakash Saini is Faculty in Marketing, Digital Marketing, Retail Management and Consumer Behavior as Assistant Professor (Selection Grade), School of Management and Liberal Studies, The NorthCap University, Gurugram, Haryana, India. Dr. Saini holds more than 14 years of experience in teaching, research, and academia. He holds a master's degree in management and commerce and has qualified UGC-NET in both disciplines and has received the Junior Research Fellowship in Management award. Dr. Saini has authored and coauthored more than 30 research papers, including ABDC, UGC-Care, Scopus, and Web of Science-listed journals and has presented his research at more than 50 conferences of national and international reputation, including IITs and IIMs, and has been awarded best research paper awards. He, with his name, has five cases published at Case Centre UK. Dr. Saini has guided four research scholars to complete their research journey in their doctoral program. Dr. Saini has been the editor of the book published by CRC Press and successfully edited a special issue on "Integration of analytics, optimization, and marketing for the growth of businesses in emerging economies" for *Transnational Marketing Journal*, published by Transnational Press London, indexed in Scopus. He has attended and conducted various seminars, workshops, and development programs in his field. He has chaired technical sessions in the international conferences of his domain and is a reviewer to journals under Inderscience and IGI Global. Dr. Saini has been invited to various places for expert lectures in research and in his domain.

Ishani Sharma

Ms. Ishani Sharma is currently pursuing her PhD in Tourism at Chitkara Business School, Chitkara University, located in Punjab, India. Specializing in the intricate fields of Bibliometric Analysis and Structural Equation Modeling, Ishani has emerged as a dynamic contributor to the academic sphere. Her research is characterized by a deep commitment to enhancing the understanding and development of the tourism industry through the application of rigorous analytical techniques. Her work not only furthers academic knowledge but also offers practical insights for the industry. Passionate about fostering collaboration and driving innovation, Ishani is open to inquiries and partnerships. Her endeavors in the field of tourism research are aimed at making a substantial and meaningful impact, both in academia and in the wider industry.

Arpita Srivastava

Dr. Arpita Srivastava is currently serving as Professor at GL Bajaj Institute of Management and Research, Greater Noida, Uttar Pradesh, India. She is a seasoned professional with a cumulative work experience of 22 years, featuring a noteworthy corporate tenure of seven years dedicated to Marketing, Product, and Brand Management in well-renowned companies like Dr Reddy's Lab, Panacea Biotech, and Win Medicare. Dr. Arpita brings a wealth of knowledge and expertise to the academic realm. Her research focus spans diverse areas such as Consumer Behavior, Brand Management, Artificial Intelligence, Gamification and Sustainability, showcasing a broad and multidimensional understanding of contemporary marketing dynamics. Dr. Arpita has significantly contributed to the academic discourse with the publication of over 30 papers in reputable journals indexed by ABDC and Scopus. Demonstrating a passion for advancing the field of marketing, Dr. Arpita actively explores new avenues and methodologies. Her commitment to staying at the forefront of her field is evident in her consistent achievements, including being the top performer in NPTEL courses on Integrated Marketing Communication (IMC) and Product and Brand Management for the past two years. Beyond her academic pursuits, Dr. Arpita has played a pivotal role in the professional development of individuals and organizations through the execution of Management Development Programs (MDPs). Her expertise has been shared with notable entities such as Anmol Industries, KRIBHCO, Haier, and Agarwal Movers and Packers, where she has conducted impactful programs. Dr. Arpita Srivastava's multifaceted career is marked by a blend of academic rigor, industry acumen, and a genuine enthusiasm for pushing the boundaries of marketing knowledge. Her contributions, both in the classroom and through research, underscore her commitment to shaping the future of marketing and business.

Aparna Tembulkar

Director. Indian Institute of Cost and Management STudies and Research (IndSearch) University of Pune. Pune, Maharashtra, India Dr. Aparna Tembulkar obtained her PhD (Marketing Management), Master of Management Science (Marketing) from the Savitribai Phule Pune University. She has also completed her bachelor's in Social Studies and diploma in Electronics and Radio Engineering. Dr. Aparna has a teaching and research experience of 18 years and has earlier worked in the industry for 13 years. She is currently the Executive Editor of the newsletter of the Association of Management Development Institutions in South Asia (AMDISA), a SAARC-recognized body. She has conducted several management development programs as well as undertaken consultancy for the corporate sector. She has authored three text books on marketing management and published several research papers in national and international journals.

Agung Prasetyo Wibowo

Dr. Agung Prasetyo Wibowo serves as Vice Dean of Student Affairs in the Faculty of Letters and Culture, Department of Literature, Gunadarma University, Indonesia. He is widely recognized for his contributions to Information Technology in Literature and Linguistics. He holds certification as a translator and has successfully completed a doctoral degree in Linguistics, with a particular focus on the field of "video game localization". He is a candidate for the position of Associate Professor in the area of Applied Linguistics. He is Lecturer, imparting knowledge on subjects such as audiovisual translation, computer-assisted translation, pop culture, and technology information in literature. Moreover, he has authored numerous articles and research papers, presenting his work as a speaker at various conferences covering a broad spectrum of topics. Dr. Wibowo is an esteemed reviewer for journals indexed by Scopus.

Pinnika Syam Yadav

Dr. Pinnika Syam Yadav is Assistant Professor at Mittal School of Business, Lovely Professional University, Phagwara, Punjab, India. He has done his MBA and PhD and is actively engaged in research. His PhD is in the area of social media marketing focused on influencers. He has published research papers in reputed journals.

Ritu Yadav

Dr. Ritu Yadav is Assistant Professor in Department of Management, Gurugram University, Gurugram, Haryana, India. Dr. Yadav holds more than five years of experience in teaching, research, and academia. She has obtained her doctorate degree in management field on the topic "Determinants of Employer Branding and Its Impact on Employer Attractiveness in Banking Sector" from Institute of Management Studies and Research (IMSAR), Maharishi Dayanand University, Rohtak, Haryana. She holds a master's degree in the field of management as well as commerce and has qualified UGC-NET with JRF in management and commerce. She has authored and coauthored more than 25 research papers in renowned journals indexed with ABDC, Scopus, WOS, etc. She has presented more than 20 research papers in national and international conferences.

Foreword

In an era where digital transformation dictates the tempo of market dynamics, the convergence of marketing and gamification emerges as a compelling narrative that reshapes the landscape of consumer engagement and brand loyalty. It is within this transformative backdrop that *Marketing and Gamification* makes its timely entrance, a pioneering text that navigates the intricate interplay between marketing strategies and gamification techniques.

Crafted by a distinguished quartet of editors – Dr. Sahil Gupta, Dr. Razia Nagina, Dr. Mandakini Paruthi, and Dr. Gaurav Gupta – this book documents the collective wisdom gleaned from diverse academic and professional vistas. Each editor brings a wealth of knowledge and a unique perspective to the discourse, setting the stage for a comprehensive exploration of gamification's multifaceted role in marketing.

The book examines the essence of gamification, not merely as a technological gimmick but as a profound cultural and societal shift that enhances the experiential aspect of consumer interactions. By examining gamification through a marketing lens, the editors and contributors illuminate its capacity to transform ordinary customer experiences into engaging, game-like journeys that foster brand loyalty, enhance customer engagement, and drive unprecedented sales growth.

Marketing and Gamification is structured to provide readers with a holistic understanding of gamification's impact across various marketing domains. From its strategic use in crowdsourcing to its predictive power in consumer engagement, the text presents an array of empirical and conceptual research that evidences gamification's potency as a marketing tool. Notably, the book does not shy away from the darker facets of gamification, offering critical insights into the ethical dilemmas and potential adverse effects on mental and emotional well-being.

What sets this book apart is its interdisciplinary approach, appealing to a broad spectrum of readers from academia to industry practitioners. It serves as an invaluable resource for businesses seeking innovative strategies to captivate and retain customers, for academics aiming to further the research frontier in consumer behavior, and for marketing professionals strategizing to enhance brand visibility and equity.

I am honored to introduce this book to readers, confident in its potential to enrich our understanding of marketing in the digital age. In its pages lies not just academic discourse but also a vision for the future of marketing – a future where engagement, enjoyment, and experiential value are paramount.

Welcome to the journey through *Marketing and Gamification*. Prepare to be inspired, challenged, and transformed.

Pratik Modi
Dean – School of Management, BML Munjal University,
Gurgaon, Haryana, India
Professor of Marketing (on Lien), Institute of Rural
Management Anand, Gujarat, India

Preface

In today's rapidly evolving digital landscape, where consumer engagement and brand loyalty are paramount, the integration of gamification into marketing strategies has emerged as a transformative force. As Roy and Jain (2022) aptly emphasize, gamification has transcended a mere entertainment value to become an integral component of business dynamics worldwide. Its pervasive influence spans industries, from corporate management to education, from wellness initiatives to professional training and development. With its roots firmly planted in the realms of psychology, technology, and design, gamification stands as a multifaceted tool reshaping how businesses interact with their customers.

Defined as the strategic infusion of game mechanics, aesthetics, and design principles into marketing endeavors, gamification offers a compelling avenue to engage and motivate customers, foster brand loyalty, and ultimately drive sales. As scholars such as Xi and Hamari (2019) elucidate, gamification encompasses a spectrum of experiential elements designed to evoke emotions, spur creativity, and cultivate engagement. The researchers provide a comprehensive definition, stating that gamification involves "technological, economic, cultural, and societal developments in which reality is becoming more gameful, and thus to a greater extent can afford the accruing of skills, motivational benefits, creativity, playfulness, engagement, and overall positive growth and happiness". By deploying techniques like points, badges, leaderboards, challenges, and rewards, marketers can craft immersive experiences that resonate deeply with their target audience, fostering a sense of community and connection around their brand (Chou, 2019). Moreover, the data and insights gleaned from gamified interactions furnish marketers with invaluable tools to refine their products, optimize campaigns, and enhance overall customer experiences (Yang et al., 2017). Thus, the adoption of gamification as a marketing strategy represents not just a trend but also a fundamental shift in how businesses engage with their clientele, underscored by its demonstrable impact on brand engagement and equity.

In this book, academics and researchers will thoroughly explore the intricate impact of gamification on marketing management dynamics, examining its nuanced effects, including those darker aspects often overlooked. These conversations are essential as they probe into the ethical challenges and the influence of gamification on branding. With a global perspective, the book will span various marketing domains, showcasing practices and insights from diverse sectors. As a pioneering effort in its field, this book aims to comprehensively assess gamification's adoption across marketing landscapes, measuring its impact on consumer engagement, brand equity, and financial outcomes. Drawing from contributions of esteemed scholars and practitioners worldwide, this volume endeavors to bridge existing gaps in social sciences literature, providing a holistic and empirically grounded examination of gamification's role in contemporary marketing management.

The first chapter, "Gamification as a Strategic Move: Redefining Storytelling through a Unique Medium", authored by Agung Prasetyo Wibowo, Reni Diah Kusumawati, and Vikas Kumar, explores the narrative aspects of video games using the case study of Until Dawn. Through qualitative analysis, the chapter examines how video games reshape traditional storytelling by incorporating narrative-limiting factors. It highlights the significance of character deaths and separate plotlines in creating engaging narrative experiences. Moreover, the chapter explores the impact of player choices on the storyline, fostering a deeper emotional connection and active involvement in crafting tales. This chapter offers insights into the transformative effects of video game storytelling on traditional narrative forms.

The second chapter, "Role of Gamification in Crowdsourcing", authored by Gesty Ernestivita, Vikas Kumar, and Tiara Nur Anisah, explores how gamification enhances motivation, collaboration, and innovation in crowdsourcing. It analyzes the integration of game elements to engage participants and emphasizes fostering cooperation. The chapter also discusses the motivational impact of rewards and anticipates future advancements, while addressing ethical considerations. It highlights the sense of belonging among participants and the importance of feedback loops for continuous improvement.

The third chapter, "Gamification as an Influencer for Consumer Behaviour and Engagement", authored by Dr. Aparna Tembulkar, explores the use of gaming elements in marketing to attract and retain consumers. The chapter analyzes the concept of gamification and its origins in marketing initiatives like rewards programs. Through a content analysis of research articles, it examines the impact of gamification on consumer behavior, focusing on its role in marketing, increasing consumer engagement, and influencing purchasing decisions. Additionally, the chapter discusses various marketing theories relevant to gamification, providing valuable insights into its implications for consumer behavior and engagement.

The fourth chapter, "Effects of Gamification on Brand Engagement of Toy Brands: First Cry and Hamleys", authored by Katyal et al., explores how gamification impacts brand engagement for "First Cry" and "Hamleys". Using mixed methods, the research examines gamification's effectiveness in increasing consumer engagement, retention, involvement, and brand satisfaction. The study identifies essential factors for successful gamification implementation, offering insights for marketers to enhance brand equity and loyalty. Additionally, the chapter discusses limitations, suggestions, and future research directions, contributing to understanding gamification's role in brand outcomes.

The fifth chapter, "Gamification and Online Shopping Experience: A Systematic Literature Review", by Dr. Ritu Yadav and Dr. Chand Prakash, provides a comprehensive overview of research on integrating gamification elements into online shopping platforms. Following the PRISMA approach, the review identifies five key themes: Customer Engagement, Brand Loyalty, Co-creation, Enjoyment, and Retailer Support. This review offers valuable insights for understanding the impact of gamification on user behavior and satisfaction in online shopping.

The sixth chapter, "Impact of Gamification on OTA Customer Engagement and Brand Love", by Malik et al. delves into how gamification influences customer engagement and brand loyalty in Online Travel Agencies (OTAs). Gamification enhances engagement by encouraging active participation and tapping into motivations like competition and social connection. Using a mixed-methods approach, the study finds that gamified interactions on OTAs lead to positive emotions and brand loyalty, fostering advocacy and willingness to pay higher prices. Overall, the study highlights gamification's power to strengthen the emotional bond between customers and OTAs, offering strategic insights for OTA managers and marketers amid digital innovation in the travel industry.

The seventh chapter, "Gamification Stimulates E-Purchase Intent: A Conceptual Analysis", by Dr. Jaspreet Kaur and Dr. Kajal Puri examines how gamification boosts customer engagement in online shopping. Amid the COVID-19 pandemic, e-marketers use gamification, offering rewards and milestones, to motivate consumers. Guided by the Stimulus-Organism-Response Model, gamification influences emotional affect, driving purchasing decisions. This highlights gamification's role as an impulse, fostering loyalty and satisfaction for corporate entities, thus emphasizing its significance in shaping modern e-commerce strategies.

The eighth chapter, "Gamification's Impact on VR Tourism", by Ishani Sharma and Arun Aggarwal, explores how gamification addresses challenges of VR-induced fatigue in the tourism industry. VR offers immersive experiences but can cause exhaustion. Gamification, integrating game elements, enhances engagement and satisfaction. The chapter assesses VR, gamification, and tourist satisfaction, highlighting research gaps and future directions.

It stresses contextually relevant gamification strategies for captivating VR tourism experiences, emphasizing the need for a meticulous research to fully leverage gamification's potential.

The ninth chapter, "Gamification's Role in Influencer Marketing", by Dr. Pinnika Syam Yadav and Dr. Mithilesh Pandey, investigates the influence of gamification on influencer traits, platform usage intentions, and electronic word-of-mouth (eWOM). Through a questionnaire administered to 252 social media users engaged in gamified events by influencers, the study employs structural equation modeling for analysis. Results indicate that gamification significantly impacts continuous platform usage intentions and eWOM, driven by both utilitarian and hedonic aspects. Attitudes also play a substantial role, influencing both user intentions and eWOM. This chapter enhances the understanding of gamification's role in influencer marketing, elucidating its impact on online shopping behavior among social media users.

The tenth chapter, "Gamified Communication in Social Media for Brand Advocacy of Start-Ups", by Baidya et al., explores the effectiveness of gamified communication strategies in fostering brand advocacy for start-up firms in social media marketing. The study investigates the deployment of gamified communication techniques, such as interactive email campaigns, quizzes, and challenges, to engage customers and promote brand advocacy. Through qualitative insights from start-up case studies and observational notes on social media platforms, the research identifies key factors contributing to successful brand advocacy through gamified communication. This study enhances the understanding of consumer engagement and advocacy in social marketing, providing practical insights for marketers to develop effective loyalty programs and deepen relationships with consumers in the digital era.

The eleventh chapter, "Gamification Strategies for Enhancing Sustainability Marketing: Engaging Consumers in Eco-Friendly Behaviors", authored by Ahmad et al., explores how gaming techniques can promote environmentally friendly consumer behavior. It examines the application of game theory to sustainable marketing, offering insights into effective strategies for encouraging practices like recycling and energy conservation. Additionally, the chapter discusses challenges and ethical considerations while emphasizing the potential of games to advance sustainability goals and foster environmental consciousness.

The twelfth chapter, "Ethical Dilemmas in Gamified Marketing Approaches", authored by Lipsa Das and Dr. T.S. Poornachandrika, scrutinizes the ethical challenges arising from the use of gamified approaches in marketing. It provides a comprehensive framework for assessing the ethical implications of gamification, considering factors such as workers' rights, autonomy, and potential harm to individuals. Drawing on various ethical perspectives, the chapter offers insights into potential regulations and emphasizes the importance of ethical considerations in the evolving landscape of gamified marketing techniques.

We sincerely hope that this edited volume will offer valuable insights into the diverse marketing strategies employed by marketers worldwide. Intended for researchers, students, practitioners, policymakers, and anyone intrigued by consumer behavior, these chapters aim to spark discussions, critiques, and advancements in our comprehension of the intersection between gamified marketing approaches and ethics. As a comprehensive academic reference, this book will benefit researchers and academicians alike, while also serving as a practical guide for practitioners navigating the evolving landscape of ethical considerations in gamified marketing techniques.

Sahil Gupta
Razia Nagina
Mandakini Paruthi
Gaurav Gupta

References

Chou, Y. K. (2019). *Actionable gamification: Beyond points, badges, and leaderboards*. Packt Publishing Ltd.

Roy, G., & Jain, V. (2022). Role of artificial intelligence in gamification for the emerging markets. In *Management and information technology in the digital era: Challenges and perspectives* (pp. 9–25). Emerald Publishing Limited.

Xi, N., & Hamari, J. (2019). Does gamification satisfy needs? A study on the relationship between gamification features and intrinsic need satisfaction. *International Journal of Information Management*, 46, 210–221.

Yang, Y., Asaad, Y., & Dwivedi, Y. (2017). Examining the impact of gamification on intention of engagement and brand attitude in the marketing context. *Computers in Human Behavior*, 73, 459–469.

Acknowledgment

The stalwart involvement of intellectuals across academia and industry has made this masterpiece of academic reference possible. First and foremost, we would like to express our deepest gratitude to all the persons and groups of individuals who have contributed to this book and have sustained us in all aspects.

We will fail in our attempt if we are not thankful enough to Routledge and their administrative and editorial staff for giving us this magnificent opportunity to serve as editors for this academic project – special thanks to the reviewers for providing us with worthy inputs and adding value to our book. We are also grateful to all the authors and contributors for reposing their confidence in us, sending their original research works and working as per the deadlines specified. We are thankful to the reviewers from academia and industry who helped us in providing their valuable suggestions and helped us complete this project effectively.

Finally, a lovely mention goes to our parents, family members, and friends for the time stolen out of their share and, last but not least, the Almighty, who has shown us the right direction and provided us with great zeal and enthusiasm to complete this project.

Dr Sahil Gupta
Dr Razia Nagina
Dr Mandakini Paruthi
Dr Gaurav Gupta

Part 1

Understanding Gamification from a Marketing Perspective

Chapter 1

Gamification as a Strategic Move
Redefining Storytelling through a
Unique Medium

*Agung Prasetyo Wibowo, Reni Diah Kusumawati
and Vikas Kumar*

Introduction

One of the most significant changes to the narrative structure occurred with the debut of video games. The advent of video games signifies a major paradigm change in the ever-changing landscape for storytelling. Video games have evolved into an enchanting blend of player agency and narrative skill in an age when digital entertainment is constantly changing the way we engage with stories (Murray, 1997). This fusion has birthed a narrative experience unlike any other – a canvas where players no longer remain passive observers but rather dynamic architects of the unfolding tales. As we traverse this ever-evolving terrain of digital entertainment, video games rise as a potent and captivating medium, their very essence bridging the chasm between interactive gameplay and the art of storytelling (Jenkins, 2004). Within this realm, a new landscape of narrative engagement is forged, one that challenges the very foundations of traditional storytelling conventions. What emerges is a dynamic, immersive experience that grants players a hitherto-unseen degree of agency – an agency that transmutes them from being mere spectators into coauthors of the stories they partake in.

The symphony of traditional storytelling has witnessed a profound alteration with the advent of video games, but this transformation extends much beyond technological evolution. It delves deep into the fabric of human interaction with narratives, reshaping the very contours of how we perceive and engage with stories. As players traverse the digital realms of these interactive narratives, they embark on journeys that intertwine the tapestries of intricate storytelling with the thrill of active participation (Aarseth, 1997). In this age, where technology and narrative unite in unprecedented ways, the interplay of interactive gameplay and intricate storytelling is not just a merger; it is a metamorphosis. The user's text is empty. This progression not only encourages players to engage with tales in new and unique ways but also requires them to actively influence and integrate their choices and actions into the core structure of the story. The concept of agency becomes palpable, as the

DOI: 10.4324/9781032694238-2

developing storylines transcend mere written narratives and transform into collective experiences that evolve in response to the player's choices and actions.

In the present age of digital innovation, when storytelling is evolving into an interactive creative medium, video games create a separate position that challenges traditional means of transmitting narratives (Kumar & Mittal, 2020). This is because video games can communicate stories in a narrative-based format. Gamers surpass the aim of being loyal spectators and the constraints of sequential narrative. Players have a significant part in creating their own stories, utilizing their freedom as the main driving force in shaping the fictional world. Video games have brought about a big change in storytelling since they have removed the traditional boundaries that previously separated the player from the tale. This has resulted in a substantial departure from the traditional approach. The resurgence of interest in participation subsequently results in the production of tales that make use of frameworks that are both imaginative and thrilling. An extremely energizing advancement is represented by this.

This event is in agreement with the narrative theory frameworks proposed by Murray (1997), well-known for promoting the concept of agency via the use of interactive storytelling. In the course of his discussion on current digital storytelling, Murray emphasizes the relevance of player involvement and the removal of barriers that stand between the artist and the audience. The research of Espen Aarseth (1997) offers a detailed examination of cybertext. It investigates the influence of player actions and choices on the creation of narratives inside virtual settings in great detail. This connects to the idea of interactive storytelling, which is a common feature in video games. In this kind of storytelling, the choices made by the player have a significant influence on the advancement of the tale. This corresponds to the concept of interactive storytelling, a prominent characteristic in video games, where the player's decisions have a substantial impact on the progression of the storyline. Aarseth's ideas effectively encapsulate the essential elements of a tale, while discarding superfluous attributes. Player actions have the capacity to impede particular narrative strands, which results in an experience that is both compelling and customized. In a more recent work, Ryan (2019) goes further into the topic by showing how video games, as a medium, boost participation in interactive storytelling while also illustrating how this engagement may be increased. While this inquiry was being conducted, the one that came before it was also being carried out. On the other hand, this also suggests that players are not only passive recipients of stories but rather actively take part in the telling of those stories. Our findings, which show the significant part of those components that hinder storytelling play in the process of redefining narrative experiences, lend credence to this conclusion and provide support for it.

Furthermore, Bogost (2008) introduced the idea of procedural rhetoric, which places an emphasis on the efficiency of gaming systems in communicating ideas and points of view. The purpose of this game is to serve as a catalyst, stimulating players to make decisions that eventually influence the narrative. The constraints that hinder the narrative's advancement toward its conclusion shape these assessments. The correlation between mechanics and storytelling offers more proof that elements that do not involve narrative have a profound impact on the perception and comprehension of tales.

Juul's 2005 study delves further into the impact of constraints and regulations on players' experiences. The narrative-inhibiting elements of interactive narratives function as structural constraints, guiding and regulating player choices in various ways. The user and game producer collaborate to provide captivating and unique experiences, consistent with the underlying concept. Juul's study on semi-realistic interactions in video games supports this concept.

Scholars like as Murray, Aarseth, Ryan, Bogost, and Juul have systematically incorporated principles into the development of digital storytelling, specifically in the context of video games. Ultimately, this transformation occurs inside the framework of video games. This topic focuses on the significant influence of narrative-limiting factors on the creation of tales that diverge from the established norms of traditional storytelling. Rather than being shown as ordinary spectators, players are presented as essential components of the narrative. The ability to enthrall, enable, and improve the audience's immersion in a narrative inside a video game has brought about a significant transformation in storytelling. The convergence of these notions offers a fundamental framework that is valuable for comprehending the process of transformation.

Present work aims to investigate the significant effects of narrative-excluding elements in video games, using *Until Dawn* as a case study. Narrating anecdotes has always constituted a fundamental aspect of human existence. The objective is to transmit significant life lessons, emotions, and conceptions from one generation to the next. The director or scriptwriter often determines the trajectory of a traditional narrative. The widespread use of video games has brought about a change in philosophical viewpoints and presented a challenge to conventional sequential standards.

The video game *Until Dawn* enables players to actively manipulate the storyline, indicating a departure from passively consuming narratives and a move toward actively engaging in their construction. Some features, such character deaths and the advancement of many storylines, in the video game *Until Dawn*, developed by Supermassive Games, restrict the length of the narrative. This condition makes the game a captivating subject for analysis. The goal of this analysis is to find out how the game reimagines storytelling in an interactive medium by using player agency, character survival, and branching storylines in a novel way. This will be accomplished by following the steps outlined in the previous sentence.

Until Dawn breaks with tradition by changing how players interact with the story with the introduction of features that make it harder to follow the chain of events, which leads up to the ending. Throughout the game, a diverse range of characters face perilous situations. Players may exert control over their characters' decisions and subsequent outcomes by choosing a sequence of acts to do. The story is heavily shaped by these options, leading to a complex web of events that are intricately connected to the player's choices. A captivating and profoundly emotional story unfolds from the complex interaction between decision-making and result.

Several approaches or methods are prevalent nowadays because of the merging of narrative and technology. The integration of intelligent storytelling with interactive gaming, influenced by the concept of gamification, signifies not just a fusion but also a revolutionary and pioneering change. Presently, gamers are able to engage with narratives using various cutting-edge techniques, but they must be vigilant in following the plot and understanding the consequences of their choices. This research examines the complex processes that lead to considerable alterations in storytelling standards as a consequence of problems faced throughout the process of tale construction. The distinctive amalgamation of intricate narrative abilities and interactive gaming inside a dynamic digital environment has been explored. The primary aim is to determine how these elements promote innovative collaboration while simultaneously eroding the established norms.

Literature Review

Gamification

Gamification is a strategic approach that tries to boost user motivation and engagement by incorporating game mechanics and design principles into areas that are not traditionally associated with gaming (Mittal et al., 2022). A variety of functional areas, such as marketing, employee training, education, and healthcare, have shown a significant amount of interest in this matter (Bhardwaj & Kumar, 2022). Through the use of game components such as points, badges, leader boards, and challenges, it is possible to tap into the intrinsic motivators that individuals possess. According to the Self-Determination Theory (SDT) developed by Deci and Ryan in 1985, individuals are motivated by three fundamental psychological needs: relatedness, competence, and autonomy. This is accomplished via the use of gamification, which provides users with the ability to make their own decisions, a feeling of mastery through the completion of fascinating activities, and a catalyst for social interaction through the inclusion of aspects that are either cooperative or competitive (Mittal & Kumar, 2020).

McGonigal (2011), a well-known game designer and author of *Reality is Broken: Why Games Make Us Better and How They Can Change the World*, is a proponent of gamification. The author is also a well-recognized supporter of the concept. McGonigal investigates the ways in which concepts from gaming may be used to address real-world problems and enhance a wide range of aspects of our lives. According to McGonigal, the fact that games are so concentrated and fully engrossing means that they have the potential to increase productivity even in circumstances in which individuals are not themselves playing games.

In addition, a study that was conducted by Deterding and colleagues (2011) highlights how important it is to have a comprehensive understanding of the psychological and motivational components of gamification. A number of significant motivational aspects, such as accomplishment, relatedness, and autonomy, are shown to be beneficial to the effectiveness of gamified applications, according to the findings of the study described earlier.

Gamification has been used into the employee training programs of both Microsoft and IBM in an attempt to improve the learning outcomes and boost the level of employee engagement within their respective organizations (Kumar & Sharma, 2021). The use of game mechanics in this circumstance is consistent with the concepts of behavioral psychology, which argue that the supply of incentives and other types of positive reinforcement fosters the development of desirable behaviors. In other words, the principles of behavioral psychology are compatible with the application of game mechanics.

Hence, gamification encompasses more than simply interesting content. As a tactical instrument that changes user experiences and behaviour in a variety of domains, it operates by using game dynamics and psychological insights to accomplish its tasks. This objective is achieved via the use of the game. A growing cohort of specialists and scholars from many disciplines are exploring the potential uses of gamification and striving to enhance its principles in order to optimize its impact across various domains. As the discourse about gamification persists, it becomes evident that this phenomenon is really occurring.

Study of the Game Linguistics

Game linguistics is an academic field that explores the complex relationships between language, discourse, and interactive video games (Bhardwaj & Gupta, 2023). The field of research is seeing rapid growth (Halenko & McLoughlin, 2021). This investigation examines the techniques by which video games use language to captivate and construct narratives, from a theoretical standpoint. Gaming linguistics is defined by Mäyrä (2017) as the study of communication inside video games. This field of study investigates the creation of narratives and characters by evaluating the vocal expressions, linguistic selections, and speech mannerisms of the characters. The study also explores the alterations that take place in language inside virtual reality and the complex relationship between cultural legacy, linguistic subtleties, and the game itself (Sundberg, 2019). This exemplifies the adaptation of language for utilitarian purposes in virtual settings.

Georgakopoulou and Spilioti (2018) explore the interactions and communication between players in multiplayer circumstances as another aspect of games linguistics. The goal is to improve our comprehension of the players' interpersonal communication. Specifically, this pertains to the analysis of content created by users inside video games. This encompasses a wide range of digital media, such as information disseminated on social media platforms, online chat rooms, and message boards. Undertaking research on the development of language and speech patterns in gaming groups is essential for accomplishing this goal.

Cybertext

Cybertext refers to a unique kind of textual involvement and interaction that is evident in digital environments, particularly in video games (Kumar & Ayodeji, 2020). Cybertext explores the dynamic relationship between users and texts that include several layers of significance, frequently contingent upon the decisions made by the users (Ryan, 2019). The reader/player actively engages in the story by traversing many narrative nodes and alternative routes, thereby assuming a co-creator role (Bizzocchi et al., 2019). Cybertextuality encompasses interactive narratives in computer games, extending beyond standard textual mediums. Players engage in intricate, diverging storylines where their five decisions determine the trajectory of the tale (Aarseth, 1997). The interactive nature of this experience enhances engagement and encourages a reevaluation of the control over the storyline within changing digital environments (Ryan, 2019). To put it concisely, cybertext provides a conceptual framework for comprehending the complex connection between users and dynamic, interactive narratives in digital settings. This framework modifies how we interact and perceive fun and textual information.

Narratology

The study of narratives in a variety of media is the area of main emphasis of the dynamic field of narrative studies. Understanding the underlying structure and interpretive subtleties of these tales is the goal (Prince, 2016). Narrative analysis is an academic discipline that examines the fundamental elements of stories, including characters, plot, and point of view (Herman, 2017). The goal of doing this is to identify the underlying patterns and traditions that are inherent in the craft of storytelling. It explores how tales engage audiences, elicit emotions, and represent cultural contexts in a way that extends beyond the purview of basic analysis (Ryan, 2019).

Narratology is used extensively and has become a part of many academic disciplines. Within the discipline of video game studies, the narrative analyzes the intricate connection between gaming and storytelling. It does this by examining how interactive technology tells stories and gives users agency over the encounter. As per Chatman's (2018) assertion, comprehension of the narrative techniques used by writers to modify perspectives and evoke a sense of immersion is beneficial.

The advantageous relationship between tales and the dynamically shifting landscape of digital media is clarified by the contemporary theory of narratives. Our comprehension of the stories that comprise our common experiences is therefore much improved.

Defining Narrative-Precluding Elements

Intentional decisions, occurrences, or circumstances in a tale that have multiple outcomes and may restrict particular narrative trajectories or character arcs are known as narrative-precluding elements. This idea highlights how interactive storytelling in video games is fluid and always evolving, with player choices having a direct impact on the story's progression.

Interactive Storytelling and Player Agency

In the realm of video games, the idea of interactive storytelling is gaining popularity. According to Juul (2001), video games have a distinct attraction because they empower players with agency, enabling them to actively influence the storyline through their choices and actions. The player-centric approach has revolutionized conventional concepts of narrative, turning players into collaborators who actively shape their own experiences (Murray, 1997). *Until Dawn* exemplifies this phenomenon by offering players the opportunity to deeply participate with the narrative through decision-making that has far-reaching consequences on the story's several routes (Bizzocchi et al., 2019).

Nonlinear Narratives and Multiple Endings

Contemporary video game storytelling is characterized by the use of nonlinear tales and numerous endings. Jenkins (2004) contends that video games provide a unique capacity for delivering branching storylines and different outcomes, stressing the dynamic nature of narrative development. *Until Dawn* utilizes this possibility by offering players with a tapestry of options that lead to different effects, echoing the rich possibilities of real-life decision-making (Schell, 2008). Nonlinear narratives present a challenge to participants as they navigate unpredictable outcomes, resulting in an increased emotional engagement and a more immersive and participatory storytelling experience (Aarseth, 1997).

Emotional Engagement and Character Survival

The emotional connection facilitated by variables that prevent the development of a storyline is a crucial aspect of how players engage with the narratives of video games. Hartmann et al. (2015a) conducted research indicating that the possibility of character fatalities in video games triggers intensified emotional reactions, as players develop strong attachments to the virtual individuals' survival and welfare. *Until Dawn* exploits this dynamic by intentionally positioning individuals in dangerous circumstances where player decisions determine their destinies. The emotional stakes that arise from this situation generate a captivating narrative tension, intensifying the player's ability to influence the outcome and producing a unique personal narrative experience (Lankoski & Björk, 2015).

Narrative Evolution and Player-Centric Experiences

The progression of narrative techniques in video games has created opportunities for player-focused experiences that challenge traditional linear frameworks. In their 2006 publication, Bateman and Boon present a model that explores player-driven narratives, wherein players actively engage in the collaborative process of shaping the story's development. *Until Dawn* demonstrates this framework by providing a complex network of interrelated options that mold the narrative landscape. This deviation from linear storytelling corresponds to the wider pattern of adaptive narratives, where the player assumes a crucial role as a participant in the process of constructing the tale (Ryan, 2004).

Immersion and Replayability

The immersive properties of interactive tales have been investigated extensively in study. Deterding et al. (2011) emphasize the significance of player immersion and engagement in video games, underscoring the relevance of narrative as a motivating factor. *Until Dawn* captivates gamers with its emotionally laden events and also entices replayability by offering many outcomes. The replayability of a game is derived from the inclination to investigate different choices and observe distinct narrative routes, so improving the total player engagement and emphasizing the significance of factors that can affect the storyline (Consalvo & Dutton, 2006).

Research Method

The present study employs a qualitative analytical methodology to comprehensively investigate the intricate details inherent in the game. The study precisely and painstakingly examines the myriad linguistic nuances found in *Until Dawn*. A thorough content study looks at the game's intricate gaming mechanics, narrative backdrop, and variety of player options. The focus is to have a closer look at the narrative structure, with particular attention to how characters interact, how the plot develops, and how player decisions affect the experience. The connection between the game mechanics and narrative frameworks is heavily emphasized to demonstrate how player actions subtly but significantly affect the story's development. By using this approach, not only is the game's plot structure illuminated, but also the intricate connection between the many narrative elements and the player's agency is also brought to light. The objective of this research is to thoroughly analyze *Until Dawn* from many perspectives in order to uncover all of its narrative complexities. The aim is to demonstrate how the game's storyline employs intricate linguistic elements and player decisions to reinterpret traditional narrative conventions. A comprehensive understanding of how narrative-blocking characteristics impact player engagement, emotional connection, and the development of storytelling in interactive media may be achieved by examining the intricate language complexities and their interaction with story elements.

Source of the Data

The primary source of information is the interactive video game entitled *Until Dawn*, created by Supermassive Games. The complicated plot of the game, which takes place in a secluded mountain lodge and is reliant on the decisions made by the player, at the end of the day determines how the characters turn out and where the narrative goes. Researching the fusion of interactive storytelling and storytelling is made possible by the creative integration of narrative-precluding elements like character deaths and branching storylines. The objective of this study is to shed light on the interactions between the game mechanics, the complexity of the narrative, and the choices made by the player. The purpose of this research is to enhance player engagement, challenge old storytelling norms, and revolutionize the area of interactive media narratives. This goal will be accomplished by using a comprehensive and in-depth examination.

Result and Discussion

Interactive Storytelling and Player Agency

The fascinating story of *Until Dawn* stems from its masterful fusion of player autonomy and interactive storytelling. The fundamental idea of player-focused storytelling is embodied in this video game, which lets users actively choose the plot and the destiny of the characters. The players are faced with a crucial decision, who then have to explore a dimly lighted chamber or stay put and avoid danger. This apparently uncomplicated decision sets in motion a sequence of occurrences, each bearing repercussions that reverberate throughout the storyline. Players, acting as virtual manipulators, dictate the actions, exchanges, and eventually the fate of the characters. Characters in the game form alliances or deal with conflicts as a result of decisions made by the player, creating a complex and deep story that weaves together several paths to form a coherent whole. Imagine that a character's destiny is determined by the decisions that players make, leading to several versions of the story. Each of them is a reflection of the player's unique decisions.

The butterfly effect is employed in *Until Dawn. It is* a phenomenon in which seemingly tiny decisions have huge and far-reaching consequences. Imagine the thrill of realizing that a seemingly little decision taken early in the game led to an unanticipated turning point later on. Players are completely immersed in a narrative experience where their decisions are not only incidental but rather crucial to the overall storyline because to the intricate web of interactivity.

The butterfly effect is a chaos theory idea that suggests that little changes made to a system over time can have big effects. This is seen in the video game *Until Dawn*, when apparently unimportant choices have a big impact on the story and the characters' fates. Interactive storytelling in *Until Dawn* surpasses conventional narratives. Players are active participants who contribute to the creation of a narrative journey. While navigating the complex labyrinth of options, the destinies of the characters are at stake, influenced by the very hands that direct them. The integration of agency and storytelling in *Until Dawn* exemplifies the immersive capacity of video games, wherein tales serve as interactive platforms for player ingenuity.

Nonlinear Narratives and Multiple Endings

Until Dawn skillfully incorporates nonlinear storylines and different endings, heightening the player involvement by providing a dynamic and individualized storytelling experience. The game's narrative structure exhibits branching and converging paths, resembling a choose-your-own-adventure story, empowering players to control the trajectory of the plot.

Until Dawn features a grand total of ten distinct conclusions, with each one being influenced by the player's decisions made during the course of the game. Consequently, there is no definitive method to engage in the game, and every player's encounter will be distinct. Envision a pivotal moment in the story where the destiny of a character hangs in the balance, as they must choose between confronting an enigmatic individual or seeking refuge. This decision splits the narrative into two separate tales, each with its own unique difficulties, revelations, and outcomes. Players assume the role of navigators, crafting a narrative that is distinct to their decisions.

As players explore these varied paths, they will encounter a complex narrative that is intricately intertwined with divergent and interconnected storylines. The actions that the characters perform not only have an effect on their alliances, rivalries, and revelations, but they also result in the development of the plot and the establishment of distinctive character dynamics. There is a mirror of actual life in the hard decisions and nonlinear tales included in the story.

Take into consideration the way in which actions have an effect on following chapters, gradually amassing into a complex web of interrelated repercussions. The revelation that a decision that appeared to be unimportant when it was being made in a previous chapter had a substantial impact on an event that occurred later on in the story is a further enhancement of the already captivating experience. As a result of the knock-on impact of this phenomenon, players are prompted to carefully consider their choices and are provided with a feeling of power and control.

One decision that was made in Chapter 1 of Until Dawn, is to look into the potential causes of the noise that was coming from the basement. It is possible that Jessica's existence is hinged on this decision, which is of utmost significance. Finding Jessica and being able to save her life are possible if you decide to explore the source of the noise and find out where it is coming from. On the other side, Jessica's death at the hands of the Wendigo might result from you choosing to ignore the interruption.

The Chapter 6 of the game Until Dawn, is about having the choice to have faith in Josh. This is yet another important choice that might influence whether or not Josh will get through this. In the event that you choose to put your faith in Josh, he has the potential to save your life. On the other hand, if you make the decision to be skeptical of him, he may turn against you and make an effort to kill you.

Choosing whether to kill Hannah or to spare her is the topic of Chapter 10 of the game. Taking this challenging decision is not something that can be solved easily. In the event that you execute Hannah, the Wendigo curse will be lifted, and she will be killed. On the other hand, if you leave Hannah alone, she will transform into a Wendigo and kill you.

The choice is to be made in Chapter 10 of the Until Dawn, over whether or not to stay in the lodge or to leave. Your playstyle will determine the option you choose. You can try to survive by staying in the lodge if you think you can fight the Wendigos. If you're unsure, though, you may always try to flee the lodge.

Chapter 11 of the game is about making the decision to save Chris or Sam. This is the hardest decision in the game and the last one to make. Only one of these characters is able to be saved. Sam's rescue means Chris's demise. Chris will die, and you will save him.

The result of these decisions is a variety of endings that reflect the many paths that gamers might take. Imagine an epilogue that reveals the destiny of characters and their surroundings based on the actions of the players. By providing results that align with their decisions, the game respects player agency and highlights the significance of their narrative contributions.

Storytelling becomes an interactive labyrinth in *Until Dawn*, enhanced by nonlinear storylines and many endings. Replayability and personalization are two aspects that contribute to the enhancement of the storytelling process. The dynamic architecture of the game recognizes players as the authors of their own tales of the game.

Until Dawn makes use of nonlinear storytelling and a variety of different conclusions in a multitude of ways, in addition to the examples that were described before. Ethical dilemmas are often presented to players in the game, for example, in circumstances in which there is no unambiguous action that may be regarded as appropriate or inappropriate. In order to do this, players will face difficult decisions that will shape the story. To further heighten the sense of mystery and tension, the game makes use of red herrings and foreshadowing. This does double duty: it builds tension for players and pulls them farther into the story than they would have been able to achieve without it.

An outstanding example of the use of several endings and a nonlinear story is Until Dawn. By putting these plans into action, we can make a game that is both entertaining and packed with surprises, so it can be replayed.

Emotional Engagement and Character Survival

Players are drawn into a fascinating and dramatic experience in *Until Dawn* by the narrative connection it constructs. The deft combination of character survival with emotional connection is what makes this possible. The game introduces a fresh approach to character survival. In this technique, the actions made by the player have a direct impact on the fates of the characters, which results in a broad variety of sentiments being generated.

Furthermore, they give players the impression that they are a part of the story and the characters, which is a factor that adds to the emotional and intimate component of the game.

Imagine a difficult situation in which a player is forced to decide whether they will face a horrific thing, which may perhaps result in their death, or whether they will escape first. The emotional stakes of the game are nicely captured by this option, as players are required to grapple with the repercussions of their choices, aware that their choices will have a direct influence on the course of events that an individual character will experience.

Players are forced to make difficult choices that have a significant impact on the characters' destinies throughout the game. In Chapter 6 of the game, for example, players are required to make a decision on whether or not they should trust Josh. Should they put their faith in him, he might be able to save them. On the other hand, if they do not trust him, he may turn on them and make an attempt to kill them. Due to the fact that Josh is a multifaceted man who possesses both admirable and deplorable characteristics, this choice appears to be challenging. There is a possibility that players are unsure about whether or not they should trust him, which might make the choice far more difficult.

Throughout the narrative, it is intriguing to see the players' emotional bond strengthen as they get more familiar with the many characters shown in the story. Player choices directly influence their likelihood of survival, resulting in a fluctuation of feelings such as apprehension, remorse, and hope. This increases the emotional engagement and immersion that players experience in the game.

For example, the player character Mike is faced with the decision of whether or not to kill a character called Emily or to save her life. This is a difficult choice because Emily has been possessed by a Wendigo, and she is trying to kill Mike. If Mike shoots Emily, she will die. However, if Mike spares Emily, she will continue to be a threat to him and the other characters.

Consider a scenario where a character's survival is dependent on a split-second choice during a chase sequence. The player's quick thinking determines whether the character escapes or falls victim to danger. This instantaneous impact underscores the emotional stakes, creating a visceral connection between player agency and character destiny. If Emily has the Flare Gun, a DON'T MOVE event will occur in the elevator. If she moves, she will still dodge the attack. If Emily doesn't have the Flare Gun, the elevator event won't happen and she will get automatically injured at the top of the conveyor belt.

Analyzing this dynamic, *Until Dawn* transforms character survival from being a mere gameplay mechanic into an emotional narrative tool. The emotional engagement stems from players' investment in the characters' journeys, as their decisions become conduits for triumphs, tragedies, and unforeseen twists.

The game forces players to make difficult choices that have a real impact on the fate of the characters. In Chapter 6, for instance, players have to decide whether or not to trust Josh. Should they put their faith in him, he might be able to save them. On the other hand, if they do not trust him, he may turn on them and make an attempt to kill them. Due to the fact that Josh is a multifaceted man who possesses both admirable and deplorable characteristics, this choice appears to be challenging. It is possible that gamers are uncertain about whether or not they should trust him, which might make the decision far more difficult.

The creation of a one-of-a-kind emotional experience is accomplished by *Until Dawn* through the deft combination of story and gameplay. The fact that players are given agency, which in turn heightens their emotional involvement, creates a strong connection between the decisions they make, the survival of their characters, and the emotional resonance they experience. The choices that players make have an emotional impact on the virtual reality, turning it into an emotional canvas. This is because of the dynamic interaction that takes place between the players.

Narrative Evolution and Player-Centric Experiences

This game provides players with a dynamic narrative journey that goes beyond the conventional linear storytelling. It is a perfect example of how storytelling and experiences that are focused on the player have progressed in the world of video games. When playing the game, players are immersed in a dynamic narrative environment, and the decisions they make have an impact on how the story develops and how it ultimately finishes.

Imagine a tranquil mountain cottage where the opening scene features a group of friends being introduced to one another. Despite the fact that the storyline of the game has already been decided upon, the players are in command of the specific choices and actions that shape the storyline. Decisions made by players operate as a brushstroke, influencing the interactions between characters, the progression of the tale, and the emotional resonance of the game.

There are nine different characters in *Until Dawn*, each of whom the player has the ability to take control of and who each have their own distinct personalities and backstories. Due to the fact that these people have intricate and ever-changing interactions with one another, the tale is significantly influenced by these relationships.

By way of illustration, in Chapter 6 of the game, if players decide to place their trust in Josh, he could be able to assist them in surviving by providing them with assistance. Nevertheless, in the event that gamers decide to put doubt on him, he has the ability to retaliate by attempting to get rid of them. The decisions that players make about the connections between characters have the potential to have a huge influence on the tale as well as on the results for the characters. Through the course of their exploration of the narrative web, players will come across a multitude of plot threads that branch off and mix together, much like in a choose-your-own-adventure book. Players are able to engage with a variety of various narratives and are encouraged to feel a strong feeling of control and immersion as a result of the choices they make, which have a variety of ramifications.

Until Dawn performs an outstanding job of putting together a complicated network of numerous alternative narrative points during the course of the game. This is one of the game's many strengths in terms of that aspect of the tale. One of the first unexpected happenings that take place is the presence of Dr. Hill, a therapist who breaches the fourth wall in the game by speaking straight to the camera. This is one of the first shocking events that take place. However, despite the fact that players are still attempting to piece together the jigsaw that is the story, these moments are filled with interesting mysteries that continue to fascinate their attention.

Take into consideration a situation in which the outcome of a character's destiny is determined by the decision that a player takes about the exploration of a mystery sound. This choice propels the narrative in a new direction, unveiling secrets that would remain hidden otherwise. The game rewards exploration with revelations, encouraging players to be active participants in the storytelling process.

Until Dawn is kind enough to play a quick recap after each scene, as well, allowing players to watch a montage of important events from the previously played section. Between Dr. Hill's role and an array of storytelling techniques within the game itself, the narrative becomes the perfect catalyst to support the game's most touted feature: the butterfly effect.

Analyzing this, *Until Dawn* stands as a paradigm of narrative evolution, as it moves beyond linear narratives to embrace the player as a coauthor. This player-centric model aligns with the trend of adaptive narratives, where players collaborate in crafting the storyline, forging a unique and personalized experience.

Until Dawn iterates that sometimes doing nothing is the right decision to make – if given the choice to shoot a squirrel or a bean bag, the player can be safe and patiently wait for the squirrel to move along. There is no right or wrong paths to take in this game, but the characters are far from immortal. Their lives depend on your ruling, a realization both terrifyingly stressful and ultimately rewarding.

The synthesis of narrative evolution and player-centric experiences has redefined storytelling within video games. Players not only consume narratives but also actively participate in their construction, rendering *Until Dawn* an epitome of the transformative potential that emerges when storytelling is approached as a collaborative endeavor.

Immersion and Replayability

Until Dawn skillfully leverages immersion and replayability to create a multifaceted and captivating gaming experience. The game's immersive qualities draw players into its world, while its replayable nature encourages them to explore different paths and outcomes, enhancing the overall engagement.

Imagine a scene where a character navigates through a dimly lit corridor, the ambiance amplified by eerie sound effects and atmospheric visuals. This sensory-rich environment immerses players, making them feel as though they're walking in the character's shoes.

With choices that directly affect character interactions and outcomes, players may create a branching plot with a multitude of possible outcomes. After the game is completed, players may have the impression that they are compelled to begin again and investigate many additional possibilities and paths; hence, each time they play, they will encounter a different narrative.

Imagine a situation in which the only thing that determines whether or not a character will live is the decision that they make. In certain iterations of the game, the protagonist is able to escape the game alive, but in others, they are doomed to a tragic end. As a result of the appeal of viewing several outcomes, players are compelled to engage in multiple replays, which serve to strengthen their emotional connection to the narrative.

More research confirms that *Until Dawn* expertly strikes a balance between immersing oneself in the experience and maintaining the ability to play it again and again. The first draws players in by engrossing them in a story world, while the latter encourages them to go back and find all the secrets, riddles, and different endings. The ability to play a game through from the beginning to end several times is what we mean when we talk about replayability.

There is a connection between these three features, and one of the factors that is associated with increased player engagement is the combination of replayability and immersion. In addition to being urged to develop an emotional investment in the plot and characters, players are also encouraged to delve deeply into their environment, try out different choices, and traverse through several stories.

The video game *Until Dawn* is a great example of how immersion and replayability can work together to create a story encounter that changes and grows with each playthrough. Playing this game will show you exactly how to get this combo. This enhances the game's longevity and enjoyment, while also enabling players to establish a profound connection with the narrative's environment. If this is really the situation, then it has a significant advantage.

Discussion

With the help of future updates, the overriding objective of this research is to investigate all of the many narrative components that are present in Until Dawn. This research intends to analyze various methods of storytelling as well as the complex relationship that exists between the framework of a narrative and the player's agency. It is necessary to take into consideration a variety of factors in order to accomplish this goal. These factors include player-centric experiences, emotional involvement, interactive narrative, and nonlinear plotlines.

The discussion will focus on analyzing the ways in which Until Dawn deviates from the conventional narrative tropes that are often used. In order to do this, it is necessary to have a complete understanding of the dynamic relationship that exists between theoretical notions and real research. Players are given the opportunity to have a voice in the narrative and to take on the role of writers when player agency is included into a tale. Because of this, the storyline begins to include a greater number of characters, and each one has the opportunity to influence the direction that the story takes. According to Juul (2001) and Bateman and Boon (2006), when players actively engage in storytelling, it not only improves the narrative but also turns the game into a dynamic platform where player decisions dictate the consequences.

Playing Until Dawn allows players to explore how their decisions impact the development of the story via its branching plots and nonlinear narratives. The game immerses players in a flexible plot in which their decisions have a huge influence on the overall telling of the tale. This is due to the fact that there are a great number of potential paths and events that might occur (Jenkins, 2004; Ryan, 2004). The objective of this discussion is to investigate the ways in which these branching stories have the potential to strengthen the emotional connection that exists between the player and the character, as well as to make it possible for the two to engage in a more customized relationship with one another.

Additionally, the emotional resonance and the idea of character survival provide a glimpse into the intricate emotional core that was included into the production of the game. This is an extra point of interest. This study yielded insights into how character deaths evoke intensified emotional responses, so building a strong emotional connection between players and the climax of the game. Hartmann et al. and Deterding et al. conducted studies in 2015 and 2011, respectively. This study aims to examine how these attributes, which hinder the advancement of a tale, go beyond being basic mechanics. Instead, they function as channels via which players might be motivated to cultivate empathy and establish connections with one other. To examine the nonmechanical aspects of these traits, the study was conducted to investigate several approaches.

Because of the player-focused experiences and the advancement of the story in *Until Dawn*, the way things are done has undergone a considerable shift. The game has instigated this modification. This research highlights the capacity of interactive narratives by demonstrating how the decisions made by players may convert storytelling into a cooperative and flexible enterprise. Furthermore, the research illustrates the potential of interactive narratives by showcasing how player choices may fundamentally transform the storyline. The aim of this study is to examine the correlation between player actions and narrative dynamics, with the intention of challenging the established standards of storytelling. *Until Dawn* is an exemplary instance of how video games provide an innovative approach to storytelling by providing a creative medium for its creation.

Lately, our focus has been on two key elements of the game that enhance its overall attractiveness: its replay value and its level of immersion. These two traits significantly enhance the overall appeal of the game. *Until Dawn* expands the limits of story involvement by offering intricately detailed settings and replayable encounters. *Until Dawn* is a game that challenges the limits of narrative involvement. Within the context of this discourse, an examination is conducted to ascertain the correlation between immersion, emotional involvement, replayability, and the duration of gameplay. It places an emphasis on the idea that the life of the game may be extended via the use of replayability and that immersion can improve emotional engagement, which in turn raises the impact of the interactive story (Consalvo & Dutton,

2006; Murray), respectively. These two aspects are highlighted during the course of the game.

The findings of the study shed light on the very significant impact that the narrative-restricting elements of the video game *Until Dawn* have had on the overall experience of playing the game. This study contributes to the ongoing discussion that is taking place concerning player control, the development of narratives, emotional involvement, and interactive storytelling. Enhanced, customized, and dynamic narrative experiences are produced as a consequence of the integration of various components, which culminates in the development of storytelling. The conventional narrative frameworks that have been used in the past are presented with a problem as a result of this.

Player agency, which refers to the capacity of players to actively impact the narratives of the games by the choices they make, is considered to be one of the most fundamental qualities of video games, according to Juul (2001). Previous research has shown that this assumption aligns with the results of that inquiry. This product is compatible with the game *Until Dawn*, where the player's actions lead to several narrative situations and outcomes that impact the characters' survival prospects throughout the events. This is the situation that occurs inside the game. This may be used in combination with the game. An illustration of the player-centric narrative creation paradigm, as proposed by Bateman and Boon (2006), may be seen in this instance. The paradigm in question promotes an interactive and ever-changing connection between the player and the narrative being conveyed. The game's unique blend of player agency and immersion perfectly illustrates this principle.

A research conducted by Hartmann et al. (2015b) delves into the emotional aspects of story-blocking components. In 2015, the study was published. According to the research, when a character dies, players have a far stronger emotional response. This makes you care deeply about the characters in the game and makes you want to help them get closer to them. Players will have more control over the characters' destiny in *Until Dawn*, thanks to this bias, which will increase their interest in the game.

Features that don't depend on narrative but instead elicit emotional resonance and promote recurrent interaction are more effective in increasing immersion, according to this study. This contradicts previous studies, as shown by the study of Consalvo and Dutton (2006), which focuses on the immersive aspects of stories. Players are encouraged to delve into different plotlines by engaging with branching pathways and encountering several endings, according to research conducted by Deterding et al. (2011) on engagement and replayability. As a result, the participants are encouraged to develop an attitude of inquiry and friendship. Several fields of study are greatly affected by this revelation. Within the field of game design, the gained information might guide designers in creating narrative-driven games that are engrossing. Furthermore, by promoting a thorough examination of the narrative dynamics inside interactive media, the study's multidisciplinary methodology offers implications for media studies and narrative theory.

With this information, educators may create engaging teaching materials that use interactive storytelling to improve student learning. Additionally, the study emphasizes the potential therapeutic applications of video games that draw players into profoundly moving narratives, encouraging emotional release and the growth of empathy. The study brings up moral questions about characteristics that obstruct the formation of a story. The inclusion of these characteristics provides players with a secure environment in which they may make challenging choices, hence fostering the development of empathy and critical thinking skills.

Conclusion

The research has examined the obstacles that could arise when attempting to portray the tale of Until Dawn using modern media in order to create an immersive storytelling experience. Conventional assumptions about narratives are challenged by research into player-centric experiences, interactive storytelling, emotional engagement, and branching storylines. Examining a constantly changing environment poses this challenge. There is a continual flux in this setting. The results show that Until Dawn gives players an enthralling and interesting story to follow. In addition, it allows users to actively participate in creating their own unique storylines. Novel narrative interactions are made possible by the game's unique choice system, which allows players to engage with other characters on an emotional level and take charge of the tale. Throughout their engagement, gamers undergo a wide range of emotions and behaviors as they are engrossed in captivating and constantly changing experiences. The event takes place inside a narrative environment that is interactive and departs from the conventional structure of a linear storyline.

In conclusion, the chapter sheds light on the significant function that narrative-limiting features perform in video games. Until Dawn is a game that entirely modifies the traditional style of narrative by combining a variety of interactive elements, a wide range of tales, emotional engagement, and experiences that are focused on the player. This game highlights the revolutionary potential of interactive media by fostering the production of collective narratives, reinventing old storytelling approaches, and increasing the amount of tales that players are exposed to.

References

Aarseth, E. (1997). *Cybertext: Perspectives on ergodic literature.* The Johns Hopkins University Press.

Bateman, C., & Boon, R. (2006). 21st century fiction: A new model of interaction. In M. Rauterberg (Ed.), *Proceedings of the 9th international conference on entertainment computing (ICEC'06)* (pp. 1–12). Springer.

Bhardwaj, A., & Gupta, A. (2023). Role of video lectures in engineering education. *International Journal of Educational Reform, 32*(2), 208–229.

Bhardwaj, A., & Kumar, V. (2022). Web and social media approach to marketing of engineering courses in India. *International Journal of Business Innovation and Research (IJBIR)*, 27(4), 541–555.

Bizzocchi, J., Tanenbaum, J., & Gutwin, C. (2019). Social roles in collaborative interactive narratives. In *Proceedings of the 2019 CHI conference on human factors in computing systems* (pp. 1–14). ACM.

Bogost, I. (2008). *Persuasive games: The expressive power of videogames*. MIT Press.

Chatman, S. (2018). *Story and discourse: Narrative structure in fiction and film*. Cornell University Press.

Consalvo, M., & Dutton, N. (2006). Game analysis: Developing a methodological toolkit for the qualitative study of games. *Game Studies*, 6(1), 1–11.

Deci, E. L., & Ryan, R. M. (1985). *Intrinsic motivation and self-determination in human behavior*. Plenum Press.

Deterding, S., Dixon, D., Khaled, R., & Nacke, L. (2011). From game design elements to gamefulness: Defining gamification. In *Proceedings of the 15th international academic MindTrek conference: Envisioning future media environments* (pp. 9–15). ACM.

Georgakopoulou, A., & Spilioti, T. (2018). *The Routledge handbook of language and digital communication*. Routledge.

Halenko, N., & McLoughlin, L. (2021). We're not moving the story, we're moving the plot: An exploratory analysis of transmedia storytelling in video games. *Communication Research and Practice*, 7(1), 16–33.

Hartmann, T., Toz, E., & Klimmt, C. (2015a). Avatar death and player identification: The impact of avatar-based compulsion loop and game demands. *Journal of Media Psychology*, 27(2), 67–78.

Hartmann, T., Toz, E., & Klimmt, C. (2015b). Exploring the enjoyment of playing video games. In P. Vorderer, D. Klimmt, & C. R. Klimmt (Eds.), *Explaining the enjoyment of playing video games: The role of competition* (pp. 221–239). Routledge.

Herman, D. (2017). *Basic elements of narrative*. John Wiley & Sons.

Jenkins, H. (2004). Game design as narrative architecture. In N. Wardrip-Fruin & P. Harrigan (Eds.), *First person: New media as story, performance, and game* (pp. 118–130). MIT Press.

Juul, J. (2001). Games telling stories? A brief note on games and narratives. *Game Studies*, 1(1), 1–13.

Juul, J. (2005). *Half-real: Video games between real rules and fictional worlds*. MIT Press.

Kumar, V., & Ayodeji, O. G. (2020). Web analytics for knowledge creation: A systematic review of tools, techniques and practices. *International Journal of Cyber Behavior, Psychology and Learning (IJCBPL)*, 10(1), 1–14.

Kumar, V., & Mittal, S. (2020). Mobile marketing campaigns: Practices, challenges and opportunities. *International Journal of Business Innovation and Research (IJBIR)*, 21(4), 523–539.

Kumar, V., & Sharma, D. (2021). E-learning theories, components and cloud computing based learning platforms. *International Journal of Web-Based Learning and Teaching Technologies*, 16(3), 1–16.

Lankoski, P., & Björk, S. (2015). *Game design research: An introduction to theory & practice*. ETC Press.

Mäyrä, F. (2017). *An introduction to game studies: Games in culture*. Sage Publications.

McGonigal, J. (2011). *Reality is broken: Why games make us better and how they can change the world*. Penguin.

Mittal, S., & Kumar, V. (2020). A framework for ethical mobile marketing. *International Journal of Technoethics (IJT)*, *11*(1), 28–42.

Mittal, S., Kumar, V., & Seppi, J. (2022). Targeting mobile gamers community for marketing campaigns. *Journal of Content, Community & Communication (JCC)*, *16*(2), 106–117.

Murray, J. H. (1997). *Hamlet on the Holodeck: The future of narrative in cyberspace.* MIT Press.

Prince, G. (2016). *A dictionary of narratology.* University of Nebraska Press.

Ryan, M. L. (2004). *Narrative across media: The languages of storytelling.* University of Nebraska Press.

Ryan, M. L. (2019). *Narration in various media.* Walter de Gruyter GmbH & Co KG.

Schell, J. (2008). *The art of game design: A book of lenses.* CRC Press.

Sundberg, S. (2019). *The player's language: A socio-material perspective on the discursive construction of gameworlds.* Bloomsbury Academic.

Chapter 2

Role of Gamification in Crowdsourcing

Gesty Ernestivita, Vikas Kumar and Tiara Nur Anisah

Role of Gamification in Crowdsourcing

Introduction

In the ever-evolving landscape of crowdsourcing, the infusion of gamification has emerged as a transformative force, reshaping the dynamics of collaboration, motivation, and innovation. The concept of crowdsourcing, harnessing the collective intelligence of a diverse group of individuals, has become a powerful paradigm for problem-solving, idea generation, and data collection. Gamification, drawing inspiration from game design principles, introduces elements such as points, badges, and leader boards to infuse a sense of play and competition into the crowdsourcing experience. This introduction sets the stage for an in-depth analysis of how these gamified elements contribute to the engagement and sustained participation of individuals in crowdsourced initiatives. Motivation lies at the heart of any successful crowdsourcing endeavour, and gamification emerges as a potent tool to ignite and sustain this motivation. By incorporating reward systems and fostering a sense of accomplishment through virtual currencies or tangible prizes, gamification incentivizes participants to actively contribute their skills and knowledge.

However, the impact of gamification extends beyond mere competition, delving into the delicate balance between competition and collaboration. Building a cooperative environment within the crowd is essential for harnessing collective intelligence effectively (Bhardwaj & Kumar, 2024). The incorporation of artificial intelligence and augmented reality is poised to reshape the gamified landscape, presenting new opportunities and challenges for both researchers and practitioners (Ayodeji & Kumar, 2023). Ethical considerations form an integral part of this exploration, as the use of gamification raises questions about responsible practices and the potential for unintended consequences (Bhardwaj & Kumar, 2022). As the ethical dimensions of gamified crowdsourcing gain prominence, it becomes important to delve into the ethical considerations and provide insights to mitigating risks associated with this dynamic interplay.

DOI: 10.4324/9781032694238-3

The ethical decision-making framework becomes a guiding principle, prompting a critical examination of the potential risks, unintended consequences, and responsible practices in the application of gamified elements (Nanda & Kumar, 2023). The unethical usage can lead to unintended consequences of gamification, such as over-competitiveness, data inaccuracies, or participant burnout. Hence, it becomes important to understand how the platforms anticipate and mitigate these unintended effects responsibly. The importance of clearly communicating gamification mechanisms to participants also becomes an interesting factor. How the platforms ensure informed consent and transparency in the use of gamified elements becomes very much important to explore? As gamification seeks to motivate participants, balancing the motivational strategies with ethical considerations is an important task. How can platforms achieve a harmonious integration of gamified elements, which motivates participants without compromising ethical standards, needs a careful consideration.

Theoretical Background

Although the applications of the gamification in crowdsourcing are very much interesting, it becomes important to consider the prominent theoretical frameworks supporting these applications. The most prominent of them have been discussed in this section.

Self-Determination Theory (SDT)

SDT posits that individuals have innate psychological needs for autonomy, competence, and relatedness. Gamification in crowdsourcing can be analysed through the lens of SDT, exploring how the design of gamified elements satisfies these psychological needs, thereby enhancing participant motivation and engagement (Deci & Ryan, 2000). The SDT key concepts are as follows: (1) autonomy that refers to the need to feel in control of one's actions and choices. In the context of SDT, individuals are motivated when they perceive themselves as the origin of their own behaviour, making choices aligned with their values and interests. Gamification in crowdsourcing can be designed to support autonomy by providing participants with choices, autonomy over task selection, and a sense of control over their contributions. (2) Competence involves the need to feel effective and capable in one's actions. SDT suggests that individuals are motivated when they can see their efforts leading to successful outcomes. In the context of gamified crowdsourcing, elements that challenge participants offer opportunities for skill development, provide clear feedback on their performance, and contribute to the satisfaction of the competence needed. (3) Relatedness pertains to the need for social connection and a sense of belonging. In gamified crowdsourcing, fostering a supportive

community, encouraging collaboration, and recognizing and valuing participants' contributions can enhance the sense of relatedness. Social interactions
within the gamified environment can contribute to the overall motivation
and engagement of individuals.

SDT provides a framework for understanding how gamification can
enhance motivation in crowdsourcing. By incorporating elements that
support autonomy, competence, and relatedness, gamified platforms can
create an environment where participants are intrinsically motivated to
contribute actively and persistently. These motivational aspects of the
SDT can be seen through three most important applications like Choice
architecture, Feedback and recognition, and the Community building.
(1) Choice architecture: the theory suggests that providing individuals
with choices and allowing them to make decisions that align with their
interests enhance motivation. In the context of gamified crowdsourcing,
designing platforms that offer participants choices in tasks, challenges, or
rewards can contribute to a more engaging and motivating experience.
(2) Feedback and recognition: SDT highlights the importance of feedback
in supporting individuals' sense of competence. Gamified crowdsourcing
platforms can leverage feedback mechanisms, such as badges, points, and
leader boards, to provide participants with clear indications of their progress and achievements, fostering a sense of competence and motivation.
(3) Community building: relatedness is facilitated through the creation
of a community within gamified crowdsourcing platforms. Encouraging
social interactions, collaboration, and recognition of participants' contributions can satisfy the need for relatedness, fostering a sense of belonging and motivation to actively engage with the community. In summary,
Self-Determination Theory provides a valuable lens for understanding the
psychological needs that drive human motivation. When applied to gamification in crowdsourcing, it offers insights into designing platforms that
support autonomy, competence, and relatedness, ultimately enhancing
participants' intrinsic motivation and engagement.

Flow Theory

Flow theory, proposed by Csikszentmihalyi (Nakamura & Csikszentmihalyi,
2009), describes a state of optimal experience where individuals are fully
immersed and focused on an activity. Gamification's role in creating a flow
state within crowdsourcing tasks can be examined, assessing how game-like
elements contribute to heightened concentration and enjoyment, fostering
sustained participation (Csikszentmihalyi, 1990). Flow occurs when individuals have clear goals and a sense of direction. Gamified elements in crowdsourcing tasks can provide participants with specific objectives, creating a
structured environment that facilitates flow. Immediate feedback is real-time
feedback that is crucial for flow. Gamification can incorporate immediate

feedback mechanisms, such as progress indicators or achievement notifications, to keep participants informed about their performance. Whereas the balanced challenge and skill flow emerge when the difficulty of a task matches the individual's skill level. Gamified crowdsourcing platforms should provide challenges that are neither too easy nor too difficult, encouraging participants to stretch their abilities without feeling overwhelmed. Conditions for flow, concentration, and focus are the following: flow requires intense concentration and focused attention on the task at hand. Gamification elements, such as immersive storytelling or interactive features, can contribute to capturing and maintaining participants' attention within crowdsourcing activities. Loss of Self-awareness: in a state of flow, individuals lose self-awareness and become fully engrossed in the activity. Gamification can create an environment where participants are so absorbed in the crowdsourcing task that they temporarily forget about external concerns.

Flow dimensions are as follows: (1) Challenge–Skill Balance: the relationship between the challenge level of a task and the individual's skill level is central to flow. Gamification elements should be designed to dynamically adjust the level of challenge based on participants' evolving skills and experiences. (2) Clear Feedback: timely and clear feedback about performance is crucial for maintaining the flow. Gamified crowdsourcing platforms can incorporate feedback loops that guide participants and help them stay immersed in the task.

Application to Gamification in Crowdsourcing are as follows – (1) Gamified Challenges: designing gamified challenges within crowdsourcing tasks that progressively align with participants' skill levels fosters a sense of flow. The challenges should be engaging and encourage participants to focus their attention on the task at hand. (2) Real-Time Feedback: Incorporating real-time feedback mechanisms, such as progress bars, achievement notifications, or interactive visuals, helps participants maintain a sense of control and awareness during crowdsourcing activities. This immediate feedback contributes to the flow experience. (3) Personalized Experiences: Gamification in crowdsourcing can offer personalized experiences by tailoring challenges and rewards based on individual preferences and performance. Personalization contributes to the challenge–skill balance, enhancing the likelihood of participants experiencing flow. (4) Storytelling and Immersion: using gamification to create immersive storytelling experiences within crowdsourcing tasks can enhance concentration and engagement. Immersive elements contribute to a loss of self-awareness as participants become absorbed in the narrative of the gamified activity. In summary, flow theory provides valuable insights into creating optimal experiences within gamified crowdsourcing platforms. By understanding and integrating the principles of flow, designers can enhance participant engagement, focus, and enjoyment, ultimately contributing to a more satisfying and productive crowdsourcing experience.

Social Identity Theory

Social Identity Theory suggests that individuals categorize themselves and others into social groups, influencing behaviour and attitudes (Pradhan & Kumar, 2016). Gamified crowdsourcing platforms often create virtual communities. Analysing these communities through the lens of Social Identity Theory can provide insights into how gamification fosters a sense of belonging and collaboration among participants (Tajfel & Turner, 2010). Social Identity Theory has been applied to understand various intergroup phenomena, including prejudice, discrimination, and conflict. It provides insights into how individuals navigate their social environment based on group affiliations and how these dynamics contribute to broader societal issues. The theory contributes to our understanding of how groups form, evolve, and interact. It explains the psychological processes that drive individuals to seek positive social identity through group membership and the consequences of such affiliations on behaviour. Critics argue that Social Identity Theory oversimplifies complex intergroup relations and may not fully account for individual differences in how people relate to their social identities. Additionally, it has been criticized for not adequately addressing the fluid and context-dependent nature of social categorization.

Goal-Setting Theory

Locke and Latham's Goal-Setting Theory emphasizes the importance of clear and challenging goals in enhancing performance. Gamification often involves setting and achieving goals within a virtual environment. This framework can be applied to understand how goal-setting elements in gamification impact participants' commitment and effort in crowdsourcing activities (Locke & Latham, 2002). Goal-Setting Theory has found an extensive application in business and management. It is often used to enhance employee performance, improve organizational productivity, and guide strategic planning (Faisol et al., 2023). In educational settings, the theory is applied to enhance student motivation and achievement (Nayar & Kumar, 2018). Setting clear academic goals, providing feedback, and fostering a goal-oriented learning environment are key applications (Kumar & Sharma, 2021). Individuals use Goal-Setting Theory to structure personal development plans. Whether it is pursuing fitness goals, learning a new skill, or achieving career milestones, the theory provides a framework for effective goal setting and attainment. Critics argue that the theory may not fully account for the complexity of human motivation. Some individuals may be motivated by factors beyond goal setting, and the theory may not address the nuanced interplay of social and psychological factors in certain contexts. Goal-Setting Theory stands as a foundational framework for understanding motivation and performance across diverse domains. By emphasizing the importance of clear, challenging, and attainable goals, the theory provides a practical guide for individuals and organizations seeking to enhance performance, foster motivation, and achieve meaningful outcomes. As a dynamic and widely applicable theory, it continues to shape how individuals approach tasks, organizations structure their objectives, and educators facilitate learning experiences.

Dual Systems Theory

Dual Systems Theory distinguishes between the reflective and impulsive systems in decision-making (Kumar & Nanda, 2022). Gamification often appeals to the impulsive, more emotional side of participants. This framework can be used to explore how gamified elements influence both rational decision-making and emotional responses, shaping the overall participant experience in crowdsourcing (Kahneman, 2011). Dual Systems Theory has been instrumental in shaping the field of behavioural economics. Understanding how individuals make decisions under the influence of both systems has implications for economic models, policy design, and consumer behaviour. The theory is applied in diverse fields, including psychology, marketing, law, and public policy, to explain and predict decision-making processes. It helps identify situations where individuals may rely on intuitive or deliberate thinking. Some critics argue that the theory oversimplifies the complexity of cognitive processes and decision-making. The clear distinction between System 1 and System 2 may not fully capture the nuances of how these systems interact in practice. From an evolutionary standpoint, some researchers suggest that both systems evolved to serve adaptive purposes. They argue that quick, intuitive thinking (System 1) may have been crucial for survival, while reflective thinking (System 2) enhances problem-solving in more complex environments. Dual Systems Theory offers valuable insights into the intricacies of human cognition and decision-making. By recognizing the interplay between intuitive, automatic thinking and reflective, deliberative processing, the theory provides a nuanced understanding of how individuals navigate a multitude of situations. Its applications extend across various disciplines, shaping our comprehension of economic behaviour, consumer choices, and the biases that influence judgment (Kusumawati et al., 2021). As researchers continue to refine and expand upon the theory, it remains a foundational framework for exploring the dynamics of human thought and decision-making processes. Hence, it finds a good application in gamification for crowdsourcing.

Technology Acceptance Model (TAM)

TAM assesses how users adopt and accept technology based on perceived ease of use and perceived usefulness (Kumar & Rewari, 2023; Paruthi et al., 2023). Applying TAM to gamification in crowdsourcing allows for the examination of how participants perceive the gamified elements, evaluating their ease of use and the perceived benefits they bring to the crowdsourcing process (Davis, 1989). TAM has been extensively applied in information systems research to understand and predict user acceptance of various technologies, including software applications, websites, and mobile apps. TAM has demonstrated a strong predictive power in explaining user acceptance behaviours across different contexts. Its simplicity and applicability make it a practical model for understanding user adoption. Critics argue that TAM has a limited scope in capturing the complexity of technology adoption. It focuses primarily on individual perceptions, neglecting the influence of social and organizational factors. Over time, TAM has evolved into extended models, such as TAM2 and Unified Theory of Acceptance and Use of Technology (UTAUT), which incorporate additional factors and address some of the limitations of the original model.

The Technology Acceptance Model continues to be a foundational framework for understanding the dynamics of user acceptance and adoption of technology. By highlighting the crucial role of perceived ease of use and perceived usefulness, TAM provides insights that inform the design, implementation, and marketing of new technologies. While acknowledging its limitations, the model's enduring influence and adaptability make it a valuable tool for researchers and practitioners seeking to unravel the complexities of technology adoption.

Ethical Decision-Making Framework

To address the ethical considerations associated with gamification in crowdsourcing, a framework based on ethical decision-making models (such as the Utilitarian, Deontological, and Virtue Ethics perspectives) can be employed. This framework will guide the analysis of the ethical implications of gamification strategies, ensuring a responsible and principled approach. (Rest, 2020). Ethical Decision-Making Frameworks are commonly applied in business, healthcare, law, and other professional domains (Mittal & Kumar, 2020). They guide individuals and organizations in navigating complex ethical challenges. Critics argue that frameworks may oversimplify complex ethical issues and that decisions are often context-dependent. Additionally, the effectiveness of a framework relies on the willingness of individuals and organizations to adhere to ethical principles. An Ethical Decision-Making Framework provides a systematic and principled approach to addressing moral dilemmas. By incorporating key components such as identifying ethical issues, clarifying values, and assessing consequences, individuals and organizations can navigate complex ethical terrain with a greater sense of responsibility and integrity. Continuous reflection and learning contribute to the refinement of ethical decision-making processes, fostering a culture of ethical awareness and accountability.

Innovation Diffusion Theory

Rogers' Innovation Diffusion Theory explores the process through which innovations spread within a social system. Gamification in crowdsourcing can be viewed as an innovation influencing participant behaviour. Analysing the adoption and diffusion of gamification features within crowdsourcing platforms using this framework provides insights into the factors influencing its integration and impact. (Rogers, 2023). The theory is widely applied in marketing to understand consumer behaviour and design strategies for introducing new products or services (Kumar & Mittal, 2020). It is also relevant in communication studies for analysing the spread of information. Critics argue that the theory may oversimplify the complexity of innovation adoption. It may not fully capture the influence of cultural, economic, or psychological factors on individuals' decision-making. The Innovation Diffusion Theory remains a cornerstone in the study of how new ideas and technologies permeate societies. By examining the patterns of adoption and the factors influencing the diffusion process, the theory provides valuable insights for innovators, marketers, policymakers, and researchers seeking to understand and facilitate the acceptance of innovations within diverse social systems.

Applications

The exploration of gamification in crowdsourcing has led us through a journey of understanding the intricate interplay between game elements and collaborative endeavours. In this extensive discussion, we delve into the multifaceted dimensions, implications, and potential future trajectories of gamification in the context of crowdsourcing. Drawing upon theoretical frameworks, practical applications, and ethical considerations, we find that there are multiple layers of this dynamic relationship.

Motivation and Engagement

The first cornerstone of our discussion revolves around the profound impact of gamification on participant motivation and engagement in crowdsourcing activities. As Self-Determination Theory posits, autonomy, competence, and relatedness are pivotal for fostering intrinsic motivation. The gamified elements, such as points, badges, and leader boards, intricately woven into crowdsourcing platforms, act as catalysts for satisfying these psychological needs. The concept of flow, as elucidated by Csikszentmihalyi, further enhances our understanding, emphasizing the importance of maintaining an optimal balance between challenge and skill to induce a state of deep engagement. Understanding the interplay between intrinsic and extrinsic motivation is crucial in the gamified crowdsourcing context, where the design of game elements influences participants' engagement and commitment. Intrinsic motivation stems from internal factors such as personal enjoyment and a sense of fulfilment, while extrinsic motivation is driven by external rewards or punishments. It needs to be explored how gamified elements leverage both types of motivation and their implications for sustaining participant engagement in crowdsourcing activities.

Achieving a state of flow in crowdsourcing is an intricate process that involves thoughtful design, personalized experiences, and a balance between challenge and skill. By integrating gamification elements that align with the components of flow, platforms can create an environment that not only enhances engagement but also fosters a sense of fulfilment and well-being among participants. The continuous fine-tuning of gamified challenges to cater to individual preferences and skill levels ensures a dynamic and evolving flow experience, contributing to the sustained success of crowdsourcing platforms. As the field progresses, the synergy between gamification and the flow state remains a cornerstone for creating a collaborative and engaging landscape within crowdsourcing environments.

Collaboration and Community Building

Moving to the second pillar, we explore how gamification fosters collaboration and community building within crowdsourcing platforms. Social Identity Theory becomes a guiding framework, shedding light on the formation of virtual communities and the sense of belonging among participants (Mittal et al., 2022). The gamified environment, with its competitive and collaborative elements, plays a pivotal role in shaping a dynamic and supportive community. First is competitive dynamics, examining the impact of leader boards and competitive elements; we discuss how gamification can strike a balance between healthy competition and collaboration. What are the potential challenges in maintaining this balance, and how can platforms optimize competitiveness for positive outcomes?. Second is recognition and relatedness; the recognition of participants' contributions emerges as a key theme in the discussion, exploring how gamification provides avenues for acknowledging and valuing individuals. How does this recognition contribute to a sense of relatedness, and what are the implications for sustained community engagement? Third is, Long-term Community Building; as communities evolve, the strategies for sustaining engagement and preventing community fatigue become very much important. How gamification adapts to the changing dynamics of virtual communities over the futuristic applications needs to be taken care of.

Skill Development and Problem-Solving

The third dimension of our discussion centres around the role of gamification in skill development and problem-solving within the crowdsourcing landscape. Goal-setting theory offers insights into how gamified challenges can be structured to encourage skill acquisition and goal attainment. Further-more, the gamified approach to problem-solving transforms complex tasks into manageable components, aligning with the principles of Innovation Diffusion Theory. The integration of gamification in crowdsourcing extends beyond engagement to encompass skill development and problem-solving. Drawing insights from Goal-Setting Theory and aligning with the principles of Innovation Diffusion Theory, this dimension explores how gamified challenges can be structured to encourage skill acquisition and goal attainment. Additionally, it delves into how a gamified approach transforms complex tasks into manageable components, fostering problem-solving within the crowdsourcing landscape. Most important considerations are:

a. Goal-Setting Theory posits that individuals are motivated by setting and achieving specific, challenging goals. In the context of gamified crowd-sourcing, this theory becomes a guiding principle for designing challenges that drive skill development and problem-solving. Most prevalent application to skill development that the gamified challenges can be structured to include clear skill-based objectives. Whether it is coding, design, or data analysis, participants set goals aligned with skill development. Achieving these goals not only enhances their competencies but also provides a tangible sense of accomplishment. The second important application can be in designing the challenges with progressive skill levels, to ensure a continuous learning curve. As participants advance through increasingly complex tasks, they gradually acquire and refine skills. This structured progression aligns with the principles of Goal-Setting Theory, fostering skill development over time. Another application of the Goal Setting Theory can be in Goal Attainment through personalized goal setting. Gamification allows for personalized goal setting, where participants can define specific skill-related objectives based on their interests and aspirations. This customization enhances motivation, as participants are invested in achieving goals that are personally meaningful. Feedback on goal progress, that is regular feedback on participants' progress towards their skill-based goals is crucial. Gamified elements such as progress bars, achievement badges, or level indicators provide real-time feedback, reinforcing their journey and contributing to a sense of goal attainment.

b. Innovation Diffusion Theory explores how new ideas or innovations spread through a population. Applied to crowdsourcing, the gamified approach to problem-solving aligns with the diffusion of innovative solutions within a collaborative environment. This is also divided into two. First one is application to problem solving where it is about breaking down complex problems (gamification excels in breaking down complex problems into manageable components). Crowdsourcing challenges can be designed as smaller, interconnected tasks that collectively address a larger issue (Kumar & Gupta, 2022).

c. This modular approach aligns with the principles of breaking down innovations into adoptable units. The second one is collaborative problem-solving (gamified crowdsourcing platforms facilitate collaborative problem-solving; participants, each contributing to a specific aspect of a complex problem, collectively work towards a solution). This collaborative approach mirrors the social aspects of innovation diffusion, where diverse contributions lead to the adoption of novel solutions.

APPLICATION TO USER ADOPTION OF SOLUTIONS

(1) Recognition and Adoption: gamification elements like leader boards, badges, or virtual rewards can recognize and highlight participants who contribute significantly to solving complex problems. This recognition fosters a sense of accomplishment and motivates users to adopt and further diffuse innovative solutions. (2) Iterative Problem-Solving: the iterative nature of gamification in crowdsourcing encourages participants to continuously refine and improve solutions. Innovation Diffusion Theory suggests that innovations are adopted through an iterative process, and gamification supports this cycle by promoting ongoing problem-solving efforts.

INTEGRATING SKILL DEVELOPMENT AND PROBLEM-SOLVING

(1) In a holistic approach to task design for skill integration, challenges can be strategically designed to integrate skill development and problem-solving. Participants engage in tasks that not only contribute to solving a larger problem but also require the application and enhancement of specific skills. (2) Skill synergy is the collaborative nature of gamified crowdsourcing that ensures that participants with diverse skill sets collaborate on multifaceted challenges. This creates a synergy where participants not only contribute their individual expertise but also learn from others, fostering a holistic skill development experience. There are some challenges and considerations in skill development and problem-solving, and they are as follows: (1) addressing potential challenges like balancing complexity, striking a balance between challenging participants to foster skill development, and avoiding overwhelming complexity are crucial. Gamified challenges should be challenging enough to stimulate growth but not so difficult that they discourage participation. (2) Ensuring collaboration – designing challenges that encourage collaboration without fostering excessive competition is essential. The goal is to create an environment where participants are motivated to share knowledge and skills for collective problem-solving (Mittal & Kumar, 2019).

The integration of gamification in crowdsourcing, guided by Goal-Setting Theory and Innovation Diffusion Theory, transforms the landscape into a dynamic space for skill development and collaborative problem-solving. By aligning challenges with participants' skill-based goals and breaking down complex problems into manageable components, gamification becomes a catalyst for continuous learning and innovation diffusion. This holistic approach not only enhances individual competencies but also contributes to the collective intelligence of the crowdsourcing community. As the field evolves, the seamless integration of gamification, skill development, and problem-solving remains a cornerstone for fostering a collaborative and innovative environment within crowdsourcing platforms.

Technological Advancements and Future Trajectories

As Innovation Diffusion Theory guides our exploration, we contemplate the integration of artificial intelligence, augmented reality, and other emerging technologies into gamified environments. Looking at the future of crowdsourcing, guided by the principles of Innovation Diffusion Theory, we anticipate the transformative impact of emerging technologies on gamification. The integration of artificial intelligence (AI), augmented reality (AR), and other cutting-edge technologies becomes important to the gamified environment. The crowdsourcing platforms envision a landscape where innovation and collaboration are propelled by the synergies between technology and gamification.

Integration of artificial intelligence can enhance and personalize the gamification experiences in crowdsourcing. What are the ethical considerations associated with AI integration, and how can responsible AI practices be implemented become very much interesting to investigate. AI algorithms can analyse user behaviours, preferences, and performance data to personalize gamified experiences (Kumar & Lata, 2022). Tailored challenges, real-time feedback, and skill recommendations contribute to a more individualized and engaging environment. The AI-driven task assignment can dynamically match participants with tasks based on their evolving skill levels and expertise (Lata & Kumar, 2021). This not only optimizes task distribution but also ensures that individuals are consistently challenged and motivated.

Predictive Analytics for Motivation

AI's predictive capabilities can anticipate user motivation patterns (Kumar & Ogunmola, 2022). By analysing historical data, AI can suggest gamification elements that are likely to motivate individuals, enhancing the overall effectiveness of motivational strategies.

The integration of augmented reality has the potential for creating more immersive and engaging gamified crowdsourcing experiences. Augmented reality can certainly redefine the boundaries of virtual collaboration and problem-solving. AR technologies can bring a new dimension to gamified crowdsourcing challenges by overlaying virtual elements onto the real world. This immersive experience enhances engagement and provides participants with a novel and dynamic way to interact with tasks. Collaborative AR can also facilitate collaborative problem-solving by creating shared virtual spaces where participants from different locations can collaboratively work on challenges. This fosters a sense of presence and teamwork, transcending geographical constraints. Augmented reality can also be leveraged for real-time recognition and rewards. Participants may receive virtual badges or rewards overlaid onto their physical surroundings, creating a tangible and augmented representation of their achievements within the gamified environment.

Considering the emerging technologies, Blockchain technology can enhance transparency and trust within gamified crowdsourcing platforms. Smart contracts and decentralized ledgers can ensure fair and transparent reward systems, providing a secure and immutable record of participants' achievements. The integration of biometric data, such as facial expressions or physiological responses, can add a new layer to gamification. Platforms could adapt challenges based on users' emotional states or measure the physiological impact of engaging in gamified tasks. Going beyond AR, the integration of Extended Reality (XR), which includes both augmented and virtual reality, can create fully immersive gamified environments. Participants may find themselves in virtual worlds, collaborating on tasks in ways that transcend the limitations of the physical world.

As technological advancements bring more data into play, ensuring robust data privacy measures and security protocols becomes paramount. Participants must have the confidence that their personal information is handled responsibly within gamified crowdsourcing platforms. AI-driven gamification elements should be designed with a commitment to algorithmic fairness. Bias detection, transparency in decision-making processes, and ongoing monitoring can mitigate potential ethical concerns related to AI integration. However, the technological advancements should not exacerbate digital divides. Efforts must be made to ensure that emerging technologies are accessible to diverse participants, fostering inclusivity within gamified crowdsourcing platforms.

The future of gamification in crowdsourcing holds immense potential, driven by the seamless integration of emerging technologies. As AI, AR, and other innovations become integral components, the gamified landscape evolves into a dynamic and immersive environment. Envisioning this future, guided by the principles of Innovation Diffusion Theory, not only propels collaboration and innovation but also prompts a thoughtful consideration of ethical and responsible integration. The gamified crowdsourcing platforms of tomorrow will not only leverage cutting-edge technologies but also uphold principles of transparency, fairness, and accessibility, ensuring a transformative and inclusive experience for participants worldwide.

Conclusions

The chapter traverses a journey that explores the present landscape and anticipates the future, guided by principles such as Self-Determination Theory, Goal-Setting Theory, and Innovation Diffusion Theory. The integration of gamification within crowdsourcing platforms emerges as a powerful catalyst, shaping engagement, motivation, skill development, and collaborative problem-solving. The symbiotic relationship between gamification and crowdsourcing holds immense promise for shaping the collaborative and innovative landscapes of the future. As participants engage with gamified challenges, find motivation in their contributions, and collaboratively solve complex problems, the gamified crowdsourcing ecosystem evolves into a dynamic and empowering space. With thoughtful integration, ethical considerations, and a commitment to ongoing improvement, gamification stands as a beacon, guiding crowdsourcing platforms towards a future of enriched collaboration, skill development, and transformative engagement.

References

Ayodeji, O. G., & Kumar, V. (2023). E-commerce research models: A systematic review and identification of the determinants to success. *International Journal of Business Information Systems (IJBIS)*, 43(1), 87–106.

Bhardwaj, A., & Kumar, V. (2022). A framework for enhancing privacy in online collaboration. *International Journal of Electronic Security and Digital Forensics (IJESDF)*, 14(4), 413–432.

Bhardwaj, A., & Kumar, V. (2024). Challenges in online collaboration to augment industry 4.0. *International Journal of Technology, Policy and Management (IJTPM)*, 24(1), 71–92.

Csikszentmihalyi, M. (1990). *Experience, F. T. psychology of optimal*. Harper & Row.

Davis, F. D. (1989). Perceived usefulness, perceived ease of use, and user acceptance of information technology. *MIS Quarterly*, 1(1), 319–340.

Deci, E. L., & Ryan, R. M. (2000). The "what" and "why" of goal pursuits: Human needs and the self-determination of behavior. *Psychological Inquiry*, 11(4), 227–268.

Faisol, F., Kumar, V., & Aliami, S. (2023). Mediating role of inter-firm linkages and innovation capability towards the sustainability of SMEs in Indonesia. *International Journal of Technology, Policy and Management (IJTPM)*, 23(4), 387–409.

Kahneman, D. (2011). *Thinking, fast and slow*. Farrar, Straus and Giroux.

Kumar, V., & Gupta, G. (Eds.). (2022). *Strategic management during a pandemic*. Routledge.

Kumar, V., & Lata, M. (Eds.). (2022). *The future of E-commerce*. Nova Science Publishers.

Kumar, V., & Mittal, S. (2020). Mobile marketing campaigns: Practices, challenges and opportunities. *International Journal of Business Innovation and Research (IJBIR)*, 21(4), 523–539.

Kumar, V., & Nanda, P. (2022). Approaching the Porter's five forces through social media analytics. *International Journal of Services Operations and Informatics (IJSOI)*, 12(2), 184–200.

Kumar, V., & Ogunmola, G. A. (2022). Web analytics applications, opportunities and challenges to online retail in India. *International Journal of Services and Operations Management*, 41(4), 463–485.

Kumar, V., & Rewari, M. (Eds.). (2023). *Pandemics in the age of social media: Information and misinformation in developing nations*. Routledge.

Kumar, V., & Sharma, D. (2021). E-learning theories, components and cloud computing based learning platforms. *International Journal of Web-Based Learning and Teaching Technologies*, 16(3), 1–16.

Kusumawati, R. D., Oswari, T., Yusnitasari, T., Mittal, S., & Kumar, V. (2021). Impact of marketing-mix, culture and experience as moderator to purchase intention and purchase decision for online music product in Indonesia. *International Journal of Business Innovation and Research (IJBIR)*, 25(4), 475–495.

Lata, M., & Kumar, V. (2021). Standards and regulatory compliances for IoT. *International Journal of Service Science Management, Engineering and Technology (IJSSMET)*, 12(5), 133–134.

Locke, E. A., & Latham, G. P. (2002). Building a practically useful theory of goal setting and task motivation: A 35-year odyssey. *American Psychologist*, 57(9), 705.

Mittal, S., & Kumar, V. (2019). Study of knowledge management models and their relevance in organisations. *International Journal of Knowledge Management Studies*, 10(3), 322–335.

Mittal, S., & Kumar, V. (2020). A framework for ethical mobile marketing. *International Journal of Technoethics (IJT)*, 11(1), 28–42.

Mittal, S., Kumar, V., & Seppi, J. (2022). Targeting mobile gamers community for marketing campaigns. *Journal of Content, Community & Communication (JCC)*, 16(2), 106–117.

Nakamura, J., & Csikszentmihalyi, M. (2009). Flow theory and research. In *Handbook of positive psychology* (pp. 195–206). Oxford University Press.

Nanda, P., & Kumar, V. (2023). Decision analytics for competitive advantage: Cases on using social media analytics. *International Journal of Technology, Policy and Management*, 23(4), 372–386.

Nayar, K. B., & Kumar, V. (2018). Cost benefit analysis of cloud computing in education. *International Journal of Business Information Systems (IJBIS)*, 27(2), 205–221.

Paruthi, M., Nagina, R., & Gupta, G. (2023, March). Measuring the effect of consumer brand engagement on brand-related outcomes in gamified mobile apps: A solicitation of technology acceptance model. In *Proceedings* (Vol. 85, No. 1, p. 10). MDPI.

Pradhan, P., & Kumar, V. (2016). Trust management models for digital identities. *International Journal of Virtual Communities and Social Networking (IJVCSN)*, 8(4), 1–24.

Rest, J. R. (2020). *Moral development: Advances in research and theory*. Praeger.

Rogers, E. M. (2023). *Diffusion of innovations* (5th ed.). Free Press.

Tajfel, H., & Turner, J. C. (2010). An integrative theory of intergroup conflict. *The Social Psychology of Intergroup Relations*, 1(1), 33–47.

Part 2

Gamification as an Influencer for Consumer Behavior and Engagement

Gamification as an Influencer for Consumer Behavior and Engagement

Aparna Tembulkar

Introduction

In this competitive, quick-paced environment, gamification is rapidly gaining the interest of different corporate organizations. Gamification is the application of gaming elements – such as leaderboards, contests, medals, and badges into contexts other than game design

(Deterding et al., 2011). Gamification techniques are being introduced by organizations, particularly in the marketing sector, in non-gaming contexts at an accelerated rate. Gamification is primarily being used to boost consumer engagement, which can help marketers achieve their objectives by getting more people involved in the process. Currently, a lot of businesses use gamification components like online forums and applications (Nike's running application or Samsung's online communities) (Streukens et al., 2019) to increase the users' experience with gamification. Customers in the non-gaming environment are acting in a particular way as a result of this usage of technology and one of the objectives of using gamification is being used by businesses to retain customers and boost revenue (Hamari et al., 2014).

Research Methodology – Content Analysis of Research Articles

This chapter follows a content analysis approach based on the review of extant literature available from Scopus, Web of Science, and Science Direct. The initial search showed 121 papers from these databases. While carrying out the review, some articles were rejected on the basis of the title while some others were rejected on the basis of the abstract. Full-text literature review was carried out for 55 research articles, leading to the major themes in alignment with the objective.

The researcher can extract themes from extensive data using content analysis. The description of content trends and the disclosure of researchers' areas of interest are advantages of content analysis. Therefore, content analysis makes sense for this research.

DOI: 10.4324/9781032694238-5

NVivo software version 14.23.2 (QSR International, Melbourne, Australia) was used to import the articles. Subsequently, using NVivo software, coding was done to understand the various theoretical frameworks contributing to gamification, resulting in five theories. Besides this, using the explore feature, word clouds were created through word frequency commands to understand the most popular theories among the five theories. Additionally, coding was carried out to comprehend how gamification affects client involvement and buy intention.

The section that follows presents the results of our content analysis.

What is gamification?

The usage of game design features outside of games is known as gamification (Deterding et al., 2011; Brigham, 2015). Previous research in a variety of areas, including education, has shown the effects of gamification (effects on behavior change) (Hew et al., 2016), that is, the financial and banking sector (for improving personal experience with the aid of the virtual assistant) (Rodrigues et al., 2016), nutrition, health (Sultan & Suhail, 2019), wellness (for improving overall fitness) (Johnson et al., 2016), and the supply chain industry (for improving ordering system) (Putz et al., 2019). Research has also attempted to look into how gamification affects the e-commerce sector.

According to Behl et al. (2020), businesses have adopted and embraced gamified apps as a result of the expanding accessibility of technology, particularly mobile technology (Eisingerich et al., 2019). The main aim of gamification is to keep the consumer engaged and positively influence his purchase intention (AlMarshedi et al., 2017).

Why does gamification work?

There are two key dynamics that make gamification work – challenges and rewards. In general, people enjoy competing and finding solutions to challenges. It is human nature to respond to challenges. Challenges give consumers a sense of competition and create an anticipation for the reward. So, it is essential that marketers not only pose challenges but also commend those who win or overcome the challenges (Brigham, 2015). Either in-game prizes or nongame rewards, such as discounts, can be used to achieve this. Receiving rewards further motivates consumers to continue with the game and the product. A well-designed game will lead to consumers' enjoyment as well as entertainment. Additionally, games help to draw a greater attention to the products, services, and website of the marketer (Raj & Gupta, 2018).

The greatest benefit of gamifying a task is that it promotes greater participation and engagement. Aspects of human competition and aspiration for improvement are used in gamification. The game will typically display the person's progress, which encourages them to complete the activity. It encourages the consumers to make the effort to finish the game/task on hand by luring them with rewards. In these ways, gamification helps people focus on achieving a personal best by thoughtfully laying out what they have accomplished and also giving them the opportunity to fail (Yang et al., 2019). Research indicates that the incorporation of gaming aspects into non-gaming activities has a noteworthy impact on consumer engagement and decision-making. In addition, it has been shown that challenges and rewards are the two most popular processes; the most tried gamification components include leader boards, badges, and points (Wen et al., 2014). The chapter will enlist various elements of gamification and focus on the ones that are popular in the context of marketing.

The ultimate goal of any marketing activity is to achieve customer satisfaction through the sale of the products and services. Although gamification is known to increase consumer engagement, the real question is whether this engagement results in the purchase of the product/service. The chapter deals with the impacts of gamification on the purchase decision of the consumers.

Literature throws light on several theories that explain the reasons why gamification works. These include the Cognitive Evaluation Theory (CET), Self-Determination Theory (SDT), Technology Acceptance Model (TAM), and the Theory of Planned Behavior (TPB). Similar to this, the gamification of consumer contexts has employed the Stimulus-Organism-Response (SOR) theory to explain why customers intend to use gamified goods or services.

The chapter will discuss these theories and their relevance to the concept of gamification and consumer engagement.

Theoretical Framework

Literature throws light on various theories that explain the usage of gamification and the reasons why gamification works.

Cognitive Evaluation Theory (CET) Theory – people have psychological needs – autonomy, competence, and relatedness – while they are working on specific activities, according to Cognitive Evaluation Theory (CET). People are intrinsically driven and experience higher satisfaction when their wants are perceived to be met, which increases their engagement in the activities thereby explaining why customers engage in gamification (Suh et al., 2018; Dikcius et al., 2021). A psychological theory, the cognitive evaluation tries to explain how extrinsic rewards affect intrinsic motivation.

According to this theory, the idea of "intrinsic incentive" is usually referred to as "intrinsic motivation". The notion holds that people are more likely to participate in an activity when they have internal motivations like enjoyment.

Drawing from theoretical underpinnings, Xu et al. (2020) use CET to develop a conceptual framework for gamification and elaborates on how gamification components are important factors in determining customer happiness and intrinsically driven purchase intent. By applying such CET features to gamification, it is possible to regard the behaviors of intrinsic regulation as driven by internal reasons like happiness and the behaviors of extrinsic regulation as driven by external factors like prizes and competition

Intrinsic motivation emerges when a person understands that the causes are the aforementioned behaviors. Enjoyment is a prime example of intrinsic motivation. People who are driven by their own intrinsic motivation will work harder and enjoy a task more.

Self-Determination Theory (SDT) – according to the concept of extrinsic and intrinsic motivation, one of the most widely used motivation theories in use today is the theory of self-determination (SDT). The definition of intrinsic motivation is when someone engages in an activity because it is essentially fascinating or enjoyable, while extrinsic motivation is when someone does because it produces a separable result (Brühlmann, 2013). According to the Self-Determination Theory, gamification is an extrinsic motivation since people are motivated to participate in gamifying activities by earning points, badges, or other prizes. However, the author also points out that these forms of rewards might develop into a type of intrinsic drive. When it comes to loyalty programs, for example, using feedback as an implicit incentive increases implicit motivation to participate more effectively than providing explicit rewards like points.

Using gamified systems enhances application engagement; this behavioral change was attributable to the impact of intrinsic motivation (Kim et al., 2020). One of the few motivational theories that concentrate on how much a person's behavior is self-determined and self-motivated is self-determination theory (SDT), which contends that people become more self-determined and self-motivated when three fundamental intrinsic needs are addressed. The three basic requirements are (1) autonomy: the capacity to accept one's own actions on an internal level, (2) relatedness: a feeling of kinship and participation with people in a group, and (3) competence: controlling the result and mastery (Costa & Castro, 2021; Groh, 2012; Micarelli et al., 2016). Gamification utilizes this theory by fulfilling these needs. For example, it provides autonomy in allowing the player to use various paths or make choices in the game and allows for competence by giving badges and relatedness through leaderboards. The literature also notes that research utilizing SDT in the video game industry has demonstrated how game features like feedback, choice, and repeatability may assist meet criteria and increase intrinsic motivation (Kam & Umar, 2018).

Technology Acceptance Model (TAM) Theory – users will interact with an application, product, or service website as long as it is user-friendly and beneficial, according to the Technology Acceptance Model (TAM). Learning a new skill is usually difficult since people are generally resistant to change. However, if companies gamify their electronic commerce platforms to make them simple and easy to use, customers will try using the new apps or websites.

For instance, people are more likely to use a page if they can first learn something about it and think it will be fun. Consumers play games more frequently when they feel it to be practical and simple to use (Tobon et al., 2020). Varannai et al. (2017) explain the applicability of the TAM model (Paruthi et al., 2023) to gamification by means of ease of use, recognition of benefits, and external motivation factors such as personal enjoyment. Perceived utility and simplicity of use, in line with the TAM framework, have a positive influence on behavioral intention and actual behavior in terms of frequency and length of usage in the gamified setting (Chen & Zhao, 2022).

The Technology Acceptance Model (TAM) states that a user's decision to utilize a technology is mostly influenced by its usability and utility, that is, to participate in the game. How easy and fun it is to use is the second factor.

Perceived ease-of-use refers to how easy a person believes a certain game to be to use. Perceived utility is the notion that using a particular gaming task could enhance task performance. The degree to which someone feels that playing a game is enjoyable is known as perceived enjoyment, and it is closely associated with perceived utility. The regular use of online gaming is largely driven by perceived delight. Similarly, when social indicators (such avatars, emotional content, or communication capabilities) are used in an online gaming application on a website, users' perceptions of other participants as social actors shift (after the social presence is detected) (Rodrigues et al., 2016).

Salimon et al. (2021) also found support for the TAM model with respect to applying gamification in the smart phone banking industry, with the aim of increased and widespread usage.

Theory of Planned Behavior (TPB) – the factors that affect behavior prediction are described by the Theory of Planned Behavior (TPB), a theory of decision-making (Kumar et al., 2023). According to this idea, every behavior begins with an intention, and the intention is influenced by a person's attitude toward the behavior, subjective norms, and perceived behavioral control.

One definition of attitude is "a favorable or unfavorable evaluation of the behaviour". Subjective norms are described as "perceived social pressure to perform, or not, the behavior in question". Perceived behavioral control is the measure of how difficult the behavior is thought to be to perform. This hypothesis has been utilized to explain customer behavior in gamified environments. Researchers have also found that because TPB lets users compare their performance to other players', it serves as an example of how badges may be a helpful tool for engaging users with gamified products. Subsequential norms then push everyone to achieve greater standards of performance (Tobon et al., 2020).

Stimulus-Organism-Response (SOR) Model – this method, which is established in psychology, defines a stimulus as an impulse that conveys a message. Reactions, outcomes, answers, and reactions for an organism – a single person – are referred to as responses. The SOR model consists of three components: stimulus, impact, and reaction. The gamification model most often cited by different writers is based on the gamification pyramid approach proposed by Werbach and Hunter (2012), which consists of game components, game mechanics, and game dynamics.

Researchers who have studied consumer behavior with respect to the SOR model claim that businesses employ numerous stimuli to get a favorable impact on consumers (Yang et al., 2019). It is believed that this positive effect will persuade the customer to use the business' products, website, or services. When it comes to gamification, companies try to use a range of incentives to promote the kind of customer behavior that is most commonly mentioned by different writers (Gatautis et al., 2016). They do this by utilizing features that are easily recognizable by consumers as being part of games, such as avatars, badges, points, levels, and virtual presents (Zhang et al., 2020).

The concept map given below in Figure 3.1 depicts various theoretical models that form the basis for gamification.

The word cloud derived from the NVivo Software, given in Figure 3.2, shows the Self-Determination Theory (SDT) and Technology Acceptance Model (TAM). These are the more popular theories to explain the impact of gamification.

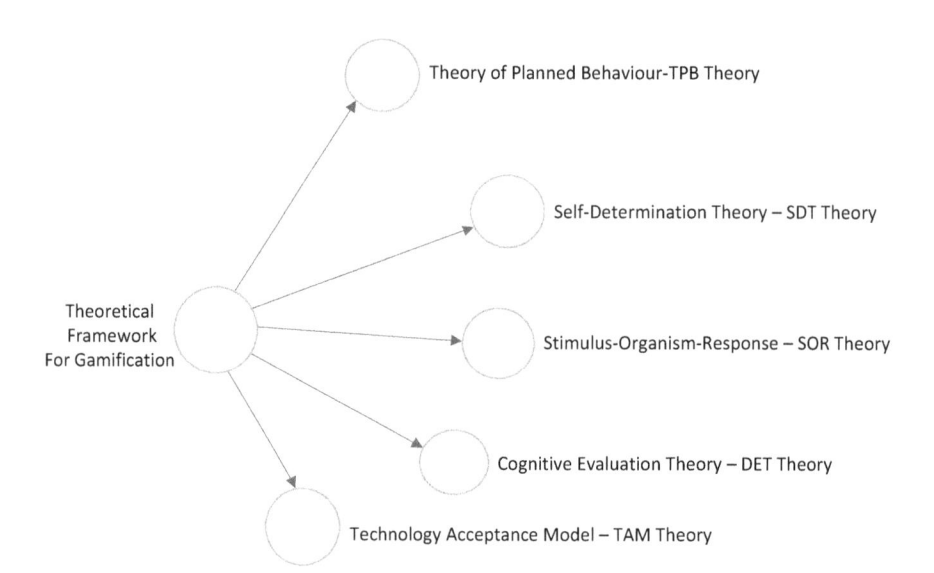

Figure 3.1 Concept map of theoretical models

Source: author's work

Figure 3.2 Word cloud showing higher word frequency for the words "SDT", "TAM", "acceptance", and "Determination"

Source: author's work

Elements of Gamification

By adding game components, gamification is viewed as a technique for energizing and engaging patients, students, volunteers, and other audiences (Haziri et al., 2019). Palmer et al. (2012) have extracted four key components of gamification from the fields of game mechanics, behavioral economic theories, and contemporary user experience design thinking. These are described later briefly:

Progress Paths – progress Paths, the first component, is defined as "the use of challenges and evolving narratives to increase task completion".

Usually, gamification begins with a straightforward task and progresses to more difficult ones over time. While a newbie is rewarded, more seasoned users stay active in the process. As a result, the advancement path gets increasingly difficult as the user proceeds. An example of this is leaderboards.

Feedback and Reward – the use of rapid indications of success through virtual and financial rewards is the second component, feedback and reward. Gamification typically uses conventional financial rewards to instantly reward consumers; but, depending on the customer's journey, it can also use delayed gratification. Some clients wish to take on more responsibility, leadership, or power as they grow. Reward points are typically used to provide rewards.

Social Connections – utilizing a customer's social networks, the third component, social connection, encourages competition and provides support.

The fact that so many gamification programs allow users to quickly access their social networks and acquaintances is one of its main draws. Badges facilitate social interaction.

Interface and user experience – the fourth component, interface and user experience, needs to have user-friendly website design and graphics from video games. Even for small and medium-sized firms, it might be challenging for a small team to achieve such complicated design standards.

For gamification to be successfully implemented and produce the intended results, including change in behavior, connection development, loyalty, repeat business, and intrinsic and extrinsic rewards, full thought must be given (Hamid & Kuppusamy, 2017). Conaway and Garay (2014) emphasized that gamification must be entertaining for the user even when it incorporates features of gaming, such as levels, prizes, badges, points, tokens, and competition (Kiryakova et al., 2013).

Points, Badges, and Leaderboards – points, badges, and leaderboards, collectively known as PBL, seem to be the most popular game elements (Thomas & Baral, 2023). Another adaptation in the form of levels, scoreboards and trophies are also found as elements of gamification in the reviewed literature (Adhytia et al., 2023; Wrona, 2012). Widyani (2021) also suggests a loyalty program as a gamification element. Storytelling, avatars, challenges, and achievements are also some of the elements used in gamification (Kam & Umar, 2018). The popular elements and corresponding game dynamics (Hamari & Koivisto, 2015; Vanduhe et al., 2020) are given in Table 3.1.

Table 3.1 Table of Various Game Elements

Game Elements	How the Element Explains Gamification	Game Dynamics
Points	It is form of reward for accomplishing a particular activity	Reward
Badges	A badge is issued or given, once a certain level is completed or a certain number of points are accumulated. It is related to task completion as well as motivation to go ahead	Achievement
Leaderboards	A leaderboard indicates your relative position in the game when compared with another player. It gives a competitive insight and helps move toward task completion	Completion
Level	It is the level of the game that has been achieved and displays the status of the player	Status
Progress bars	These help track the progress and also how much of a task/game has been completed.	Completion

Source: author's work

Figure 3.3 Word cloud of elements showing badges, points, and leaderboards as words with higher frequency

Source: author's work

A synthesis of literature using the NVivo software has also highlighted points, badges, and leaderboards as words with higher frequency in the word cloud shown in Figure 3.3.

Consumer Engagement through Gamification

Engaging and motivating customers are challenges that most organizations face (Haziri et al., 2019). Over the past few years, gamification has drawn a lot of attention as a trending solution for boosting user engagement.

Lu and Ho (2020) suggest that gamification is promoting beneficial service use patterns, such as boosting user activity, social connection, or the quality and productivity of actions (Streukens et al., 2019). According to Sigala (2015), the incorporation of game/motivational affordances is assumed to produce "gameful" experiences that are intrinsically driven, fulfilling, and desirable use patterns. Because of this, gamification is commonly described as the next wave of customer involvement and marketing tactics. Lorenzo-Lledó et al. (2023) opine that gamification is known to improving advantageous service usage patterns, such as increasing user activity, social connection, or the caliber and productivity of actions. Hamari et al. (2014) focus on the function of gamification in evoking the same psychological sensations as games (usually) do. In their article "Does gamification work?", they opine that indeed gamification works. The majority of the research works that were analyzed showed that gamification had good effects or results (Hamari et al., 2014).

The study's results (Xu et al., 2020) show that the autonomy, absorption, and game incentives of gamification positively enhance people's sense of enjoyment and help them meet their psychological needs, which in turn affect consumers' intention to make a purchase (Harwood & Garry, 2015).

The greatest benefit of gamifying a task is that it promotes greater participation and engagement (Seaborn & Fels, 2015; Tiwari, 2023). These characteristics are desired by the majority of enterprises. Engagement, brand loyalty, and brand awareness are three fundamental marketing ideas that perfectly match the main objectives of gamification (Lucassen & Jansen, 2014). Gamification, when done properly, can also give users a feeling of progress and accomplishment (Rasool et al., 2020). Gamification uses aspects of human competition and aspiration for improvement (Brigham, 2015). People are influenced and motivated to engage in activities linked to education, marketing, training, networking, tourism, and health through the application of gamification (Abou-Shouk & Soliman, 2021/2020). It is a very new way of interacting with people.

The broad consensus is that enjoyment of an activity is a significant intrinsic motivator. Rewards, autonomy, and the use of gamification aspects are found to increase consumer enjoyment, which encourages shopping. Through particular activities, such as earning incentives, being absorbed in games, competing, and feeling self-control, consumer enjoyment can foster positive attitudes and affect purchase decision (Hollebeek et al., 2021; Xu et al., 2020). Customer engagement generally refers to a customer's continued encounters with a business, which deepen their emotional and psychological relationships with it (Mitchell et al., 2017). Their propensity to interact with marketers and their brand loyalty toward goods that employ marketing gamification are both impacted by gamification aspects. Customer interaction with gamification and gamified shopping experiences have a favorable impact on views about gamification as well as on brand loyalty (Raj & Gupta, 2018). Another study (Kim et al., 2020) demonstrated that gamification may be a potential distinctive feature utilized to draw customers to a platform, particularly those who have a penchant for novelty.

Overall literature provides evidence that gamification increases consumer engagement and creates a positive effect on the intention to purchase. In addition to this are several marketing theories that explain the relationship between gamification, consumer engagement, and purchase decision.

Impact of Gamification on Consumer Purchase Decision

According to Harindranath and Sivakumaran (2021), promotion is a crucial element to boost sales. Gamification is frequently used as a marketing tactic to advertise goods and services. Gamification is commonly suggested as a way to close knowledge gaps, promote learning, and influence behavior (Beck et al., 2019/2018). However, very little is known about how it impacts a consumer's real buy intention (Zhang et al., 2020). Viewing the consumers' decision-making process is essential to understanding how gamification affects consumers' purchase decisions. The external elements that can have an impact on the Consumer's decision should be taken into account when making the final product choice. The consumer attempts to evaluate a product by attempting to determine its advantages and features. A product's appraisal also takes into account the views of the reference groups (such as friends, family, and salespeople). In addition to the aforementioned variables, social norms and individual characteristics may also have an impact on these decisions as intrinsic motivation (Ryan & Deci, 2000a, 2000b) and uninterrupted experiences. According to research (Wen et al., 2014), gamification has a considerable influence on consumers' purchase decisions (Sailer et al., 2017; Che et al., 2023) as well as on online purchase decisions (Berger et al., 2014; Tobon et al., 2020). Additionally, studies (Lucassen & Jansen, 2014) show that gamification increases engagement through fruitful interaction. Similar research suggests that gamification components are favorably associated with brand app experiences (Lee & Jin, 2019). Similarly, according to Xu et al. (2020), gamification helps people achieve their psychological requirements and increases sense of enjoyment, all of which have a favorable impact on consumers' intentions to make online purchases (García-Jurado et al., 2019). Another study (Raman, 2020) posits that gamification positively affects young female consumers' purchasing intentions.

Another study (Raj & Gupta, 2018) showed that gamification's effect on brand loyalty was significantly and favorably predicted by customer engagement (Shang & Lin, 2013) with it and good purchasing intention on gamified websites.

The word cloud extracted through the word frequency query in NVivo software depicted in Figure 3.4 brings out "Consuming" (with "Consumer" as a stemmed word), "engagement", "motivation", "Behavior" as words with high frequency, further reinforcing the impact of gamification on consumer engagement and purchase intention.

Conclusion

Gamification is the use of game elements in nongame contexts (Deterding et al., 2011). Various theories like the Self-Determination Theory (SDT), Technology Adoption Model (TAM), and Cognitive Evaluation Theory (CET) explain the reasons why gamification works. Increasingly, literature throws light on the use of gamification in marketing to attract, engage, and influence the consumer buying behavior and further to retain them. The chapter presents a synthesis of 55 research articles to further elucidate the role of gamification in attracting, engaging, influencing, and retaining customers. It is found that gamification

Figure 3.4 Word cloud depicting high-frequency words like "Gamification", "Consuming", "Behavior", and "Engagement"

Source: author's work

does have a positive impact on customer engagement and purchase intention. Literature also suggests that the use of gamification in marketing would help foster brand loyalty. The research does bring out that gamification increases customer engagement and impacts the purchase decision positively.

References

Abou-Shouk, M., & Soliman, M. (2021). The impact of gamification adoption intention on brand awareness and loyalty in tourism: The mediating effect of customer engagement. *Journal of Destination Marketing and Management*, *20*, 100559. https://doi.org/10.1016/j.jdmm.2021.100559 (Original work published 2020, August)

Adhytia, M., Putra, W., Sensuse, D., Suryono, R. R., Indonesia, U. T., & Kautsarina, K. (2023, April). Trends and applications of gamification in E-commerce: A systematic literature review. *Journal of Information Systems Engineering and Business Intelligence*. https://doi.org/10.20473/jisebi.9.1.28-37

AlMarshedi, A., Wanick, V., Wills, G. B., & Ranchhod, A. (2017). Gamification and behaviour. In S. Stieglitz, C. Lattemann, S. Robra-Bissantz, R. Zarnekow, & T. Brockmann (Eds.), *Gamification. Progress in IS* (pp. 19–29). Springer. https://doi.org/10.1007/978-3-319-45557-0_2

Beck, A. L., Chitalia, S., & Rai, V. (2019). Not so gameful: A critical review of gamification in mobile energy applications. *Energy Research and Social Science, 51*, 32–39. https://doi.org/10.1016/j.erss.2019.01.006 (Original work published 2018, August)

Behl, A., Sheorey, P., Pal, A., Veetil, A. K. V., & Singh, S. R. (2020). Gamification in E-commerce. *Journal of Electronic Commerce in Organizations. 18*(2), 1–16. https://doi.org/10.4018/jeco.2020040101

Berger, V., Miesler, L., & Hari, J. (2014, November 1–11). *The potential of gamification in changing consumer behaviour towards a more sustainable nutrition behaviour*. Academy of Marketing Conference, Bournemouth.

Brigham, T. J. (2015). An introduction to gamification: Adding game elements for engagement. *Medical Reference Services Quarterly, 34*(4), 471–480. https://doi.org/10.1080/02763869.2015.1082385

Brühlmann, F. (2013, April). *Gamification from the perspective of self-determination theory and flow* [Bachelor thesis, Institute of Psychology University of Basel], 28.

Che, T., Peng, Y., Zhou, Q., Dickey, A., & Lai, F. (2023, May). The impacts of gamification designs on consumer purchase: A use and gratification theory perspective. *Electronic Commerce Research and Applications, 59*, 101268. https://doi.org/10.1016/j.elerap.2023.101268

Chen, Y., & Zhao, S. (2022). Understanding Chinese EFL learners' acceptance of gamified vocabulary learning apps: An integration of self-determination theory and technology acceptance model. *Sustainability (Switzerland), 14*(18). https://doi.org/10.3390/su141811288

Conaway, R., & Garay, M. C. (2014). Gamification and service marketing. *SpringerPlus, 3*(1). https://doi.org/10.1186/2193-1801-3-653

Costa, J., & Castro, R. (2021). SMEs must go online – E-commerce as an escape hatch for resilience and survivability. *Journal of Theoretical and Applied Electronic Commerce Research, 16*(7), 3043–3062. https://doi.org/10.3390/jtaer16070166

Deterding, S., Dixon, D., Khaled, R., & Nacke, L. (2011). From game design elements to gamefulness: Defining "gamification". In *Proceedings of the 15th international academic MindTrek conference: Envisioning future media environments, MindTrek 2011* (pp. 9–15). https://doi.org/10.1145/2181037.2181040

Dikcius, V., Urbonavicius, S., Adomaviciute, K., Degutis, M., & Zimaitis, I. (2021). Learning marketing online: The role of social interactions and gamification rewards. *Journal of Marketing Education, 43*(2), 159–173. https://doi.org/10.1177/0273475320968252

Eisingerich, A. B., Marchand, A., Fritze, M. P., & Dong, L. (2019). Hook vs. hope: How to enhance customer engagement through gamification. *International Journal of Research in Marketing, 36*(2), 200–215. https://doi.org/10.1016/j.ijresmar.2019.02.003

García-Jurado, A., Castro-González, P., Torres-Jiménez, M., & Leal-Rodríguez, A. L. (2019). Evaluating the role of gamification and flow in E-consumers: Millennials versus generation X. *Kybernetes, 48*(6), 1278–1300. https://doi.org/10.1108/K-07-2018-0350

Gatautis, R., Vitkauskaite, E., Gadeikiene, A., & Piligrimiene, Z. (2016). Gamification as a mean of driving online consumer behaviour: Sor model perspective. *Engineering Economics, 27*(1), 90–97. https://doi.org/10.5755/j01.ee.27.1.13198

Groh, F. (2012). Gamification: State of the art definition and utilization. In *Proceedings of the 4th seminar on research trends in media informatics (RTMI'12)*, 39–46. http://vts.uni-ulm.de/docs/2012/7866/vts_7866_11380.pdf

Hamari, J., & Koivisto, J. (2015). "Working out for likes": An empirical study on social influence in exercise gamification. *Computers in Human Behavior*, 50, 333–347. https://doi.org/10.1016/j.chb.2015.04.018

Hamari, J., Koivisto, J., & Sarsa, H. (2014). Does gamification work? – A literature review of empirical studies on gamification. In *Proceedings of the annual Hawaii international conference on system sciences*, 3025–3034. https://doi.org/10.1109/HICSS.2014.377

Hamid, M., & Kuppusamy, M. (2017). Gamification implementation in service marketing: A literature review. *Electronic Journal of Business & Management*, 2(1), 38–50. http://enterprise-gamification.com

Harindranath, R. M., & Sivakumaran, B. (2021). Perceived impact of promotional support: Issues and scale. *Journal of Promotion Management*, 27(1), 77–102. https://doi.org/10.1080/10496491.2020.1809592

Harwood, T., & Garry, T. (2015). An investigation into gamification as a customer engagement experience environment. *Journal of Services Marketing*, 29(6–7), 533–546. https://doi.org/10.1108/JSM-01-2015-0045

Haziri, F., Shabani, L., & Chovancova, M. (2019, January). Customer game experience impact on gamification and online purchasing. *Contemporary Issues in Business, Management and Economics Engineering*. https://doi.org/10.3846/cibmee.2019.078

Hew, K. F., Huang, B., Chu, K. W. S., & Chiu, D. K. (2016). Engaging Asian students through game mechanics: Findings from two experiment studies. *Computers & Education*, 92, 221–236.

Hollebeek, L. D., Das, K., & Shukla, Y. (2021, January). Game on! How gamified loyalty programs boost customer engagement value. *International Journal of Information Management*, 61. https://doi.org/10.1016/j.ijinfomgt.2021.102308

Johnson, D., Deterding, S., Kuhn, K. A., Staneva, A., Stoyanov, S., & Hides, L. (2016). Gamification for health and wellbeing: A systematic review of the literature. *Internet Interventions*, 6, 89–106.

Kam, A. H. T., & Umar, I. N. (2018). Fostering authentic learning motivations through gamification: A self-determination theory (SDT) approach. *Journal of Engineering Science and Technology*, 13(Special Issue), 1–9.

Kim, C., Costello, F. J., & Lee, K. C. (2020, July). The unobserved heterogeneous influence of gamification and novelty-seeking traits on consumers' repurchase intention in the omnichannel retailing. *Frontiers in Psychology*, 11. https://doi.org/10.3389/fpsyg.2020.01664

Kiryakova, G., Angelova, N., & Yordanova, L. (2013). Gamification in education. In *Proceedings of 9th international Balkan education and science conference*.

Kumar, S., Gupta, G., & Kumar, M. (2023). A bibliometric analysis of religiosity and purchase intentions: Overview, insights and future research directions. *International Journal of Business Information Systems*, 1(1), 1. https://doi.org/10.1504/ijbis.2023.10055663

Lee, J. Y., & Jin, C. H. (2019). The role of gamification in brand app experience: The moderating effects of the 4Rs of app marketing. *Cogent Psychology*, 6(1), 1–18. https://doi.org/10.1080/23311908.2019.1576388

Lorenzo-Lledó, A., Pérez Vázquez, E., Andreu Cabrera, E., & Lorenzo Lledó, G. (2023, September). Application of gamification in early childhood education and primary education: Thematic analysis. *Retos*, 50, 858–875. https://doi.org/10.47197/retos.v50.97366

Lu, H., & Ho, H. (2020, May). Exploring the impact of gamification on users' engagement for sustainable development: A case study in brand applications. *Sustainability*, 12(10), 4169. https://doi.org/10.3390/su12104169

Lucassen, G., & Jansen, S. (2014, August). Gamification in consumer marketing – future or fallacy? *Procedia – Social and Behavioral Sciences*, *148*, 194–202. https://doi.org/10.1016/j.sbspro.2014.07.034

Micarelli, A., Stamper, J., & Panourgia, K. (2016). Preface. In *Lecture notes in computer science (including subseries lecture notes in artificial intelligence and lecture notes in bioinformatics)* (Vol. 9684, pp. v–vi). https://doi.org/10.1007/978-3-319-39583-8

Mitchell, R., Schuster, L., & Drennan, J. (2017). Understanding how gamification influences behaviour in social marketing. *Australasian Marketing Journal*, *25*(1), 12–19. https://doi.org/10.1016/j.ausmj.2016.12.001

Palmer, D., Lunceford, S., & Patton, A. J. (2012). The engagement economy: How gamification is reshaping businesses. *Deloitte Review*, *11*, 52–69.

Paruthi, M., Nagina, R., & Gupta, G. (2023, March). Measuring the effect of consumer brand engagement on brand-related outcomes in gamified mobile apps: A solicitation of technology acceptance model. In *Proceedings* (Vol. 85, No. 1, p. 10). MDPI.

Putz, L. M., Hofbauer, F., & Mates, M. (2019, April). A vignette study among order pickers about the acceptance of gamification. In *GamiFIN* (pp. 154–166).

Raj, B., & Gupta, D. (2018). Factors influencing consumer responses to marketing gamification. *2018 International Conference on Advances in Computing, Communications and Informatics, ICACCI 2018*, 1538–1542. https://doi.org/10.1109/ICACCI.2018.8554922

Raman, P. (2020). Examining the importance of gamification, social interaction and perceived enjoyment among young female online buyers in India. *Young Consumers*. https://doi.org/10.1108/YC-05-2020-1148

Rasool, A., Shah, F. A., & Islam, J. U. (2020). Customer engagement in the digital age: A review and research agenda. *Current Opinion in Psychology*, *36*, 96–100. https://doi.org/10.1016/j.copsyc.2020.05.003

Rodrigues, L. F., Oliveira, A., & Costa, C. J. (2016). Playing seriously – how gamification and social cues influence bank customers to use gamified E-business applications. *Computers in Human Behavior*, *63*, 392–407. https://doi.org/10.1016/j.chb.2016.05.063

Ryan, R. M., & Deci, E. L. (2000a). Intrinsic and extrinsic motivations: Classic definitions and new directions. *Contemporary Educational Psychology*, *25*, 54–67. https://doi.org/10.1006/ceps.1999.1020

Ryan, R. M., & Deci, E. L. (2000b). Self-determination theory and the facilitation of intrinsic motivation, social development, and well-being. *American Psychologist*, *55*, 68. https://doi.org/10.1037/0003-066x.55.1.68

Sailer, M., Hense, J. U., Mayr, S. K., & Mandl, H. (2017). How gamification motivates: An experimental study of the effects of specific game design elements on psychological need satisfaction. *Computers in Human Behavior*, *69*, 371–380. https://doi.org/10.1016/j.chb.2016.12.033

Salimon, M. G., Aliyu, O. A., Yusr, M. M., & Perumal, S. (2021). Smartphone banking usage in Nigeria: Gamification, technology acceptance and cultural factors empirical perspectives. *Electronic Journal of Information Systems in Developing Countries*, *87*(4), 1–19. https://doi.org/10.1002/isd2.12174

Seaborn, K., & Fels, D. I. (2015). Gamification in theory and action: A survey. *International Journal of Human Computer Studies*, *74*, 14–31. https://doi.org/10.1016/j.ijhcs.2014.09.006

Shang, S. S. C., & Lin, K. Y. (2013). An understanding of the impact of gamification on purchase intentions. *19th Americas Conference on Information Systems, AMCIS 2013 – Hyperconnected World: Anything, Anywhere, Anytime*, *1*, 439–448.

Sigala, M. (2015). The application and impact of gamification funware on trip planning and experiences: The case of TripAdvisor's funware. *Electronic Markets*, *25*(3), 189–209. https://doi.org/10.1007/s12525-014-0179-1

Streukens, S., van Riel, A., Novikova, D., & Leroi-Werelds, S. (2019). Boosting customer engagement through gamification: A customer engagement marketing approach. In *Handbook of Research on Customer Engagement* (pp. 35–54). https://doi.org/10.4337/9781788114899.00008

Suh, A., Wagner, C., & Liu, L. (2018). Enhancing user engagement through gamification. *Journal of Computer Information Systems*, 58(3), 204–213. https://doi.org/1 0.1080/08874417.2016.1229143

Sultan, Y. H., & Suhail, K. S. (2019). The impact of significant factors of digital leadership on gamification marketing strategy. *International Journal for Advance Research and Development*, 4(5), 29–33. www.IJARND.com

Thomas, N. J., & Baral, R. (2023). Mechanism of gamification: Role of flow in the behavioral and emotional pathways of engagement in management education. *International Journal of Management Education*, 21(1), 100718. https://doi. org/10.1016/j.ijme.2022.100718

Tiwari, R. (2023). The tourism pursuit app – can tourism destinations be gamified? In *Teaching Cases in Tourism, Hospitality and Events* (pp. 48–57). https://doi. org/10.1079/9781800621022.0005

Tobon, S., Ruiz-Alba, J. L., & García-Madariaga, J. (2020, October). Gamification and online consumer decisions: Is the game over? *Decision Support Systems*, 128, 113167. https://doi.org/10.1016/j.dss.2019.113167

Vanduhe, V. Z., Nat, M., & Hasan, H. F. (2020). Continuance intentions to use gamification for training in higher education: Integrating the technology acceptance model (TAM), social motivation, and task technology fit (TTF). *IEEE Access*, 8, 21473–21484. https://doi.org/10.1109/ACCESS.2020.2966179

Varannai, I., Sasvari, P., & Urbanovics, A. (2017). The use of gamification in higher education: An empirical study. *International Journal of Advanced Computer Science and Applications*, 8(10), 1–6. https://doi.org/10.14569/ijacsa.2017.081001

Wen, D. M. H., Chang, D. J. W., Lin, Y. T., Liang, C. W., & Yang, S. Y. (2014). Gamification design for increasing customer purchase intention in a mobile marketing campaign app. In *Lecture notes in computer science (including subseries lecture notes in artificial intelligence and lecture notes in bioinformatics)*, 8527 LNCS (pp. 440–448). https://doi.org/10.1007/978-3-319-07293-7_43

Werbach, K., & Hunter, D. (2012). *For the win: How game thinking can revolutionize your business*. Wharton Digital Press.

Widyani, D. (2021). Gamification as a marketing strategy for Garuda Indonesia loyalty program. *International Journal of Research in Business and Social Science (2147–4478)*, 10(7), 418–422. https://doi.org/10.20525/ijrbs.v10i7.1405

Wrona, K. (2012). Gamification and games, their potential for application in marketing strategies. *Transactions of the Institute of Aviation*, 227(6), 93–105. https://doi. org/10.5604/05096669.1076720

Xu, Y., Chen, Z., Peng, M. Y. P., & Anser, M. K. (2020). Enhancing consumer online purchase intention through gamification in China: Perspective of cognitive evaluation theory. *Frontiers in Psychology*. https://doi.org/10.3389/fpsyg.2020.581200

Yang, P., Zhao, Y., Xu, T., & Feng, Y. (2019). The impact of gamification element on purchase intention. *2019 16th International Conference on Service Systems and Service Management, ICSSSM 2019*, 1–6. https://doi.org/10.1109/ ICSSSM.2019.8887654

Zhang, L., Shao, Z., Li, X., & Feng, Y. (2020). Gamification and online impulse buying: The moderating effect of gender and age. *International Journal of Information Management*, 102267. https://doi.org/10.1016/j.ijinfomgt.2020.102267

Chapter 4

Effects of Gamification on Brand Engagement of Toy Brands

First Cry and Hamleys

Shweta Katyal, Ruhi Lal and Ravinder Rena

Introduction

In today's dynamic business environment, brand engagement is essential for the success of a brand across all sectors (Paruthi et al., 2022). Toy brands target children and their parents; therefore, the goal is to grab and hold their interest. In recent years, gamification has grown in popularity as a way to boost brand engagement. Deterding et al. (2011) have defined gamification as adding game elements to non-gaming environments. It may increase engagement and positive attitudes toward brands. Previous studies also indicate that gamification increases consumers' intrinsic motivation, involvement, and overall experience (Domínguez et al., 2013; Kankanhalli et al., 2011; Witt, 2011; Von Ahn & Dabbish, 2008).

Technological growth approach in 2011–2015 gamification was discussed. Gartner (2012) predicted that over 80% of gamified applications will fail commercially in 2012 due to poor design. Gamification solutions will take 5–10 years to become viable, according to a 2014 poll (Gartner, 2014). Technology improves consumer–brand relationships instead (Rahman et al., 2022). These features boost customer engagement and profitability via frequent and extended interactions. These encounters are crucial to consumer–company relations (Gatautis, 2016).

This research examines how gamification impacts brand engagement at 'First Cry' and 'Hamleys'. 'First Cry' and 'Hamleys' are popular toy brands that cater to kids and families. In the digital world, many firms recognizing conventional tactics of engaging teens may not work.

Research Questions

1. How do gamification strategies affect brand engagement for both '*First Cry*' and '*Hamleys*' among their respective customer bases?
2. What is the relationship between gamification, consumer retention, repeat purchase behavior, and overall satisfaction with the brands '*First Cry*' and '*Hamleys*'?

DOI: 10.4324/9781032694238-6

3. How do gamified experiences influence consumer perceptions and preferences for *'First Cry'* and *'Hamleys'*?
4. To what extent do existing customers of *'First Cry'* and *'Hamleys'* exhibit brand engagement?

Research Objectives

- To examine the effects of gamification strategies on the brand engagement of *'First Cry'* and *'Hamleys'*.
- To examine the relation between gamification, consumer retention, repeat purchase behavior, and satisfaction with the brand.
- To assess the influence of gamified experiences on consumer perceptions, and preferences toward *'First Cry'* and *'Hamleys'*.
- To measure the level of gamified engagement among the existing customers of *'First Cry'* and *'Hamleys'*.

Conceptual Framework

A conceptual framework has been developed to examine the impact of gamified methods on brand engagement within the context of toy brands, namely *'First Cry'* and *'Hamleys'*. The construction of the model involves the use of variables that are pertinent to the field of research. The three primary factors under consideration are gamification, Consumer, and Brand Engagement (Figure 4.1). The concept of gamification involves using the customer as a mediating variable in order to foster brand engagement, hence resulting in the desired outcome variable (Singla & Gupta, 2019). The use of gamification tactics, such as loyalty points, challenges, awards, badges, and leaderboards, is specified within the framework employed by toy companies *'First Cry'* and *'Hamleys'*. However, the impact of gamification tactics on brand engagement varies depending on customer characteristics such as age, gender, and socioeconomic status.

Background of the Study

The rapid development of digital platforms has encouraged research into new tactics to improve brand engagement. This study examines the effects of gamification, a contemporary approach, on two well-known companies, *'First Cry'* and *'Hamleys'*, in the context of the toy market. Gamification can drastically alter brand–consumer relationships as consumer preferences for interactive experiences change. An improved understanding of the influence of gamification on consumer perceptions and behaviors within the dynamic world of toy brands will result from examining its application in these brand engagement strategies, showing its relevance and potency in promoting engagement.

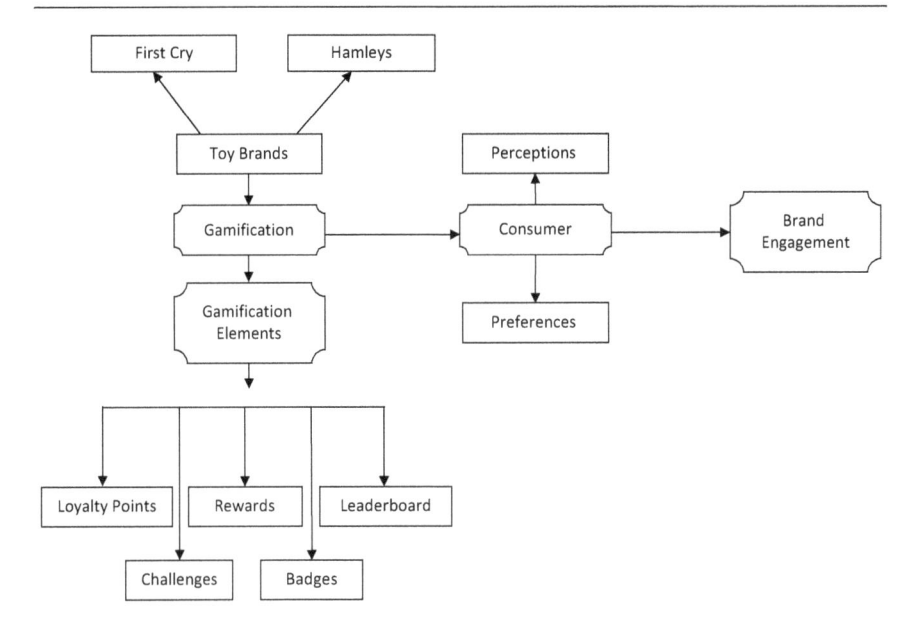

Figure 4.1 Conceptual framework

Source: researchers' own analysis

Scope of the Study

This study examines how gamification affects brand engagement in the toy industry, focusing on two prominent brands, '*First Cry*' and '*Hamleys*'. The primary objective of this study is to evaluate how effectively gamification strategies increase brand engagement among various client bases. The research will look at the relationship between gamification aspects and brand engagement measures through a comparative analysis of these businesses. The results will shed light on the prospective benefits and consequences of implementing gamification strategies for enhancing brand engagement, providing insights into how gamification might affect consumer opinions of and interactions with toy brands '*First Cry*' and '*Hamleys*'.

Review of Literature

Various published resources were accessed to understand the effectiveness of gamification strategies in brand engagement. In this review of literature, we focused on four streams as derived from the framework of the study. These are: (1) Gamification Strategies of Toy Brands, (2) Effectiveness of Gamification for Brand Engagement, (3) Consumer Characteristics and Responses toward Gamification, and (4) Influence of Consumer Characteristics on Brand Engagement.

Gamification Strategies of Toy Brands

Gamification helps toymakers produce enjoyable products. Gamification enhances nongame settings to boost engagement, enjoyment, and achievement. Toy brands may gamify. You may purchase various toys to complete a collection or acquire specific features from different manufacturers. Action figure lines frequently include unique characters that may be combined to build larger toys or access digital content. QR stickers or codes may be used in toys. One can scan these codes for virtual goodies, points, or in-game cash. Toy brand-related online games, applications, and virtual worlds may use these incentives (Kim, 2015). Games and interactive packaging are feasible for corporations. LEGO instruction books usually include puzzles. Smartphones and tablets may interact with toys using AR. Users might watch characters or interact with virtual toys using this technology. Toy manufacturers may create digital leaderboards or tournaments to showcase users' skills and accomplishments (Karać & Stabauer, 2017). These all will encourage friendly competition and involvement. QR Code scavenger companies may host real or virtual hunts for toy QR codes to provide gamers with exclusive content, discounts, or incentives. With toys as characters, youngsters may create their own tales (Merhabi et al., 2021). Brands may inspire creativity with stories and context. Product designers usually build applications that enhance play. These applications provide toy-themed games, puzzles, and interactive stories. Brands may use toys or objectives to advance customers (Karać & Stabauer, 2017). Tiers may add features or content. Toymakers that need teamwork promote a collaborative play. Group collaboration and social involvement may enhance (Merhabi et al., 2021). Companies use blind bags or surprise boxes to entice consumers. These packages surprise consumers with toys and accessories. Combining toys and digital experiences may be intriguing. Digital games overcome physical difficulties, while board games may include apps to enhance the experience. Customization may promote toy inventiveness and ownership. Gamification increases customer loyalty and engagement for toys.

Effectiveness of Gamification for Brand Engagement

Gamification adds game aspects to nongame circumstances as an important brand engagement strategy. Gamification uses competition, incentives, and challenges to engage people. Gamification boosts nongame user engagement and behavior, according to Deterding et al. (2011). Domínguez et al. (2013) demonstrate how gamification may enhance user engagement, loyalty, and interactions in digital branding. Gamification may work because it motivates consumers. According to Deci and Ryan's 1985 Self-Determination Theory, relatedness, competence, and autonomy drive individuals. Gamification satisfies these psychological needs, increasing brand engagement. Gamification makes users feel accomplished and growing, say Kankanhalli et al. (2011) and Von Ahn and Dabbish (2008). Gamification increases user engagement (Katyal & Lal, 2023). Landers and Callan (2011) say that gamified websites boost user engagement and duration. Leaderboards, awards, and points boost brand learning and engagement. Games with engaging content may boost brand loyalty. Morschheuser et al. (2017) say that gamification creates brand loyalty via emotional relationships. Loyalty rewards help organizations build long-term engagement. Gamification engages clients by satisfying their needs and enhancing their experience. Engaging and rewarding brand experiences may promote brand loyalty via gamification.

Consumer Characteristics and Responses Toward Gamification

Numerous studies have explored consumer attributes and brand involvement. Demographics, psychographics, and behavioral patterns affect brand engagement, as shown. Smith and Johnson (2018) research found that younger customers are more engaged with brands than older consumers. Brand participation influences brand loyalty and online shopping (Witt, 2011). Chen and Lee (2019) found that online shoppers were more engaged with brands on digital platforms in a longitudinal study. Brand engagement is complexly influenced by consumer attributes. Demographic, psychographic, behavioral, and cultural factors affect consumer–brand relationships.

Influence of Consumer Characteristics on Brand Engagement

Gamification aids user engagement, motivation, education, innovation, and personal growth (Gartner, 2012). Gamification improves consumer and corporate relationships. Experts have researched consumer involvement for decades. Customers' dynamic emotional or cognitive relationship with an item was explored. These studies studied value co-creation and post-purchase customer behavior. Brodie et al. (2013), Cheung et al. (2011), Gambetti and Graffigna (2010), Hollebeek et al. (2014), and Vivek et al. (2012) studied it. Companies, products, brands, and advertising are being researched. Numerous research studies have examined how virtual brand communities and social media affect customer involvement (Algeshcimer et al., 2005; Brodie et al., 2013; Chan et al., 2014; Cheung et al., 2011; Di Gangi & Wasko, 2009). Each company's audience and gamification approach decide its effect.

Research Methodology

The study employs mixed research methods and techniques of qualitative and quantitative analysis (Table 4.1). For a qualitative analysis, the case

Table 4.1 Research Tool Mapping

Sr No	Research Question	Research Objective	Research Tool
1	How does the implementation of gamification strategies affect brand engagement levels for both 'First Cry' and 'Hamleys' among their respective customer bases?	To examine the effects of gamification on the brand engagement of 'First Cry' and 'Hamleys'.	1. Survey 2. Observational notes from social media pages of the brands 'First Cry' and 'Hamleys'. 3. Case study
2	What is the relationship between gamification efforts and customer retention, repeat purchase behavior, and overall satisfaction with the brands First Cry' and 'Hamleys'?	To examine the effects of gamification on customer retention, repeat purchase behavior, and satisfaction with the brand.	1. Case study 2. Survey 3. Observational notes from social media pages of brands 'First Cry' and 'Hamleys'.
3	How do gamified experiences influence customer perceptions and preferences for 'First Cry' and 'Hamleys', and how does this influence their decision-making processes?	To assess the influence of gamified experiences on customer views, perceptions, and choices toward 'First Cry' and 'Hamleys'.	1. Survey 2. Observational notes from social media pages of the brands 'First Cry' and 'Hamleys' case studies.
4	To what extent do the existing customers of 'First Cry' and 'Hamleys' exhibit brand engagement, and how does this engagement vary between the two brands?	To measure the level of existing brand engagement among "First Cry' and 'Hamleys' customers.	1. Survey 2. Observational notes from social media pages of the brands 'First Cry' and 'Hamleys' case studies.

Source: researchers' own analysis

study method will be used to explore and monitor the gamification strategies. On the other hand, the survey research method has been used as a quantitative analysis method to measure awareness and effectiveness of gamification strategies among customers of both toy brands.

Research Design

The research design section discusses the blueprint for the collection and analysis of data under the study in a structured way.

Research Type – exploratory and descriptive.
Sampling Strategy – case study and survey – non-probabilistic and purposive sampling for interview (case study) and simple random sampling for survey.

Research Purpose – to examine, assess, and measure.
Research Approach – deductive for the case study.

Data Collection

Case Study Method

Primary data was collected for both method case study and survey. For the case study method, an interview was conducted with the brand managers and employees of franchise stores of '*First Cry*' and '*Hamleys*' which led to the development of the case story.

Sample Size: fifteen stores of First Cry and Hamleys, where 30 brand owners and managers were interviewed
Sampling Technique: non-probabilistic and purposive
Time Horizon: from April 2023 to July 2023 (three months)
Data Collection Instrument: semi-structured open-ended interview
Type of Questions: grand and mini tour questions
Interview technique: probing (verbal and nonverbal)

Survey Method

The survey questionnaire is designed on the basis of the inverted funnel sequence. The questionnaire comprises 18 items, and the responses have been collected using the Likert Scale and Nominal Scale. The survey questionnaire was shared among potential respondents as parents and relatives of children as potential buyers of the brand '*First Cry*' and '*Hamleys*' to gather relevant data as per the instrument designed.

An N-Test was performed to establish the sample size needed for this survey. Given the anticipated effect size and required degree of statistical power, the analysis intended to guarantee the sample size was adequate to identify statistically significant effects.

Total household population in Delhi/NCR: 3,435,999.
Calculated survey sample size: 385
Sample frame: customer database of '*First Cry*' & '*Hamleys*', online purchase records, in-store purchase records, membership programs, loyalty programs run by toy brands '*First Cry*' and '*Hamleys*', market research panels by collaborating with the research agencies to get the database of potential buyers of the toy brands.
Structure of survey: questionnaire (close-ended questions)
Respondents: parents/relatives of children and potential buyers of toy brands '*First Cry*' and '*Hamleys*' from Delhi/NCR
Sample size: 385

Time horizon: From April 2023 to July 2023 (three months)
Survey statistical analysis: correlation using SPSS

Rationale behind Selection and Implementation of Method

Case studies evaluated brand engagement gamification in practice. Gamification qualitative case studies interviewed and measured brand engagement. Multi-case analysis revealed trends and variability and higher research validity and theoretical application. Researchers comprehended qualitative data via interpretive case studies. The research needed thorough case narrative development and analysis. This strategy revealed case studies' various complexities, interpretations, and locations. This extensive research evaluated how gamification increases brand engagement in varied settings. Interpretive case analysis illuminated qualitative data.

To generalize about the population, quantitative analysis used a representative sample. This research examines gamification's brand engagement impacts.

Data Analysis and Interpretation

Case Study Method

Case Study 1: 'First Cry' – Enhancing Brand Engagement through Gamification

'*First Cry*' is a leading online and offline baby and maternity retailer. It was launched in India in 2010 and is now a major newborn and childcare retailer of the Mahindra Group. '*First Cry*' is a prominent platform that provides an extensive selection of items catering to the needs of infants and children. '*First Cry*' sells apparel, toys, diapers, and newborn and maternity supplies in one place. It highlights busy parents' convenience and accessibility. '*First Cry*' targets parents, especially new and expecting parents, who want a wide choice of baby and maternity supplies. Online shopping, home delivery, and physical stores make shopping easy for them.

'*First Cry*' successfully employed gamification tactics on its website and mobile app to enhance brand engagement, leading to significant effects.

The gamification strategies used by '*First Cry*' are the following: '*First Cry*' has implemented a tiered loyalty program that allows consumers to accumulate points via their purchases and interactions with the company. As clients amass points, they have access to unique privileges and discounts, therefore cultivating a feeling of accomplishment and loyalty.

'*First Cry*' implemented interactive quizzes on their site, providing clients with the opportunity to assess their knowledge and earn incentives. The quizzes include subject matters pertaining to parenting, child development, and product knowledge, so fostering an immersive and instructive encounter.

'*First Cry*' has implemented virtual sticker collections as a means for clients to acquire stickers via the completion of certain activities or by making purchases. Through the process of collecting stickers, users can get access to exclusive discounts or earn unique prizes, thus fostering a sense of continuing engagement with the business.

Case Study 2: 'Hamleys' – Elevating Brand Engagement through Gamification

'*Hamleys*', one of Reliance Retails' oldest and best-known toy stores, was founded in 1760 in London, the United Kingdom, and has a long history of offering high-quality toys and an engaging in-store experience. '*Hamleys*', which sells a large choice of toys, games, and entertainment, positions itself as a premium price and iconic toy store. It highlights the remarkable and immersive in-store experience with live demonstrations, experiential displays, and amazement.

'*Hamleys*', having worldwide reach, has embraced the digital era by using gamification tactics across its online platforms and brick-and-mortar establishment. Hamleys targets families with children of all ages. Parents and caregivers looking for quality toys and unique gifts and children looking for a magical and exciting shopping experience are their target customers.

'*Hamleys*' has implemented augmented reality (AR) experiences by means of its smartphone application, enabling consumers to engage in digital interactions with toys. Through the process of scanning certain items, individuals can access interactive games, virtual experiences, and personalized material, fostering an immersive and fascinating brand interaction. '*Hamleys*' has used gamification strategies inside its brick-and-mortar locations to provide consumers with a dynamic and engaging retail atmosphere. The implementation of interactive stations, treasure hunts, and quizzes within the retail environment effectively captivates visitors and stimulates their curiosity, thus fostering a deeper engagement with the brand. Consequently, this heightened level of contact contributes to an overall rise in the visitors' involvement with the brand.

Case Study Research Strategy

A systematic, step-by-step case study analysis in the gamification strategies of the toy brands is the research study strategy. Clarity, choice, and operationalization of qualitative data are taken into account in this study. According to Rashid et al. (2019), the research study's analysis was divided into four phases: (1) the foundation phase, (2) the pre-field phase, (3) the field phase, and (4) the reporting phase. The study examined the relationship between the learning from the evaluation of the literature, the theoretical underpinnings for in-depth numerous cases with descriptions and theme analysis, and each of the four case study phases. For a parallel investigation, many case studies are used. The simultaneous analysis of the case studies is documented for records.

This is the initial and most important stage in carrying out the case study. The foundation phase is the initial step and is based on factors to minimize ambiguity and to concentrate on the literature to provide the context for each factor. The familiarity with concepts and theories led to the emergence of the philosophical paradigm (Lincoln et al., 2011). Inductive and deductive reasoning are the two types of research logic that are frequently used. The deductive research methodology utilized in this study enhances theoretical strength and strives to test claims. The idea is based on subjective reports of experience that were the foundation of the investigation. The study looked at philosophical issues as well as the link between language and concepts defining the research stages and the best approach for each phase (Evely et al., 2008). Theoretical literature was read and examined early on to help with idea creation and to determine the goal of the research. In order to comprehend the social phenomena, the researcher talked to the participants. To generalize the theory, the researcher tested the theory and the underlying assumptions. To evaluate particular occurrences or actions in a constrained environment and uncover critical factor processes and linkages, individual behavioral traits actions, and interactions, the context and the processes involved in the phenomena were thoroughly explored (Punch, 2013). Because there is limited control over the occurrence within the framework of real life, case studies are taken into consideration for the research (Yin, 1994).

Case Study Analysis and Interpretations

Four stages of case analysis are employed in the research study as a framework for analysis to examine the wide range of perspectives revealed in the stories through in-depth interviews. Understanding how to enhance efforts and methods that can provide an alternative for a variety of opportunities for growth and development was aided by this.

Four Phases of Case Analysis

The cases are developed on the basis of the interviews conducted with the brand managers of the toy brands '*First Cry*' and '*Hamleys*'. The analyses of the four phases of the case study (Table 4.2) are based on the study proposed by Yin (2013). The research maintained a level of theoretical flexibility in order to generate case studies based on the data obtained through field notes. Dedicated endeavors yielded enhanced foundations for creating instruments and protocols (Tables 4.3 and 4.4) that incorporate the diverse perspectives of the respondents.

Outcomes and Benefits of 'First Cry' Gamification Strategies

The implementation of a gamified loyalty program of '*First Cry*' effectively motivated clients to participate in frequent brand interactions and make

Table 4.2 Phases of Case Study Analysis

Four Phases of Case Study Analysis

Foundation Phase	Pre-Field Phase	Field Phase	Reporting Phase
1. Philosophical and sociological consideration	Decision upon the conceptualization of the case	Contact and collect data for the development of the case study	Reporting of the case study
2. Research logic consideration	Case design and deciding upon the methodology for achieving the goal. Case study protocol	Interact with the participants on ethical grounds for accurate data collection.	
3. Ethical consideration			

Source: Researcher's own analysis

Table 4.3 Process of Data Analysis from the Case Study

Case Description	Participant Description	Relationship Description	Field Protocol
A case study of two toy brands 'First Cry' and 'Hamleys' utilizes gamification for brand engagement strategy through the Gamified Rewards System.	Brand managers of franchise stores of 'First Cry' and 'Hamleys'.	The gamification strategies were monitored, and in-depth discussions took place with the brand managers to find out the effects of loyalty programs, interactive online game challenges, personalized experiences through virtual events and activities, and parent engagement programs.	The interactions and discussions took place with brand managers of toy brands to get data for case story development while interviewing them. The experiences of the event of the brand managers of the participating companies, including their motivations, processes, lessons learned, and outcomes, and interviews with them were shared. Investigation probed deeper than the first impression.

Source: researchers' own analysis

repeated purchases, resulting in a notable enhancement in brand loyalty. The motivation of customers to accumulate points and advance through several stages resulted in heightened levels of brand loyalty and improved consumer retention.

The use of gamification components, such as quizzes and sticker collections, contributed to an augmented customer experience by introducing an

Table 4.4 Framework of Case Study Consideration

Philosophical Consideration	Research Logic Consideration	Ethical Consideration
Loyalty programs of '*First Cry*' and '*Hamleys*' cultivate emotional bonds between consumers and brands, ultimately fostering enduring brand engagement and association. Implementation of brand engagement strategies has the potential to exert influence over consumers, thereby potentially leading them to make decisions that may not align with their optimal interests.	The data collected from the interview was gathered to better understand the strategy and survey the customer to check emotional bond, positioning in the mind of the customer, and brand association. It was ensured that the research was up-to-date and customer insights were taken. In order to get qualitative data and avoid depending entirely on a single data point, 15 franchise stores were examined, and survey data from the customers were recorded.	Inquiries emerged concerning the ethical implications associated with the utilization of diverse psychological and emotional strategies used by the brands, and researchers used the methodologies aimed at measuring the influence on consumer behaviour.

Source: researchers' own analysis

enjoyable and entertaining aspect to the whole customer journey. As a consequence, this led to a heightened level of consumer engagement and recollection, making a positive impact on total customer satisfaction.

The implementation of gamified experiences prompted consumers to actively share their accomplishments and encounters on various social media platforms, resulting in heightened brand exposure and the generation of organic word-of-mouth promotion.

While exploring social media platforms to review the user engagement insights of '*First Cry*', the study observed a significant increase in engagement of posts related to gamification strategies than in other posts by the brand. On observing a few posts on the social media accounts of the brand, it was noticed that there is approximately 96% (10,000+ likes) increase in engagement on content/posts related to gamification while other posts only had 4% of the above engagement which rounds about from 200 to 400 likes. However, engagement on comments was constantly very few on both types of content/post.

Outcomes and Benefits of 'Hamleys' Gamification Strategies

The outcomes and benefits of a certain situation or action are the results and advantages that are derived from it. The incorporation of augmented reality (AR) experiences into the Hamleys mobile application has contributed to an elevated level of customer experience. This integration has introduced an additional element of thrill and engagement to the process of purchasing. The lifelike interactions with virtual characters and games were well-received by customers, resulting in a memorable and delightful experience throughout their visit to '*Hamleys*'.

The implementation of gamified experiences inside physical retail spaces, such as treasure hunts and interactive stations, has resulted in a notable rise in shop visits. These engaging activities have effectively incentivized consumers to dedicate a greater amount of time to exploring the various offerings within the store. The rise in customer traffic resulted in an expansion of chances for consumers to interact with the brand and complete transactions.

The use of gamification allowed '*Hamleys*' to enhance its brand image by positioning itself as a forward-thinking and immersive business that caters to the changing desires of its target audience. This strategic approach aided in distinguishing Hamleys from its rivals and further solidified its standing as a prominent toy store.

While exploring social media platforms to review the user engagement insights of '*Hamleys*', the study observed a significant increase in the engagement of posts related to gamification strategies than in other posts by the brand. On observing a few posts on the social media accounts of the brand, it was noticed that there is approximately a 99% (50,000+ likes) increase in engagement on content/posts related to gamification while other posts only had 1% of the above engagement which rounds about from 400 to 600 likes. Moreover, engagement on comments was constantly increasing (2,000–4,500) on gamified content/posts, while others had a low engagement of 20 to 30 comments individually.

In conclusion, it can be seen that both '*First Cry*' and '*Hamleys*' have successfully used gamification techniques in order to augment brand engagement. The gamified loyalty program and interactive quizzes used by '*First Cry*' effectively cultivated consumer engagement. Similarly, the employment of augmented reality experiences and in-store gamified activities by '*Hamleys*' successfully generated immersive and lasting customer experiences. The aforementioned case studies demonstrate the potential of gamification as a strategy to enhance brand engagement, foster consumer loyalty, and establish a brand distinction.

Interviewing reputable brands like 'First Cry' and 'Hamleys' provides an array of challenging obstacles that call for vigilant navigation. Acquiring access to executives who can provide vital information about the brand's gamification tactics and consumer engagement practices is one of the main challenges. Additionally, because they are the curators of confidential information, these businesses frequently take caution when disclosing sensitive information, raising questions about data privacy and compliance. Maintaining brand reputation and image in this situation becomes of utmost importance, which may cause hesitation in revealing any difficulties or negative aspects of their gamification initiatives. As a result, there may be some response bias as interviewers may be inclined to promote their brand favorably. Establishing a clear study aim, maintaining confidentiality and anonymity, and highlighting the research's potential benefit to these businesses are necessary for overcoming these obstacles. To obtain a comprehensive understanding of gamification tactics, it is also beneficial to interact with employees at all organizational levels. Building trust and establishing a professional rapport with brand representatives are essential tactics for obtaining the needed insights while adhering to the needs and limitations of the businesses.

Survey Method

Survey Result Findings

The levels of agreements being set, the responses of the frequency tests are mentioned in Table 4.5.

Survey Analysis and Interpretations

The research discovered that the use of gamification tactics led to better levels of engagement among consumers of 'First Cry' and 'Hamleys', as well as improved engagement rates.

According to the results, gamification motivates 59% of consumers to actively engage in brand-related activities like competitions, challenges, and interactive quizzes. This increased engagement helped to create a consumer base that was more engaged and devoted.

According to the survey, gamification raised consumer retention rates for both businesses by 61.2%. Customers were more likely to feel attached to and loyal to businesses after participating in gamified experiences, which encouraged long-term brand engagement. Gamified experiences improved brand loyalty and increased the possibility that consumers would return to 'First Cry' and 'Hamleys' for more purchases. Results showed that customer satisfaction levels are favorably impacted by gamified interactions. Gamification experiences that are entertaining and engaging might improve how consumers feel about businesses as a whole.

According to the research, gamification helped 'First Cry' and 'Hamleys' develop more dynamic and compelling brand personalities. Gamified interactions may give companies a reputation for being forward-thinking, imaginative, and customer-focused. The results demonstrated that distinct consumer groups within 'First Cry' and 'Hamleys' customer bases responded better to particular gamification tactics. Gamified material may elicit varied responses from various demographic groups. With 57.2% of consumers who have taken part in gamified events demonstrating maintained engagement over

Table 4.5 Frequency Test Results of the Survey

Sr. No.	Item	Response	Response	Response	Response	Response
1.	Age group	18-25 35.8%	26-35 41.35%	36-45 11.9%	46 and above 10.4%	-
2.	Buyer of toy products	Yes 73.9%	No 14.9%	Maybe 11.2%	-	-
3.	Frequency of purchase from the toy store	Yes 69.4%	No 25.4%	Maybe 5.2%	-	-
4.	Purchaser of *First Cry or Hamleys* or both	First Cry 6%	Hamleys 18.7%	Both 59.7%	None 15.7%	-
5.	Participation of buyers in gamified strategies offered by brands	Yes 59%	No 28.4%	Maybe 12.7%	-	-
6.	Gamification experiences and increased brand engagement	Strongly disagree 1.5%	Disagree 8.2%	Neutral 32.1%	Agree 15.7%	Strongly agree 42.5%
7.	Gamification experiences and positive brand satisfaction	Strongly disagree 1.5%	Disagree 6%	Neutral 35.1%	Agree 16.4%	Strongly agree 41%
8.	Gamification experience and positive brand perception	Strongly Disagree 0%	Disagree 7.5%	Neutral 26.9%	Agree 26.1%	Strongly agree 39.6%
9.	Enjoyable and engaging gamified experiences with *'First Cry'* and *'Hamleys'*	Strongly disagree 1.5%	Disagree 6%	Neutral 30.6%	Agree 20.1%	Strongly agree 41.8%
10.	Gamified experiences leading to positive brand views and opinion	Strongly disagree 0.7%	Disagree 6%	Neutral 32.8%	Agree 19.4%	Strongly agree 41%
11.	Preferred toy brand (*'First Cry'* and *'Hamleys'*) due to gamified experiences	Strongly disagree 3%	Disagree 8.2%	Neutral 22.4%	Agree 23.1%	Strongly agree 43.3%
12.	Gamification and overall brand experience	Strongly disagree 0.7%	Disagree 6%	Neutral 27.6%	Agree 23.9%	Strongly agree 41.8%
13.	Gamification leading to brand loyalty and brand retention	Strongly disagree 3.7%	Disagree 3%	Neutral 32.1%	Agree 20.9%	Strongly agree 40.3%
14.	The uniqueness of gamified strategies of *'First Cry'* and *'Hamleys'* over other toy brands	Strongly disagree 0.7%	Disagree 7.5%	Neutral 27.6%	Agree 20.1%	Strongly agree 44%
15.	Satisfactory gamified experience offered by *'First Cry'* and *'Hamleys'*	Strongly disagree 2.2%	Disagree 4.5%	Neutral 24.6%	Agree 24.6%	Strongly agree 44%

Source: researchers' own analysis

time, the research may show that gamification has a long-lasting effect on brand engagement levels.

According to the poll findings, 20.9% of consumers are more inclined to stick with a brand if they have participated in gamification activities. Gamification and repeat purchase behavior are positively correlated, with participants who had gamified encounters expressing a stronger desire to stick with the brand over the long term.

Gamification increases consumer happiness, according to survey replies. Gamification provides value and fun to participants' interactions, as shown in the 24.6% of participants who stated increased satisfaction with their overall brand experiences after interacting with gamified features. Gamified encounters led to greater sentiments of connection and loyalty among participants, which improved participant perceptions of the brand. It also revealed that various client categories respond differently to gamification.

According to survey results, 44% of participants tend to have a more positive opinion of both 'First Cry' and 'Hamleys' after they have participated in gamified encounters. Participants' impressions of the brands improved as a result of gamification, seeming to be more creative, participatory, and customer-focused. According to research, gamification strengthens users' emotional bonds with businesses. Participating in gamified activities may arouse pleasant sentiments and a sense of delight, deepening one's connection to 'First Cry' and 'Hamleys'.

After participating in gamified events, roughly 40.3% of participants reported having a greater degree of brand recall and awareness. Gamification helped create a more recognizable and memorable brand identity, which raised brand awareness and consideration. Results indicated that individuals who had favorable gamified experiences were more likely to tell their social networks about their encounters with 'First Cry' and 'Hamleys'. As a result, advocacy and word-of-mouth referrals grew. The poll also showed that 'First Cry' and 'Hamleys' had different levels of brand engagement.

A crucial impetus was the emergence of gamified experiences, which showed how important it is to promote continuing communication and engagement. These results, combined, helped researchers better understand how gamified experiences affect consumers' opinions, perceptions, purchasing decisions, and brand loyalty for 'First Cry' and 'Hamleys'. They provide insightful information on how well gamification has shaped consumer relationships with these firms.

Correlation Analysis of Survey

The research used IBM SPSS to determine the strength and direction of the association between two variables using Spearman's rank–order correlation statistical analysis. The variables were produced via survey data cleaning and

Table 4.6 Comprehensive Results of Correlation Analysis

	Variable Combinations	Correlation Coefficient	Sig. (Two-Tailed)	Interpretation
	Gamification Engagement and Brand Engagement	−0.705	$p < 0.001$ N = 385	Significantly negative correlation
	Gamification Engagement and Brand Satisfaction	−0.519**	$p < 0.001$ N = 385	Significantly negative correlation
	Gamification Engagement and Brand Perception	−0.498	$p < 0.001$ N = 385	Significantly negative correlation
	Gamification Engagement and Enjoyment from Gamified Experiences	−0.454**	$p < 0.001$ N = 385	Significantly negative correlation
Spearman's rho	**Brand Perception and Views/ Opinions**	0.613**	$p < 0.001$ N = 385	Significantly positive correlation
	Gamification Engagement and Brand Choice	−0.391	$p < 0.001$ N = 385	Significantly negative correlation
	Gamification Engagement and Value Addition	−0.444**	$p < 0.001$ N = 385	Significantly negative correlation
	Gamification Engagement and Loyalty/Retention	−0.436**	$p < 0.001$ N = 385	Significantly negative correlation
	Uniqueness of Gamification Experiences and Brand Engagement	0.555	$p < 0.001$ N = 385	Significantly positive correlation
	Overall Satisfaction and Brand Engagement	0.593	$p < 0.001$ N = 385	Significantly positive correlation

Source: researchers' own analysis

coding. The following are comprehensive explanations of correlation data (Table 4.6) between variable sets:

- A correlation value of −0.705 indicates a substantial unfavorable association between gamification engagement and brand engagement. The correlation coefficient p value is less than 0.001, making it statistically significant. It seems improbable that such a big negative correlation was observed by coincidence. A negative correlation means brand engagement falls and gamification engagement rises. This suggests that brand engagement and client gamification strategies are adversely connected.

- The correlation value of –0.519 indicates a substantial negative correlation between brand satisfaction and gamification participation. The correlation coefficient's p value of less than 0.001 indicates statistical significance. The found negative correlation is unlikely to be random. Brand satisfaction decreases when gamification participation increases, and vice versa. Lower brand satisfaction is connected to more gamified methods.
- Gamification engagement has a somewhat negative correlation with brand perception (-0.498). This association is significant since the correlation coefficient p-value is less than 0.001. The observed negative correlation is unlikely to be due to a mistake. Brand impression decreases as gamification involvement increases and vice versa. Thus, greater gamification reduces brand perception.
- The research found a substantial negative correlation (Spearman's rho = –0.454, p < 0.001) between gamification involvement and satisfaction of gamified encounters. The negative correlation is unlikely to be a coincidence. When gamification involvement grows, the enjoyment of gamified events decreases and vice versa. In other words, more gamified engagement decreases enjoyment.

The correlation score of 0.613 indicates a high positive correlation between views and opinions and brand perception. The correlation coefficient's p-value of less than 0.001 indicates that this correlation is significant. It seems unlikely that the positive correlation was found by chance. A positive correlation shows that brand perception increases views and opinions and vice versa. More positive thoughts and feelings about a brand lead to a better brand image. Buyers with a positive image of 'First Cry' and 'Hamleys' as toys are more likely to have positive attitudes toward these products. Gamification engagement negatively correlates with brand choice, with a correlation value of −0.391. The correlation coefficient's p-value of less than 0.001 indicates this association is significant. The found negative correlation is unlikely to be an accident. A negative connection shows brand choice decreases when gamification participation increases and vice versa. Increased gamification approach engagement decreases the likelihood of choosing other toy brands over 'First Cry' and 'Hamleys'.

- A substantial negative correlation exists between gamification engagement and Value Addition (Spearman's rho = −0.444, p < 0.001). The observed negative correlation is unlikely to be due to a mistake. This negative correlation suggests that gamification engagement decreases value addition and vice versa. Increased gamification participation decreases perceived customer experience value. These findings suggest that consumer value and gamification engagement may conflict. Gamified experiences may boost consumer engagement, but they may not improve customer value.
- A substantial negative correlation exists between gamification engagement and loyalty/retention (Spearman's rho = −0.436, p < 0.001). Gamification engagement decreases loyalty and retention, and vice versa. Thus, more

gamified participation decreases customer loyalty and retention. Gamification engagement and customer loyalty and retention may conflict, according to these findings. Gamified experiences may boost consumer engagement but not brand loyalty and retention (First Cry and Hamleys).

- The correlation analysis found a substantial positive correlation (Spearman's rho = 0.555, $p < 0.001$) between unique gamification experiences and brand engagement. It seems that brand engagement increases with gamification experience uniqueness, and vice versa. 'First Cry' and 'Hamleys' enjoy increased brand engagement from consumers who find their gamified experiences unique. This suggests that brand engagement is positively connected with gamified experience uniqueness. Unique gamification experiences make First Cry and Hamleys more appealing to consumers. This favorable correlation underscores the need for unique and cutting-edge gamified experiences to boost brand engagement.
- The research found a substantial positive correlation (Spearman's rho = 0.593, $p < 0.001$) between brand engagement and overall satisfaction. Brand involvement increases overall satisfaction and vice versa, according to the positive correlation. Overall satisfaction is linked to 'First Cry' and 'Hamleys' brand participation. These findings suggest a strong positive correlation between brand involvement and customer pleasure. Brand involvement is associated with an increased consumer satisfaction. The link between brand engagement and customer satisfaction emphasizes its importance.

Conclusion

The extensive analysis of gamification's effects on brand engagement, customer behavior, perceptions, and brand engagement levels for 'First Cry' and 'Hamleys' revealed the complex relationship between gamified experiences and consumer–brand interactions.

Gamification has a beneficial and transforming influence on consumers' interactions with 'First Cry' and 'Hamleys'. Gamification has helped these companies engage customers across several touchpoints by capturing their attention and active involvement. Gamification creates an immersive and pleasant brand experience, strengthening consumer–company emotional bonds. This has made the 'First Cry' and 'Hamleys' more appealing. Gamification has been found to encourage client retention, repeat purchases, and satisfaction. Gamified events have increased brand loyalty to 'First Cry' and 'Hamleys'.

Gamified interactions increase brand engagement and connection, which may boost additional advantages beyond repeat purchases. Gamification increases the overall brand experience, increasing customer pleasure and loyalty. Gamified experiences' effects on customer attitudes, perceptions, and choices show how gamification changes participants' preferences and decision-making processes.

Gamified interactions have elevated 'First Cry' and 'Hamleys' to distinctive and fascinating brands. Participants liked how gamification and brand values and identity worked together, which affected their decisions and motivated them to support firms on social media. The amount of brand involvement between 'First Cry' and 'Hamleys' clients shows different customer affinities. The survey's results show how successfully each brand's engagement strategies built connections and facilitated communication with its customers. This study proves that gamification affects consumer behavior, brand engagement, and views regarding 'First Cry' and 'Hamleys'.

These companies' gamified experiences have created engaging and enjoyable interactions, increasing consumer loyalty, repeat purchases, and satisfaction (Lal & Rahman, 2013). Gamification has become a key tool for organizations to interact with their target audiences, create brand advocates, and lead the industry.

Suggestions

1. Brands should tailor gamified experiences to their audience needs. 'First Cry' and 'Hamleys' may adjust gamification methods to customer engagement and happiness by learning consumer preferences and behavior patterns.
2. Marketers must stay involved to optimize gamification. Gamified content should be updated often to keep customers interested.
3. Gamification with incentive-based rewards may increase client retention and repeat purchases. Gamified activities may earn discounts, early product access, and other incentives from 'First Cry' and 'Hamleys'.
4. Gamifying customer feedback may boost interest and give relevant data. Brands may engage and collect feedback using interactive surveys, quizzes, and challenges.
5. Improved social media gamification may improve brand advocacy. Sharing participants' successes and interactions on social media may help the company spread word-of-mouth.
6. Gamification provides numerous advantages, but firms must be transparent and ethical. Customer trust requires an explicit communication of gamified interaction rules, rewards, and data usage.
7. 'First Cry' and 'Hamleys' should see gamification as a long-term strategy, not a fad. Brand experiences may be gamified to develop customer loyalty and long-term partnerships.
   Gamification boosted 'First Cry' and 'Hamleys' brand engagement, customer behavior, and perceptions. The results and proposed strategies may help both firms utilize gamification to improve customer interactions and stand out in the market.

Limitations of the Study

1. Gamification influences brand engagement, customer behavior, and 'First Cry' and 'Hamleys' perceptions, according to the study. Noting several restrictions that might affect results' reproducibility and applicability is crucial.

Chapter 5

Gamification and Online Shopping Experience

A Systematic Literature Review

Ritu Yadav and Chand Prakash Saini

Introduction

Gamification, the application of game design elements in nongame contexts, has gained significant attention and adoption across various industries, including marketing and consumer engagement. In online shopping, where retailers strive to enhance customer experiences and drive sales, gamification techniques have emerged as a promising strategy to captivate and retain customers. By leveraging the principles of game mechanics, such as challenges, rewards, and competition, online retailers can create immersive and engaging shopping experiences beyond traditional transactional interactions.

The integration of gamification elements into online shopping platforms can transform how consumers perceive and engage with e-commerce. By adding fun, excitement, and interactivity elements, gamification aims to enhance user motivation, increase time spent on websites, foster brand loyalty, and ultimately drive customer satisfaction and purchase behavior. However, the implementation of gamification in the context of online shopping is still a relatively new and evolving phenomenon, necessitating a comprehensive examination of the existing literature to understand its impact and effectiveness.

Motivation and Engagement

One of the primary objectives of gamification in online shopping is to enhance user motivation and engagement. Several studies have examined the impact of gamification elements (Paruthi et al., 2023) such as badges, leaderboards, and progress tracking on user behavior. For instance, Lee (2023) reported that gamification features, including rewards and challenges, enhanced user satisfaction and loyalty, leading to repeat purchases.

User Experience and Satisfaction

Gamification can potentially create a more enjoyable and satisfying online shopping experience. Research has shown that gamified elements, such as

DOI: 10.4324/9781032694238-7

interactive product visualization, personalized recommendations, and social interactions, can contribute to a positive user experience. For example, Huotari and Hamari (2017) found that personalized recommendations and social sharing features increased user satisfaction and trust in online shopping platforms. Additionally, Lee and Xu (2020) reported that interactive virtual try-on features in the fashion industry positively influenced user satisfaction and purchase intention.

Influence on Consumer Behavior

Gamification techniques in online shopping platforms have also been found to impact consumer behavior. Several studies have explored the effects of gamification on purchase intention, brand loyalty, and repeat purchases. For instance, Hamari and Koivisto (2015) found that gamification elements, such as virtual currencies and achievements, positively influenced users' purchase intentions. Similarly, Gatautis et al. (2021) reported that gamification strategies, including loyalty points and rewards, increased brand loyalty and customer retention.

This chapter presents a systematic literature review exploring the relationship between gamification and the online shopping experience. By synthesizing and analyzing a range of scholarly articles, research studies, and industry reports, this study seeks to identify the key themes, theories, and empirical evidence regarding the impact of gamification on various aspects of the online shopping experience. This study's findings will contribute to academia and industry by offering insights and implications for the effective design and implementation of gamified online shopping platforms. Additionally, it will identify areas for further research and development, ultimately guiding the future direction of gamification in e-commerce.

Methodology

The literature review is an essential part of developing any theory and model. It suggests the gaps and provides future research directions to researchers (Chen & Zheng, 2019). This research was conducted to provide a systematic and realistic sketch of gamification and its relation with the online shopping experience. To attain the study's goal, the review's quantitative and qualitative aspects were assessed. Bibliometric analysis was done to provide quantitative information for review, and the qualitative aspect of the review was studied through a systematic literature review using the PRISMA technique (Chen & Zheng, 2019)

PRISMA refers to Preferred Reporting Items for Systematic Reviews and Meta-Analyses. It represents an evidence-based minimum set of items for reporting in systematic reviews and meta-analyses. PRISMA flow diagram was used to show the flow of studies through each phase of the review process.

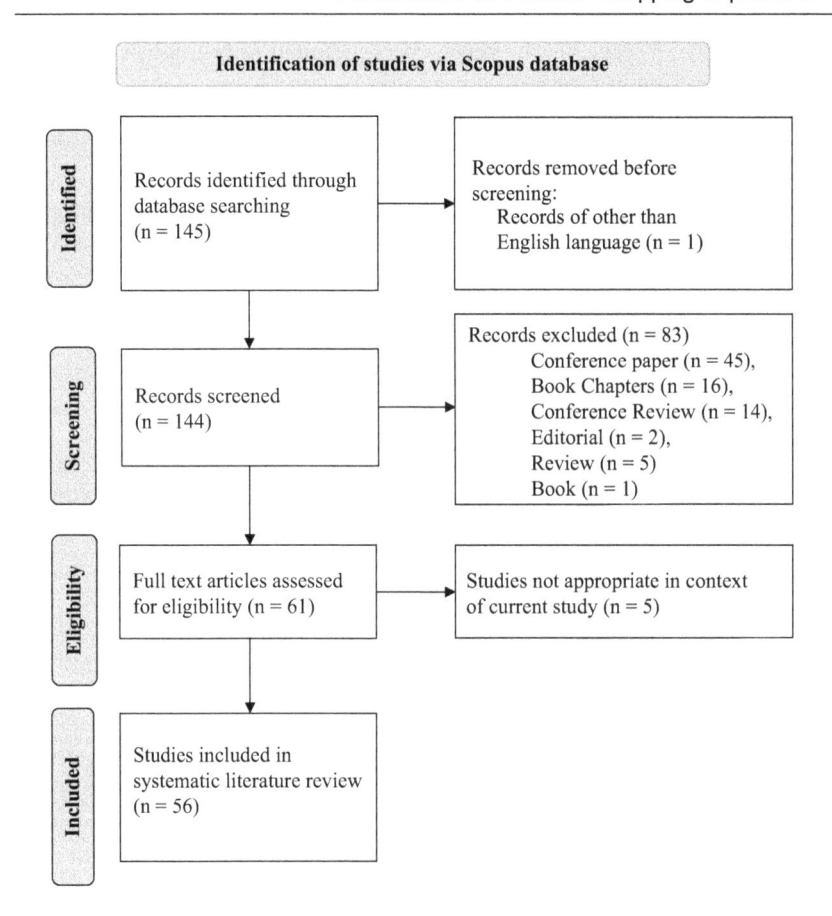

Figure 5.1 PRISMA technique

Source: researchers' analysis

The phases of the flow diagram (Figure 5.1) are identification, screening, eligibility, and included (Page et al., 2021).

Identification of Literature

Gamification and online shopping have been associated and referred to in different terms. For including a maximum number of studies in a systematic review, Boolean operators (And, OR) (Cronin et al., 2008) were used for literature identification. The search terms for the literature identification were "gamification" OR "gamified" AND "Online Shopping" OR "Online Retail", OR "Buying Behavior", OR "Customer Satisfaction", OR "Customer Engagement". Using these search terms, 145 records were identified from the Scopus database. One record was found in Spanish, hence excluded at the identification stage, as the researchers included only English language records in this systematic review.

Screening

A total of 145 articles were entered under the screening stage, of which 83 records were removed under inclusion and exclusion criteria (Page et al., 2021). The researcher was focused only on research articles and removed records of conference papers (n = 45), book chapters (n = 16), conference reviews (n = 14), editorial (n = 2), review (n = 5), and book (n = 1). Thus, 61 articles were entered under eligibility criteria.

Eligibility

Out of 61 articles, 5 records were removed as the researcher didn't find them appropriate in the current study context.

Inclusion

Finally, 56 articles were considered appropriate for bibliometric analysis, systematic literature review, and content analysis.

Descriptive Analysis of Literature

After selecting studies for final review, the data was recorded in Microsoft Excel for descriptive analysis. The published literature on gamification and online shopping experience was presented as graphs and charts.

Year Base

Chart 5.1 shows that the first article on the application of gamification in utilitarian services was published in 2013 by Hamari in the *Electronic Commerce Research and Applications* journal. Maximum records (14 articles) were published in 2023 (January to June 2023). The year 2021 also witnessed much research on gamification applications in online retailing. A minimum number of articles on gamification were witnessed in 2013 and 2015.

Chart 5.2 highlights that the maximum number of research on gamification and online retailing experiences was published in India. Out of 56 articles, 12 were published in India, followed by the UK (10) and China (5). The United States, Italy, and Iran published equal research works (three articles each), and Portugal and Spain published similar research (4 articles each).

Chart 5.3 demonstrated that the maximum number (31.7%) of research was presented under the Business, Management, and Accounting category, followed by Computer Science (16.3%), Social Science (12.2%),

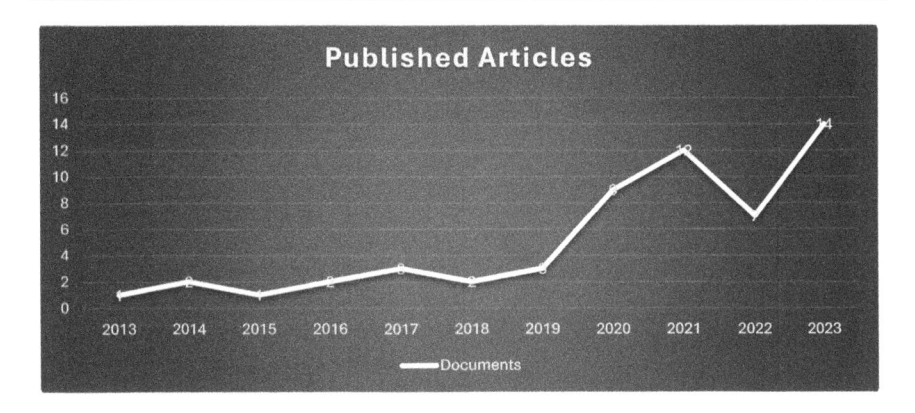

Chart 5.1 Published articles
Source: secondary data (Scopus database)

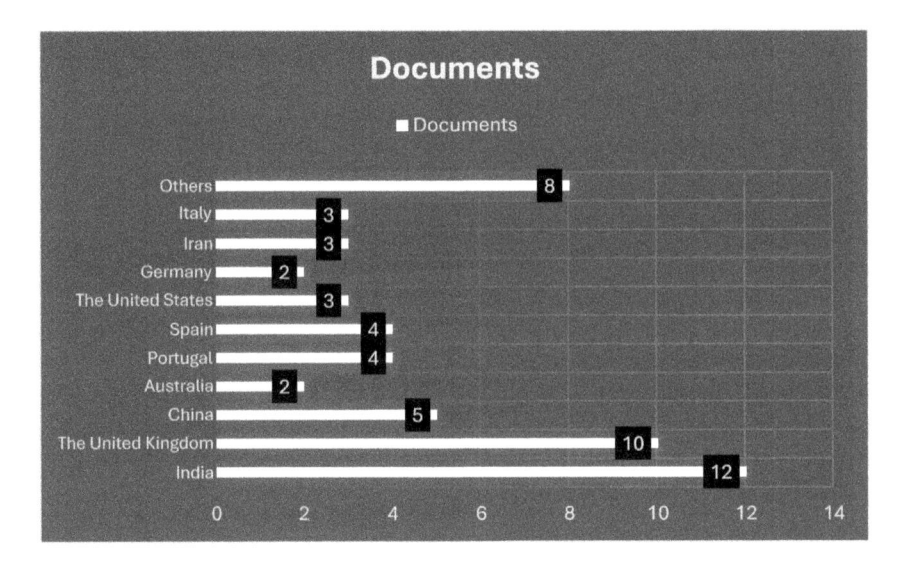

Chart 5.2 Country base
Source: secondary data (Scopus database)

Engineering (6.5%) etc. These statistics clarified that the Business, Management, and Accounting field draws more attention from researchers working on Gamification.

Table 5.1 demonstrates that the most cited article included in the review was authored by Hamari (2013) on "Transforming homo economicus into homo ludens: A field experiment on gamification in a utilitarian peer-to-peer trading service" published in *Electronic Commerce Research and Applications*

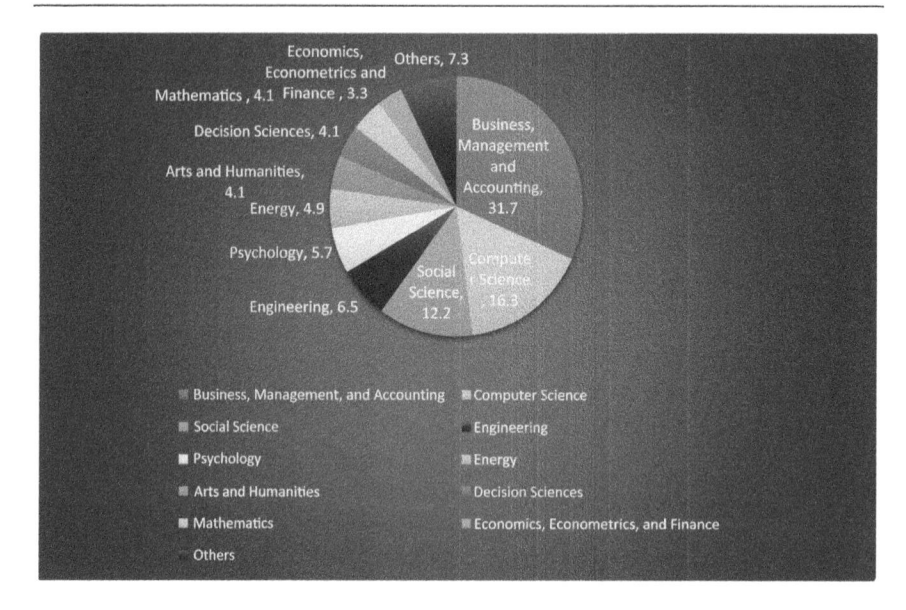

Chart 5.3 Subject area

Source: secondary data (Scopus database)

journal, and the number of citations for this article was 495. Yang et al.'s (2017a) article "Examining the impact of gamification on the intention of engagement and brand attitude in the marketing context" was the second most cited article with 222 citations in the systematic review. Harwood and Garry's (2015) article got 176 citations and was the third most cited. The study by Robson et al. (2016) was the fourth most cited article, with 170 citations. Some other most frequently cited articles are shown in Table 5.1.

Review Analysis and Findings

After the descriptive literature presentation, content analysis was done by briefly reporting literature, identifying themes, and suggesting future research directions (Rodrigues & Mendes, 2018). Initially, articles were analyzed author-centrically and then concept-centrically (theme based) to extract relevant information (Webster & Watson, 2002). Although the term gamification was introduced in the year 2002 by Nick Pelling, the first study directed toward gamification applications in trading activities was conducted by Hamari (2013) on "Transforming homo economicus into homo ludens: a field experiment on gamification in a utilitarian peer-to-peer trading service". A summary in Table 5.2 is prepared to highlight the key findings of the selected articles:

Table 5.1 Citation Base

Title	Author	Year	Citation
Transforming homo economicus into homo ludens: a field experiment on gamification in a utilitarian peer-to-peer trading service	Hamari J.	2013	495
Examining the impact of gamification on intention of engagement and brand attitude in the marketing context	Yang Y., Asaad Y., Dwivedi Y.	2017	222
An investigation into gamification as a customer engagement experience environment	Harwood T., Garry T.	2015	176
Game on: engaging customers and employees through gamification	Robson K., Plangger K., Kietzmann J.H., McCarthy I., Pitt L.	2016	170
Gamification: making work fun, or making fun of work?	Dale S.	2014	166
Gamification and the online retail experience	Insley V.; Nunan D.	2014	98
Hook vs. hope: how to enhance customer engagement through gamification	Eisingerich A.B., Marchand A., Fritze M.P., Dong L.	2019	97
Playing seriously – how gamification and social cues influence bank customers to use gamified e-business applications	Rodrigues L.F., Oliveira A., Costa C.J.	2016	94
Gamification-based framework for engagement of residential customers in energy applications	AlSkaif T., Lampropoulos I., van den Broek M., van Sark W.	2018	72
Gamification and online impulse buying: the moderating effect of gender and age	Zhang L., Shao Z., Li X., Feng Y.	2021	57

Source: secondary data (Scopus database)

Based on the above-reported review, five key themes were identified: *customer brand engagement, brand loyalty, co-creation, enjoyment and retailer support.*

Themes Identification

Impact of Gamification on Customer Engagement: AlSkaif et al. (2018) found that gamified systems increased customer participation, time spent on websites, and social interaction. Rodrigues et al. (2016) also reported that

Table 5.2 Relevant Review of Literature

Author (Year)	Key Findings
Hamari (2013)	Mere implementation of game mechanisms in utilitarian service does not automatically lead to significant increases in user activity. But those users who actively observed their badges showed an increased user activity.
Insley and Nunan (2014)	Game elements played an important role in enhancing the retail experience.
Dale (2014)	Gamification serves as a corporate transformation agent that aids in producing a workforce that is more motivated and engaged.
Harwood and Garry (2015)	Virtual gamified platforms impact the customer experience (CE) experience.
Rodrigues et al. (2016)	The Technology Acceptance Model (TAM) in the case of gamified apps predicted the behavioral intention of users in e-banking that benefits the business in terms of customer engagement.
Robson et al. (2016)	Using illustrative examples, this study noted the important role of game elements in customer and employee engagement.
Gupta and Mathad (2017)	Using a factor analysis approach, this study explored eight major factors influencing the adoption of gamification: personal perspective, usefulness, ease of use, price consciousness, perceived critical mass, flow experience, awareness, and personal innovativeness.
Yang et al. (2017a)	Gamification leads to higher retailer revenues and greater long-term engagement by other customers as customers register through multiple accounts.
Yang et al. (2017b)	The results provide an empirical support for perceived usefulness, ease of use, and enjoyment as predictors of the intention of engagement and brand attitude with the gamification process. It was discovered that people's brand attitudes, not their intentions to engage, were connected to their perception of social impact.
Miller et al. (2018)	The gamification training strategy positively impacted customer satisfaction with the performance of the IT service desk.
AlSkaif et al. (2018)	Employment of game design elements in nongame contexts helps to enhance energy applications by driving customer engagement and energy-related behavior change.
Kumar and Ravi Kumar (2019)	Intrinsic rewards, along with extrinsic rewards, should be used for good game designs.
Haziri et al. (2019)	The results showed that the association between products and services in the context of the game mechanism via social media was statistically significant, and the relationship between them is weak or moderated.
Eisingerich et al. (2019)	Gamification principles (social interaction, sense of control, goals, progress tracking, rewards, and prompts) promote customers' hopes and consequently increase customer engagement and digital sales.

(Continued)

Table 5.2 (Continued)

Author (Year)	Key Findings
Liu and Tanaka (2020)	Two experiments were conducted in this study. Gamification increased user participation in online shopping in the first experiment, while the second experiment found that social cues motivated users to participate in the use of a gamified point system.
Viega and Napitupulu (2020)	Using Structure Equation Modeling (SEM), the study found that brand attitude and customer satisfaction fully mediated the impact of gamification marketing practices on brand loyalty. In contrast, social media marketing and consumer brand engagement did not significantly affect brand loyalty.
Ruengaramrut et al. (2020)	Results of structural equation modeling (SEM) identified the role of gamification as a moderator variable strengthening the relationship between customer engagement and the new service development process.
Prott and Ebner (2020)	Results of the study highlighted that users preferred the design of gamified questionnaires and took longer completion time. But the customer satisfaction remains the same.
Syrjala et al. (2020)	The research demonstrates four consumer benefits of gamified packaging, including utilitarian, hedonic, social, and educational benefits. These benefits are also related to three dimensions (cognitive, emotional, and behavioral) of consumer brand engagement.
Xu et al. (2020a)	Gamification was found to be an important factor for cognitive and emotional consumer behavior.
Bauer et al. (2020)	When gamification is paired with financial incentives, its beneficial impacts are lessened since customers are more likely to play games for the extrinsic reward of a discount rather than for intrinsic delight.
Raman (2020)	Using PLS-SEM, the study found that gamification positively influenced young female consumers' behavioral intention (BI). Gamification also has a favorable and indirect influence on BI through social interaction and perceived enjoyment.
Xu et al. (2020b)	Game rewards, absorption, and autonomy of gamification positively enhanced the sense of enjoyment that helped people meet their psychological needs, ultimately impacting consumers' online purchase intention.
Hosseini and Rezvani (2021)	This study argued that customer satisfaction alone cannot inspire loyalty. Customers' satisfaction with gamified services can lead to developing trust and, in turn, loyalty during online shopping.
Srivastava and Bag (2021)	This study confirmed that distinct marketing strategy was required for different segments of consumers. Also, convenience, entertainment, engagement, age, and income significantly impact gamification.

(Continued)

Table 5.2 (Continued)

Author (Year)	Key Findings
Jami Pour et al. (2021)	Over a sample of grocery retailers, this study found that gamification had a significant and positive impact on customer experience directly and through the mediating effect of customer brand engagement.
Lau and Ki (2021)	Results found that VR fashion apps create a game environment and affect users' purchase intention.
Merhabi et al. (2021)	Customer service, insight sharing word-of-mouth, random tasks, and other activities co-created by online users and positively influenced by gamification were all explored in this study.
Kiguchi et al. (2021)	Tariffs are likely to create positive and negative financial outcomes for individuals because of customer engagement
De Canio et al. (2021)	The intention to purchase when using a gamified mobile app is indirectly influenced by intrinsic motives (such as shopping gamification, focused attention, shopping delight, and socialness). Most astonishingly, the findings indicate that the convenience of online buying positively modifies the level of buying engagement.
Garcia-Jurado et al. (2021)	Using the User Engagement Scale (UES), the study confirmed that gamification significantly affects user engagement in Spanish e-commerce activities.
Hollebeek et al. (2021)	Based on a literature review, this study hypothesized the relationship between gamified loyalty programs (GLPs) with customer engagement, where extrinsic/intrinsic motivators are the important drivers for GLP.
Whittaker et al. (2021)	This study provided proof that the value-in-behavior generated by a gamified app increases users' intentions to use the app going forward as well as their behavioral intents to engage in gamification.
Abou-Shouk and Soliman (2021)	The study's findings using structural equation modeling showed that tourism firms have favorable intents to utilize gamification to boost consumer engagement and build brand awareness and loyalty for tourist destinations.
Zhang et al. (2021)	Gamification mechanisms that offer rewards and upgrade badges are favorably correlated with perceived satisfaction and social engagement, which have a significant impact on consumers' impulse purchases.
Sinha and Srivastava (2022)	This study established the relationship between augmented reality (AR) and preexisting consumer brand engagement (CBE) dimensions (affective, cognitive, and activation), to brand satisfaction (BS) and brand loyalty (BL).
Arcas et al. (2022)	Customer engagement with the gamified loyalty program promotes brand engagement, favoring brand loyalty and increasing share-of-purchase and share-of-wallet.

(Continued)

Table 5.2 (Continued)

Author (Year)	Key Findings
Sheetal et al. (2022)	The application of gamification in online retail, customer experiences in gamified retail, and obstacles and ethical issues with gamification were themes that were discovered through qualitative research. The semantic analysis showed that there are numerous unethical marketing techniques and that gamification is perceived negatively in terms of ethics.
Yadav et al. (2022)	Considering the Technological Acceptance Model (TAM), the results of structural equation modeling found that perceived usefulness, perceived ease of use, convenience, and enjoyment significantly lead to customer engagement during online shopping.
Dzandu et al. (2022)	This study used structural equation modeling (SEM) to demonstrate a strong and favorable association between the social impact theory components of internalization, compliance, and identification and the gamified mobile money payment (Gmmp).
Potseluyko et al. (2022)	Game-like platform combined with BIM could provide simplified data delivery to a client, leading to customer satisfaction, confidence, and increased sales.
Shi et al. (2022)	Results showed that gamification provides opportunities for tourists' various value perceptions on the OTA platforms, which affects their intention to buy during the online shopping festival.
Lopes et al. (2023a)	This study discovered that online shopping can be enjoyable and have a favorable emotional impact on a sample of Portuguese customers. However, game mechanics do not increase online customer engagement, nor is gamification in online retail stores driven by a co-creation process.
Lin et al. (2023)	Using Starbucks branded app as a tool, the study showed that game elements positively influence customer engagement and perceived playfulness. Gamification enhances customer engagement on the Starbucks branded app, creating joyful emotion and sustainable consumption.
Saxena et al. (2023)	The findings confirm that self–brand connection and customer–brand engagement play a constructive moderating role in the relationship between affective commitment and motivation to engage in gamification.
Elgarhy et al. (2023)	Adopting gamification has a favorable impact on consumer engagement, repurchase intent, and intrinsic incentives. Additionally, the association between gamification, repurchase intention, and intrinsic incentives has been partially mediated by consumer involvement. Furthermore, repurchase intention had an impact on intrinsic motives.

(Continued)

Table 5.2 (Continued)

Author (Year)	Key Findings
Lopes et al. (2023b)	On the basis of conducted interviews, this study found that most respondents do not consider online shopping as a substitute for other entertainment activities like gamification. Respondents stressed that in online shopping, the important thing is personal satisfaction and their needs. Regarding co-creation, the findings show that most respondents do not value the features on shop websites that let consumers design their own products.
Akbari and Bigdeli (2023)	Based on SEM results, this study revealed that gamification positively affects customer engagement (CE) and customer experience (CX).
Jain et al. (2023)	Using SEM, this study revealed that consumers' social and personal integrative motives for gaming positively influence customer engagement with luxury brands.
Hsu (2023)	This study revealed the moderating effect of gamification on the relationship between brand love and customer engagement.
Martin-Pena et al. (2023)	Using Structural Equation Modeling, the study found that value co-creation mediates the relationship between the emotional mechanics of gamification and service design.
Patharia and Jain (2023)	This study found that a variety of personal characteristics (such as trust and experience), website features (such as perceived behavioral tracking), and product aspects (such as perceived service quality) cause users to quit their electronic shopping carts.
Silva et al. (2023)	Any point of the customer journey may support customer value development through gamification design. It can increase consumer motivation and information search during the pre-service stage of brand engagement, and it can increase customer participation and brand relationships during the core and post-service phases of brand engagement.
Disse and Olsson (2023)	Distinct affordances induced by game elements in retail led to a more exciting customer experience (CX). The connections between affordances and the holistic CX led to a GCX-influencing customer engagement, satisfaction, and brand attitude.
Xu et al. (2023)	Gamification features such as social connectedness, rewardability, playfulness, and novelty significantly affect the immersive experience.
Kaur et al. (2023)	This study identified perceived delight as a crucial factor in determining whether or not consumers will use gamification.

Source: authors' compilation

gamification techniques enhanced user engagement by tapping into intrinsic motivators such as autonomy, mastery, and purpose. The inclusion of specific gamification elements has been explored in customer engagement. Points, badges, leaderboards, and virtual rewards are common gamification features for motivating and engaging customers. Eisingerich et al. (2019) found that points and badges positively influenced customer engagement and perceived enjoyment. Similarly, Eisingerich et al. (2019) reported that leaderboards and virtual rewards increased customer engagement and loyalty.

Impact of Gamification on Brand Loyalty: Sinha and Srivastava (2022) found that gamified elements, such as rewards and challenges, positively influenced brand loyalty by enhancing customer engagement and satisfaction. Similarly, Viega and Napitupulu (2020) reported that gamification features, such as loyalty programs and virtual rewards, increased brand loyalty and repeat purchases. Different gamification elements have been investigated in brand loyalty. Research has shown that these gamification elements contribute to positive brand perceptions and enhance customer loyalty. Viega and Napitupulu (2020) found that gamification elements positively influenced customers' loyalty intentions, specifically virtual currencies and achievements.

Impact of Gamification on Co-Creation: numerous studies have explored the impact of gamification on co-creation in online platforms. For instance, Silva et al. (2023) found that gamified platforms increased customer participation and motivation to contribute ideas and feedback. Gamification techniques, such as challenges, rewards, and leaderboards, effectively fostered co-creation by incentivizing and recognizing participants. Similarly, Merhabi et al. (2021) reported that gamification positively influenced the quantity and quality of customer contributions in co-creation initiatives (Lopes et al., 2023b; Silva et al., 2023).

Impact of Gamification on Enjoyment: Kaur et al. (2023) found that gamified elements, such as rewards and achievements, increased users' enjoyment and overall satisfaction. Similarly, Srivastava and Bag (2021) and Yang et al. (2017b) reported that gamification techniques positively influenced users' perceived enjoyment and engagement in online environments.

Gamification in Retailer Support: gamification techniques offer a unique approach to enhancing retailer support and engaging customers (Srivastava & Bag, 2021). By incorporating game-like elements such as challenges, rewards, progress tracking, and interactive interfaces, retailers can create a more immersive and enjoyable support experience. Studies have shown that gamified support interfaces can increase customer engagement, motivation, and satisfaction (Eisingerich et al., 2019; Potseluyko et al., 2022; Sheetal et al., 2022).

Discussion, Conclusion, and Implications

The study's SLR findings presented gamification's role in online shopping. Various studies identified the need for gamified apps to engage customers (Silva et al., 2023; Disse & Olsson, 2023; Yadav et al., 2022; Jami Pour et al., 2021) and make them brand loyal (Viega & Napitupulu, 2020; Abou-Shouk & Soliman, 2021; Sinha & Srivastava, 2022; Bauer et al., 2020). Gamification proved its significant contribution to co-creation activities (Merhabi et al., 2021; Lopes et al., 2023a; Silva et al., 2023) as adding a game element to online shopping apps creates entertainment and enjoyment (Srivastava & Bag, 2021; Kaur et al., 2023; Yang et al., 2017a) and develops user-friendly environment. The use of game elements in retailing benefited the customer and retailer both. For users, it makes shopping entertaining and creative (Srivastava & Bag, 2021), and for retailers, gamification helps to find engaged and loyal customers (Yadav et al., 2022; Jami Pour et al., 2021; Sinha & Srivastava, 2022) that benefits the retailer in terms of increased sales (Eisingerich et al., 2019; Potseluyko et al., 2022; Sheetal et al., 2022).

The study presented the potential implications for academicians, practitioners, marketers, game developers, and web designers. This research provided adequate systematic literature on gamification and customer experience. This pool of systematic review helps the academicians, practitioners, and researchers working in this direction. This study provides them with valuable insights into the literature.

This study identified five major themes: customer engagement, brand loyalty, co-creation, enjoyment, and retailer support that guide marketer in developing their marketing strategies. The study noticed that the game element increases the average time spent on shopping websites, increasing customer engagement with retailing sites and helping convert occasional users into loyal users. So, marketers should add game elements to their shopping websites to find engaged and loyal customers. Users also want an entertaining and friendly interface for shopping. In this case, designers add augmented reality and virtual reality check features along with game elements on their websites with fewer complications. Also, game developers should focus on personalized and tailored gamified experiences to cater to individual user preferences and motivations. Developers should be aware of the ill effects of gamified applications in terms of over-reliance on extrinsic rewards, potential privacy concerns, etc., which may undermine intrinsic motivation.

Future Research Agenda

This research tried to include an extensive review of the Scopus database on gamification and its applications in marketing. In the future, SLR and bibliometric analysis can be done again by taking other databases like Web of Science, EBSCO, PubMed, etc. Meta-analysis can be done on current data accessed from Scopus, and data can be accessed from other databases.

Through a systematic review, the researcher noticed that more research should be conducted on the type of gamified content published on websites. More research is required on gamification's role in different stages of consumer buying. Further research is also needed to explore the long-term effects, sustainability, and effectiveness of gamification strategies in online shopping and the potential integration with emerging technologies such as virtual reality and augmented reality.

References

Abou-Shouk, M., & Soliman, M. (2021). The impact of gamification adoption intention on brand awareness and loyalty in tourism: The mediating effect of customer engagement. *Journal of Destination Marketing and Management*, 20. https://doi.org/10.1016/j.jdmm.2021.100559

Akbari, M., & Bigdeli, M. (2023). Gamified customer experience and engagement in Amazon online retailing company in the Covid-19 era. *International Journal of Electronic Commerce Studies*, 13(4), 135–158. https://doi.org/10.7903/ijecs.2055

AlSkaif, T., Lampropoulos, I., van den Broek, M., & van Sark, W. (2018). Gamification-based framework for engagement of residential customers in energy applications. *Energy Research and Social Science*, 44, 187–195. https://doi.org/10.1016/j.erss.2018.04.043

Arcas, P. B., Gil, S. C., & Moreno, J. M. (2022). Boosting brand engagement and loyalty through gamified loyalty programmes. *UCJC Business and Society Review*, 19(75), 144–181. https://doi.org/10.3232/UBR.2022.V19.N4.04

Bauer, J. C., Linzmajer, M., Nagengast, L., Rudolph, T., & D'Cruz, E. (2020). Gamifying the digital shopping experience: Games without monetary participation incentives increase customer satisfaction and loyalty. *Journal of Service Management*, 31(3), 563–595. https://doi.org/10.1108/JOSM-10-2018-0347

Chen, Y., & Zheng, B. (2019, March 1). What happens after the rare earth crisis: A systematic literature review. *Sustainability (Switzerland)*. https://doi.org/10.3390/su11051288

Cronin, P., Ryan, F., & Coughlan, M. (2008). Undertaking a literature review: A step-by-step approach. *British Journal of Nursing*, 17, 38–43. https://doi.org/10.12968/bjon.2008.17.1.28059

Dale, S. (2014). Gamification: Making work fun, or making fun of work? *Business Information Review*, 31(2), 82–90. https://doi.org/10.1177/0266382114538350

De Canio, F., Fuentes-Blasco, M., & Martinelli, E. (2021). Engaging shoppers through mobile apps: The role of gamification. *International Journal of Retail and Distribution Management*, 49(7), 919–940. https://doi.org/10.1108/IJRDM-09-2020-0360

Disse, I. K., & Olsson, M. (2023). Uncovering the gamified customer experience in the retail environment. *International Journal of Retail and Distribution Management*. https://doi.org/10.1108/IJRDM-07-2022-0268

Dzandu, M. D., Hanu, C., & Amegbe, H. (2022). Gamification of mobile money payment for generating customer value in emerging economies: The social impact theory perspective. *Technological Forecasting and Social Change*, 185. https://doi.org/10.1016/j.techfore.2022.122049

Eisingerich, A. B., Marchand, A., Fritze, M. P., & Dong, L. (2019). Hook vs. hope: How to enhance customer engagement through gamification. *International Journal of Research in Marketing*, 36(2), 200–215. https://doi.org/10.1016/j.ijresmar.2019.02.003

Elgarhy, S. D., Abdel Rahieem, W. M. A. N., & Abdulmawla, M. (2023). Influences of gamification on repurchase intention and intrinsic motivations in Egyptian hotels and travel agencies: The mediating role of customer engagement. *Journal of Quality Assurance in Hospitality and Tourism*. https://doi.org/10.1080/15280 08X.2023.2194705

Garcia-Jurado, A., Torres-Jimenez, M., Leal-Rodriguez, A. L., & Castro-Gonzalez, P. (2021). Does gamification engage users in online shopping? *Electronic Commerce Research and Applications*, 48. https://doi.org/10.1016/j.elerap.2021.101076

Gatautis, R., Gadeikienė, A., & Vitkauskaitė, E. (2021). Expression of the concept of gamification in the context of ICT development. *Gamification and Consumer Engagement: Creating Value in Context of ICT Development*, 69–97. https://doi.org/10.1007/978-3-030-54205-4_4

Gupta, R., & Mathad, K. (2017). A study of factors affecting consumer behavioural intentions towards adoption of gamification. *Indian Journal of Marketing*, 47(7), 7–19. https://doi.org/10.17010/ijom/2017/v47/i7/116471

Hamari, J. (2013). Transforming homo economicus into homo Ludens: A field experiment on gamification in a utilitarian peer-to-peer trading service. *Electronic Commerce Research and Applications*, 12(4), 236–245. https://doi.org/10.1016/j.elerap.2013.01.004

Hamari, J., & Koivisto, J. (2015). Why do people use gamification services? *International Journal of Information Management*, 35(4), 419–431. https://doi.org/10.1016/j.ijinfomgt.2015.04.006

Harwood, T., & Garry, T. (2015). An investigation into gamification as a customer engagement experience environment. *Journal of Services Marketing*, 29(7), 533–546. https://doi.org/10.1108/JSM-01-2015-0045

Haziri, F., Chovancov, M., & Fetahu, F. (2019). Game mechanics and aesthetics differences for tangible and intangible goods provided via social media. *Management and Marketing*, 14(2), 176–187. https://doi.org/10.2478/mmcks-2019-0012

Hollebeek, L. D., Das, K., & Shukla, Y. (2021). Game on! How gamified loyalty programs boost customer engagement value. *International Journal of Information Management*, 61. https://doi.org/10.1016/j.ijinfomgt.2021.102308

Hosseini, E., & Rezvani, M. H. (2021). E-customer loyalty in gamified trusted store platforms: A case study analysis in Iran. *Bulletin of Electrical Engineering and Informatics*, 10(5), 2899–2909. https://doi.org/10.11591/eei.v10i5.3165

Hsu, C.-L. (2023). Enhancing brand love, customer engagement, brand experience, and repurchase intention: Focusing on the role of gamification in mobile apps. *Decision Support Systems*. https://doi.org/10.1016/j.dss.2023.114020

Huotari, K., & Hamari, J. (2017). A definition for gamification: Anchoring gamification in the service marketing literature. *Electronic Markets*, 27(1), 21–31.

Insley, V., & Nunan, D. (2014). Gamification and the online retail experience. *International Journal of Retail and Distribution Management*, 42(5), 340–351. https://doi.org/10.1108/IJRDM-01-2013-0030

Jain, S., Mishra, S., & Saxena, G. (2023). Luxury customer's motivations to adopt gamification. *Marketing Intelligence and Planning*, 41(2), 156–170. https://doi.org/10.1108/MIP-05-2022-0207

Jami Pour, M., Rafiei, K., Khani, M., & Sabrirazm, A. (2021). Gamification and customer experience: The mediating role of brand engagement in online grocery retailing. *Nankai Business Review International*, 12(3), 340–357. https://doi.org/10.1108/NBRI-07-2020-0041

Kaur, J., Lavuri, R., Parida, R., & Singh, S. V. (2023). Exploring the impact of gamification elements in brand apps on the purchase intention of consumers. *Journal of Global Information Management*, 31(1). https://doi.org/10.4018/JGIM.317216

Kiguchi, Y., Weeks, M., & Arakawa, R. (2021). Predicting winners and losers under time-of-use tariffs using smart meter data. *Energy, 236.* https://doi.org/10.1016/j. energy.2021.121438

Kumar, G. A., & Ravi Kumar, A. (2019). Employing gamification methods to increase customer engagement in digital marketing. *International Journal of Recent Technology and Engineering, 8*(2 Special Issue 8), 869–872. https://doi.org/10.35940/ ijrte.B1366.0882S819

Lau, O., & Ki, C.-W. C. (2021). Can consumers' gamified, personalized, and engaging experiences with VR fashion apps increase in-app purchase intention by fulfilling needs? *Fashion and Textiles, 8*(1). https://doi.org/10.1186/s40691-021-00270-9

Lee, H., & Xu, Y. (2020). Classification of virtual fitting room technologies in the fashion industry: From the perspective of consumer experience. *International Journal of Fashion Design, Technology and Education, 13*(1), 1–10. https://doi.org/10. 1080/17543266.2019.1657505

Lee, Y. J. (2023). Gamification and the festival experience: The case of Taiwan. *Current Issues in Tourism, 26*(8), 1311–1326. https://doi.org/10.1080/13683500.202 2.2053074

Lin, C.-W., Chien, C.-Y., Ou Yang, C.-P., & Mao, T.-Y. (2023). Encouraging sustainable consumption through gamification in a branded app: A study on consumers' behavioral perspective. *Sustainability (Switzerland), 15*(1). https://doi.org/10.3390/ su15010589

Liu, B., & Tanaka, J. (2020). Integrating gamification and social interaction into an AR-based gamified point system. *Multimodal Technologies and Interaction, 4*(3), 1–19. https://doi.org/10.3390/mti4030051

Lopes, J. M., Gomes, S., Lopes, P., Silva, A., Lourenco, D., Esteves, D., Cardoso, M., & Redondo, V. (2023a). Exploring the role of gamification in the online shopping experience in retail stores: An exploratory study. *Social Sciences, 12*(4). https://doi. org/10.3390/socsci12040235

Lopes, J. M., Gomes, S., Santos, N., Cussina, H., Vieira, I., Escudeiro, M., Maio, L., & Magalhaes, Y. (2023b). The epic game of creating a successful gamified co-creation strategy. *Administrative Sciences, 13*(1). https://doi.org/10.3390/admsci13010011

Martin-Pena, M. L., Garcia-Magro, C., & Sanchez-Lopez, J. M. (2023). Service design through the emotional mechanics of gamification and value co-creation: A user experience analysis. *Behaviour and Information Technology.* https://doi.org/ 10.1080/0144929X.2023.2177823

Merhabi, M. A., Petridis, P., & Khusainova, R. (2021). Gamification for brand value co-creation: A systematic literature review. *Information (Switzerland), 12*(9). https://doi.org/10.3390/info12090345

Miller, C. L., Grooms, J. C., & King, H. (2018). To infinity and beyond gamifying IT service-desk training: A case study. *Performance Improvement Quarterly, 31*(3), 249–268. https://doi.org/10.1002/piq.21263

Page, M. J., McKenzie, J. E., Bossuyt, P. M., Boutron, I., Hoffmann, T. C., Mulrow, C. D., Shamseer, L., Tetzlaff, J. M., Akl, E. A., Brennan, S. E., Chou, R., Glanville, J., Grimshaw, J. M., Hróbjartsson, A., Lalu, M. M., Li, T., Loder, E. W., Mayo-Wilson, E., McDonald, S., . . . Moher, D. (2021). The PRISMA 2020 statement: An updated guideline for reporting systematic reviews. *BMJ, 372*(71). https://doi.org/10.1136/bmj.n71

Paruthi, M., Nagina, R., & Gupta, G. (2023, March). Measuring the effect of consumer brand engagement on brand-related outcomes in gamified mobile apps: A solicitation of technology acceptance model. In *Proceedings* (Vol. 85, No. 1, p. 10). MDPI.

Patharia, I., & Jain, T. (2023). Antecedents of electronic shopping cart abandonment during online purchase process. *Business Perspectives and Research*. https://doi.org/10.1177/22785337221148810

Potseluyko, L., Pour Rahimian, F., Dawood, N., Elghaish, F., & Hajirasouli, A. (2022). Game-like interactive environment using BIM-based virtual reality for the timber frame self-build housing sector. *Automation in Construction*, *142*. https://doi.org/10.1016/j.autcon.2022.104496

Prott, D., & Ebner, M. (2020). The use of gamification in gastronomic questionnaires. *International Journal of Interactive Mobile Technologies*, *14*(2), 101–118. https://doi.org/10.3991/ijim.v14i02.11695

Raman, P. (2020). Examining the importance of gamification, social interaction and perceived enjoyment among young female online buyers in India. *Young Consumers*, *22*(3), 387–412. https://doi.org/10.1108/YC-05-2020-1148

Robson, K., Plangger, K., Kietzmann, J. H., McCarthy, I., & Pitt, L. (2016). Game on: Engaging customers and employees through gamification. *Business Horizons*, *59*(1), 29–36. https://doi.org/10.1016/j.bushor.2015.08.002

Rodrigues, L. F., Oliveira, A., & Costa, C. J. (2016). Playing seriously – how gamification and social cues influence bank customers to use gamified E-business applications. *Computers in Human Behavior*, *63*, 392–407. https://doi.org/10.1016/j.chb.2016.05.063

Rodrigues, M., & Mendes, L. (2018, April). Mapping of the literature on social responsibility in the mining industry: A systematic literature review. *Journal of Cleaner Production*. https://doi.org/10.1016/j.jclepro.2018.01.163

Ruengaramrut, V., Ribiere, V., & Mariano, S. (2020). The moderating effect of gamification on the relationship between customer engagement and new service development process involvement. *International Journal of Innovation and Learning*, *27*(1), 93–119. https://doi.org/10.1504/IJIL.2020.103895

Saxena, G., Jain, S., & Mishra, S. (2023). Enhancing affective commitment through gamified services of luxury brands: Role of game mechanics and self-congruity. *Journal of Services Marketing*. https://doi.org/10.1108/JSM-06-2022-0217

Sheetal, Tyagi, R., & Singh, G. (2022). Gamification and customer experience in online retail: A qualitative study focusing on ethical perspective. *Asian Journal of Business Ethics*. https://doi.org/10.1007/s13520-022-00162-1

Shi, S., Leung, W. K. S., & Munelli, F. (2022). Gamification in OTA platforms: A mixed-methods research involving online shopping carnival. *Tourism Management*, *88*. https://doi.org/10.1016/j.tourman.2021.104426

Silva, J. H. O., Mendes, G. H. S., Teixeira, J. G., & Braatz, D. (2023). Gamification in the customer journey: A conceptual model and future research opportunities. *Journal of Service Theory and Practice*, *33*(3), 352–386. https://doi.org/10.1108/JSTP-07-2022-0142

Sinha, M., & Srivastava, M. (2022). Augmented reality-enabled Instagram game filters: Key to engaging customers. *Journal of Promotion Management*, *28*(4), 467–486. https://doi.org/10.1080/10496491.2021.2008577

Srivastava, G., & Bag, S. (2021). Diagnosing key factors for gamification in marketing using hierarchical clustering technique. *International Journal of Technology Marketing*, *15*(4), 354–378. https://doi.org/10.1504/ijtmkt.2021.119074

Syrjala, H., Kauppinen-Raisanen, H., Luomala, H. T., Joelsson, T. N., Konnola, K., & Makila, T. (2020). Gamified package: Consumer insights into multidimensional brand engagement. *Journal of Business Research*, *119*, 423–434. https://doi.org/10.1016/j.jbusres.2019.11.089

Viega, M. T., & Napitupulu, T. A. (2020). Impact analysis of experience on gamification marketing activities, social media marketing, and other factors toward brand loyalty in online marketplace application. *Journal of Theoretical and Applied Information Technology, 98*(20), 3180–3197.

Webster, J., & Watson, R. T. (2002). Analyzing the past to prepare for the future: Writing a literature review. *MIS Quarterly, 26*(2), 13–23.

Whittaker, L., Mulcahy, R., & Russell-Bennett, R. (2021). Go with the flow for gamification and sustainability marketing. *International Journal of Information Management, 61.* https://doi.org/10.1016/j.ijinfomgt.2020.102305

Xu, X., Wang, L., & Zhao, K. (2020a). Exploring determinants of consumers' platform usage in "double eleven" shopping carnival in China: Cognition and emotion from an integrated perspective. *Sustainability (Switzerland), 12*(7). https://doi.org/10.3390/su12072790

Xu, X.-Y., Tayyab, S. M. U., Jia, Q.-D., & Wu, K. (2023). Exploring the gamification affordances in online shopping with the heterogeneity examination through REBUS-PLS. *Journal of Theoretical and Applied Electronic Commerce Research, 18*(1), 289–310. https://doi.org/10.3390/jtaer18010016

Xu, Y., Chen, Z., Peng, M. Y.-P., & Anser, M. K. (2020b). Enhancing consumer online purchase intention through gamification in China: Perspective of cognitive evaluation theory. *Frontiers in Psychology, 11.* https://doi.org/10.3389/fpsyg.2020.581200

Yadav, K., Arora, A., Yadav, R., & Prakash, C. (2022). Gamified apps and customer engagement: Modeling in online shopping environment. *Transnational Marketing Journal, 10*(3), 593–605. https://doi.org/10.33182/tmj.v10i3.2199

Yang, Y., Asaad, Y., & Dwivedi, Y. (2017a). Examining the impact of gamification on intention of engagement and brand attitude in the marketing context. *Computers in Human Behavior, 73,* 459–469. https://doi.org/10.1016/j.chb.2017.03.066

Yang, Z., Algesheimer, R., & Dholakia, U. (2017b). When ethical transgressions of customers have beneficial long-term effects in retailing: An empirical investigation. *Journal of Retailing, 93*(4), 420–439. https://doi.org/10.1016/j.jretai.2017.09.005

Zhang, L., Shao, Z., Li, X., & Feng, Y. (2021). Gamification and online impulse buying: The moderating effect of gender and age. *International Journal of Information Management, 61.* https://doi.org/10.1016/j.ijinfomgt.2020.102267

Part 3

Gamification and Branding

Chapter 6

Impact of Customer Engagement and Brand Love through Gamification and Brand Love on Online Travel Agencies (OTAs)

Garima Malik, Sunetra Saha and Arpita Srivastava (Corresponding Author)

Introduction

Online Travel Agencies (OTAs) refer to internet-based enterprises that operate websites facilitating direct consumer access to a diverse array of travel-oriented services for booking purposes. The utilization of these online platforms for making travel reservations has gained considerable traction in contemporary times. This trend can be attributed to the modern consumer's inclination towards seamless mobility and the advantageous attributes intrinsic to the booking engines and reservation mechanisms offered by OTAs. These attributes encompass instantaneous payment processing and expeditious booking confirmation. It is noteworthy that the online travel sector is characterized by an intense landscape of competition among industry participants.

The concept of gamification is creating a buzz in OTA as it offers an integrated framework for customer engagement and brand Love. Gamification can be delineated as the strategic integration of game design tenets and the incorporation of ludic components within domains outside the realm of traditional gaming (Deterding et al., 2011). In the present scenario, OTA companies use gamified marketing applications to engage their customers and increase human–computer interaction time in the context of their websites.

Technological advancements have significantly transformed customer acquisition strategies and marketing approaches for companies (Al-Zyoud, 2020). Presently, consumers possess a broader range of tools and devices, enabling them to actively participate and contribute more frequently in the co-creation processes within business operations. As a result, they possess the capacity to directly exert influence on and affect the operational workflows of the organization (Kennedy & Guzmán, 2016; Rodrigues, Lopes et al., 2021).

Brand love represents the most intensive customer–brand relationship (Bagozzi, 1992). This is done by understanding the customer's needs and expectations of the brand and then finding a way to meet those needs or exceed them. In doing so, it fosters an enduring and trust-centric rapport between the customer and the brand. Gamification through improved

DOI: 10.4324/9781032694238-9

customer experience and brand loyalty encourages customer brand love (Batra et al., 2012).

During periods of online shopping festivals, Online Travel Agencies (OTAs) heavily rely on a combination of inventive digital and offline promotional strategies to captivate the attention of their clientele, drawing them into the festive ambience (Mata & Quesada, 2014). Consequently, numerous OTA platforms have incorporated gamification elements into their offerings, aiming to motivate customers to actively partake in the festivities and engage in transactions during these online shopping events. Gamification, as a concept, pertains to the integration of game design principles within non-gaming activities, with the primary objective of engrossing individuals (Deterding et al., 2011). This involves the implementation of gamification elements such as rewards, provision of coupons, and progression through badge systems, typically intended to heighten enjoyment, amusement, and involvement (Shao et al., 2019).

The integration of gamification strategies within the operations of OTAs has emerged as a prospective avenue for elevating the digital shopping experience of tourists (Lopes et al., 2023). Nonetheless, there exists a dearth of comprehensive study regarding the pivotal gamification features that hold significance for tourists, along with the fundamental incentives driving their engagement with gamified OTA platforms.

Thus, this study explores the impact of gamified marketing activities on OTA and also investigates the relationship between gamification and customer engagement. The research questions are:

Q1. How do consumers respond to the gamification mechanism used by companies on online platforms?
Q2. Does gamification affect the customer engagement of the brand, which develops the co-creation between service providers and customers?

Gamification strives to improve user experiences, encourage desired behaviours, and promote deeper engagement by integrating game components and ideas into non-game environments. Building brand love – the emotional bond and loyalty that customers form with a business – is one area where gamification has shown to be particularly successful. This study explores the idea of gamification and how it affects brand loyalty, as well as the tactics and systems that may be used to apply gamification to forge closer bonds between customers and brands.

Gamification has emerged as one of the most significant technological trends in the past ten years (Singh et al., 2022). One of the principal catalysts propelling shopping involvement and indirectly shaping consumers' inclination to make purchases through a mobile application is the implementation of shopping gamification (Insley & Nunan, 2014; Hofacker et al., 2016).

According to research, gamification can improve a number of elements related to brand love. Gamification can increase customers' feelings of accomplishment and satisfaction by offering fun tasks and incentives, further cementing their relationship with the business (Chen & Chen, 2019). A sense of community among consumers can be fostered through gamification tactics including social engagement and competitiveness (Vos et al., 2018). This results in an increase in brand loyalty and advocacy.

Gamification can also improve brand interactions by making them more engaging, entertaining, and memorable (Pour et al., 2021). Brands may capture consumers' attention and foster favourable associations with their goods or services by turning ordinary tasks into fun, game-like experience. Insights and data about consumer preferences, behaviours, and motivations can help firms develop more effective marketing campaigns and individualized products through the use of gamification (Prusty, 2018). Additionally, customer brand engagement yields a noteworthy and positive influence on user engagement within the gamified context. It showed that gamification and customer experience are mediated by customer brand involvement (Pour et al., 2021). Mobile applications that have been enhanced with gamified components may thus be more adaptable, practical, interactive, and interesting. It is essential for digital players to establish gamification and marketing strategies that are consistent with one another.

A comprehensive analysis of existing literature was conducted to comprehensively grasp the impact of gamification on the concept of brand affection, along with its underlying mechanisms, while also pinpointing areas within the research that require further exploration.

Literature Review

OTAs – given the prominence of online platforms for hotel bookings and ticket acquisition compared to traditional offline methods, the competitive landscape within the OTA service marketing sector has witnessed a noticeable escalation. Entities capable of delivering heightened customer satisfaction possess the potential to achieve performance outcomes that surpass customer anticipations, consequently eliciting a state of elevated satisfaction or delight among customers (Armstrong & Kotler, 2011). This satisfaction doesn't merely result in contented customers but also engenders a willingness to evolve into collaborative marketing partners.

Gamification – gamification is delineated as the strategic deployment of principles inherent to game design, coupled with the incorporation of ludic elements, within domains that extend beyond the conventional realm of gaming (Deterding et al., 2011). In today's digitalized market, it has become essential to employ innovative business strategies. One such strategy that has gained prominence is the integration of "Gamification" to enhance customer engagement (Spais et al., 2022). It has been recognized as a promising instrument within tourism marketing, adept at engaging customers to advocate for various tourism destinations. Tourists, in the course of their enjoyment, utilize serious games as a means to extract information concerning their intended destinations, with the ultimate goal of achieving a distinctive and enduring experiential outcome (Buhalis et al., 2019; Bulencea & Egger, 2015; Xu et al., 2017). Moreover, gamification offers significant potential benefits for bolstering both brand awareness and loyalty within these destinations (Xu et al., 2017). The work of Buhalis et al. (2019) asserts that gamification stands as a valuable technological tool within the tourism sector, adept at fortifying the development of tourist relationships, facilitating human resources management, and fostering sustainable community support for the realm of tourism.

According to a Forbes report (2021), a significant majority of Forbes 2000 companies, specifically 70%, have embraced gamification as a crucial component of their mobile marketing strategies (Park & Bae, 2014). Technological advancements have significantly transformed customer acquisition strategies and marketing approaches for companies (Al-Zyoud, 2021)

Gamification is the utilization of game elements within non-game environments (Merhabi et al., 2021; Yang et al., 2017). It involves incorporating game mechanics, such as points or leaderboards, to activate players' motivations, leading to increased competition and rewards (Rodrigues, Soares et al., 2021). Companies can employ gamification as a strategy in online retail stores to enhance customer retention and foster marketing activities (Park & Bae, 2014). The proliferation of social software and online games has revolutionized e-business, offering novel experiences for online consumers.

Some instances of gamification in the travel and tourism sector have been provided by Xu et al. (2013). Location-based games could facilitate interactions between tourists and augmented reality, destination marketing organizations also use storytelling techniques to entice tourists to visit specific locations. Restaurants use games to entice patrons to win free food, and airlines use gamification to enhance their passengers' loyalty programmes.

The present study seeks to fill the existing gaps in the field of tourism marketing by responding to the call for empirical investigations into the effects of innovative technologies, particularly gamification, on the efficacy of tourism marketing endeavours. With this objective in mind, the study endeavours to forecast both the factors influencing the intention to adopt gamification within travel agencies and the subsequent outcomes stemming from this adoption.

Customer Engagement

Engagement can be characterized as the dual concept of actively engaging users on an emotional level and the state of harmonious interaction with a system (O'Brien, 2010, p. 345). This phenomenon epitomizes the capacity of technology to captivate users' attention, fostering a profound sense of community and enjoyment (O'Brien & Toms, 2008).

It is recognized that the advent of social media has empowered customers to endorse or critique companies publicly (Bernritter et al., 2016; Dessart et al., 2015; Scheinbaum, 2016). In certain aspects, this phenomenon referred to as "customer engagement behavior" (van Doorn et al., 2010) enables traditional marketing strategies to leverage the enhanced interactivity offered by social media platforms, potentially leading to higher levels of "consumer brand engagement" (Hollebeek, 2011; Brodie et al., 2013).

Customer engagement encompasses the experiential interaction between customers and brands, websites, or other entities, while also reflecting the psychological and motivational state of the relationship (Vivek et al., 2012; Paruthi et al., 2023). Customer engagement stands as the ultimate aim in the realm of gamification across various related fields (Ng et al., 2020; Syrjälä et al., 2020). Nonetheless, its implementation within the marketing domain presents additional complexities (Jang et al., 2018; Hollebeek et al., 2019).

The incorporation of gamification strategies by companies aims to elicit diverse stimuli in consumers, ideally of a positive nature, with the subsequent intention of influencing their responses and behaviours (Jami Pour et al., 2021). These stimuli encompass elements commonly found in games, such as points, virtual goods, achievements, gifts, levels, and rewards. Depending on whether this state is pleasant or unpleasant, it will engender a particular behaviour, either action or avoidance, or lack thereof (Gatautis et al., 2016; Ma et al., 2021). Consequently, these stimuli will shape the cognitions and emotions of consumers, exerting an influence on their behaviour and eliciting a response. Notably, individuals with a higher degree of online shopping experience possess a greater quantity, content, and organization of cognitions derived from previous encounters. These past positive experiences contribute to enhancing customer engagement with the brand (De Canio et al., 2021).

Brand Love

The notion of brand love has its roots in interpersonal love theories (Shimp & Madden, 1988), specifically drawing upon the triangular theory of love (Sternberg, 1986). Over the past few years, brand love has gained considerable prominence as a noteworthy subject within the realm of consumer branding research.

Brand love holds great significance within the literature on consumer–brand relationships, as it has been associated with a range of positive outcomes. Batra et al. (2012), in their study across various product contexts, identified three fundamental elements of brand love: a favourable emotional attachment, a strong sense of brand integration, and passion-driven behaviours. Additionally, Singla and Gupta (2019) observed substantial impacts of brand love on word-of-mouth and online loyalty within Portuguese brand communities, while Bairrada et al. (2018) confirmed the substantial influence of brand love on desirable behavioral outcomes, including positive word-of-mouth, a willingness to pay a premium price, and enhanced customer loyalty.

Brand love surpasses the mere notion of "liking" and possesses a heightened intensity. Consequently, it has emerged as a crucial construct that influences various other constructs, such as brand loyalty, brand sacredness, and brand advocacy (Drennan et al., 2015; Joshi & Yadav, 2020; Palusuk et al., 2019; Wang et al., 2019). Hence, it becomes crucial for researchers to scrutinize the pivotal factors that contribute to the formation of brand affection and its subsequent interconnections with other constructs. Investigating these antecedents and associations is imperative for acquiring a holistic comprehension of the ramifications and intricacies associated with brand affection.

Previous studies conducted by Sarkar and Sreejesh (2014) and Sarkar et al. (2019) have examined the impact of brand love on active engagement and loyalty intention, respectively. Additionally, Dwivedi (2015) investigated the influence of brand engagement on loyalty intention. Nonetheless, the precise function of brand engagement as a substantial mediator within the link connecting brand affection and intention for loyalty has not yet been investigated. Brand love has been linked to various advantages for organizations (Rossiter, 2012). Among these benefits, brand loyalty and positive word-of-mouth (WOM) are frequently mentioned. Brand loyalty represents a consumer's commitment to maintaining a valued relationship with a specific brand, demonstrating an enduring desire (Moorman et al., 1992; Assael, 1987). The influence of brand affection on brand loyalty frequently transpires by means of the intermediary influence of enhanced consumer attitudes, leading to heightened loyalty and an increased willingness to invest in a premium pricing structure (Park et al., 2006).

Committed patrons also have the potential to evolve into brand advocates and representatives participating in constructive word-of-mouth communication (Batra et al., 2012; Carroll & Ahuvia, 2006; Far & Dinani, 2015; Ismail & Spinelli, 2012; Karjaluoto et al., 2016; Wallace et al., 2014). Brand advocacy includes speaking favourably about the brand, being open to trying new products, and being willing to resist negative information or occasional brand missteps, as described by Wallace et al. (2014).

These behaviours not only provide positive information about the brand but also help mitigate the potential negative implications associated with adverse information (Du et al., 2007).

Conceptual Framework

The basic framework of the study shows how gamification, customer engagement, and brand love all work together, and how this fact affects online tourism platforms. The structure depicts how important gamification is a way to keep customers interested and build emotional ties that lead to brand love. By adding game-like features to the platform, businesses can make experiences

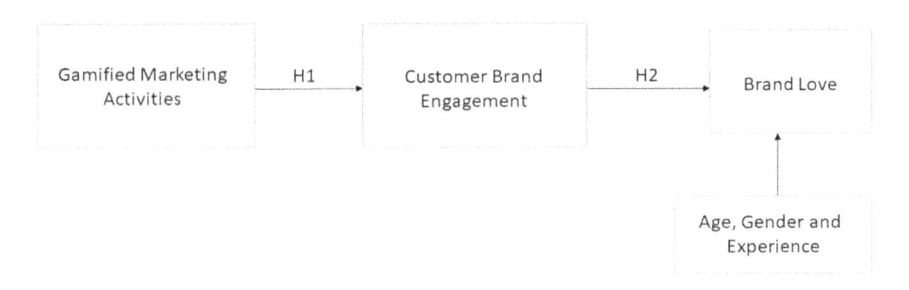

Figure 6.1 Conceptual framework
Source: researchers' own analysis

that are fun and immersive. This increases the number of users who stay on the platform and encourages them to book again. The framework shows how important it is to think about ethics when designing gaming, so that users have good experiences without their addictions being taken advantage of. Overall, this conceptual framework gives OTA businesses useful information about how to use gamification well and improve their competitive edge in the fast-changing online tourist market (refer to Figure 6.1).

Hypotheses Development

1. Hypothesis: Gamified Marketing Activities Positively Impact Customer Brand Engagement

Null Hypothesis (H0): there is no significant relationship between gamified marketing activities and customer brand engagement.

Alternative Hypothesis (Ha): gamified marketing activities have a significant positive impact on customer brand engagement.

Customer engagement is increased via gamified marketing, which incorporates game features into non-game conditions. Gamified components, according to Huang and Soman (2013), boost consumer perception and brand loyalty. Gamification, according to Zichermann and Cunningham (2011), stimulates intrinsic motives, increasing engagement and loyalty. Gamification increases engagement, according to Hamari et al. (2014), and is influenced by element quality and brand alignment. According to the literature, gamified marketing fosters brand engagement through interactive elements and intrinsic incentive. Design must reflect the brand's ideals in order to succeed.

The hypothesized favourable association between gamified marketing activities and client brand engagement is strongly substantiated by the body of existing studies. The objectives of brand engagement strategies are aligned with gamification's potential to tap into innate motivations and generate engaging experiences.

2. Hypothesis: Customer Brand Engagement Is Positively Related to Brand Love

Null Hypothesis (H0): there is no significant relationship between customer brand engagement and brand love.

Alternative Hypothesis (Ha): there exists a noteworthy and constructive correlation between customer brand engagement and the sentiment of brand affection.

Customer brand engagement fosters advocacy and loyalty through active participation and an emotional connection with a brand (Amoah et al., 2022). Brand love denotes a strong emotional connection that goes beyond fulfilment. Deeper engagement fosters emotional ties that result in brand love, according to research, which shows a high correlation between brand love and engagement. Involvement has a crucial part in creating brand love, according to studies by Batra et al. (2012) and Fournier (1998), while Bhattacharya and Sen (2003) stress the impact of emotional involvement on loyalty and attachment. According to literature, loyal clients are more likely to be engaged. As a result, the alternative hypothesis (Ha) that suggests a favourable relationship between brand involvement and love is supported.

3. Hypothesis: Gender Differences Influence Brand Love

Null Hypothesis (H0): there is no significant difference in brand love between different genders.

Alternative Hypothesis (Ha): gender differences have a significant impact on brand love.

Numerous studies on the emotional ties that consumers have with brands and the distinctions between male and female consumers have helped us understand customer preferences, attitudes, and behaviour. According to Pine and Gilmore (1999), research demonstrates that when creating strong emotional connections with organizations, men and women have different emotional triggers and priorities. According to Lafferty and Goldsmith (1999), women are more likely to form stronger emotional relationships and exhibit higher degrees of brand loyalty. Inconclusive results from some studies, however, imply that brand love formation may differ between the sexes. According to the literature, brand love may be influenced by gender differences in emotional attachment to products.

4. Hypothesis: Age Differences Impact Brand Love

Null Hypothesis (H0): there is no significant relationship between age and brand love.

Alternative Hypothesis (Ha): age differences have a significant impact on brand love.

Studies indicate that brand love is influenced by age and that age has a substantial impact on brand perception and involvement. Schmitt (2010) found that younger consumers are more drawn to organizations that offer unique experiences, whereas older consumers may be more prone to sentimentality and nostalgia, which can foster stronger emotional bonds. Carroll and Ahuvia (2006) report that several studies did not discover any appreciable age-related differences in brand love. A research study could evaluate if there are appreciable age-related differences in brand love by using a broad sample of consumers from various age groups using statistical analyses to test this hypothesis. The research and alternative hypothesis (Ha) support the idea that brand love can be affected by age.

5. Hypothesis: Positive Brand Experiences Foster Brand Love

Null Hypothesis (H0): there is no significant relationship between brand experience and brand love.

Alternative Hypothesis (Ha): positive brand experiences have a significant positive relationship with brand love.

The fundamental concepts in consumer behaviour and marketing include the concepts of brand experience and brand love. While brand love denotes a deep emotional attachment and fondness, brand experience involves customer perceptions, feelings, and interactions with a brand across numerous touchpoints (Brakus et al., 2009). Positive brand experiences are frequently connected to heightened emotional responses and greater brand ties, according to studies that repeatedly point to a positive relationship between the two variables. The "experience economy" was first discussed by Pine and Gilmore (1998), who emphasized the value of developing engaging and memorable experiences. The idea of brand experience quality was put up by Brakus et al. (2009), focusing on the role that sensory, emotive, intellectual, and behavioural aspects have in defining brand experiences. Carroll and Ahuvia (2006) concluded that positive emotional responses are important predictors of brand love, indicating that organizations that can arouse positive feelings are more likely to forge enduring and intense connections with customers.

Research Design and Methodology

The primary objective of this research endeavour is to appraise the influence of gamification on the degrees of customer engagement and brand affinity, specifically within the domain of OTAs. This section provides an extensive examination of the research problem's nature, significance, and study objectives. The research methodology involves a combined utilization of qualitative and quantitative methods, strategically designed to provide a comprehensive understanding of customer involvement and brand affinity within OTAs. This multifaceted approach encompasses the deployment of a survey to gather quantitative data, complemented by qualitative insights through in-depth interviews or focus group discussions.

The survey phase of the research involves the administration of structured questions to individuals utilizing OTAs, focusing on elements related to gamification, customer engagement, and brand affinity. Simultaneously, the qualitative component entails conducting in-depth interviews and focus group discussions to delve into users' perspectives, experiences, and emotional connections concerning gamification within OTAs. In this study, the gamified marketing activities used by the OTA are considered, such as points, badges, cards, uploading throwback photos, and storytelling. The sampling frame used in this study is purposive sampling. The data are collected online using Google Forms. The criteria for selecting the samples are that at least the customers of the OTA have used one or two gamified marketing activities. The research population comprises individuals who have interacted with OTAs and have prior exposure to gamification aspects, totalling 230 participants. The selection of survey and interview participants follows a combination of methodologies, encompassing convenience and random sampling.

For data collection, an online questionnaire is prepared and disseminated via OTA platforms and social media channels to the targeted demographic. In-depth interviews and focus group discussions are carried out purposively, with participants chosen based on deliberate selection to provide insightful qualitative data.

Data Analysis and Results

Common Method Bias

To assess the potential influence of common method bias, an application of Harman's single-factor test was executed. To establish the number of factors that are required to adequately explain the variance, all six latent variables were plugged into an unrotated factor solution. This was done in order to find the optimal number of factors. The analysis showed that a single-factor solution could only account for 34.61% of the total variation, which is significantly lower than the cut-off value of 50%. Based on this conclusion, it appears that the common technique bias that was investigated in this study was not a significant issue.

Reliability and Validity

For the purpose of determining the extent to which the variables can be trusted, Cronbach's alpha and Composite Reliability (CR) have been applied.

The recorded values of Cronbach's Alpha and Composite Reliability (CR) surpassed the predefined threshold of 0.700. This was the case for both of these measures. Convergent validity was demonstrated by the fact that the Average Variance Extracted (AVE) and CRs both had values that were greater than 0.500 and 0.700, respectively. Cross-loadings were used to determine whether or not a discriminant analysis was legitimate. It was also determined that there was a multicollinearity, and the value of the Variance Inflation Factor (VIF) for each indicator was found to be less than 5. To evaluate the discriminant validity of the test, the researchers employed the Fornell–Lacker criterion, which is a method that is more conservative than the cross-loadings method. Due to the fact that the square root of the AVE of each construct has a value that is greater than its correlation with all of the other constructs (Klarner et al., 2013), the data indicate that the discriminant validity has been established.

Structural Model and Hypotheses Testing

The second stage of the research was examining the connections between the latent variables. The R2 value test gauges how well the latent variables fit into the least-squares model. Additionally, the Q2 value produced by a blind-folding method was higher than zero, demonstrating the structural model's predictive usefulness (Hair et al., 2010). Additionally, at a significance level of 5%, the bootstrapping method is utilized to determine the t-value for each related path coefficient. The path coefficients' t-value significance at the 5% level of significance is 1.96. The value here should be greater than 1.96 for all corresponding path coefficients. The path analysis indicates that gamified marketing activities are positively related to customer brand engagement ($p < 0.01$).

H1: Gamified Marketing Activities -> Customer Brand Engagement: this signifies the hypothesis that there's an investigation into how gamified marketing activities influence customer brand engagement. A coefficient of 0.497 indicates the strength and direction of the relationship between gamified marketing activities and customer brand engagement. The positive sign suggests a positive correlation, meaning that as gamified marketing activities increase, customer brand engagement is predicted to increase as well.

2: Customer Brand Engagement -> Brand Love: this indicates a relationship or transition from customer brand engagement to brand love. A coefficient of 0.787 indicates a positive correlation, meaning that as customer brand engagement increases, the predicted brand love also increases. The results show a positive impact of customer brand engagement on the brand love for OTA clients ($p < 0.05$).

Similarly, the findings presented in Table 6.1 show age, gender, and experience having a significant impact on the brand love of OTA users. Table 6.2 reveals structural model analysis.

Table 6.1 Hypothesis Testing

	Original Sample (O)	Sample Mean (M)	Standard Deviation (STDEV)	T Statistics (|O/STDEV|)	p Values
H1: Gamified Marketing Activities -> Customer Brand Engagement	0.497	0.499	0.065	7.652	0.000***
H2: Customer Brand Engagement -> Brand Love	0.787	0.077	0.084	1.026	0.005**
Gender -> Brand Love	0.373	0.384	0.059	4.139	0.000***
Age -> Brand Love	0.215	0.235	0.062	3.445	0.001**
Experience -> Brand Love	0.614	0.087	0.056	5.124	0.000***

***$p < 0.000$, **$p < 0.05$, *$p < 0.10$
Source: researchers' own analysis

Table 6.2 Structure Model Analysis

Endogenous Construct	R^2	$Q^2 (= 1 - SSE/SSO)$
Customer Brand Engagement	0.627	0.522
Brand Love	0.546	0.043

Note: The cross-validated redundancy Q^2 was obtained using blindfolding procedure with an omission distance of seven

Source: researchers' own analysis

Conclusion

Implications of the Study

The research has significant ramifications for OTA companies. The findings underscore the significant potential of gamification as an effective mechanism for augmenting customer engagement on OTA platforms. By integrating game-like components such as incentives, obstacles, and interactive functionalities, organizations can enhance user engagement and satisfaction by creating more immersive and pleasurable experiences. The heightened level of user involvement has the potential to result in improved user retention rates, extended session durations, and ultimately, an enhanced probability of conversions and recurring reservations. This study emphasizes the significance of developing gamified experiences that effectively resonate with the intended audience and are consistent with the brand identity of the platform in order to cultivate emotional connections and promote brand affection.

Furthermore, the research highlights the importance of utilizing gamification strategies as a means to enhance brand loyalty within the fiercely competitive online tourist industry. When clients have pleasant and satisfying interactions on the platform, they are more inclined to build a favourable emotional connection with the brand. The emotional attachment that customers develop towards a brand results in heightened levels of customer loyalty, as they are incentivized to repeatedly engage with the platform for subsequent reservations and experiences. In addition, it is common for committed customers to transform into brand champions, effectively disseminating their favourable experiences to others via word-of-mouth and social media channels, so augmenting the platform's scope and prominence. In order to properly harness the potential of gamification, it is imperative for OTA firms to give due regard to ethical factors. This entails ensuring that gamification methods are designed in a manner that not only enhances user well-being but also avoids the exploitation of addictive behaviours.

Limitations of the Study

This study has inherent limitations that open up avenues for further investigation (Singh et al., 2022). Firs, the applicability of the findings to diverse service contexts is constrained by the utilization of a limited market sample and a specific consumer group (namely, OTA consumers). To enhance the scope, future research could extend the examination of the research model to other service domains, such as electronic banking and online booking services, aiming to assess the broader applicability of the conclusions presented herein.

Second, the experimental setup involved a simulated service scenario, wherein participants engaged in a hypothetical badge system with the awareness of its transient nature. The participants were provided a badge signifying their participation in the experiment. As Hamari and Koivisto (2015) highlight, relying on self-reported data may result in imaginative or amplified perceptions concerning the incorporation of game mechanics. To elevate the research's validity, it might be beneficial to consider implementing a field experiment within an operational service environment to enhance the practical relevance and authenticity of the findings in subsequent studies.

References

Al-Zyoud, M. F. (2020). The impact of gamification on consumer loyalty, electronic word-of mouth sharing and purchase behavior. *Journal of Public Affairs*, 2263. Advance online publication. https://doi.org/10.1002/pa.2263

Amoah, J., Jibril, A. B., Bankuoru Egala, S., & Keelson, S. A. (2022). Online brand community and consumer brand trust: Analysis from Czech millennials. *Cogent Business & Management*. https://doi.org/10.1080/23311975.2022.2149152

Armstrong, G., & Kotler, P. (2011). *Marketing: An introduction*. Pearson Education.

Assael, H. (1987). *Consumer behavior and marketing action* (pp. 1–13). Kent Publishing Co. https://doi.org/10.1016/0167-8116(88)90003-1

Bagozzi, R. P. (1992). The self-regulation of attitudes, intentions, and behavior. *Social Psychology Quarterly*, 178–204. https://doi.org/10.2307/2786945

Bairrada, C. M., Coelho, F., & Coelho, A. (2018). Antecedents and outcomes of brand love: Utilitarian and symbolic brand qualities. *European Journal of Marketing*, 52(3–4), 656–682. https://doi.org/10.1108/EJM-02-2016-0081

Batra, R., Ahuvia, A., & Bagozzi, R. P. (2012). Brand love. *Journal of Marketing*, 76(2), 1–16. https://doi.org/10.1509/jm.09.0339

Bernritter, S. F., Verlegh, P. W. J., & Smit, E. G. (2016). Why non profits are easier to endorse on social media: The roles of warmth and brand symbolism. *Journal of Interactive Marketing*, 33, 27–42. https://doi.org/10.1016/j.intmar.2015.10.002

Bhattacharya, C. B., & Sen, S. (2003). Consumer-company identification: A framework for understanding consumers' relationships with companies. *Journal of Marketing*, 67(2), 76–88. https://doi.org/10.1509/jmkg.67.2.76.18609

Brakus, J. J., Schmitt, B. H., & Zarantonello, L. (2009). Brand experience: What is it? How is it measured? Does it affect loyalty? *Journal of Marketing*, 73(3), 52–68. http://doi.org/10.1509/jmkg.73.3.52

Brodie, R. J., Ilic, A., Juric, B., & Hollebeek, L. (2013). Consumer engagement in a virtual brand community: An exploratory analysis. *Journal of Business Research*, 66(1), 105–114.

Buhalis, D., Leung, R., & Jun, M. (2019). Smart hospitality – interconnectivity and interoperability towards an ecosystem. *International Journal of Hospitality Management*, 79, 77–87. https://doi.org/10.1016/j.ijhm.2017.11.011

Bulencea, L., & Egger, R. (2015). *Gamification in tourism designing memorable experiences* (1. Aufl). Books on Demand GmbH.

Carroll, B. A., & Ahuvia, A. C. (2006, April). Some antecedents and outcomes of brand love. *Marketing Letters*, 17, 79–89. https://doi.org/10.1007/s11002-006-4219-2

Chen, C. F., & Chen, F. S. (2019). Gamification marketing strategy and brand loyalty: Focusing on the moderating role of technology acceptance. *International Journal of Information Management*, 45, 191–203. https://doi.org/10.1016/j.ijinfomgt.2018.09.010

De Canio, F., Fuentes-Blasco, M., & Martinelli, E. (2021). Engaging shoppers through mobile apps: The role of gamification. *International Journal of Retail & Distribution Management*, 49(7), 919–940. https://doi.org/10.1108/IJRDM-09-2020-0360

Dessart, L., Veloutsou, C., & Morgan-Thomas, A. (2015). Consumer engagement in online brand communities: Asocial media perspective. *Journal of Product & Brand Management*, 24(1), 28–42. https://doi.org/10.1108/JPBM-06-2014-0635

Deterding, S., Dixon, D., Khaled, R., & Nacke, L. (2011, September). From game design elements to gamefulness: Defining "gamification". In *Proceedings of the 15th international academic MindTrek conference: Envisioning future media environments* (pp. 9–15). https://doi.org/10.1145/2181037.2181040

Drennan, J., Bianchi, C., Cacho-Elizondo, S., Louriero, S., Guibert, N., & Proud, W. (2015). Examining the role of wine brand love on brand loyalty: A multi-country comparison. *International Journal of Hospitality Management*, 49, 47–55. https://doi.org/10.1016/jijhm.2015.04.012

Du, S., Bhattacharya, C. B., & Sen, S. (2007). Reaping relational rewards from corporate social responsibility: The role of competitive positioning. *International Journal of Research in Marketing*, 24(3), 224–241. https://doi.org/10.1016/j.ijresmar.2007.01.001

Dwivedi, A. (2015). A higher-order model of consumer brand engagement and its impact on loyalty intentions. *Journal of Retailing and Consumer Services*, 24, 100–109. https://doi.org/10.1016/j.jretconser.2015.02.007

Far, M. S., & Dinani, H. G. (2015). Investigating effect rate of brand love on mouth marketing and consumers' purchase intention. *Indian Journal of Fundamental and Applied Life Sciences*, 5(S4), 1450–1457. An Open Access, Online International Journal. www.cibtech.org/sp.ed/jls/2015/04/jls.htm

Fournier, S. (1998). Consumers and their brands: Developing relationship theory in consumer research. *Journal of Consumer Research*, 24(4), 343–353. https://doi.org/10.1086/209515

Gatautis, R., Vitkauskaite, E., Gadeikiene, A., & Piligrimiene, Z. (2016). Gamification as a mean of driving online consumer behaviour: SOR model perspective. *Inzinerine Ekonomika-Engineering Economics*, 27, 90–97. https://doi.org/10.5755/j01.ee.27.1.13198

Hamari, J., & Koivisto, J. (2015). Why do people use gamification services? *International Journal of Information Management*, 35(4), 419–431.

Hamari, J., Koivisto, J., & Sarsa, H. (2014). Does gamification work? – A literature review of empirical studies on gamification. In *2014 47th Hawaii international conference on system sciences* (pp. 3025–3034). IEEE. https://doi.org/10.1109/HICSS.2014.377

Huang, W. H. Y., & Soman, D. (2013). Gamification of education. *Report Series: Behavioural Economics in Action*, 29(4), 37.

Hofacker, C. F., de Ruyter, K., Lurie, N. H., Manchanda, P., & Donaldson, J. (2016). Gamification and mobile marketing effectiveness. *Journal of Interactive Marketing*, 34, 25–36. https://doi.org/10.1016/j.intmar.2016.03.00

Hollebeek, L. D. (2011). Demystifying customer brand engagement: Exploring the loyalty nexus. *Journal of Marketing Management*, 27(7–8), 785–807. https://doi.org/10.1080/0267257X.2010.500132

Hollebeek, L. D., Srivastava, R. K., & Chen, T. (2019). SD logic–informed customer engagement: Integrative framework, revised fundamental propositions, and application to CRM. *Journal of the Academy of Marketing Science*, 47, 161–185.

Insley, V., & Nunan, D. (2014). Gamification and the online retail experience. *International Journal of Retail and Distribution Management*, 42(5), 340–351. https://doi.org/10.1108/IJRDM-01-2013-0030

Ismail, A. R., & Spinelli, G. (2012). Effects of brand love, personality and image on word of mouth: The case of fashion brands among young consumers. *Journal of Fashion Marketing and Management*, 16(4), 386–398. https://doi.org/10.1108/13612021211265791

Jami Pour, M., Rafiei, K., Khani, M., & Sabrirazm, A. (2021). Gamification and customer experience: The mediating role of brand engagement in online grocery retailing. *Nankai Business Review International*, 12(3), 340–357. https://doi.org/10.1108/NBRI-07-2020-0041

Jang, S., Kitchen, P. J., & Kim, J. (2018). The effects of gamified customer benefits and characteristics on behavioral engagement and purchase: Evidence from mobile exercise application uses. *Journal of Business Research*, 92, 250–259. https://doi.org/10.1016/j.jbusres.2018.07.056

Joshi, R., & Yadav, R. (2020). Brand desire: Scale development and empirical examination. *Journal of Asia-Pacific Business*, 21(3), 169–184.

Karjaluoto, H., Munnukka, J., & Kiuru, K. (2016). Brand love and positive word of mouth: The moderating effects of experience and price. *Journal of Product & Brand Management*, 25(6), 527–537. https://doi.org/10.1108/JPBM-03-2015-0834

Klarner, P., Sarstedt, M., Hoeck, M., & Ringle, C. M. (2013). Disentangling the effects of team competences, team adaptability, and client communication on the performance of management consulting teams. *Long Range Planning*, 46(3), 258–286.

Kennedy, E., & Guzmán, F. (2016). Co-creation of brand identities: Consumer and industry influence and motivations. *Journal of Consumer Marketing, 33*(5), 313–323. https://doi.org/10.1108/JCM-07-2015-1500

Lafferty, B. A., & Goldsmith, R. E. (1999). Corporate credibility's role in consumers' attitudes and purchase intentions when a high versus a low credibility endorser is used in the ad. *Journal of Business Research, 44*(2), 109–116. https://doi.org/10.1016/S0148-2963(98)00002-2

Lopes, J. M., Gomes, S., Durão, M., & Pacheco, R. (2023). The Holy Grail of luxury tourism: A holistic bibliometric overview. *Journal of Quality Assurance in Hospitality & Tourism, 24*(6), 885–908.

Ma, L., Zhang, X., Ding, X., & Wang, G. (2021). How social ties influence customers' involvement and online purchase intentions. *Journal of Theoretical and Applied Electronic Commerce Research, 16*, 395–408. https://doi.org/10.3390/jtaer16030025

Mata, F. J., & Quesada, J. (2014). Online travel agencies in Spain: Determining factors and impact on the tourist decision-making process. *Journal of Hospitality Marketing & Management, 23*(5), 518–536. https://doi.org/10.18089/tms.2019.15020

Merhabi, M. A., Petridis, P., & Khusainova, R. (2021). Gamification for brand value co-creation: A systematic literature review. *Information, 12*(9), 345. https://doi.org/10.3390/info12090345

Moorman, C., Zaltman, G., & Deshpande, R. (1992). Relationships between providers and users of market research: The dynamics of trust within and between organizations. *Journal of Marketing Research, 29*(3), 314. https://doi.org/10.2307/3172742

Ng, S. C., Sweeney, J. C., & Plewa, C. (2020). Customer engagement: A systematic review and future research priorities. *Australasian Marketing Journal, 28*(4), 235–252. https://doi.org/10.1016/j.ausmj.2020.05.004

O'Brien, H. L. (2010). The influence of hedonic and utilitarian motivations on user engagement: The case of online shopping experiences. *Interacting with Computers, 22*(5), 344–352. https://doi.org/10.1016/j.intcom.2010.04.001

O'Brien, H. L., & Toms, E. G. (2008). What is user engagement? A conceptual framework for defining user engagement with technology. *Journal of the American Society for Information Science and Technology, 59*(6), 938–955. https://doi.org/10.1002/asi.20801

Palusuk, N., Koles, B., & Hasan, R. (2019). 'All you need is brand love': A critical review and comprehensive conceptual framework for brand love. *Journal of Marketing Management, 35*(1–2), 97–129. https://doi.org/10.1080/0267257X.2019.1572025

Park, C. W., MacInnis, D. J., & Priester, J. R. (2006). Beyond attitudes: Attachment and consumer behavior. *Seoul National Journal, 12*(2), 3–36.

Park, H., & Bae, J.-H. (2014). Study and research of gamification design. *International Journal of Software Engineering and its Applications, 8*, 19–28. https://doi.org/10.14257/ijseia.2014.8.8,03

Paruthi, M., Nagina, R., & Gupta, G. (2023, March). Measuring the effect of consumer brand engagement on brand-related outcomes in gamified mobile apps: A solicitation of technology acceptance model. In *Proceedings* (Vol. 85, No. 1, p. 10). MDPI.

Pine, B. J., & Gilmore, J. H. (1998). *Welcome to the experience economy* (Vol. 76, No. 4, pp. 97–105). Harvard Business Review Press.

Pour, A. R., Marimon, F., & Foroudi, P. (2021). Fostering hotel customers' brand loyalty: The roles of gamification and customer experience. *International Journal of Hospitality Management, 94*, 102919.

Prusty, A. K. (2018). Gamification: An effective technique to enhance customer engagement. *Journal of Marketing and Consumer Research, 50*, 43–51.

Rodrigues, I., Lopes, J. M., Borges, A., Oliveira, J., & Oliveira, M. (2021). How can gamified applications drive engagement and brand attitude? The case of Nike run club application. *Administrative Sciences*, *11*, 92. https://doi.org/10.3390/admsci11030092

Rodrigues, I. M., Soares, N. F., Lopes, J. M., Oliveira, J. C., & Lopes, J. M. N. G. (2021). Gamification as a new trend in the co-creation process. *RAM. Revista de Administração Mackenzie*, *22*, 1–33. https://doi.org/10.1590/1678-6971/eramr210132

Rossiter, J. R. (2012). A new C-OAR-SE-based content-valid and predictively valid measure that distinguishes brand love from brand liking. *Marketing Letters*, *23*(3), 905–916. https://doi.org/10.1007/s11002-012-9173-6

Sarkar, A., Sarkar, J. G., & Bhatt, G. (2019). Store love in single brand retailing: The roles of relevant moderators. *Marketing Intelligence & Planning*, *37*(2), 168–181. https://doi.org/10.1108/MIP-05-2018-0148

Sarkar, A., & Sreejesh, S. (2014). Examination of the roles played by brand love and jealousy in shaping customer engagement. *Journal of Product & Brand Management*, *23*(1), 24–32.

Scheinbaum, A. C. (2016). Digital engagement: Opportunities and risks for sponsors. *Journal of Advertising Research*, *56*(4), 341. https://doi.org/10.2501/JAR-2016-040

Schmitt, B. H. (2010). *Customer experience management: A revolutionary approach to connecting with your customers*. John Wiley & Sons.

Shao, Z., Zhang, Y., Zhang, J., & Pan, Y. (2019). How can gamification strengthen tourist loyalty? The role of perceived value and trust. *Sustainability*, *11*(12), 3435.

Shimp, T. A., & Madden, T. J. (1988). Consumer-object relations: A conceptual framework based analogously on Sternberg's triangular theory of love. *Advances in Consumer Research*, *15*(1), 163–168.

Singh, M., Singh, S., Raman, R. K., Thakur, R., Johar, I. P., & Singh, P. (2022). Exploring dimensions of financial inclusion from stakeholders' perspectives: Evidence from rural areas of Jammu District. *Acta Universitatis Bohemiae Meridionalis*. https://doi.org/10.32725/acta.2022.004

Singla, V., & Gupta, G. (2019, August 2). Emotional branding scale and its role in formation of brand trust. *Paradigm*, *23*(2), 148–163. https://doi.org/10.1177/0971890719859668

Spais, G., Behl, A., Jain, K., Jain, V., & Singh, G. (2022). Promotion and branding from the lens of gamification in challenging times. *Journal of Promotion Management*, *28*(4), 413–419. https://doi.org/10.1080/10496491.2021.2008849

Sternberg, R. J. (1986). A triangular theory of love. *Psychological Review*, *93*, 119–135. https://doi.org/10.1037/0033-295X.93.2.119

Syrjälä, H., Kauppinen-Räisänen, H., Luomala, H. T., Joelsson, T. N., Könnölä, K., & Mäkilä, T. (2020). Gamified package: Consumer insights into multidimensional brand engagement. *Journal of Business Research*, *119*, 423–434. ISSN 0148-2963. https://doi.org/10.1016/j.jbusres.2019.11.089

Van Doorn, J., Lemon, K. N., Mittal, V., Nass, S., Pick, D., Pirner, P., & Verhoef, P. C. (2010). Customer engagement behavior: Theoretical foundations and research directions. *Journal of Service Research*, *13*(3), 253–266. https://doi.org/10.1177/1094670510375599

Vivek, S. D., Beatty, S. E., & Morgan, R. M. (2012). Customer engagement: Exploring customer relationships beyond purchase. *Journal of Marketing Theory and Practice*, *20*(2), 122–146. http://www.jstor.org/stable/23243811

Vos, M., Moller, L., & Odekerken-Schröder, G. (2018). The gamification of brands: Branding consequences of gamified advertising experiences. *Journal of Business Research*, *90*, 286–297. https://doi.org/10.1016/j.jbusres.2018.04.030

Wallace, E., Buil, I., & de Chernatony, L. (2014). Consumer engagement with self-expressive brands: Brand love and WOM outcomes. *Journal of Product & Brand Management*, 23(1), 33–42. https://doi.org/10.1108/JPBM-06-2013-0326

Wang, C. L., Sarkar, J. G., & Sarkar, A. (2019). Hallowed be thy brand: Measuring perceived brand sacredness. *European Journal of Marketing*, 53(4), 733–757. https://doi.org/10.1108/EJM-08-2017-0551

Xu, F., Weber, J., & Buhalis, D. (2013). Gamification in tourism. In *Information and communication technologies in tourism 2014: Proceedings of the international conference in Dublin, Ireland, January 21–24, 2014* (pp. 525–537). Springer International Publishing.

Xu, X., Buhalis, D., & Weber, J. (2017). Serious games and the gamification of tourism. *Tourism Management*, 60, 244–256. https://doi.org/10.1016/j.tourman.2016.11.020

Yang, Y., Asaad, Y., & Dwivedi, Y. (2017). Examining the impact of gamification on intention of engagement and brand attitude in the marketing context. *Computers in Human Behavior*, 73, 459–469. https://doi.org/10.1016/j.chb.2017.03.066

Zichermann, G., & Cunningham, C. (2011). *Gamification by design: Implementing game mechanics in web and mobile apps*. O'Reilly Media, Inc.

Chapter 7

Gamification Stimulates Customer E-Purchase Intention

A Conceptual Analysis

*Jaspreet Kaur and Kajal Puri**

Introduction

New technological advancements and the COVID-19 pandemic have given e-tailers numerous options to increase their earnings in a cutthroat industry (Gupta, 2016). One strategy that has great promise for marketers looking to engage their target audience is digital marketing. Digital marketing uses gamification as one of its promotional strategies. To maintain the interest of consumers in a specific brand, marketers use game concepts. These concepts are based on tailored conversations concerning a particular brand (Gupta, 2016).

Consumers play games on digital platforms to earn bonus points which are mostly utilized to receive rebates and discounts at the time of virtual shopping. Many marketers have engaged consumers in playing digitalized games to attract them as well as bolster their products. This use of games in non-gaming contexts, that is to boost sales, to promote the product, and to provide better service, etc., is called gamification. Gamification is done to have the intended result. It has been widely used in physical fitness, teaching, for making reforms in the government sector, for the welfare of the general public, etc. Gamification is not a new technique; it has been used by 70% of the top 2,000 global players in the form of various badges, reward points, coupons, etc.[1] Playfulness is a method of improving services through the use of inspirational outcomes to encourage engaging gameplay and promote behavioural outcomes (Hamari et al., 2014). Playfulness results in three types of outcomes which are explained next:

1. *Inspirational Outcomes*: these components stimulate inspiration among players in the form of acknowledgment, rewards, badges, recognitions, and advancements (Koestner & Hope, 2014). These components are akin to those found in games that evoke sensations among players. When people behave in the absence of any visible outward benefit, a person's underlying values, goals, and moral principles are the source of this internal drive. It can also result from the enjoyment of pursuit and the impulse

* Kajal Puri is corresponding author.

DOI: 10.4324/9781032694238-10

to grow personally (Ackerman, 2020). An extrinsic outcome is an urge to act in a definite manner that is built on outside influence (Koestner & Hope, 2014). Fundamentally, extrinsic outcomes consider the benefit of the action, but intrinsic outcomes are concerned with enjoying and appreciating the activity irrespective of the results. Although these two inspirational approaches may appear to be at odds with one another at first look, both are essential for an effective goal setting.

2. *Intellectual Inference*: as a result of inspirational outcomes, the player has intellectual changes that affect his or her thoughts and sentiments.
3. *Conduct or Behavioral Inference*: playfulness results can be seen in the action of the players, after responding to intellectual inferences (Vdov, 2020).

Review of Literature

Gamification

Gamification has nothing to do with digitalization. In the 1900s, there was a system prevailing in the market economy for the benefit of both marketers and consumers, in which rewards and gifts were offered to customers to boost sales for marketers. Charles Coonradt wrote a book titled *The Game of Work* in 1973. The author pointed out that as sales revenue was decreasing rapidly, employees should engage customers by using gamification techniques, which would ultimately enhance consumer loyalty, contentment, and pleasure. However, the older textual version was not attractive, while contemporary models of digitalized community games were more appealing. In 1979, American Airlines launched its recurring leaflet programme[2] referred to as advantage. This programme helped travelers accumulate points, which were used for purchasing tickets, receiving services, obtaining discounts on hiring cabs, staying in hotels, and buying items. Thomas W. Malone, at the Massachusetts Institute of Technology in 1981, studied computer exergaming to enhance students' interest in academics. In 1983, Holiday Inn Hotels Chain also launched a commitment and faithfulness initiative. By 2002, significant game activities were invented by the Woodrow Wilson International Center for Scholars. Because these games were used to enhance students' interest in studies, they were referred to as Serious Games. Moreover, the term "gamification" was coined by Nick Pelling in 2002; the inventor was tasked with creating vending machines and automated teller machines with game-like interfaces. Nick recognized the importance of games in commerce (Paruthi et al., 2023). The inventor manifested that he would utilize his mastery of games in commerce. He applied the stimulus in business for selling and marketing. He discerned that gamification had the potential to persuade and captivate employees by creating a pleasant atmosphere, magnifying their passion and zeal, and generating eagerness.

Bunchball, a hosted computing technique, was invented by Rajat Paharia in 2005. It helped business houses use the power of playfulness and substantially promoted the usage of scoreboards, points accumulation and redemption, earning badges, and more. In 2007, Kevan Davis invented the use of playfulness in doing household chores, like beating a rat that had hidden itself, through an app called Chore Wars. In 2009, American schools used this concept to educate students in sixth grade onwards by rewarding participants with points, badges, and other accomplishments. This was done to spark their interest in studies, with a software program that featured game-like modules. In 2010, DevHub used gamification on its webpage to increase user traffic, resulting in a 70% hike in visits. The term "gamify" was first used by Nathan Lands, who applied game-like structures to various fields such as business, health, and education, which traditionally did not incorporate playfulness.

In 2012, a digital playfulness course was initiated by Kevin Werbach, enrolling forty-five thousand mentees. In the same year, researchers at Gartner forecasted that nearly 70% of multinational corporations would be using gamified apps by 2014. In 2013, a survey was conducted in which Managing Directors, Chief Executive Officers, and other high-ranking officials admitted that they played games to reduce work pressure. By 2014, top officials reported that playfulness had a positive effect on the profitability and viability of their organizations.

Game Elements

The incorporation of an entertaining element into the game may cause a customer response that manifests as perceived delight. According to Davis et al. (1992), perceived pleasure is an inherent incentive that drives people to undertake tasks. Petkus (2004) and Smilansky (2017) have stated that the entertaining features in the game's content have been identified as a key component that could enhance the customer's enjoyment of the game's sensory and experiential effects. The essential aspects of a gamification design are games, which may be thought of as building bricks. While playing, badges serve as a visual depiction of an accomplishment or awards for efforts that highlight users' individuality. Badges boost user engagement and encourage users to select particular tasks to obtain a desired recognition. Obtaining badges may also signify membership in a social group with particular characteristics and prestige (Werbach et al., 2012). In earlier times, there had been a focus on the fundamental components of games, such as scores, credits, points, and prizes (extrinsic motivation) while overlooking other aspects including enjoyment, fun, and praise (intrinsic motivation) (Conaway & Garay, 2014). According to Pe-Than et al. (2014), players would find an activity more pleasurable if they have believed that it would improve societal connectivity. Gamification features aim to stimulate people's inner responses and societal interactions (Koivisto & Hamari, 2014) rather than their external responses (Suh et al., 2017; Zheng et al., 2019). Entertaining features in a game could improve the consumer's emotional perception (Tasci & Ko, 2016). Additionally, it has been found that customers are willing to employ innovations that include fun elements when they believe that they are enjoying playful activities. As a result, this propensity encourages users to utilize gaming applications more frequently to get gratification and delight (Collier & Barnes, 2015). The usage of pleasure as a game feature has been demonstrated to produce hedonistic benefits for the consumer (Chen et al., 2017; Ozturk et al., 2016). Game design components are visual representations of ratings, rankings, or badges that are placed in a particular context and offer the chance to advance by achieving new levels. The users can gradually accumulate points while carrying out particular tasks (Mekler et al., 2017). Playful techniques are frequently employed to motivate people to reach their intended levels and goals. Levels and accomplishments are managed by using efficiency charts, points' accumulation, and feedback displayed on a progress bar. These charts provide a historical record of each player's performance. This component fosters a competency perspective, which promotes continued growth, following the concept of motivation. Points make it easier to keep track of progress and for comparison among participants because these points are simple to evaluate (Sailer et al., 2017). Giving feedback is an essential part of excellent game design, and points are the ideal method for doing so (Hall & Toke, 2018). Tu et al. (2019) have pointed out that interaction with others and enjoyable gaming features boost consumer engagement. So, several businesses have begun incorporating game elements into their apps. Gaming elements give successful company-related digital experiences through apps and online portals to the intended audience (Lee & Jin, 2019). Participants' accomplishment is taken into account when ranking them on a leader board. A leader board is a form of a chart that compares the accomplishments of participants in a contest. The participant details are placed on a chart based on a particular aspect, like the quantum of points they have earned, encouraging their growth. Participants who are on the last position have community pressure which further leads to an unfavourable effect on their performance. While some participants are negatively motivated and try to advance further, it is a debatable issue. Some competitors are in the same position on the leader board, and out of them some would lag. So, there is a chance that players would become disheartened, which could have a detrimental impact and prevent them from participating actively (Szyszka, 2019).

Joy is an important playing experience that makes gaming enjoyable. This contrasts with games that lack any enjoyable components and have serious substance. A key component of gaming is enjoyment, which may be seen as one of the factors that influence users' behaviour while adopting new technology (Joe et al., 2022). The incentive of the gamer can be increased by game components (scores, accomplishments, digital prizes, and badges, etc.) (Bitrián et al., 2021). Gamification may be categorized as gamefulness, gamely communication, and gamely architecture. All these allow a user to fully engage in the gaming procedure (Kim, 2021). Consequently, as it pertains to the customer's buying selection, gaming components may cause consumers to sense pleasure, satisfaction, and societal responses. To increase client engagement with a good or service, gaming components ranging from contests to prizes to point-scoring competitions can be used as promotional and advertising material (Wang, 2021).

Game Mechanics

The elements of games that include data structure and gaming techniques are referred to as game mechanics. Regulations, procedures, and other game artefacts that programmers devise are created by mechanics (Hunicke et al., 2004; Walk et al., 2017). Good technological advancements in game mechanics increase the perceived value of the playing experience and also enhance its practical advantage (Hong & Tam, 2006). Consumers have found games entertaining and interesting because of the mechanics' design, which includes building a fantasy setting, audiovisual impacts, scripting plots, etc. Customers anticipate the mechanics of games to provide them with entertaining instances, which may alter their purchasing habits when they are exposed to a firm's diverse offerings of goods and services (Zichermann & Cunningham, 2011). Gamified techniques can alter the desired behaviour by fostering an eco-conscious attitude and raising customer allegiance knowledge. The effectiveness of changing behaviour is increased through the pattern of games. When a game's architecture is poor, the game becomes less enjoyable and replayable. To obtain an intended behaviour modification while implementing games, each component of the setting must be taken into account (Haque et al., 2014). Gamification can affect consumer involvement, stimulate certain behaviours, and assist consumers to accomplish goals. Hedonistic worth is preferable to incentives. Increased ongoing involvement is offered by hedonic worth (Hsu & Chen, 2018). Gaming with ongoing involvement is beneficially connected to a business commitment. WeChat application is progressively adding new features, and it has become China's foremost multifunctional application, with daily users spending more than six hours on it. The game mechanics boost the morale of enticed individuals as well as encourage loyalty (Högberg et al., 2019). A community of players communicates socially with the aid of the game's dynamics, which alters their buying habits (Koivisto & Hamari, 2014). Playfulness improves customer comprehension, perspectives, and behaviour. Aspects of award-based games have improved the consequences for long-lasting behaviour. Serious game components are being used by organizations to encourage positive and enduring behaviour among customers (Shevchuk et al., 2019). To incorporate playful features into portable merchandizing apps, businesses should use difficulty levels similar to those used in video games (Aydınlıyurt et al., 2021). In digital selling apps, playfulness helps consumers to accumulate points. Customer purchasing behaviour is altered due to the psychological effects of gaming inducements (Gatautis et al., 2021). To achieve enhanced results, it is necessary for a builder of a game to experiment with it with the intended gamers as well as with those who require it in everyday settings of their lives. Players would get their preferred outcome, that is pleasure, by involving themselves in gaming activities (Epstein et al., 2021). Employing an AI (artificial intelligence) app helps in analysing settings, transmitting personalized communications, and overseeing gaming competitors, which simulates customer involvement and inspires behavioural change (Soares et al., 2021).

Gamification and Retail Experiences

Transparency is a shopper's trait that encourages him to intuitively and imaginatively connect with automation (Webster & Martocchio, 1992). That is why internet merchants struggle to involve buyers in gameplay dynamics, with the aid of advertising and special deals and discounts, which are highly appreciated by shoppers (Andrews & Currim, 2004). Shoppers, with a greater degree of clarity, have an increasingly favourable interaction with digital vendors' apps. Fortunately, they view competition with other shoppers as a sport while they shop via the internet (Ahn et al., 2007). Customers perceive that looking for the greatest deals on goods is a leisure activity motivated by fascination and the pursuit of knowledge (Füller, 2010). Playfulness has the power to change bad customer habits like returning and exchanging products. Sellers can use the playful technique that offers free delivery on purchases and charges for the cost of return shipment. Gamification features allow an online selling app to compare the price of a product to other online stores and display the prices of various online stores. So that customers can decide to purchase the product at the lowest price from the online store (Insley & Nunan, 2014). When customers purchase online, gaming can have a profound effect on the outcomes of e-sellers (Hofacker et al., 2016). Consumers are motivated to shop online due to fun and enjoyment as well as by real returns. Consumers purchase online because they identify it with the pursuit of joy and contentment. There are a variety of reasons why people purchase through the internet, including the desire for enjoyment or delight, the need for product knowledge, and the want to compare prices. Additionally, it has been revealed that respondents do not employ any particular online shopping techniques, but they are enticed by retailers' attractions and inducements like sales, gifts, coupons, price reductions, and discounts (Geraldo & Mainardes, 2017). They look for things that grab their attention. Most internet shoppers refrain from returning their purchases, and they favour common items over uncommon or hard-to-find ones. Karać and Stabauer (2017) have highlighted that digital store customers are unacquainted with playfulness. Because playfulness is a non-compulsory or discretionary activity, internet shoppers can leverage the advantages of using playfulness strategies. Its execution depends upon the type of customers. Alatalo et al. (2018) have stated that prior research has indicated gamification to be a crucial component in examining the perspective of digital buyers in online store settings. By integrating gaming features in web-based stores, digital sellers want to enhance the online buying experience for clients. Businesses can use impulses to a certain degree to impact the consumer's engagement (Pecorari & Lima, 2021). Bauer et al. (2020) have pointed out that gamification diminishes its effectiveness and good impact when paired with financial prizes because gamers do not contend with these financial incentives, but the external drive to get coupons, price reductions, gifts, etc., as a result of playfulness promotes loyalty among consumers towards the business house. Consumer demand, technological advances, and tools for decision-making assistance, etc., are all contributing to the growth of price dynamics. A questionnaire survey has been undertaken to further understand shopper and businessman opinions on playfulness and dynamic pricing. Because of price dynamics, business organizations must be ready for alterations and adjustments in distribution. Retailers maintain the distribution network to meet customer orders (Guvenc et al., 2020). Gamification can be viewed as a situation, where there are numerous ways to engage customers in gameful activities while buying digitally (Hwang & Choi, 2020). Kapp et al. (2020) have quoted that playfulness encourages participants to revisit the page of the marketer who is engaging them in cause-related activity. Marketers struggle to persuade shoppers to participate in an information-sharing procedure. Businesses need to enhance the safety standards to encourage buyers to share their information with them because buyers do not trust the security standards of online shopping portals. Moreover, gaming features enhance the beneficial impact of digital buying and boost pleasure among digital buyers as well as result in a pertinent involvement of online customers (Bidler et al., 2020).

The firms in the industry are implementing cutting-edge techniques including playfulness to cope with the industry's fierce rivalry, and playfulness effectively executes their promotional campaigns (Jayasooriya et al., 2020). A good implementation of playful marketing and advertising will increase customer brand loyalty. A key element of playful selling is amusement and entertainment. Before buyers can engage in these initiatives, their initial interest must be ignited by the knowledge and rewards, incentives, coupons, and gifts offered by the sales force. Because customers enjoy engaging in games while shopping online and unintentionally enter the competition in search of glory. Moreover, researchers have also revealed the reasons behind such engagements to be the system design's motivations, which include fun and attractiveness, and distinguishing feedback systems (Lu & Ho, 2020; De Canio et al., 2021). Playfulness increases consumer interest and engagement. An engaging playfulness experience improves the perception of the brand as well as the mindset and attitude of customers towards the company. Gaming can significantly improve the relationship between customers

and businesses and boost digital shopper involvement as well as affect customer behaviour (Xu et al., 2020). Sellers can enhance the understanding
of their existing and potential buyers about digital shopping with the help
of promotional measures. These promotional campaigns can bolster customer commitment, enhance internet-based purchasing experiences, and
boost their propensity for digital buying (Dwivedi et al., 2021). Playfulness
and social media marketing can significantly increase buyers' involvement,
affect consumer behaviour, and enhance customer engagement with digital
buying as well as strengthen the relationship between customers and business houses. Digital buyers are encouraged to participate in a playful system
through social interaction (Gajanova & Radišić, 2021). Consumers use the
app for incentives, price comparisons, successful purchases at competitive
prices, discounts, offers, gifts, successful completion of challenges, and information acquisition. Playfulness has an impact on the loyalty of customers
(Kunkel et al., 2021). Consumer pleasure can be influenced by trustworthiness, sense of security, accuracy of data, diversification, and the distribution
of goods. Buyers are more inclined to browse digitally for recreational activities and tangible benefits than for competitive reasons. Likewise, shoppers
make transactions digitally – not because they feel lonely, bored, etc., but
instead, because they perceive them to be connected to the search for happiness, delight, and pleasure. The game-based strategy has recently gained
popularity as an emerging technique for boosting consumer involvement in
business-to-customer settings (Mofokeng, 2021). Sreejesh et al. (2021) have
noted the extensive usage of gaming mechanisms in formulating games with
three main components – feedback, presents, and challenges. Moreover, these
mechanisms are more effective at retaining consumers. Ushakov and Shatila (2021) have stated that an inspirational method for increasing consumer
engagement is playfulness. Motivating people to achieve their targets through
emotional engagement is the secret to the success of playfulness. Two categories encompass human inspiration: inner inspiration and outer inspiration.
External inspiration is fuelled by an outside factor that encourages someone
to act in a certain way in anticipation of earning an incentive. Contrarily,
internal drive describes behaviour that is motivated by internal factors like
joy, delight, happiness, excitement, or pleasurable feelings. Gaming deployment has advantages for assisting behaviour modification (Zain et al., 2021).
Digital buying has become essential. The primary goal for retailers is to keep,
maintain, and retain customers because it helps to increase profits. Gamification commerce, if properly and effectively created, may also help in consumer
communication. In the present economic climate, businesses struggle to offer
a rich customer experience (Sheetal et al., 2022). Gaming is a successful
strategy for boosting client retention, promoting favourable word of referral, and raising involvement. Additionally, offering hedonistic values, one of
the fundamental tenets of gamification has been shown to work as an effective method for attracting shoppers and boosting their propensity to make

additional purchases (Shi et al., 2022). Lopes et al. (2023) have conducted interviews of 30 participants and revealed that participants' electronic purchasing requirements are met by expert-designed games. Comfort, efficiency, velocity, acceleration, accessibility to digital deals, promotions, and premium products are the factors that drive customer demand. These variables imply that participants find internet buying to be a desirable alternative since it provides an even more comfortable, accessible, and favourable environment than traditional in-store purchasing.

Gamification as a Means of Driving Online Consumer Purchase Behaviour

Corporate houses and marketers will be in the profitable and growth stage if they recognize the needs and requirements of buyers and further run their businesses based on the information acquired from their marketing segment (Urbanskiene et al., 2000). In comparison to a conventional marketing arrangement, modernized digital online marketing arrangement has distinctive features like customization which makes customers satisfied and businesses more reliable, etc. (Gatautis & Vitkauskaite, 2009). Customers consider functional (usability, cost comparison, and supply differentiation) and voluptuous features (alluring portal or site arrangement) while shopping digitally (Bilgihan et al., 2015). Kazakevičiūtė and Banytė (2012) pointed out that hedonistic features, that is enticing characteristics are more significant for buyers and users.

A large number of scientists like Eroglu et al. (2001), Sautter et al. (2004), Mummalaneni (2005), Richard (2005), Oh et al. (2008), Kim et al. (2009), Manganari et al. (2009), and Björk (2010) have recommended Stimulus-Organism-Response model that had been developed by Mehrabian and Russell in the year 1974. This model should be used while studying the digital buyers' buying behaviour (Gatautis et al., 2016). Components of digital marketing act as impetus, encouragement, and provocation in inducing psychological influence (emotional affect) on buyers, which further generates buyer decisions, that is either to buy the product or to keep away from it. Appropriately and adequately outlined merchandizing and marketing design has psychological aftermath on customers and buyers and inflates their purchasing probability. So, it is pertinent on the part of the marketers and corporate houses to fabricate and design such a domain that would generate affirmative reactions in buyers (Kotler, 1973). Eroglu et al. (2001) have formulated digital buyers' buying behaviour representation. The researchers have divided the impulse of digital buying into two types, that is eminent and anonymous impulses. These eminent and anonymous impulses of digital buying generate passionate and intellectual reasoning in buyers, which leads to either buying decisions or avoiding resolution. Anonymous impulse is the buyer's conception, observation, and evaluation of a good or service.

The researchers have suggested measuring eminent impulse with the aid of Pleasure (P), Arousal (A), and Dominance (D) representation (PAD) model. According to Donovan et al. (1994) and Massara et al. (2010), pleasure, arousal, and dominance are not dependent on each other.

Gatautis and Vaiciukynaite (2013) have pointed out that there are numerous reasons that provoke customers in the digital environment to buy items such as sections of online buying portals, portal conversational links, portal contents, data and information surfing, and browsing on the portal. Gatautis et al. (2016) have revealed that corporate houses are using these playful tools to constructively influence buyers. So, gamification acts as the impulse that instigates consumers to buy, and ultimately the motive of the corporate houses to make customers loyal and satisfied is achieved. Figure 7.1 portrays a theoretical representation of the influence of playfulness on digital shopper behaviour.

Companies use offers, badges, online points, digital acknowledgments, personifications, or icons and discounts on buying certain quantities or certain

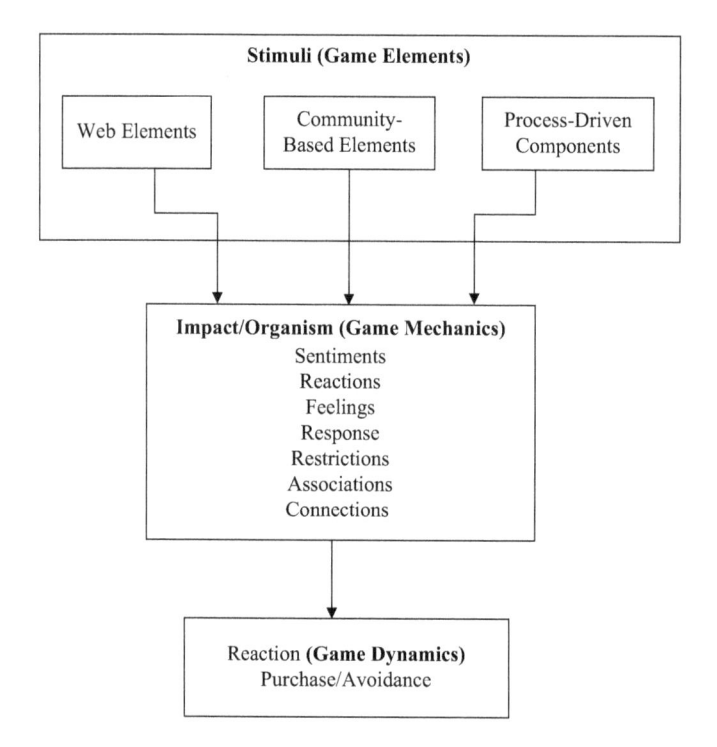

Figure 7.1 Theoretical representation of the influence of playfulness on digital shopper behaviour

Source: *adapted from* Gatautis, R., Vitkauskaite, E., Gadeikiene, A., & Piligrimiene, Z. (2016). Gamification as a means of driving online consumer behaviour: SOR model perspective. *Engineering Economics, 27*(1), 90–97, (page 94)

values of items. These components of playfulness act as impulses that motivate buyers to buy. There are three types of impulses, that is portal components (available on the website in the form of online gifts, acknowledgments, rewards, points, avatars, badges, etc.), community-based elements (accomplishments recognized by others, association with recognized groups, etc.), and process-driven game components (moving from one stage to another, checking by the gamer or the player about his or her performance, and comparing it with other contestants and unbolting higher levels).

These types of impulses affect the buyer's or customer's mindset. It is game mechanics that will generate sentiments, reactions, feelings, and responses' connections. It is the impact part of the model, that is the result of the impulse. Werbach et al. (2012) have stated that impact is not the result of a single element of playfulness, rather several components of playfulness are used in different proportions to make up the mind of the player. Then, finally, player takes his or her decision, that is either he or she will be engrossed in doing these playful activities or repudiate to play a part in these activities (Gatautis et al., 2016).

Use of Gamification by Online Sellers

Gamification is an effective strategy for fostering relationships with customers and increasing online sales. Its primary goal is to create games for customers, which encourage them to use online portals for purchasing goods and services.

Validation, accomplishment, and rewards are the three key ways that create consumers' interest in gamification marketing strategies. Rewards may arrive in the form of preferential brooches, coupons, savings, or loyalty points. These kinds of small acts go a long way towards improving client satisfaction with products, which makes online business more profitable. As per profound thought by Yu-kai Chou, an entrepreneur and experienced designer, gamification requires eight core drives of human motivation to make customers satisfied:

- Epic meaning.
- Accomplishment.
- Empowerment.
- Ownership.
- Social influence.
- Scarcity.
- Avoidance.
- Unpredictability.

Consumer behaviour is likely to be affected by gamification strategies that are working in the present scenario which keeps pace with ongoing culture.

Companies are creating apps that are consumer-friendly in the fields of education, retail, banking, food, beverage, and e-commerce that are working on gamification strategies that are out-of-box strategies to be ahead of their competitors. For having a win-win situation, different companies use these to satisfy their customers.

Consumer electronics company *Fitbit* uses gamification to advertise its wireless wearable and other technologies. By installing the Fitbit fitness app and connecting it with their Fitbit gadget, such as a smartwatch, with the aid of Bluetooth, they can simply keep track of the general health of customers. The device displays heart rate, blood oxygen levels, calories burned, and many other body functions.

Due to the difficulty in communicating, *Duolingo* has created a special language-learning programme that aids gamification. Duolingo's creators have released 98 instructional courses in 39 languages in which any individual from any nation can enroll himself or herself. Their main interface page has animated characters and vibrant colours to grab customers' attention. Gamification has also been used by *Coca-Cola* and *Nescafe* to improve the in-store product experience. They have produced engaging "Moments of Joy" for their customers in collaboration with Ksubaka (a personalization engine). When a customer is near the outlet of Coca-Cola or Nescafe, he receives a notification on his smartphone, and if he desires to redeem the offer, he can click on the notification and redeem that by going to the nearby outlet. By doing this, both brands have received lots of likes and shares, which has helped to increase their sales turnover. For instance, Coca-Cola has developed the concept of gamified vending machines where, if a consumer hugs a machine, scratches a card, or says a different word to it, he receives a reward.

When it comes to being sped up with tech trends, no one does it better than the Starbucks coffee chain. With the "My Rewards" programme of the Starbucks application, customers earn a few stars or points every time they place an order. On the completion of a specific number of stars, consumers can use these stars to avail of discounts at the nearest coffee outlet. The free offer of coffee or a sandwich at Starbucks has increased the customers' visits to the outlets. Starbucks' digital app also has a seamless digital interface with integrated features like online ordering, pay later, and customized music playlists via Spotify. Starbucks is known for the world's best coffee and providing the best user experience. The *Uber* app uses gamification from a business perspective. Launched in 2018, a reward system or playful loop is activated in the driver's account that monitors the driver's performance and progress throughout the day and includes a tier system that unlocks various rewards and incentives for drivers. For example, if a potential rider intentionally cancels a driver, the driver will not be charged a cancellation fee. The cancellation fee will be charged to the rider for cancellation of the ride. Moreover, these charges will be paid to the next driver who will be hired by the rider. The next driver will further pass it to the driver, whose ride has been canceled by the rider. This strategic programme by Uber aims to maintain the driver base and stabilize the employee workforce. *Flipped Classroom* concept has been put to use in several different fields, and one such field is education. It is a type of blended learning. To discuss the pros and cons of gamification of education, the researcher has experimented and conducted a primary survey using a questionnaire for e-learning with gamification elements, for English as well as for foreign language education. The results of this study have highlighted the importance of well-designed tutorials, tasks, interfaces, and feedback for effective game-based e-learning (Matsumoto, 2016).

Conclusion

This chapter highlights game elements, mechanics, gamification, and retail experiences as well as their effect on digital consumer purchase behaviour. Gamification as a means of driving online consumer purchase behaviour contemplates a learning process that aims at improving customer intention towards online buying. Different types of game components are used which serve as stimulus for online buyers to engage in games and buy products and services. Game dynamics ensures an increased involvement of consumers in games resulting in increased sales of concerned marketers. Game stimulus helps a person to interact with a combination of game elements, which ensures consumers' ongoing participation in gamified business activities. Gamification induces customers to purchase, and ultimately the goal of the company to boost sales is achieved. It would generate different experiences for different customers. Gamers will either purchase or avoid the product (Gatautis et al., 2016). Young and free customers might be interested in gamification, while aged and busy customers might not engage with it, that is customers' perception will vary depending upon their situation, subjectivity, and mental makeup (Jayasingh & Eze, 2010). Moreover, their future engagement will be based on their present experience. Because nowadays, customers think rationally – they do not immediately purchase the products; they evaluate various online portals and shopping apps and put the product in a cart and wait for various offers and over the period. Their interest also vanishes in some products while the products are in their shopping cart. So, e-marketers should focus on the aspects that insist consumers to purchase, and accordingly e-marketers should plan their gamification strategies. The major goal of gamification strategies is to alter the behaviour and trigger the flow from negative to positive motivation for the consumer. Future research can comprehend both qualitative and quantitative data which will intensify the importance of online consumer behaviour through gamification. The inclusion of various elements like chatbots based on artificial intelligence can be ensured to increase and stimulate Customer E-Purchase Intention (Shafi et al., 2020). It can be extended to compare different brands available in online shopping and for the creation of their value. Therefore, gamification must provide game aesthetics to make the environment adaptable for ultimate consumers.

Notes

1 https://www.hurix.com/unlock-the-potential-of-gamification-what-is-how-it-works-much-more/
2 https://spinify.com/blog/gamification-history/#:~:text=The%20gamification%20 history%20spans%20years,with%20the%20S%26H%20Green%20Stamps

References

Ackerman, C. E. (2020). Self-determination theory of motivation: Why intrinsic motivation matters. Positive Psychology.

Ahn, T., Ryu, S., & Han, I. (2007). The impact of web quality and playfulness on user acceptance of online retailing. *Information & Management, 44*(3), 263–275.

Alatalo, S., Oikarinen, E. L., Reiman, A., Tan, T. M., Heikka, E. L., Hurmelinna-Laukkanen, P., & Vuorela, T. (2018). Linking concepts of playfulness and well-being at work in retail sector. *Journal of Retailing and Consumer Services, 43*, 226–233.

Andrews, R. L., & Currim, I. S. (2004). Behavioural differences between consumers attracted to shopping online versus traditional supermarkets: Implications for enterprise design and marketing strategy. *International Journal of Internet Marketing and Advertising, 1*(1), 38–61.

Aydınlıyurt, E. T., Taşkın, N., Scahill, S., & Toker, A. (2021). Continuance intention in gamified mobile applications: A study of behavioral inhibition and activation systems. *International Journal of Information Management, 61*, 102414.

Bauer, K. N., Garcia-Marquez, C., & Gandara, D. A. (2020). Teaching with games and gamification: Best practices and future research needs. In *Handbook of teaching with technology in management, leadership, and business* (p. 322–336). Edward Elgar Publishing.

Bidler, M., Zimmermann, J., Schumann, J. H., & Widjaja, T. (2020). Increasing consumers' willingness to engage in data disclosure processes through relevance-illustrating game elements. *Journal of Retailing, 96*(4), 507–523.

Bilgihan, A., Nusair, K., Okumus, F., & Cobanoglu, C. (2015). Applying flow theory to booking experiences: An integrated model in an online service context. *Information & Management, 52*(6), 668–678. https://doi.org/10.1016/j.im.2015.05.005. Retrieved June 10, 2023, from https://www.sciencedirect.com/science/article/abs/pii/S0378720615000518

Bitrián, P., Buil, I., & Catalán, S. (2021). Enhancing user engagement: The role of gamification in mobile apps. *Journal of Business Research, 132*, 170–185.

Björk, P. (2010). Atmospherics on tour operators' websites: Website features that stimulate emotional response. *Journal of Vacation Marketing, 16*(4), 283–296.

Chen, W. K., Chang, D. S., & Chen, C. C. (2017). The role of utilitarian and hedonic values on users' continued usage and purchase intention in a social commerce environment. *Journal of Economics and Management, 13*(2), 193–220.

Collier, J. E., & Barnes, D. C. (2015). Self-service delight: Changing the focus of traditional self-service technology. *Journal of Business Research, 68*(5), 986–993.

Conaway, R., & Garay, M. C. (2014). Gamification and service marketing. *SpringerPlus, 3*(1), 1–11.

Davis, F. D., Bagozzi, R. P., & Warshaw, P. R. (1992). Extrinsic and intrinsic motivation to use computers in the workplace 1. *Journal of Applied Social Psychology*, 22(14), 1111–1132.

De Canio, F., Fuentes-Blasco, M., & Martinelli, E. (2021). Engaging shoppers through mobile apps: The role of gamification. *International Journal of Retail & Distribution Management*, 49(7), 919–940.

Donovan, R. J., Rossiter, J. R., Marcoolyn, G., & Nesdale, A. (1994). Store atmosphere and purchasing behavior. *Journal of Retailing*, 70(3), 283–294.

Dwivedi, Y. K., Ismagilova, E., Hughes, D. L., Carlson, J., Filieri, R., Jacobson, J., Jain, V., Karjaluoto, H., Kefi, H., Krishen, A. S., Kumar, V., Rahman, M. M., Raman, R., Rauschnabel, P. A., Rowley, J., Salo, J., Tran, G. A., & Wang, Y. (2021). Setting the future of digital and social media marketing research: Perspectives and research propositions. *International Journal of Information Management*, 59, 102168.

Epstein, D. S., Zemski, A., Enticott, J., & Barton, C. (2021). Tabletop board game elements and gamification interventions for health behavior change: Realist review and proposal of a game design framework. *JMIR Serious Games*, 9(1), e23302.

Eroglu, S. A., Machleit, K. A., & Davis, L. M. (2001). Atmospheric qualities of online retailing. *Journal of Business Research*, 54(2), 177–184.

Füller, J. (2010). Refining virtual co-creation from a consumer perspective. *California Management Review*, 52(2), 98–122.

Gajanova, L., & Radišić, M. (2021). Self-determination theory as mediator in the nexus of gamification and customer purchasing behaviour. In *SHS web of conferences* (Vol. 90, p. 01005). EDP Sciences.

Gatautis, R., Banytė, J., Kuvykaitė, R., Virvilaitė, R., Dovalienė, A., Piligrimienė, Ž., Gadeikienė, A., Vitkauskaitė, E., & Tarutė, A. (2021). The conceptual model of gamification-based consumer engagement in value creation. In *Gamification and consumer engagement: Creating value in context of ICT development* (pp. 99–108). Springer.

Gatautis, R., & Vaiciukynaite, E. (2013). Website atmosphere: Towards revisited taxonomy of website elements. *Economics & Management*, 18(3).

Gatautis, R., & Vitkauskaite, E. (2009). eBusiness policy support framework. *Inzinerine Ekonomika-Engineering Economics*, 65(5), 35–46. Retrieved June 12, 2023, from https://www.researchgate.net/publication/235464807_eBusiness_policy_support_framework

Gatautis, R., Vitkauskaite, E., Gadeikiene, A., & Piligrimiene, Z. (2016). Gamification as a mean of driving online consumer behaviour: SOR model perspective. *Engineering Economics*, 27(1), 90–97.

Geraldo, G. C., & Mainardes, E. W. (2017). Research on the factors that affect the intention of online shopping. *REGE-Revista de gestão*, 24(2), 181–194.

Gupta, R. (2016). *A study on consumer behavioural intentions towards adoption of gamification–a digital promotion technique* [Doctoral dissertation, Christ University].

Guvenc, O., Kazybayeva, A., & Abeshev, K. (2020). Dynamic prices in retail and its impacts on logistics. In *Proceedings of the 6th international conference on vehicle technology and intelligent transport systems (VEHITS 2020)* (pp. 659–666). Science and Technology Publications, Lda.

Hall, D., & Toke, Z. (2018). *Gamification: Gamified elements' impact on online trust* [Theseis, Department of Informatics, Lund School of Economics and Management, Lund University].

Hamari, J., Koivisto, J., & Sarsa, H. (2014, January). Does gamification work?–A literature review of empirical studies on gamification. In *2014 47th Hawaii international conference on system sciences* (pp. 3025–3034). IEEE.

Haque, M. F., Haque, M. A., & Islam, M. S. (2014). Motivational theories-a critical analysis. *ASA University Review, 8*(1).

Hofacker, C. F., Kode, R., Nicholas, H., Luriec, P. M., & Donaldson, J. (2016). Gamification and mobile marketing effectiveness. *Journal of Interactive Marketing, 34,* 25–36. Advance online publication. https://doi.org/10.1016/j.intmar.2016.03.001

Högberg, J., Ramberg, M. O., Gustafsson, A., & Wästlund, E. (2019). Creating brand engagement through in-store gamified customer experiences. *Journal of Retailing and Consumer Services, 50,* 122–130.

Hong, S. J., & Tam, K. Y. (2006). Understanding the adoption of multipurpose information appliances: The case of mobile data services. *Information Systems Research, 17*(2), 162–179.

Hsu, C. L., & Chen, M. C. (2018). How gamification marketing activities motivate desirable consumer behaviors: Focusing on the role of brand love. *Computers in Human Behavior, 88,* 121–133.

Hunicke, R., LeBlanc, M., & Zubek, R. (2004, July). MDA: A formal approach to game design and game research. In *Proceedings of the AAAI workshop on challenges in Game AI* (Vol. 4, No. 1, p. 1722).

Hwang, J., & Choi, L. (2020). Having fun while receiving rewards?: Exploration of gamification in loyalty programs for consumer loyalty. *Journal of Business Research, 106,* 365–376.

Insley, V., & Nunan, D. (2014). Gamification and the online retail experience. *International Journal of Retail & Distribution Management, 42*(5), 340–351.

Jayasingh, S., & Eze, U. C. (2010). The role of moderating factors in mobile coupon adoption: An extended TAM perspective. *Communications of the IBIMA.* Retrieved June 14, 2023, from https://ibimapublishing.com/articles/CIBIMA/2010/596470/596470.pdf

Jayasooriya, S., Alles, T., & Thelijjagoda, S. (2020, September). Demystifying the concept of IoT enabled gamification in retail marketing: An exploratory study. In *2020 International research conference on smart computing and systems engineering (SCSE)* (pp. 234–241). IEEE.

Joe, S., Kim, J., & Zemke, D. M. V. (2022). Effects of social influence and perceived enjoyment on Kiosk acceptance: A moderating role of gender. *International Journal of Hospitality & Tourism Administration, 23*(2), 289–316.

Kapp, K. M., Valtchanov, D., & Pastore, R. (2020). Enhancing motivation in workplace training with casual games: A twelve month field study of retail employees. *Educational Technology Research and Development, 68*(5), 2263–2284.

Karać, J., & Stabauer, M. (2017, July 9–14). Gamification in E-commerce: A survey based on the octalysis framework. In *HCI in business, government and organizations. Supporting business: Proceedings of the 4th international conference, HCIBGO 2017, held as part of HCI international 2017, Part II 4* (pp. 41–54). Springer International Publishing.

Kazakevičiūtė, A., & Banytė, J. (2012). The relationship between retail crowding and consumers' satisfaction. *Economics and Management, 17*(2), 652–658.

Kim, J. H., Kim, M., & Lennon, S. J. (2009). Effects of web site atmospherics on consumer responses: music and product presentation. *Direct Marketing: An International Journal, 3*(1), 4–19.

Kim, S. (2021). How a company's gamification strategy influences corporate learning: A study based on gamified MSLP (mobile social learning platform). *Telematics and Informatics, 57,* 101505.

Koestner, R., & Hope, N. (2014). A self-determination theory approach to goals. In *The Oxford handbook of work engagement, motivation, and self-determination theory* (pp. 400–413). Oxford University Press.

Koivisto, J., & Hamari, J. (2014). Demographic differences in perceived benefits from gamification. *Computers in Human Behavior*, *35*, 179–188.

Kotler, P. (1973). Atmospherics as a marketing tool. *Journal of Retailing*, *49*(4), 48–64.

Kunkel, T., Lock, D., & Doyle, J. P. (2021). Gamification via mobile applications: A longitudinal examination of its impact on attitudinal loyalty and behavior toward a core service. *Psychology & Marketing*, *38*(6), 948–964.

Lee, J. Y., & Jin, C. H. (2019). The role of gamification in brand app experience: The moderating effects of the 4Rs of app marketing. *Cogent Psychology*, *6*(1), 1576388.

Lopes, J. M., Gomes, S., Lopes, P., Silva, A., Lourenço, D., Esteves, D., Cardoso, M., & Redondo, V. (2023). Exploring the role of gamification in the online shopping experience in retail stores: An exploratory study. *Social Sciences*, *12*(4), 235.

Lu, H. P., & Ho, H. C. (2020). Exploring the impact of gamification on users' engagement for sustainable development: A case study in brand applications. *Sustainability*, *12*(10), 4169.

Manganari, E. E., Siomkos, G. J., & Vrechopoulos, A. P. (2009). Store atmosphere in web retailing. *European Journal of Marketing*, *43*(9/10), 1140–1153.

Massara, F., Liu, S. S., & Melara, R. D. (2010). Adapting to a retail environment: Modeling consumer–environment interactions. *Journal of Business Research*, *63*(7), 673–681.

Matsumoto, T. (2016). Motivation strategy using gamification. *Creative Education*, *7*(10), 1480.

Mekler, E. D., Brühlmann, F., Tuch, A. N., & Opwis, K. (2017). Towards understanding the effects of individual gamification elements on intrinsic motivation and performance. *Computers in Human Behavior*, *71*, 525–534.

Mofokeng, T. E. (2021). The impact of online shopping attributes on customer satisfaction and loyalty: Moderating effects of E-commerce experience. *Cogent Business & Management*, *8*(1), 1968206.

Mummalaneni, V. (2005). An empirical investigation of web site characteristics, consumer emotional states and on-line shopping behaviors. *Journal of Business Research*, *58*(4), 526–532.

Oh, J., Fiorito, S. S., Cho, H., & Hofacker, C. F. (2008). Effects of design factors on store image and expectation of merchandise quality in web-based stores. *Journal of Retailing and Consumer Services*, *15*(4), 237–249.

Ozturk, A. B., Nusair, K., Okumus, F., & Hua, N. (2016). The role of utilitarian and hedonic values on users' continued usage intention in a mobile hotel booking environment. *International Journal of Hospitality Management*, *57*, 106–115. https://doi.org/10.1016/j.ijhm.2016.06.007

Paruthi, M., Nagina, R., & Gupta, G. (2023, March). Measuring the effect of consumer brand engagement on brand-related outcomes in gamified mobile apps: A solicitation of technology acceptance model. In *Proceedings* (Vol. 85, No. 1, p. 10). MDPI.

Pe-Than, E. P. P., Goh, D. H. L., & Lee, C. S. (2014). Making work fun: Investigating antecedents of perceived enjoyment in human computation games for information sharing. *Computers in Human Behavior*, *39*, 88–99.

Pecorari, P. M., & Lima, C. R. C. (2021). Correlation of customer experience with the acceptance of product-service systems and circular economy. *Journal of Cleaner Production*, *281*, 125275.

Petkus, E., Jr. (2004). Enhancing the application of experiential marketing in the arts. *International Journal of Nonprofit and Voluntary Sector Marketing*, *9*(1), 49–56.

Richard, M. O. (2005). Modeling the impact of internet atmospherics on surfer behavior. *Journal of Business Research*, *58*(12), 1632–1642.

Sailer, M., Hense, J. U., Mayr, S. K., & Mandl, H. (2017). How gamification motivates: An experimental study of the effects of specific game design elements on psychological need satisfaction. *Computers in Human Behavior*, *69*, 371–380.

Sautter, P., Hyman, M. R., & Lukosius, V. (2004). E-tail atmospherics: A critique of the literature and model extension. *Journal of Electronic Commerce Research*, *5*(1), 14–24.

Shafi, P. M., Jawalkar, G. S., Kadam, M. A., Ambawale, R. R., & Bankar, S. V. (2020). AI assisted chatbot for E-commerce to address selection of products from multiple products. In *Internet of things. Smart computing and technology, a roadmap ahead* (pp. 57–80). Springer.

Sheetal, Tyagi, R., & Singh, G. (2022). Gamification and customer experience in online retail: A qualitative study focusing on ethical perspective. *Asian Journal of Business Ethics*, 1–21.

Shevchuk, N., Degirmenci, K., & Oinas-Kukkonen, H. (2019, December 15–18). Adoption of gamified persuasive systems to encourage sustainable behaviors: Interplay between perceived persuasiveness and cognitive absorption. In *International conference on information systems ICIS 2019 proceedings*. Association for Information Systems.

Shi, S., Leung, W. K., & Munelli, F. (2022). Gamification in OTA platforms: A mixed-methods research involving online shopping carnival. *Tourism Management*, *88*, 104426.

Smilansky, S. (2017). *Experiential marketing: A practical guide to interactive brand experiences*. Kogan Page Publishers.

Soares, F., Madureira, A., Pagès, A., Barbosa, A., Coelho, A., Cassola, F., Ribeiro, F., Viana, J., Andrade, J. P., Dorokhova, M., Morais, N., Wyrsch, N., & Sørensen, T. (2021). Feedback: An ICT-based platform to increase energy efficiency through buildings' consumer engagement. *Energies*, *14*(6), 1524.

Sreejesh, S., Ghosh, T., & Dwivedi, Y. K. (2021). Moving beyond the content: The role of contextual cues in the effectiveness of gamification of advertising. *Journal of Business Research*, *132*, 88–101.

Suh, A., Cheung, C. M., Ahuja, M., & Wagner, C. (2017). Gamification in the workplace: The central role of the aesthetic experience. *Journal of Management Information Systems*, *34*(1), 268–305.

Szyszka, N. D. (2019). *Gamification in marketing: Aspects influencing intention of engagement and brand attitude* [Dissertation]. https://repositorio-aberto.up.pt/bitstream/10216/123349/2/362346.pdf

Tasci, A. D., & Ko, Y. J. (2016). A fun-scale for understanding the hedonic value of a product: The destination context. *Journal of Travel & Tourism Marketing*, *33*(2), 162–183.

Tu, R., Hsieh, P., & Feng, W. (2019). Walking for fun or for "likes"? The impacts of different gamification orientations of fitness apps on consumers' physical activities. *Sport Management Review*, *22*(5), 682–693.

Urbanskiene, R., Clothey, B., & Jakstys, J. (2000). *Vartotojuelgsena*. Kaunas.

Ushakov, D., & Shatila, K. (2021). The impact of workplace culture on employee retention: An empirical study from Lebanon. *The Journal of Asian Finance, Economics and Business (JAFEB)*, *8*(12), 541–551.

Vdov, K. (2020). *The effect of gamification on customer experience in the digital environment* [Thesis]. www.theseus.fi/handle/10024/339309

Walk, W., Görlich, D., & Barrett, M. (2017). Design, dynamics, experience (DDE): An advancement of the MDA framework for game design. In *Game dynamics: Best practices in procedural and dynamic game content generation* (pp. 27–45). Springer Link. https://link.springer.com/chapter/10.1007/978-3-319-53088-8_3

Wang, C. L. (2021). New frontiers and future directions in interactive marketing: Inaugural editorial. *Journal of Research in Interactive Marketing*, *15*(1), 1–9.

Webster, J., & Martocchio, J. J. (1992). Microcomputer playfulness: Development of a measure with workplace implications. *MIS Quarterly*, 201–226.

Werbach, K., Hunter, D., & Dixon, W. (2012). *For the win: How game thinking can revolutionize your business* (Vol. 1). Wharton Digital Press.

Xu, Y., Chen, Z., Peng, M. Y. P., & Anser, M. K. (2020). Enhancing consumer online purchase intention through gamification in China: Perspective of cognitive evaluation theory. *Frontiers in Psychology*, *11*, 581200.

Zain, N. H. M., Johari, S. N., Aziz, S. R. A., Teo, N. H. I., Ishak, N. H., & Othman, Z. (2021). Winning the needs of the Gen Z: Gamified health awareness campaign in defeating COVID-19 pandemic. *Procedia Computer Science*, *179*, 974–981.

Zheng, X., Men, J., Yang, F., & Gong, X. (2019). Understanding impulse buying in mobile commerce: An investigation into hedonic and utilitarian browsing. *International Journal of Information Management*, *48*, 151–160.

Zichermann, G., & Cunningham, C. (2011). *Gamification by design: Implementing game mechanics in web and mobile apps*. O'Reilly Media, Inc.

Part 4

Gamification and Specific Marketing Domains

Chapter 8

The Effect of Gamification on Virtual Tourist Experiences in the Tourism Industry

Ishani Sharma and Arun Aggarwal

Introduction

The rapid pace of digital evolution in recent years has had a profound impact on multiple sectors, among which the tourism industry stands as a notable example. As an early adopter of innovative technologies, tourism has significantly leveraged digital advancements to augment tourist experiences and adapt to the evolving demands of tourists (Femenia-Serra et al., 2019). At the forefront of this technological integration is Virtual Reality (VR), a groundbreaking innovation that permits a digital replica of physical environments and thereby allows tourists to experience a diverse array of cultural and regional experiences virtually, transcending geographical barriers (Guttentag, 2010; Huang et al., 2020; Gupta et al., 2022). By revolutionizing the process of destination exploration, VR has significantly expanded the reach of the tourism industry and provided an engaging platform for tourists to explore unfamiliar territories (Tussyadiah et al., 2018).

Nonetheless, the integration of VR within the tourism industry has also given rise to a multitude of challenges. Prominent among these are the physiological effects of VR-induced motion sickness and feelings of isolation (Chirico et al., 2018; Slater & Sanchez-Vives, 2016). However, one of the most pivotal concerns emanating from VR usage is the fatigue that users experience, which comprises both physical and cognitive exhaustion (Wei et al., 2023). This fatigue hampers the quality of user experience, thereby posing a significant impediment to the extensive implementation of VR within the tourism sector (Li et al., 2021; Fan et al., 2022). The mitigation of these adverse effects is critical for realizing the potential of VR as an immersive and interactive medium for enhancing the tourism experience.

In the quest for solutions to these challenges, the potential of gamification emerges as a promising prospect. Gamification, the strategic incorporation of game design elements and principles in non-gaming contexts, has witnessed an extensive application across various sectors as a tool to foster user engagement and enhance satisfaction (Deterding et al., 2011). By utilizing motivational constructs inherent in gaming systems, gamification fosters a

DOI: 10.4324/9781032694238-12

sense of accomplishment and competition, consequently encouraging active participation (Hamari, 2017; Lin et al., 2023). Its efficacy in promoting user motivation, enhancing engagement, and improving overall user experience has been empirically validated in diverse domains, including education (Rojas-Sánchez et al., 2023), healthcare (Mäkinen et al., 2022), and marketing (Alcañiz et al., 2019).

The application of gamification within the context of VR-based tourism appears to be a natural progression and a potentially effective strategy for addressing VR-induced fatigue. Indeed, games themselves are built to engage users for extended periods; hence, the principles of gamification could potentially reduce the perceived fatigue by making the VR experience more enjoyable and less tiring (Porter, 2017). Despite the proven potential of gamification in various sectors and its theoretical relevance to VR tourism, its specific capability to counter fatigue and enhance the VR tourist experience remains largely unexplored.

In light of these considerations, this chapter endeavors to delve into the potential of gamification to enhance the VR tourism experience, with a particular focus on the alleviation of VR-induced fatigue and the consequent enhancement of tourist satisfaction. We undertake a two-phase experimental study, wherein we investigate the influence of various gamification elements on the tourist's level of fatigue and satisfaction within the context of VR-based tourism. This inquiry seeks not only to bridge a significant research gap but also to offer valuable insights for tourism operators, VR developers, and policymakers as they navigate the ever-evolving digital landscape of the tourism industry. Furthermore, the objective of our exploration is to augment the existing body of scholarship surrounding digital tourism. By providing a comprehensive analysis of the intersection between Virtual Reality, gamification, and tourist satisfaction, we strive to lay a solid foundation for future research in this fascinating and rapidly evolving field.

Virtual Reality in Tourism: A Double-Edged Sword

Transformation of Tourism by Virtual Reality

Virtual Reality (VR) has emerged as a game-changer in the tourism industry, offering immersive and interactive experiences that enable globetrotters to virtually traverse desired destinations (Guttentag, 2010). This cutting-edge technology allows for a deeper connection with various locations, artifacts, and diverse cultures, free from the typical constraints of geography, time, and physical attendance (Lim et al., 2022). Particularly striking is the capacity of VR to allow exploration of areas that are either inaccessible or delicate in nature, such as archaeological sites or endangered ecosystems. In these scenarios, VR enables a rich, immersive experience without compromising the preservation of these vulnerable locations (Femenia-Serra et al., 2019).

Beyond its utility as an exploration tool, VR acts as a potent enabler for trip planning and visualization. Leveraging the power of virtual tours and extensive 360-degree vistas, future travelers can gain a preview of their intended destinations, thereby contributing to more thoughtful and well-informed travel choices (Fan et al., 2022). From a marketing perspective, VR serves as a highly effective promotional conduit for the tourism sector, offering an interactive and immersive stage for showcasing tourist spots and attractions, and thereby amplifying customer engagement (Tussyadiah et al., 2018).

Challenges Posed by Virtual Reality in Tourism

While the impact of VR on tourism is undoubtedly transformative, its adoption in the sector does not come without its unique set of hurdles, including access constraints, a need for technological adeptness, and user experience considerations. Sustained engagement with VR can lead to undesirable physical side effects, commonly referred to as VR-induced motion sickness. This condition presents symptoms such as nausea, disorientation, and visual discomfort, posing further challenges to widespread acceptance of this technology (Souchet et al., 2023). Moreover, the solitary nature of VR experiences can give rise to psychological problems such as feelings of isolation and loneliness due to the absence of authentic social interaction (Appel et al., 2020). Notably, fatigue has been identified as a significant deterrent to VR adoption, resulting directly from extended VR usage (Merkx & Nawijn, 2021).

VR-induced fatigue can be bifurcated into two types – physical, which arises from operating VR equipment, and cognitive, resulting from the mental effort and sensory overload inherent to the VR environment (Kemeny et al., 2020; Zhang et al., 2020). Since these negative experiences can drastically impact the overall enjoyment of VR tourism experiences, devising strategies to mitigate their effects and enhance the benefits of VR in the tourism industry is crucial (Dandotiya & Aggarwal, 2022).

The Promise of Gamification in VR Tourism

One promising solution lies in the realm of gamification – the process of integrating game-like elements into non-gaming contexts to boost user engagement and motivation across various sectors (Deterding et al., 2011). Applied to VR tourism, gamification could add an interactive and engaging dimension to the virtual experience, potentially easing VR-related issues such as fatigue and loneliness. Integrating gamified elements like scoring systems, achievements, and competitive or collaborative gameplay could significantly enrich the VR tourism experience, making it more appealing and satisfying, which could encourage repeat usage and improve overall user satisfaction (Hamari, 2017; Caldas et al., 2022).

The Unexplored Territory of Gamification in VR Tourism

The potential of gamification to mitigate VR-induced fatigue, specifically in the context of tourism, warrants thorough exploration. While numerous studies have attested to the effectiveness of gamification in enhancing user motivation and fostering engagement across diverse domains, its specific application in addressing fatigue related to prolonged VR usage remains an under-explored domain (Sousa et al., 2022). An investigation of this nature could provide valuable academic insights into the interface between VR and gamification, contributing to the emerging body of knowledge on the implementation of digital technologies in tourism. Furthermore, it would yield practical guidance for tourism operators and policymakers aiming to augment the VR tourism experience, leading to more sustainable and inclusive tourist experiences in the digital age (Yung et al., 2021).

Given the advent of digital tourism and the acceleration of VR adoption, understanding the potential of gamification in this context is of critical importance. This chapter aims to contribute to this understanding by reviewing relevant literature and proposing a conceptual framework for integrating gamification into VR tourism experiences.

In conclusion, while the use of VR in tourism presents both opportunities and challenges, the application of gamification elements may provide a means to mitigate the negative impacts and enhance the benefits of VR for a more engaging, satisfying, and enjoyable tourist experience. The integration of gamification strategies into VR environments could have far-reaching implications for the development and sustainability of the tourism industry in the digital era. This chapter seeks to shed light on this potential and pave the way for further academic and practical exploration of this fascinating and promising field.

The Game Factor: Understanding Gamification

Concept and Evolution of Gamification

Gamification, as initially proposed by Nick Pelling in 2002 and later widely adopted within the digital media industry in the ensuing decade, implies the employment of game design principles and mechanics within nongame contexts (Bigdeli et al., 2016; Deterding et al., 2011). The primary objective of gamification is to foster user engagement and stimulate individuals to achieve specified goals. This is accomplished by incorporating elements traditionally associated with games, such as scoring systems, badges, leaderboards, and interactive challenges (Hamari, 2017).

The allure of gamification lies in its ability to tap into the intrinsic motivation of individuals, eliciting psychological responses similar to those experienced during gameplay. This, in turn, boosts their level of engagement, performance metrics, and overall satisfaction (Bartholomew et al., 2011). The efficacy of gamification strategies has been empirically demonstrated across various fields like education, healthcare, marketing, and environmental conservation, thereby validating its potential to augment user engagement and satisfaction (Hsu & Chen, 2021; Seaborn & Fels, 2015; Hamari et al., 2014; Paruthi et al., 2023)

Application of Gamification in Virtual Reality Tourism

In the context of VR tourism, gamification could offer an effective strategy to address prevailing challenges and elevate the user experience. The integration of game elements into VR tourism experiences can lead to a more immersive and enjoyable tourist experience. Such gamified experiences may counter the fatigue often associated with prolonged VR use by integrating gameplay elements such as timed challenges, rest intervals, and rewards, consequently enhancing user satisfaction and engagement (Nicholson, 2015).

Moreover, the integration of social gaming components into VR could address feelings of solitude and isolation, frequently cited as drawbacks in solo VR experiences. This could be accomplished by encouraging a communal spirit among users, thereby promoting social interaction and paving the way for collective experiences within the virtual realm (Xu et al., 2014/2013). By engendering a sense of shared accomplishment and connection, these gaming elements could lead to more gratifying and rewarding experiences in VR tourism (Lin & Wang, 2021).

Research Gaps and Future Directions

While the potential advantages are evident, the incorporation of gamification in the sphere of VR tourism remains an emergent area of study. To fully grasp its implications and effectiveness, it necessitates further examination. Specifically, we must identify the gaming components that can best amplify the VR tourism experience and comprehend the methods through which gamification can alleviate exhaustion and improve user satisfaction. This calls for a cross-disciplinary methodology, fusing knowledge from game design, psychology, and tourism studies to cultivate a comprehensive understanding of the potential and constraints of gamification in VR tourism. For instance, the application of self-determination theory (Ryan & Deci, 2000) may provide valuable perspectives on the motivational aspects of gamification. Concurrently, flow theory (Csikszentmihalyi, 1990) can provide insight into the optimal equilibrium between challenge and ability in game elements to maintain user engagement and lessen fatigue. Furthermore, considering the swift progression in VR and gamification technologies, it is vital to ponder how these developments might steer their utilization in the tourism sector. For instance, advancements in AI and machine learning could present opportunities for tailored, adaptive game elements that cater to individual user requirements and inclinations (Yannakakis & Togelius, 2018).

In conclusion, while gamification holds promise as a solution to challenges inherent in VR tourism, meticulous research is vital to unlock its full potential. This includes empirical examinations to assess the efficiency of various game elements and theoretical contemplations to understand the underlying dynamics. These endeavors will aid in the effective assimilation of gamification in VR tourism, ensuring that the benefits of these technologies are optimized while their drawbacks are minimized. Not only is this research academically significant, but it also offers practical guidance for industry professionals aiming to create more captivating and rewarding VR tourism experiences.

Gamification and Fatigue: An Experimental Approach

The Prevalence of VR-Induced Fatigue in Tourism

As the tourism industry embraces the ever-increasing use of Virtual Reality (VR) technology, there is growing awareness of the debilitating aftermath of VR-induced fatigue. This fatigue, manifested through both physical and cognitive stress, significantly influences the user experience. It could potentially curtail satisfaction levels and deter future utilization of VR, thereby undermining the enduring feasibility of VR as an instrument in the tourism sector (Kim & Shin, 2021; Chardonnet et al., 2017).

VR-induced fatigue may stem from physical discomfort associated with donning VR gear or from the cognitive burden imposed by processing immersive 3D environments. These effects can present themselves as symptoms such as headaches, vertigo, nausea, and confusion (Souchet et al., 2023). Furthermore, in the context of tourism, prolonged VR use could possibly conflict with the inherent objectives of relaxation and leisure typically associated with tourism experiences (Stanney et al., 2020). As such, it is imperative to explore methods that can alleviate the burden of fatigue, while preserving the immersive and interactive benefits of VR.

The Potential of Gamification to Mitigate Fatigue

In light of these hurdles, gamification presents itself as a potential countermeasure to offset the negative impacts of VR-induced fatigue. Gamification, defined as the application of game-like elements in nongame environments, has proven to be successful in enhancing engagement and motivation across numerous domains (Deterding et al., 2011; Hamari, 2017). Gamification's potential in fatigue reduction is attributed to its capacity to maintain user interest and disrupt the tedium commonly associated with extended task performance (Zichermann & Linder, 2010). For instance, components such as point systems and leaderboards can instill a sense of achievement and progression, while challenges and quests can infuse diversity and sustain user intrigue (Nicholson, 2015). Moreover, social aspects such as group play or communal leaderboards could cultivate a sense of camaraderie and collective success, which might help alleviate feelings of solitude and amplify satisfaction derived from the VR experience (Han et al., 2022; Guo et al., 2020).

Experimental Approach to Study Gamification and VR-induced Fatigue

Given the proven effectiveness of gamification in various fields, it is worthwhile to investigate empirically its potential to offset VR-induced fatigue within the tourism sector. A dual-phase experimental research method could be implemented. The initial phase could be designed to determine the role of VR-induced fatigue as a mediating factor in the correlation between gamification and tourist satisfaction. This could involve participants engaging in VR tourism experiences, both with and without gamification aspects, and subsequently evaluating their levels of fatigue, engagement, and satisfaction. Employing standardized fatigue and satisfaction scales, along with physiological metrics such as heart rate variability or eye tracking, could yield objective data to complement self-reported measures (Hancock & Choudhury, 2023).

The secondary phase of the experiment could investigate the distinctive effects of diverse gamification elements on the VR tourism experience, with an emphasis on fatigue mitigation. For example, which proves to be more effective in reducing fatigue: a scoring system or a leaderboard? Do cooperative or competitive gaming elements give a more substantial boost to engagement and satisfaction? In addition, it would be insightful to study the influence of user characteristics like age, gender, or gaming experience on the effectiveness of gamification, thereby contributing to a more comprehensive understanding of gamification's impact.

Limitations and Future Research Directions

Although the potential of gamification in alleviating VR-induced fatigue is encouraging, it is crucial to understand that gamification isn't a cure-all solution for every challenge encountered in VR tourism. The design of gamified VR experiences must be contextually relevant and adhere to user preferences to ensure their efficacy (Böckle et al., 2017). For instance, competitive game elements may be engaging for some users but stressful for others, potentially contradicting the leisure goals of tourism (Hanus & Fox, 2015). Thus, user-centric design principles and context-specific gamification strategies form an essential area for future research. Moreover, potential negative implications of gamification must be examined. Over-stimulation of users due to excessive game elements and fostering competitive environments that might contradict relaxation goals inherent in tourism are potential pitfalls.

Also, the longer-term impact of gamification on the perceived authenticity of the tourism experience should be explored (Leung et al., 2023).

In conclusion, the incorporation of gamification into VR tourism offers significant potential to enhance user engagement and reduce VR-induced fatigue. However, this approach requires a careful implementation and further empirical exploration to maximize its benefits while minimizing potential drawbacks. A thoughtful, evidence-based approach to gamification can help unlock the full potential of VR in the tourism industry, offering users rich, immersive, and satisfying experiences.

Results and Discussion

In building upon the theoretical groundwork and the research methodology delineated earlier, the ensuing discourse aims to evaluate prospectively the findings derived from the posited experiment. Given the unavailability of actual empirical data at this juncture, the following deliberation will be premised on hypothetical outcomes and their associated implications in the realm of VR tourism.

If the proposed experiment hypothetically elicits results demonstrating that the assimilation of gamification within VR tourism experiences leads to a decline in fatigue and an enhancement in satisfaction, it would thereby provide compelling evidence advocating the potential merits of gamification within VR tourism. In particular, the empirical findings could emphasize how disparate game elements are instrumental in mitigating fatigue and elevating user satisfaction. Prior research in other domains indicates that game elements such as points and badges can amplify user motivation and engagement (Hamari, 2017). Similarly, leaderboards could induce a sense of healthy competition, thereby further augmenting user engagement (Bai et al., 2021). Such elevated levels of engagement could potentially counteract fatigue experienced in VR tourism ventures. Furthermore, the social dimensions of games, encompassing multiplayer modes or collaborative tasks, could potentially address feelings of isolation frequently associated with VR tourism experiences (Xu et al., 2014/2013). By affording VR tourists opportunities for social interaction, a sense of community and collective experience could be fostered, thereby enhancing the overall user experience.

However, it is of paramount importance to exercise caution in interpreting these hypothetical results. While gamification showcases potential to enrich VR tourism experiences, the efficacy of this approach is significantly contingent upon the nuances of its implementation. For instance, game elements that are poorly designed or irrelevant might have minimal positive impact or may even detract from the user experience (Nicholson, 2015). Moreover, it is essential to recognize the variability among users. For example, while some users may respond positively to competitive game elements such as leaderboards, others might perceive them as discouraging (Hamari et al., 2014).

Thus, it becomes crucial to tailor the gamification strategy to correspond to the specific context and the characteristics of the user group.

In conclusion, the hypothetical positive findings from the proposed experiment could provide promising insights into the potential of gamification in augmenting VR tourism experiences. However, further research is necessitated to gain a comprehensive understanding of the best practices for implementing gamification in VR tourism and to validate its potential benefits. Future research endeavors should strive to confirm these findings with empirical data, thereby deepening our understanding of the optimal ways to design and implement gamified VR experiences within the sphere of tourism. Moreover, understanding the influence of individual differences and preferences will be critical in ensuring the wide applicability and success of gamification strategies in this field. The ultimate objective is to curate VR tourism experiences that are not only immersive and engaging but also accessible, pleasurable, and gratifying for a diverse array of users.

Implications for the Tourism Industry

Investigating the potential of gamification as a tool to alleviate VR-induced fatigue and enrich tourist experiences could offer invaluable insights pertinent to the tourism industry. Should our hypothetical results conform to our expectations, several crucial implications could be drawn for tourism service providers, policymakers, and research scholars.

Primarily, the capacity of gamification to ameliorate VR tourist experiences and diminish fatigue indicates that tourism service providers could consider incorporating game elements into their VR offerings. However, as highlighted by Nicholson (2015), meaningful gamification should not be an exercise of merely appending game mechanics to a system. Rather, it should entail designing game elements in a manner that is congruent with user objectives and the context of application. For instance, service providers could develop challenges or quests that are integral to the VR tourist experience, bestowing points or badges upon successful completion (Xu et al., 2014/2013).

Second, the potential benefits of gamification in VR tourism also signify that policymakers could endorse the use of gamification as a recommended practice within the tourism industry. Policymakers could formulate guidelines or propose incentives to encourage tourism service providers to implement gamification strategies (Sigala, 2015).

Finally, for researchers in this field, these findings could catalyze further investigations into the optimal ways to implement gamification in VR tourism. Avenues for exploration could include the evaluation of various game elements, the understanding of individual differences in response to gamification, and the examination of the long-term effects of gamification on VR tourism experiences. For tourism marketers, understanding the impact of gamification on VR experiences could inform marketing strategies. If gamification elements increase user satisfaction and reduce fatigue, they might be incorporated into marketing messages to appeal to potential tourists (Femenia-Serra et al., 2019). For instance, marketing campaigns could highlight the unique game elements integrated into VR experiences, emphasizing how these can enhance enjoyment and minimize discomfort.

For VR software developers in the tourism industry, the findings could shape the development process. Developers could be encouraged to include options for gamification in their software design. They might incorporate systems for points, achievements, or social interaction directly into VR platforms, allowing tourism providers to create custom game elements relevant to their specific VR content (Pospíšil, 2023).

The potential success of gamification in enhancing VR tourism could also spur technology innovation. Companies might be motivated to explore new technologies that enable more immersive and engaging gamified experiences. This could lead to advancements in VR technology, such as better motion tracking for more interactive game elements or improved social features to enhance the sense of shared experience in VR (Guttentag, 2010).

Lastly, the education sector could benefit from these insights. Courses related to tourism could integrate sections on VR and gamification, preparing future professionals to effectively use these tools. Furthermore, the findings could encourage educational institutions to adopt similar gamified approaches in their teaching methodologies, particularly in courses related to VR and tourism (Yung et al., 2021; Beck et al., 2019).

Moreover, if our hypothesis proves accurate, it could open new avenues for research. Scholars could delve deeper into the specifics of gamification in VR tourism, examining which game elements are most effective in reducing fatigue and enhancing satisfaction, or how these effects vary among different user groups (Hamari et al., 2014).

Finally, it's important to note the ethical considerations. While gamification can potentially enhance user engagement and satisfaction, it is critical to ensure that these strategies are not used manipulatively to exploit users. In this regard, both tourism providers and policymakers should prioritize ethical considerations in the design and regulation of gamified VR tourist experiences (Gelter et al., 2021). While these implications paint an exciting picture for the future of VR tourism, it is crucial to reiterate the need for responsible and ethical implementation of gamification. The ultimate goal should always be to enhance user experiences and satisfaction, not just to prolong their time in VR or maximize profit (Gelter et al., 2021).

Conclusion

As we consider the prospective role of gamification in enhancing VR tourism experiences, our understanding remains shaped by a series of hypothetical scenarios and potential experimental results. The theories presented herein align with the broader literature on gamification and its applications (Deterding et al., 2011), as well as studies specific to VR experiences (Dubois et al., 2021), but empirical research in the intersection of these two fields – particularly regarding the issue of VR-induced fatigue – is still emerging. The proposition that gamification can reduce VR-induced fatigue and subsequently improve the tourism experience underscores a promising pathway for enhancing digital tourism offerings. Gamification has the potential to transform VR tourism from a novelty into a genuinely satisfying and immersive experience, surpassing traditional tourism in unique and compelling ways (Xu et al., 2014/2013). However, a successful implementation will require careful consideration of various factors such as the user's needs and preferences, the relevance and design of the game elements, and the potential for negative side effects (Nicholson, 2015). Understanding and applying these principles could help tourism providers, policymakers, and researchers alike optimize the use of gamification in VR tourism.

Moreover, while the potential benefits of gamification are promising, it is equally crucial to consider the ethical implications. Policymakers and providers must ensure that gamified VR experiences are designed responsibly and do not exploit users Fuchs (2014). Looking forward, additional research will be critical to fully understand the potential of gamification in VR tourism and establish best practices for its implementation. In the context of the rapidly evolving digital landscape, this topic represents a promising and rich area of exploration that could significantly reshape the future of the tourism industry.

References

Alcañiz, M., Bigné, E., & Guixeres, J. (2019). Virtual reality in marketing: A framework, review, and research agenda. *Frontiers in Psychology, 10,* 1530.

Appel, L., Appel, E., Bogler, O., Wiseman, M., Cohen, L., Ein, N., Abrams, H. B., & Campos, J. L. (2020). Older adults with cognitive and/or physical impairments can benefit from immersive virtual reality experiences: A feasibility study. *Frontiers in Medicine, 6,* 329.

Bai, S., Hew, K. F., Sailer, M., & Jia, C. (2021). From top to bottom: How positions on different types of leaderboard may affect fully online student learning performance, intrinsic motivation, and course engagement. *Computers & Education, 173,* 104297.

Bartholomew, K. J., Ntoumanis, N., Ryan, R. M., & Thøgersen-Ntoumani, C. (2011). Psychological need thwarting in the sport context: Assessing the darker side of athletic experience. *Journal of Sport and Exercise Psychology, 33*(1), 75–102.

Beck, J., Rainoldi, M., & Egger, R. (2019). Virtual reality in tourism: A state-of-the-art review. *Tourism Review, 74*(3), 586–612.

Bigdeli, Z., Haidari, G., Haji Yakhchali, A., & Basirian Jahromi, R. (2016). Gamification in library websites based on motivational theories. *Webology, 13*(1), 1–12.

Böckle, M., Novak, J., & Bick, M. (2017, June 5–10). Towards adaptive gamification: A synthesis of current developments. In *Proceedings of the 25th European conference on information systems (ECIS) Guimarães, Portugal*. ISBN 978-989-20-7655-3. Research Papers: http://aisel.aisnet.org/ecis2017_rp/11

Caldas, O. I., Sanchez, N., Mauledoux, M., Avilés, O. F., & Rodriguez-Guerrero, C. (2022). Leading presence-based strategies to manipulate user experience in virtual reality environments. *Virtual Reality, 26*(4), 1507–1518.

Chardonnet, J. R., Mirzaei, M. A., & Mérienne, F. (2017). Features of the postural sway signal as indicators to estimate and predict visually induced motion sickness in virtual reality. *International Journal of Human–Computer Interaction, 33*(10), 771–785.

Chirico, A., Ferrise, F., Cordella, L., & Gaggioli, A. (2018). Designing awe in virtual reality: An experimental study. *Frontiers in Psychology, 8*, 2351.

Csikszentmihalyi, M. (1990). *Flow: The psychology of optimal experience*. Harper and Row.

Dandotiya, R., & Aggarwal, A. (2022). An examination of tourists' national identity, place attachment and loyalty at a dark tourist destination. *Kybernetes. 52*(12), 6063–6077.

Deterding, S., Dixon, D., Khaled, R., & Nacke, L. (2011, September). From game design elements to gamefulness: Defining "gamification". In *Proceedings of the 15th international academic MindTrek conference: Envisioning future media environments* (pp. 9–15). ACM Digital Library.

Dubois, L. E., Griffin, T., Gibbs, C., & Guttentag, D. (2021). The impact of video games on destination image. *Current Issues in Tourism, 24*(4), 554–566.

Fan, X., Jiang, X., & Deng, N. (2022). Immersive technology: A meta-analysis of augmented/virtual reality applications and their impact on tourism experience. *Tourism Management, 91*, 104534.

Femenia-Serra, F., Neuhofer, B., & Ivars-Baidal, J. A. (2019). Towards a conceptualisation of smart tourists and their role within the smart destination scenario. *The Service Industries Journal, 39*(2), 109–133.

Fuchs, C. (2014). *Digital labour and Karl Marx*. Routledge.

Gelter, J., Lexhagen, M., & Fuchs, M. (2021). A meta-narrative analysis of smart tourism destinations: Implications for tourism destination management. *Current Issues in Tourism, 24*(20), 2860–2874.

Gupta, G., Gupta, A., & Joshi, M. C. (2022, December 14). A conceptual and bibliometric study to understand marketing in metaverse: A new paradigm. *2022 5th International Conference on Contemporary Computing and Informatics (IC3I)*. https://doi.org/10.1109/ic3i56241.2022.10073455

Guo, Y., You, X., Gu, Y., Wu, G., & Xu, C. (2020). A moderated mediation model of the relationship between quality of social relationships and internet addiction: Mediation by loneliness and moderation by dispositional optimism. *Current Psychology, 39*, 1303–1313.

Guttentag, D. A. (2010). Virtual reality: Applications and implications for tourism. *Tourism Management, 31*(5), 637–651.

Hamari, J. (2017). Do badges increase user activity? A field experiment on the effects of gamification. *Computers in Human Behavior, 71*, 469–478.

Hamari, J., Koivisto, J., & Sarsa, H. (2014, January). Does gamification work?-A literature review of empirical studies on gamification. In *2014 47th Hawaii international conference on system sciences* (pp. 3025–3034). IEEE.

Han, D. I. D., Bergs, Y., & Moorhouse, N. (2022). Virtual reality consumer experience escapes: Preparing for the metaverse. *Virtual Reality, 26*(4), 1443–1458.

Hancock, T. O., & Choudhury, C. F. (2023). Utilising physiological data for augmenting travel choice models: Methodological frameworks and directions of future research. *Transport Reviews*, 1–29.

Hanus, M. D., & Fox, J. (2015). Assessing the effects of gamification in the classroom: A longitudinal study on intrinsic motivation, social comparison, satisfaction, effort, and academic performance. *Computers & Education, 80*, 152–161.

Hsu, C. L., & Chen, M. C. (2021). Advocating recycling and encouraging environmentally friendly habits through gamification: An empirical investigation. *Technology in Society, 66*, 101621.

Huang, H. L., Hwang, G. J., & Chang, C. Y. (2020). Learning to be a writer: A spherical video-based virtual reality approach to supporting descriptive article writing in high school Chinese courses. *British Journal of Educational Technology, 51*(4), 1386–1405.

Kemeny, A., Chardonnet, J. R., & Colombet, F. (2020). *Getting rid of cybersickness: In virtual reality, augmented reality and simulators.* Springer. https://doi.org/10.1007/978-3-030-59342-1

Kim, E., & Shin, G. (2021). User discomfort while using a virtual reality headset as a personal viewing system for text-intensive office tasks. *Ergonomics, 64*(7), 891–899.

Leung, W. K., Chang, M. K., Cheung, M. L., & Shi, S. (2023). VR tourism experiences and tourist behavior intention in COVID-19: An experience economy and mood management perspective. *Information Technology & People, 36*(3), 1095–1125.

Li, S., Fong, L. H. N., Zhang, C. X., & Chen, M. (2021). Investigating the motivations and constraints of Chinese peer-to-peer accommodation hosts. *International Journal of Contemporary Hospitality Management, 33*(1), 305–326.

Lim, W. M., Aggarwal, A., & Dandotiya, R. (2022). Marketing luxury services beyond affluence in the new normal: Insights from fine dining during the coronavirus pandemic. *Journal of Retailing and Consumer Services, 66*, 102936.

Lin, C. W., Chien, C. Y., Ou Yang, C. P., & Mao, T. Y. (2023). Encouraging sustainable consumption through gamification in a branded app: A study on consumers' behavioral perspective. *Sustainability, 15*(1), 1–14.

Lin, Y. J., & Wang, H. C. (2021). Using virtual reality to facilitate learners' creative self-efficacy and intrinsic motivation in an EFL classroom. *Education and Information Technologies, 26*(4), 4487–4505.

Mäkinen, H., Haavisto, E., Havola, S., & Koivisto, J. M. (2022). User experiences of virtual reality technologies for healthcare in learning: An integrative review. *Behaviour & Information Technology, 41*(1), 1–17.

Merkx, C., & Nawijn, J. (2021). Virtual reality tourism experiences: Addiction and isolation. *Tourism Management, 87*, 104394.

Nicholson, S. (2015). A RECIPE for meaningful gamification. In T. Reiners & L. C. Wood (Eds.), *Gamification in education and business* (pp. 1–20). Springer. https://doi.org/10.1007/978-3-319-10208-5_1

Paruthi, M., Nagina, R., & Gupta, G. (2023, March). Measuring the effect of consumer brand engagement on brand-related outcomes in gamified mobile apps: A solicitation of technology acceptance model. In *Proceedings* (Vol. 85, No. 1, p. 10). MDPI.

Porter, K. J. (2017). How to talk about videogames by Ian Bogost. *American Studies, 56*(1), 224–226.

Pospíšil, P. (2023). Moving indoors: A systematic literature review of locomotion in virtual indoor environments. *International Journal of Cartography*, 1–23. https://doi.org/10.1080/23729333.2023.2183553

Rojas-Sánchez, M. A., Palos-Sánchez, P. R., & Folgado-Fernández, J. A. (2023). Systematic literature review and bibliometric analysis on virtual reality and education. *Education and Information Technologies, 28*(1), 155–192.

Ryan, R. M., & Deci, E. L. (2000). Self-determination theory and the facilitation of intrinsic motivation, social development, and well-being. *American Psychologist*, 55(1), 68–78. https://doi.org/10.1037/0003-066x.55.1.68

Seaborn, K., & Fels, D. I. (2015). Gamification in theory and action: A survey. *International Journal of Human-Computer Studies*, 74, 14–31.

Sigala, M. (2015). Gamification for crowdsourcing marketing practices: Applications and benefits in tourism. *Advances in Crowdsourcing*, 129–145. https://doi.org/10.1007/978-3-319-18341-1_11

Slater, M., & Sanchez-Vives, M. V. (2016). Enhancing our lives with immersive virtual reality. *Frontiers in Robotics and AI*, 3, 74.

Souchet, A. D., Lourdeaux, D., Pagani, A., & Rebenitsch, L. (2023). A narrative review of immersive virtual reality's ergonomics and risks at the workplace: Cybersickness, visual fatigue, muscular fatigue, acute stress, and mental overload. *Virtual Reality*, 27(1), 19–50.

Sousa, N., Alén, E., Losada, N., & Melo, M. (2022). Virtual reality in tourism promotion: A research agenda based on a bibliometric approach. *Journal of Quality Assurance in Hospitality & Tourism*, 1–30. https://doi.org/10.1080/1528008x.2022.2112807

Stanney, K., Lawson, B. D., Rokers, B., Dennison, M., Fidopiastis, C., Stoffregen, T., Weech, S., & Fulvio, J. M. (2020). Identifying causes of and solutions for cybersickness in immersive technology: Reformulation of a research and development agenda. *International Journal of Human–Computer Interaction*, 36(19), 1783–1803.

Tussyadiah, I. P., Wang, D., Jung, T. H., & Tom Dieck, M. C. (2018). Virtual reality, presence, and attitude change: Empirical evidence from tourism. *Tourism Management*, 66, 140–154.

Wei, Z., Zhang, J., Huang, X., & Qiu, H. (2023). Can gamification improve the virtual reality tourism experience? Analyzing the mediating role of tourism fatigue. *Tourism Management*, 96, 104715.

Xu, F., Weber, J., & Buhalis, D. (2014, January 21–24). Gamification in tourism. In *Information and communication technologies in tourism 2014: Proceedings of the international conference in Dublin* (pp. 525–537). Springer International Publishing. (Original work published 2013)

Yannakakis, G. N., & Togelius, J. (2018). *Artificial intelligence and games* (Vol. 2, pp. 2475–1502). Springer.

Yung, R., Khoo-Lattimore, C., & Potter, L. E. (2021). Virtual reality and tourism marketing: Conceptualizing a framework on presence, emotion, and intention. *Current Issues in Tourism*, 24(11), 1505–1525.

Zhang, Y., Liu, H., Kang, S. C., & Al-Hussein, M. (2020). Virtual reality applications for the built environment: Research trends and opportunities. *Automation in Construction*, 118, 103311.

Zichermann, G., & Linder, J. (2010). *Game-based marketing: Inspire customer loyalty through rewards, challenges, and contests*. John Wiley & Sons.

Chapter 9

Role of Gamification in Influencer Marketing
Studying the Mediating Role of Utilitarian, Hedonic, and Attitude on eWOM

Mithilesh Pandey, Pinnika Syam Yadav and Rajshekar Reddy Pothireddy

Introduction

The ubiquity of smartphones and the widespread adoption of augmented reality technologies across all generations have set the stage for the integration of gamification in marketing endeavors. This involves infusing marketing activities with gamified elements, enabling consumers to actively participate and interact with brands. Social media platforms serve as a communal space where consumers can congregate and be incentivized to engage in various activities. Leveraging data derived from these interactions, companies gain valuable insights into consumer perspectives, allowing them to tailor their products according to prevailing consumer preferences.

Numerous brands are proactively incorporating gamification strategies to remain abreast of industry trends and provide an immersive brand experience to their clientele. In adapting to the contemporary landscape and creating an environment conducive to consumer engagement through gamification on social media platforms, brands position themselves strategically. Unlike traditional mass media platforms, social media empowers users to express and share their opinions, a dynamic impossible in traditional mass media channels. Nevertheless, brands often struggle to generate substantial participation in gamified events on their own. This gap can be effectively bridged through collaborations with influencers on social media platforms.

These activities are intricately linked to e-commerce, serving as the digital conduit between consumers and products. Content generated by influencers, coupled with e-commerce practices such as affiliate marketing, has proven to be an effective strategy. Gamification, in essence, entails leveraging game dynamics to transform programs and platforms in a nontraditional manner. By offering interactive features and catering to customer needs, gamification aims to instigate attitudinal and behavioral changes that inspire consumers

DOI: 10.4324/9781032694238-13

to actively participate, stay informed, and make more frequent purchases within social media platforms.

In the realm of e-commerce, gamification acts as a tool to captivate users and stimulate them to develop a stronger connection with the platform. Yudhoatmojo and Ramadana (2016) posit that gamification is instrumental in engaging digital customers for marketing activities, encouraging repurchases, and fostering brand loyalty. Despite its significance in e-commerce applications, there exists a dearth of knowledge regarding the interplay between influencer-driven gamification and the shopping motivations influencing consumer behavior.

This study endeavors to bridge this gap by delving into the gamification literature within the context of influencer marketing, exploring both extrinsic and intrinsic values and their correlation with attitudes toward e-commerce apps. Gamification in influencer marketing not only sustains user engagement with the platform but also yields benefits that may prompt individuals to consider purchasing and recommending the featured products to friends and family. Previous research, such as Sumarliah et al. (2021), has explored the shopping motivation associated with attitudes and behavioral patterns of consumers but has not comprehensively addressed gamification in e-commerce. Thus, the study aims to identify the influence of influencer and shopping motivation in shaping attitudes toward e-commerce apps in the context of gamification. Therefore, the findings of this study will enable e-commerce platforms to actively engage with customers to boost their sales and further strengthen their connection with consumers. Due to the "digital revolution", all the brands right now are trying to associate with all the digital platforms to engage with digital consumers as more and more people are now trying to engage with these platforms instead of offline activities. Furthermore, these platforms also generate huge streams of revenue with a heap load of customers engaging in these platforms 24/7 in multiple intervals. Lots of research articles and even various countries' top officials are trying to deliver messages on these platforms to reach their potential audience (Acikgoz & Burnaz, 2021; Belanche et al., 2021). The current study revealed that "Near one-third of the world population engage in these social media platforms (Facebook, Instagram, YouTube, LinkedIn & Twitter "Tweet-x" etc.) every minute". The trend to engage with social media consumers has been in the market for the last decade; we can say that "Micromax" was the first to start engaging with social media influencers to promote their brand through giveaways. Later on, this trend was moved a bit further by the popular brands like Samsung and Apple as the consumers' focus has been shifted to these platforms instead of these traditional channels (Barnes, 2015; Lee et al., 2021; Lou et al., 2019). Even now, for some brands, instead of digital marketing activities, the main aim is to engage with social media influencers as these platforms focus on instant delivery of awareness and increase in organic search for the products (Bashari & Fazl-ersi, 2020;

Belanche et al., 2020). Based on these developments and the enormous amount of time spent by consumers on social media platforms, marketers have started to encourage influencers to increase their organic search to earn profit from these platforms (Tabellion & Esch, 2019). In the current era, marketers increasingly face problems in that consumers regard traditional information forms of advertising as disturbing and untrustworthy for their purchasing decisions (Wenzel, 2016; Chen & Xie, 2008; Masuda et al., 2022). This will ultimately lead to the re-occurrence and rise of influencers on social media platforms which can be regarded as word-of-marketing (Lin et al., 2018) on online platforms where some research termed it as eWOM. Here is the catch – WOM is generally referred to as the transfer of information between the group after receiving information from the peer group: "Individual willingness to distribute the information to other group or not". If this individual tries to share the information or is willing to share the information, this concept can be regarded as WOM. But in the case of influencer marketing, "influencer" is the one who is triggering information in these platforms to all (Wavemaker, 2019; Oracle & Brent Leary, 2022). Once the information has been shared from the source "influencer" based on credibility and trustworthiness, it will trigger WOM in these platforms. However, in the meantime, influencer marketing has suffered from some considerable drawbacks as it is currently struggling with sincerity issues: consumers increasingly doubt the authenticity of influencers, who are more and more arbitrarily cooperating with diverse companies and multiple brands at the same time (Audrezet et al., 2020; Edelman, 2019).

As such, this study aims to uncover the influence of influencers and shopping motivation in shaping attitudes toward e-commerce apps in the context of gamification. The insights gained from this research will empower e-commerce platforms to actively engage with customers, enhance sales, and fortify their connection with consumers.

Literature Review

Gamification represents a strategic approach tailored to attract consumers with diverse needs, garnering considerable attention and necessitating a dynamic platform for interactive engagement. Coined relatively recently, this concept is closely associated with gaming elements, including elements of fun, competition, and rewards, strategically employed in nongame contexts such as websites or applications to augment brand engagement. The underlying theory centers on the idea that engaged consumers are more inclined to make purchases compared to their non-engaged counterparts. Additionally, it is conceptualized as a rather inclusive term, encompassing the integration of game mechanisms into service design to provide consumers with a game-like experience, primarily aimed at influencing user behavior (Hamari & Koivisto, 2013).

The study conducted by Bui et al. (2015) has significantly broadened the scope of gamification, extending beyond services to encompass nongame products or services aimed at steering user behavior toward the desired objectives of the brand. Integrating gaming aspects into products and services endorsed by influencers has demonstrated heightened engagement rates compared to non-gamified activities. This content not only captivates customers but also encourages them to actively participate, fostering positive word-of-mouth (WOM) for both the product and the influencer (Hsu & Chen, 2018). Hamari and Koivisto (2013) posit that social motivation serves as a mediating construct capable of shaping consumer behavior attitudes.

Social influence holds the potential to shape consumer behavioral intentions, as indicated by Hamari and Koivisto (2013), and further extends its impact to influence consumer attitudes. Nivedhitha and Manzoor's (2019) study suggests that the extent of social media usage can impact the attitudes of followers. The pivotal role of hedonic and utilitarian values in gamification is underscored, with a focus on purchase intention in studies such as those by Babin et al. (1994), Park et al. (2006), and Muruganantham and Bhakat (2013) evaluating the impact of these factors. Yang's (2010) research highlights that gamification strategies are activated through utilitarian and hedonic factors, influencing consumers. Moreover, Yang et al. (2017) identify that gamification factors significantly influence consumer attitudes, emphasizing the role of fun, entertainment, and enjoyable experiences derived from gamified activities.

In the fiercely competitive market, e-commerce and social media platforms are eager to infiltrate customers' personal chat spaces, leveraging influencers to propagate positive word-of-mouth (WOM) about their products. Survival in this competitive landscape is contingent on engaging with influencers, and success is measured by the number of followers actively involved.

The formulated hypotheses contribute to understanding the intricate relationships within influencer-driven gamification:

H1. There is a significant influence of influencer traits on hedonic factors.
H2. There is a significant influence of influencer traits on utilitarian factors.
H3. There is a significant influence of influencer traits on attitude.
H4a. There is a significant influence of utilitarian factors on continued use intention.
H4b. There is a significant influence of utilitarian factors on eWOM.
H5a. There is a significant influence of hedonic factors on continued use intention.
H5b. There is a significant influence of hedonic factors on eWOM.
H6a. There is a significant influence of attitude on continued use intention.
H6b. There is a significant influence of attitude on eWOM.
H7a and b. There is a significant influence of influencers on continued use intention and eWOM.

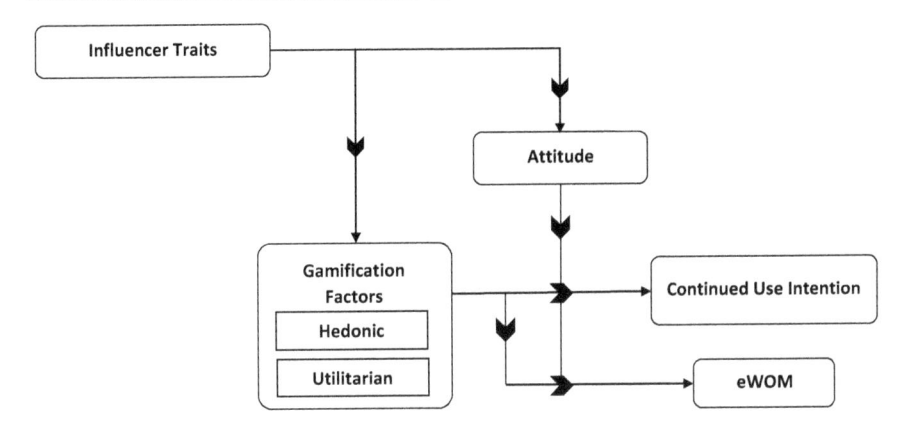

Figure 9.1 Conceptual model
Source: researchers' analysis

The influencers on social media platforms play a pivotal role in providing answers to questions, attracting people, and stimulating positive attitudes or emotions, as indicated by Kusumawardani and Putri (2020). Through gamification, consumers' continuous intention to use platforms is heightened, aligning with past research asserting that WOM is an expression of deliberate actions influenced by various needs, subsequently impacting friends' opinions and decisions (Ren et al., 2013; Berger, 2014; Kim & Son, 2009). Based on these insights, a theoretical framework has been constructed and is illustrated in Figure 9.1.

The studies related to consumer attitude have been considered to reach a level, but the studies related to consumer attitude from the perspective of consumption digital advertisement and their response to it are still in a nascent stage. The researchers study the process and consequences of across national transmission of media forms, lifestyles, and attitudes. Some researchers argue that consumers' images, preferences, and lifestyles are manipulated by social media which are substituting individual perceptions from their traditional and local cultures. Consumer attitudes toward advertisements have been generally found to be negative, though the early studies revealed that somewhat positive results have been found through informative advertisements. Those advertisements which are found to be informative have positively influenced the consumers. Bauer and Greyser study reported that if more people are favorable toward an advertisement, then unfavorable will also respond positively toward the brand. Later on, studies have only quoted that positive public opinion will positively influence the attitude of consumers. A study by Dhun and Dangi (2023) suggested that influencer source credibility describes how these influencers' perceived credibility will have a significant impact on the consumers as the influencer campaigns trigger significant engagement so that consumers can exhibit their attitude and make conversations in these platforms. In the study by Tiwari et al. (2024), influencer and consumer purchase intentions are mediated by the attitudes of these individual consumers. Furthermore, consumers' mixed attitudes influence the purchase decisions of other consumers, and influencers on social media platforms will identify and analyze consumer attitudes based on trust and distribute information – this conflicting information will influence consumers to modify their purchasing decisions (Ki et al., 2023).

Research Methodology

The study employed a quantitative survey questionnaire, incorporating a five-point Likert scale, to validate the constructed model, adapting all constructs to align with the context of gamification in social media platforms involving influencers. Responses were solicited from individuals actively engaged with influencers on social media platforms – specifically, those consistently participating in influencer activities. A total of 252 responses were gathered, chosen for their ease of data acquisition and cost-effectiveness. Additionally, data was collected through Google Forms, and questionnaires were distributed via various instant messaging services and social media platforms to ensure a diverse dataset. Following the data collection phase, Smart-PLS was employed to rigorously test the formulated hypotheses and assess the overall model. The experiment consisted of an online English language survey that asked participants to read information about the social media influencers on social media platforms. For the manipulation, we have utilized influencers' images to generate some positive output from the consumers. The online survey from the influencer pages is generally filled out by highly engaged consumers. Influencer selection has been based on criteria, to ensure we are focusing on influencers rather than celebrities. Influencers with more than 35k likes for the last ten posts have been selected as the reach for them is in millions based on observations, and an easy identification of the influencer is also a criterion.

Results

To validate the constructed model, the study employed SmartPLS, opting for Partial Least Squares Structural Equation Modeling (PLS-SEM) due to its versatility in handling non-normally distributed data. PLS-SEM is particularly advantageous in mitigating various potential human errors associated with the analysis of latent variables, rendering it a more suitable choice for research conditions when compared to alternative statistical analyses (Hair et al., 2017). The terminology shorts used for the ease of statistical analysis are mentioned in Table 9.1.

The evaluation of the constructed model involved the application of Cronbach's alpha and Composite Reliability (CR) for the constructs, while the Average Variance Extracted (AVE) was employed as a measure of latent variable

Table 9.1 Variable Heads' Terminologies

Influencer Traits	IT
Hedonic Factors	HF
Utilitarian Factors	UF
Attitude	AT
Continued Use Intention	CUI
Electronic Word-of-Mouth	eWOM

Source: researchers' analysis

Table 9.2 Model Construct

Construct	Item	Outer Loading	AVE	CR	Cronbach's Alpha	Rho_A
Reliability						
IT	IT1	0.873	0.892	0.815	0.741	0.756
	IT2	0.840				
	IT3	0.855				
	IT4	0.702				
HF	HF1	0.889	0.813	0.816	0.798	0.801
	HF2	0.715				
	HF3	0.822				
UF	UF1	0.856	0.789	0.788	0.726	0.741
	UF2	0.817				
	UF3	0.866				
AT	AT1	0.789	0.812	0.815	0.789	0.791
	AT2	0.803				
	AT3	0.816				
CUI	CUI1	0.845	0.826	0.827	0.801	0.804
	CUI2	0.855				
	CUI3	0.782				
eWOM	eWOM1	0.776	0.741	0.741	0.788	0.781
	eWOM2	0.833				
	eWOM 3	0.818				

Source: researchers' analysis

components. To enhance the robustness of the analysis, the scores were adjusted to a minimum threshold of 0.7, aligning with established practices derived from previous studies (Hair et al., 2019). The analysis is given in Table 9.2.

To establish the discriminant validity between the latent variables, the study has adopted the HTMT (Hetrotrait–Monotrait) ratio of correlations method to understand the multicollinearity issues. Table 9.3 shows that the study has established the discriminant validity.

The suggested model's R^2 values vary between 0.495 *and* 0.672, suggesting that the model has sufficient predictive capacity. All the construct hypotheses have been satisfied as the *p* value is less than 0.05 and the T-statistics is more than 1.96, as shown in Table 9.4.

Table 9.3 HTMT

	IT	HF	UF	AT	CUI	eWOM
IT						
HF	0.852					
UF	0.786	0.752				
AT	0.702	0.825	0.692			
CUI	0.825	0.872	0.789	0.825		
eWOM	0.692	0.652	0.802	0.689	0.786	

Source: researchers' analysis

Table 9.4 Construct Hypothesis

Hypothesis	Path	Path Coefficient	SE	T Statistics	p Values	Decision
H1	IT->HF	0.264	0.021	2.362	0.001	Supported
H2	IT->UF	0.41	0.253	3.215	0.000	Supported
H3	IT->AT	0.312	0.001	12.850	0.018	Supported
H4a	HF->CUI	0.125	0.074	13.520	0.000	Supported
H4b	HF->eWOM	0.047	0.002	6.890	0.000	Supported
H5a	UF->CUI	0.637	0.006	15.960	0.000	Supported
H5b	UI-> eWOM	0.551	0.221	8.570	0.011	supported
H6a	AT->CUI	0.287	0.071	3.017	0.003	Supported
H6b	AT-> eWOM	0.367	0.086	7.526	0.021	Supported
H7a	IT->CUI	0.282	0.201	1.990	0.000	Supported
H7b	IT-> eWOM	0.129	0.105	2.023	0.000	Supported

Source: researchers' analysis

From the above table observation, we can conclude that there is a significant relationship between the influencer traits and hedonic factors with ($t = 2.362; p = 0.001$) supporting the hypothesis H1. There is a significant influence of influencer traits on hedonic factors. Similarly, the relationship between influencer traits and utilitarian factors has a significant relationship with ($t = 3.215; p = 0.00$) supporting the hypothesis H2. There is a significant influence of influencer traits on utilitarian factors. The relationship between influencer traits and attitude has a significant relationship with ($t = 12.850; p = 0.018$) supporting hypothesis H3. There is a significant influence of influencer traits on attitude. Not only that, this relationship is exhibiting the strong relationship which furthermore suggests that influencer will influence the consumer attitude. The relationship between the utilitarian factor and continued use intention has a significant relationship with ($t = 15.960, p = 0.00$) supporting the hypothesis H5a as well. There is a significant influence of utilitarian factors on continued use intention. The relationship H5a exhibits the strongest relationship out of all the constructs. Stating the utilitarian factors of consumers will strongly influence consumers' continued use intention. Similarly, the relationship between the utilitarian factor and electronic word-of-mouth has a significant influence with (t = 8.570, p = 0.011) supporting the hypothesis H5b. There is a significant influence of utilitarian factors on eWOM.

The relationship between the hedonic factor and continued use intention has a significant relationship with (t = 13.520, p = 0.00) supporting the hypothesis H4a. There is a significant influence of hedonic factors on continued use intention. The relationship H4a exhibits the strongest relationship out of all the constructs. Stating the hedonic factors of consumers will strongly influence consumers' continued use intention comparatively but not as strongly as the utilitarian factor. Similarly, the relationship between the utilitarian factor and electronic word-of mouth has a significant influence with (t = 6.890, p = 0.00) supporting the hypothesis H4b. There is a significant influence of hedonic factors on eWOM.

The relationship between attitude and continued use intention has a significant relationship with (t = 3.017; p = 0.003) supporting hypothesis H6a. There is a significant influence of attitude on continued use intention.

The relationship between attitude and electronic word of mouth has a significant relationship with (t = 7.526; p = 0.021) supporting hypothesis H6b. There is a significant influence of attitude on eWOM. The relationship between influencer traits and continued use intention has a significant relationship with (t = 1.990; p = 0.00) supporting hypothesis H7a. There is a significant influence of influencers on continued use intention. The relationship between influencer traits and electronic word of mouth has a significant relationship with (t = 2.023; p = 0.00) supporting hypothesis H7b. There is a significant influence of influencers on eWOM.

Discussion and Conclusion

Owing to its surging popularity, gamification has found application across diverse nongame products and services. However, scant attention has been given to studies examining gamification within the e-commerce industry, particularly those integrating both social motivations and shopping value. The success of gamification, particularly in the e-commerce context, hinges significantly on its social dimensions. Notably, there is a notable gap in research concerning the influence of influencers in conjunction with gamification. Additionally, the study's findings revealed the fulfillment of all hypotheses. The convergence of gamification, influencer marketing, and eWOM presents a compelling opportunity for brands to not only capture attention in a crowded digital space but also nudge consumers toward purchase decisions. Gamification techniques, when thoughtfully integrated into influencer campaigns, can transform brand promotion into an interactive and engaging experience. This fosters a sense of community and motivates participation, leading to the generation of valuable user-generated content (UGC).

The investigation demonstrated that the incorporation of influencers into gamified events enhances consumer engagement, allowing brands to actively interact with users. Furthermore, this synergy can mold consumer decisions, influencing purchasing choices and fostering word-of-mouth activities on social media platforms.

The current study offers valuable insights and practical applications for marketers seeking to establish a digital presence for their brands. First, marketers can leverage influencers to create instant brand awareness and reach a vast niche audience. These influencers can be segmented on the basis of their follower base in respective fields (mega, macro, and micro) (Bergkvist & Zhou, 2016).

Establishing authenticity is a crucial factor for marketers when selecting influencers to promote brand content on social media platforms (Das et al., 2022; Eigenraam et al., 2021). This can be achieved by evaluating the level of engagement and interaction influencers have with their followers. Additionally, marketers can employ other selection methods based on influencer popularity. Several studies suggest that an influencer's credibility significantly affects consumer purchasing behavior (Chapple & Cownie, 2017; Djafarova & Rushworth, 2017). For future research suggestions, researchers could explore the mediating effect of loyalty programs with gamification elements and their impact on consumer purchase intention (Colliander & Erlandsson, 2015).

Beyond authenticity, influencer credibility significantly affects consumer purchasing behavior (Chapple & Cownie, 2017; Djafarova & Rushworth, 2017). Credible influencers who resonate with the target audience are more likely to generate positive eWOM and user-generated content (UGC) that further amplifies brand awareness and social proof. Consider an influencer who promotes a fitness tracker they genuinely use and integrates it seamlessly into their lifestyle content. Their audience is more likely to trust their recommendation and create their own UGC showcasing their experience with the tracker. This creates a snowball effect, fostering a sense of community and brand loyalty. However, the influencer-marketing landscape is constantly evolving. Future research could explore the mediating effect of loyalty programs with gamification elements on consumer purchase intention (Colliander & Erlandsson, 2015). Furthermore, investigating the interplay between influencer marketing strategies, eWOM, UGC, and even short-form video content (e.g., Reels, TikTok) could provide valuable insights into building brand communities and fostering long-term customer engagement. Optimizing influencer selection, content strategy, and engagement tactics based on these factors will be crucial for brands to stay ahead of the curve in the ever-changing digital marketing landscape.

Influencers, acting as trusted guides, can leverage gamified elements to create content that resonates with their audience. Authentic endorsements paired with interactive experiences can significantly increase brand awareness, build trust, and, ultimately, drive purchase intention. Consumers become active participants, sharing their positive experiences and recommendations through eWOM, further amplifying the brand message and influencing the behavior of others. Looking ahead, the future of marketing lies in creating a holistic experience that transcends traditional advertising methods. By embracing gamification, influencer marketing, and the power of eWOM, brands can cultivate loyal communities of engaged consumers who are not just informed but also actively involved in the brand journey. This multifaceted approach will be key to achieving sustainable success in the ever-evolving digital marketing landscape. In terms of future research directions, it is suggested that researchers explore the mediation effects, particularly focusing on loyalty in the context of gamification and its impact on consumers' purchase intentions. This would contribute to a deeper understanding of the nuanced relationships and dynamics within the gamification landscape in e-commerce.

References

Acikgoz, F., & Burnaz, S. (2021). The influence of "influencer marketing" on YouTube influencers. *International Journal of Internet Marketing and Advertising*, *15*(2), 201–219. https://doi.org/10.1504/IJIMA.2021.114331

Audrezet, A., de Kerviler, G., & Moulard, J. (2020). Authenticity under threat: When social media influencers need to go beyond self-presentation. *Journal of Business Research*, *117*, 557–569.

Babin, B. J., Darden, W. R., & Griffin, M. (1994). Work and/or fun: Measuring hedonic and utilitarian shopping value. *Journal of Consumer Research*, *20*(4), 644–566.

Barnes, B. K. (2015). The ethics of influence: Doing well by doing good. In *Exercising Influence* (pp. 93–98). https://doi.org/10.1002/9781119158523.ch16

Bashari, B., & Fazl-ersi, E. (2020). Influential post identification on Instagram through caption and hashtag analysis. *Measurement and Control*, 1–7. https://doi.org/https://doi.org/10.1177%2F0020294019877489

Belanche, D., Casaló, L. V., Flavián, M., & Ibáñez-Sánchez, S. (2021, March). Understanding influencer marketing: The role of congruence between influencers, products and consumers. *Journal of Business Research*, *132*, 186–195. https://doi.org/10.1016/j.jbusres.2021.03.067

Belanche, D., Flavián, M., & Ibáñez-Sánchez, S. (2020). Followers' reactions to influencers' Instagram posts. *Spanish Journal of Marketing – ESIC*, *24*(1), 37–54. https://doi.org/10.1108/SJME-11-2019-0100

Berger, J. (2014). Word-of-mouth and interpersonal communication: A review and directions for future research. *Journal of Consumer Psychology*, *24*(4), 586–607.

Bergkvist, L., & Zhou, K. Q. (2016). Celebrity endorsements: A literature review and research agenda. *International Journal of Advertising*, *35*(4), 642–663.

Bui, A., Veit, D., & Webster, J. (2015). *Gamification – a novel phenomenon or a new wrapping for existing concepts?* (pp. 1–21). Thirty Sixth International Conference on Information Systems, International Conference on Information Systems, Fort Worth, TX.

Chapple, C., & Cownie, F. (2017). An investigation into viewers' trust in and response towards disclosed paid-for endorsements by YouTube lifestyle vloggers. *Journal of Promotional Communications*, *5*(2).

Chen, Y., & Xie, J. (2008). Online consumer review: Word-of-mouth as a new element of marketing communication mix. *Management Science, 54*(3), 477–491.

Colliander, J., & Erlandsson, S. (2015). The blog and the bountiful: Exploring the effects of disguised product placement on blogs that are revealed by a third party. *Journal of Marketing Communications, 21*(2), 110–124.

Das, M., Jebarajakirthy, C., & Sivapalan, A. (2022). How consumption values and perceived brand authenticity inspire fashion masstige purchase? An investigation. *Journal of Retailing and Consumer Services, 68*, 103023.

Dhun, & Dangi, H. K. (2023). Influencer marketing: Role of influencer credibility and congruence on brand attitude and eWOM. *Journal of Internet Commerce, 22*(sup1), S28–S72.

Djafarova, E., & Rushworth, C. (2017). Exploring the credibility of online celebrities' Instagram profiles in influencing the purchase decisions of young female users. *Computers in Human Behavior, 68*, 1–7.

Edelman, R. (2019). *Edelman trust barometer special report: In brands we trust?* Edelman.

Eigenraam, A. W., Eelen, J., & Verlegh, P. W. (2021). Let me entertain you? The importance of authenticity in online customer engagement. *Journal of Interactive Marketing, 54*, 53–68.

Hair, J. F., Black, W. C., Babin, B. J., & Anderson, R. E. (2019). *Multivariate data analysis* (8th ed.). Cengage Learning.

Hair, J. F., Hult, G. T., Ringle, C. M., & Sarstedt, M. (2017). *A primer on partial least squares structural equation modeling (PLS-SEM)* (2nd ed.). Sage.

Hamari, J., & Koivisto, J. (2013). Social motivations to use gamification: An empirical study of gamifying exercise. In *Proceedings of the 21st European conference on information system, ECIS 2013 Proceedings, Utrecht, 105–117.* http://aisel.aisnet.org/ecis2013_cr

Hsu, C.-L., & Chen, M.-C. (2018). How does gamification improve user experience? An empirical investigation on the antecedences and consequences of user experience and its mediating role. *Technological Forecasting and Social Change, 132*, 118–129.

Ki, C. W., Chow, T. C., & Li, C. (2023). Bridging the trust gap in influencer marketing: Ways to sustain consumers' trust and assuage their distrust in the social media influencer landscape. *International Journal of Human–Computer Interaction, 39*(17), 3445–3460.

Kim, S. S., & Son, J.-Y. (2009). Out of dedication or constraint? A dual model of post-adoption phenomena and its empirical test in the context of online services. *MIS Quarterly, 33*(1), 49–70.

Kusumawardani, K. A., & Putri, F. R. (2020). Exploring the behavioural intention in culinary tourism: A study on Bandung tourist destination. *Global Research on Tourism Development and Advancement, 2*(1), 63–81.

Lee, J. A., Bright, L. F., & Eastin, M. S. (2021). Fear of missing out and consumer happiness on Instagram: A serial mediation of social media influencer-related activities. *Cyberpsychology, Behavior, and Social Networking.* https://doi.org/10.1089/cyber.2020.0431

Lin, H. C., Bruning, P., & Swarna, H. (2018). Using online opinion leaders to promote the hedonic and utilitarian value of products and services. *Business Horizons, 61*, 431–442.

Lou, C., Tan, S. S., & Chen, X. (2019). Investigating consumer engagement with influencer- vs. brand-promoted ads: The roles of source and disclosure. *Journal of Interactive Advertising, 19*(3), 169–186. https://doi.org/10.1080/15252019.2019.1667928

Masuda, H., Han, S. H., & Lee, J. (2022). Impacts of influencer attributes on purchase intentions in social media influencer marketing: Mediating roles of characterizations. *Technological Forecasting and Social Change, 174,* 121246.

Muruganantham, G., & Bhakat, R. (2013). A review of impulse buying behavior. *International Journal of Marketing Studies, 6*(10), 55–59.

Nivedhitha, K. S., & Manzoor, A. K. (2019). Gamification inducing creative ideation: A parallel mediation model. *Behaviour and Information Technology, 39*(9), 1–25.

Oracle & Brent Leary. (2022, May 3). *37% of consumers trust social media influencers over brands* [Press release]. https://www.oracle.com/at/news/announcement/consumers-turn-to-social-media-influencers-2022-05-03/

Park, E. J., Kim, E. Y., & Forney, J. C. (2006). A structural model of fashion-oriented impulse buying behavior. *Journal of Fashion Marketing and Management, 1*(5), 28–34.

Ren, L. C., Wu, M., & Lu, J. T. (2013). Research on the classification of reviewers in online auction. *International Journal of Computer Science Issues, 2*(10), 26–35.

Sumarliah, E., Usmanova, K., Mousa, K., & Indriya, I. (2021). E-commerce in the fashion business: The roles of the COVID-19 situational factors, hedonic and utilitarian motives on consumers' intention to purchase online. *International Journal of Fashion Design, Technology and Education, 15*(2), 1–11.

Tabellion, J., & Esch, F.-R. (2019). Influencer marketing and its impact on the advertised brand. In *Advances in advertising research X* (pp. 29–41). https://doi.org/10.1007/978-3-658-24878-9_3

Tiwari, A., Kumar, A., Kant, R., & Jaiswal, D. (2024). Impact of fashion influencers on consumers' purchase intentions: theory of planned behaviour and mediation of attitude. *Journal of Fashion Marketing and Management, 28*(2), 209–225.

Wavemaker. (2019). *Spotlight influencer 4.0 [report].* Retrieved September 28, 2022, from https://wavemakerglobal.com/de/wp-content/uploads/sites/4/2020/10/mSCIENCE_Spotlight-Influencer-4.0_Oktober-2019.pdf

Wenzel, B. (2016). Einfluss gewinnen mit influencer marketing. *Internet World Business, 14,* 18–19.

Yang, Y. (2010). Determinants of US consumer mobile shopping services adoption: Implications for designing mobile shopping services. *Journal of Consumer Marketing, 27*(3), 262–270.

Yang, Y., Asaad, Y., & Dwivedi, Y. (2017). Examining the impact of gamification on intention of engagement and brand attitude in the marketing context. *Computers in Human Behavior, 73,* 459–469.

Yudhoatmojo, S. B., & Ramadana, R. (2016). *Analysis on gamification features usage on Indonesia E-commerce sites using catalysis framework.* The 2nd International HCI and UX Conference, Parahyangan Catholic University, Jakarta.

Chapter 10

Gamified Communication in Social Media for Brand Advocacy of Start-Ups

Radhika Baidya, Dharmendra Kumar and Daniel Omer Livvarcin

Introduction

Start-ups struggle to create an online presence and build a dedicated following in the highly competitive social media market (AlSaad & Durugbo, 2021). They use creativity to stand out and succeed. Gamified communication has improved brand support for social media start-ups (Hamari et al., 2014). Gamified communication combines gaming with persuasive communication to create an engaging experience (Cavalcanti et al., 2021). Start-Ups may increase audience engagement and create an immersive experience by gamifying social media interactions (Hamari et al., 2023). Points, rewards, badges, and leaderboards encourage user engagement in debates, brand sharing, and start-up promotion (Mesko et al., 2015).

Gamified communication makes loyal customers enthusiastic brand champions. Users may earn points and prizes for advocacy and interactions, strengthening their start-up relationship (Love et al., 2016). Success and recognition promote loyalty and motivate individuals to share their positive experiences with friends and online. Challenges and quests may boost brand advocacy for start-ups (Lam et al., 2022). Referral networks and user-generated content contests may attract customers. Incentives and the pleasure of significant contributions and a thriving community motivate users to give their time, knowledge, and resources, fostering continuous engagement and collaboration within the platform (AlSaad & Durugbo, 2021).

Brand supporters may follow and evaluate start-ups' growth via progress tracking. As they advance in their employment, their start-up allegiance rises (Arroyo & Wan, 2019). Progress motivates people to enthusiastically support a company, providing unbeatable word-of-mouth marketing (Kapp, 2012). Gamified communication needs fast feedback. Start-ups may use it to increase communication, discover audience preferences, and address problems swiftly (Marcial et al., 2021). Start-ups may build relationships with advocates via proactive involvement, creating inclusiveness and appreciation (Al-Zyoud, 2021).

The immersive and rewarding experience of gaming in communication may inspire brand champions on many social media platforms (Armstrong, 2013).

DOI: 10.4324/9781032694238-14

Gamified communication has helped start-ups compete on social media. The product inspires, empowers, and engages consumers (Jakubowski, 2014). Let the games begin, and may bold start-ups succeed in digital brand marketing (Al-Zyoud, 2021).

Background of the Study

Gamified social media brand marketing may aid competitive start-ups. Start-ups may reach numerous clients and brand evangelists via social media (Marczewski, 2013). Start-ups face challenges in establishing their brand recognition and building trust (Huotari & Hamari, 2012). Gamified communication solves these issues creatively and interactively. Gamification in social media marketing may enhance start-up brand engagement (Aparicio et al., 2012; Paruthi et al., 2023).

Gamification components like points, incentives, and badges encourage content sharing, start-up promotion, and social media engagement (Armstrong, 2013) Customer loyalty and brand advocacy grow. Leaderboards enhance start-up word-of-mouth and organic spreading by encouraging competition (Huseynov, 2020). Quests and challenges help start-ups attract clients and highlight USPs. Users' brand loyalty increases with rank, generating a sense of community (Basten, 2017).

Start-up communication and products may benefit from real-time client feedback. Social media establishes startup-brand advocate trust and authenticity (Bilro et al., 2021). Social media gamification engages customers and turns them into brand ambassadors, increasing corporate growth (Kankanhalli et al., 2012).

Research Questions

1. How does the use of gamified communication techniques affect brand advocacy for start-ups on social media platforms?
2. What gamified communication strategies do start-ups use to promote brand advocacy on social media, and how do these strategies affect user engagement and loyalty?
3. What challenges and limitations do start-ups encounter when using gamified communication strategies on social media platforms for brand advocacy?
4. How do start-ups incorporate gamified communication techniques into their marketing and branding strategies?

Research Objectives

The objectives of the research are to:

• Evaluate the influence of gamified communication techniques on the development of brand advocacy for start-ups in social media platforms.

- Identify and analyze successful gamified communication strategies employed by start-ups to promote brand advocacy on social media.
- Examine the level of social gratification of gamified communication initiatives in the context of brand advocacy for start-ups.
- Investigate the challenges and limitations faced by start-ups when implementing gamified communication strategies on social media platforms for brand advocacy.

Review of Literature

Gamification and Gamification Communication

Gamification is applying game aspects and tactics to nongame circumstances to boost engagement and motivation (Wood & Reiners, 2015). Gamification uses points, certificates, leaderboards, and prizes to make tedious and repetitive tasks fun and interesting (Conaway & Garay, 2014; Mitchell et al., 2017). This method is used in education, marketing, and staff training to encourage good behavior and achieve goals (De-Marcos et al., 2016).

User engagement via gamification harnesses human instincts for competitiveness, achievement, and acknowledgment. Leaderboards promote friendly competition, while points and symbols demonstrate achievements (Arroyo & Wan, 2019). Challenges and goals boost excitement, while incentives motivate involvement (Widawska-Stanisz, 2014). Users are engaged by several levels or stages, and narrative aspects improve immersion (Hewapathirana & Caldera, 2023; Amelia, 2020).

Effective communication in gamification is essential for user understanding and adoption. Simple interfaces and instructions aid gamification (Basten, 2017; Mustikasari et al., 2022). A compelling story connects consumers emotionally, while timely feedback helps them grow (Xi & Hamari, 2019). Organizations clearly communicate the gamified system's rules, goals, and rewards to inspire players (Hofacker et al., 2016).

Gamification motivates and engages different workers. This system appeals to our drive for success and rivalry with points, badges, challenges, and prizes (Hsu, 2023; Mitchell et al., 2017). Gamification requires good communication to guide users and provide a meaningful experience (Mustikasari et al., 2022). Gamification increases engagement and helps accomplish goals by integrating game elements and strong communication (Kim et al., 2019).

Establishment of Feedback Loop

Users should be allowed to provide comments and questions about gamification. Addressing user concerns boosts engagement (Volkova, 2013). Effectively communicating gamification's benefits, principles, and goals may boost user engagement and encourage desired behaviors (Vitkauskaitė & Gatautis, 2018). Effective gamification communication connects consumers' understanding and active engagement, resulting in positive results (Hsu & Chen, 2018).

Gamification and Social Media

Social networking and gamification may work. Gamification may make social media more engaging, rewarding, and meaningful to retain users (Sultan & Suhail, 2019). Here are some examples of how gamification may be used in social media.

Contests and challenges are social media-friendly – examples being user contributions, sharing, and brand behavior. Rewards encourage content sharing and engagement (Huang & Saravanakumar, 2018). Users may get virtual tokens or rewards for social media actions. They may proudly display these honors on profiles (Zatwarnicka-Madura, 2015; Seaborn & Fels, 2015). User-generated content and engagement leaderboards encourage friendly rivalry. Leaderboards encourage climbs (Robson et al., 2015). Firms may incentivize likes, shares, and remarks and use experience points to reward user progress (Sgueo, 2018). Gamification may provide your most engaged social media followers exclusive content, discounts, and more. Belonging and recurring business increase as loyal followers feel valued and are incentivized to return, leading to stronger brand loyalty and long-term customer relationships (Marczewski, 2013; Kim, 2015). Consumers can be invited to post brand tales and comments on social media. Videos and photographs should be created and hashtagged (Sailer et al., 2017). Polls, quizzes, and trivia may be used in Facebook Live and Instagram Live broadcasts and seminars (Spais et al., 2022). Instant communication activates real-time interaction, fostering engagement and enhancing the viewer experience by making it more dynamic and participatory. Voting and commenting on polls involve people in important choices (Richter et al., 2015). Customers are involved and decide the company's future. Interactive advertising that feels like games (Stieglitz et al., 2017) enhances user engagement by making marketing efforts more enjoyable, thereby increasing brand loyalty and the likelihood of customer participation in promotional activities. Offering discounts and other incentives to advertising users may enhance the experience (Garcia et al., 2022). To boost self-esteem and belonging, users should be encouraged to work together on problems. User-generated content matters most (Streukens et al., 2019). Gratitude may be shown by highlighting user-generated content on social media. Collaboration and respect and friendliness may increase (Kim et al., 2019).

Matching brand personality and audience preferences makes social media gamification perform best (Thorpe & Roper, 2019). Social media may benefit from game-like activities and rewards to boost user engagement and brand loyalty (Dymek & Zackariasson, 2016).

Social Gratification through Gamified Communication

Gamification aids socializing. Gamification and social interaction make this method rewarding and community-driven (Nicholson, 2015). A thorough description of social pleasure via gamified communication is given next.

Gamification rewards users with badges, levels, and leaderboards. Social prestige comes with this acknowledgment (Ebrahim, 2021). Badges or leaderboards for engaged users, quality content, and goal accomplishment strengthen communities. Gamification fosters community (Fuchs et al., 2014). Participants collaborate on challenges, conversations, and objectives. This group fosters networking, support, and sociability (Nobre & Ferreira, 2017). Gaming is competitive and cooperative. Teamwork on missions and challenges promotes camaraderie. Leaderboards and tournaments spark energy (Kim, 2013). Gamified communication includes likes, remarks, and shares. Instant social feedback gives buyers peer acceptance (Noorbehbahani et al., 2019). Positive engagement incentives improve conduct. Sharing stories, images, and videos engages (Lam et al., 2022). Highlighting user-generated content (UGC) strengthens communities and voices. Participation in gamified communication may unlock special material or perks (Robson et al., 2015). We encourage user participation and involvement to get these special advantages (Permana et al., 2021). Gamified communication enables profiles to have badges and medals. Personalization enhances group recognition and user satisfaction (Sgueo, 2018). Experiences are shared via collaboration. Charity and group projects foster togetherness (Richter et al., 2015). Live-streaming quizzes and competitions increase engagement. Competing, answering questions, and chatting with hosts and other players make the game social and competitive (Seaborn & Fels, 2015). Gamified communication combines social interaction with gamification's driving qualities to engage, connect, and satisfy users (Lam et al., 2022). Sharing experiences and triumphs increases user loyalty, engagement, and community pleasure (Sailer et al., 2017).

Gamification Strategy to the Increase Brand Advocacy of Start-Ups

Happy customers, workers, and other stakeholders enthusiastically advocate for a company's products and services (Pellikka, 2014). Advocacy happens when customers enthusiastically recommend a firm, share positive experiences, and spread word-of-mouth marketing (Noorbehbahani et al., 2019). This kind of marketing is generally driven by loyalty, trust, and an emotional connection to the brand (Singla & Gupta, 2019; Papamichael et al., 2022).

Well-planned gamification may improve brand support by engaging users. Start-ups should first determine audience preferences, drives, and pain points (Öztürk & Hersono, 2023). User-friendly gaming systems will follow this concept. Points, medals, and leaderboards may reward consumers for utilizing start-ups' goods (Hamari et al., 2014). By encouraging users to share their triumphs on social media and earn more prizes in the gamified system, businesses may build brand support (Dymek & Zackariasson, 2016). Start-ups may use social sharing to capitalize on consumers' thirst for attention and organically grow their brand (Gatautis et al., 2016). Gamification may also establish referral schemes. Gain incentives and levels by adding friends or connections, fostering community and passion. Word-of-mouth advertising increases users (Permana et al., 2021; Ebrahim, 2021), amplifying brand reach as users become advocates, spreading the message organically and contributing to the platform's growth through personal endorsements and network effects. Progress increases users' emotional engagement in the tale and relationship with the firm and its goal. Personalized gamification is key (Öztürk & Hersono, 2023; Groh, 2012). User engagement demands constant change. Start-ups should provide fresh challenges, events, and incentives to engage users (Papamichael et al., 2022; Prince, 2013). Start-ups may engage brand champions by offering a gratifying, social, and tailored experience that feeds their interests and promotes organic growth and long-term success (Raj & Gupta, 2018).

Conceptual Framework

The research study on this chapter is grounded on established ideas and concepts, which serve as a robust basis for the investigation. The Social Identity Theory suggests (Figure 10.1) that gamified social media communication enhances brand advocacy by connecting customers to a business. The Uses and Gratifications Theory explains user engagement, while the Psychological Ownership Theory suggests that engaging experiences boost psychological ownership.

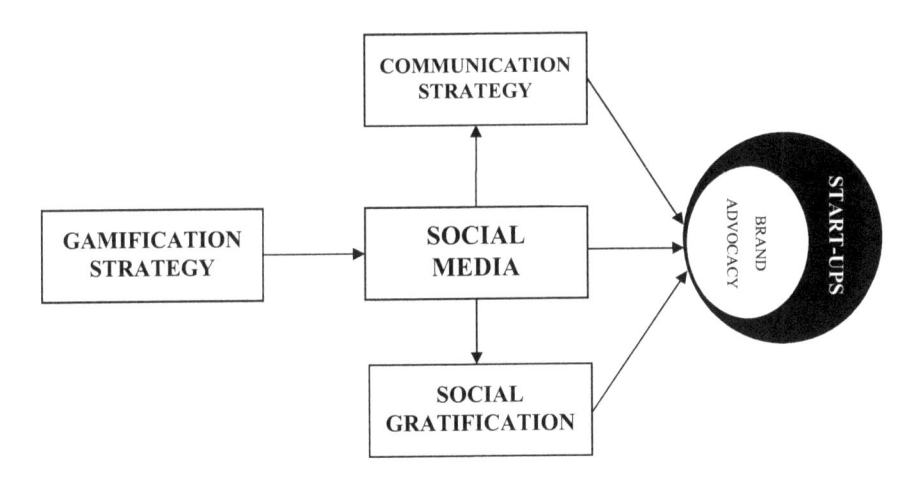

Figure 10.1 Conceptual framework

Source: researchers' own analysis

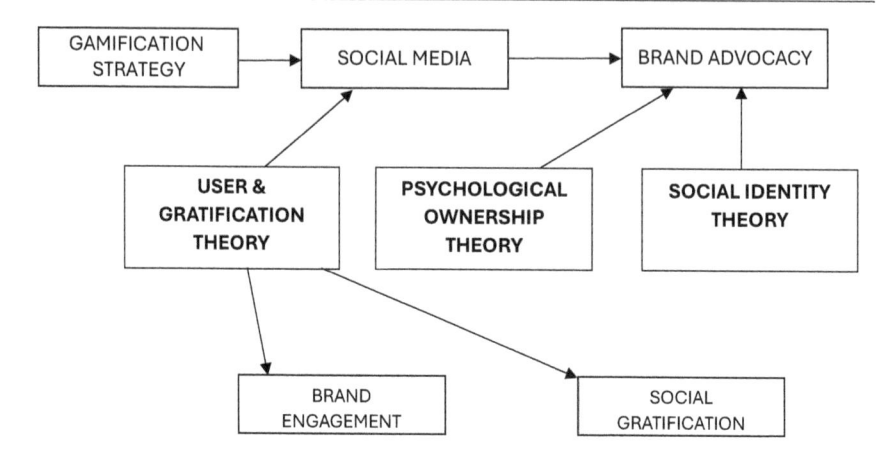

Figure 10.2 Theoretical framework
Source: researchers' own analysis

Constructs Applied in the Research Study

The study explores the relationship between gamified communication and brand advocacy for start-ups on social media (Figure 10.2). It uses Social Identity Theory, Uses and Gratifications Theory, Psychological Ownership Theory, and Brand Attachment to understand the motivations, social gratification, and brand engagement of users. The findings will guide empirical research to test the relationship between gamified communication and brand advocacy in social media marketing.

Research Methodology

The research employed qualitative case study analysis that analyses via interpretation. This research also uses qualitative content analysis to assess case study material, providing a deeper understanding of the underlying themes and patterns. This approach enables the researcher to explore complex phenomena within their real-life context, offering rich insights that contribute to the development of theoretical frameworks and practical applications. Case study data analysis should spark qualitative content analysis. Secondary data supports theoretical concepts and discussion in this study. Descriptive analysis was used to draw conclusions from several sources based on comprehensive and relevant real-world qualities. The case study matches theoretical data collection and analysis assumptions with triangulation data convergence. Comprehensive interview data was used to create a case study for analysis and conclusions.

Research Strategy

The study used a specific field technique for ethical case studies, collecting data from social media and website sources. The researcher obtained informed permission from participants and ensured data security and validity. The study used published material, bean social media, and website observations, and all participants were anonymous. Data interpretation and reporting provided objective results, and ethics in data collection addressed privacy, permission, and biases. The researchers used four rounds of case analysis to explore various viewpoints in the stories created from start-up brand websites. The study employed four-stage analysis, including foundational research, literature search, four rounds of case study analysis, and a well-established theoretical framework. The study also examined complex event context and mechanisms, focusing on behavior, interactions, and traits.

Data Analysis and Interpretation

The researcher collected ethical data from social media and website sources, obtaining informed permission and safeguarding data. They coded and analyzed the data, removing duplicates and privacy-risky PII. The study's credibility was maintained through anonymous participants, and ethical data management was employed. The researcher used four rounds of case analysis to explore diverse viewpoints from start-up brand websites, enhancing efforts and techniques for growth and development.

Four Phases of Case Analysis

Example data came from start-up websites and social media channels. Case study stages are examined using the case study technique. Website and social media observational notes were used to build case studies, preserving theoretical flexibility. Instrument and strategy that encompassed varied responder opinions were built on dedicated labor. The analysis is given in Tables 10.1, 10.2, 10.3, 10.4, and 10.5.

Table 10.1 Phases of Case Analysis

Four Phases of Case Study Analysis			
Foundation Phase	*Pre-Field Phase*	*Field Phase*	*Reporting Phase*
i. Philosophical and Sociological Consideration	Data selection and observation	Choosing relevant content for case development	Case study reporting
ii. Research Logic Consideration	Design the methodology for goal achievement	Interaction on social media pages of the brand	Case study reporting
iii. Ethical Consideration	Case study protocol	Securing the personal information of users on social media	Clearly disclosed the potential outcome of the case study to the participants

Source: researchers' own analysis

Table 10.2 Process of Data Analysis from the Case Study

Sl. No.	Case Description	Participant Description	Relationship Description	Field Protocol
1.	The BYJU'S Case study	The participants of BYJU'S are school students, competitive exam aspirants, college students, parents	Personalized learning, engaging content, convenience and accessibility, exam preparation, holistic learning, continuous support, positive brand image, lifelong learning	Identification of specific social media pages and websites for the collection of relevant data. Compliance of ethical standards by obtaining an informed consent from the participants on the social media.
2.	Oyo Rooms	Travelers and guests seeking affordable and comfortable accommodation, budget-conscious tourists, business travelers, property owners/partners, OYO staff and employees	Convenience and affordability, consistency and standardization, user-friendly platform, customer support, property partnerships, feedback loop, promotions, and loyalty programs	The identification of specific social media pages and websites for the collection of relevant data. Compliance of ethical standards by obtaining informed consents from the participants on the social media.
3.	Swiggy	Swiggy's social media and apps are used by families, office workers, and groups searching for quick meals at many restaurants, cafés, fast-food chains, and fine-dining places. Swiggy support, delivery partners	Convenience and variety, efficiency and timeliness, reliability, restaurant visibility, delivery partners' feedback and improvement, restaurant partnership, promotions, and offers	Identification of specific social media pages and websites for the collection of relevant data. Compliance of ethical standards by obtaining informed consent from the participants on the social media.

(Continued)

Table 10.2 (Continued)

Sl. No.	Case Description	Participant Description	Relationship Description	Field Protocol
4.	Paytm	Users, individuals, businesses, and organizations. Users' mobile recharges, bill payments, money transfers, online shopping, booking tickets, and more. Paytm caters to people looking for convenient digital payment options, merchants and businesses, banking customers, service providers	Digital convenience and accessibility, cashless transactions, user engagement and loyalty, merchant empowerment, financial inclusion, consumer services, e-commerce platform, digital wallet, customer support	Identification of specific social media pages and websites for the collection of relevant data. Compliance of ethical standards by obtaining informed consent from the participants on the social media.
5.	Zomato	Users, clients, participants are individuals who use the platform to explore restaurants, view menus, read reviews, and place orders for food delivery; food enthusiasts, diners, and people seeking convenient food options, restaurants and food establishments, delivery partners	Restaurant discovery, convenience and food delivery, reviews and recommendations, business for restaurants, delivery efficiency, customer support, promotions and offers, contactless ordering and payments, technology integration for restaurants, global presence	Identification of specific social media pages and websites for the collection of relevant data. Compliance of ethical standards by obtaining informed consent from the participants on the social media.
6.	Cure.fit	Cure.fit's primary participants are individuals who are interested in improving their overall health and well-being, access a variety of fitness classes, healthy meals, mental wellness resources, and healthcare services through the platform; fitness enthusiasts; nutrition seekers; mental wellness advocates	Convenience and accessibility, engagement and motivation, health tracking, healthy meals, mental wellness, healthcare services, customer support, branding and community, subscription models	Identification of specific social media pages and websites for the collection of relevant data. Compliance of ethical standards by obtaining the informed consent from the participants on the social media.

Source: researchers' own analysis

Table 10.3 Framework of Case Study Consideration

Sl. No.	Philosophical Consideration	Research Logic Consideration	Ethical Consideration
1.	Interpretive paradigm was explored.	Through semi-structured interviews and deductive approach, experiences were considered.	The participants were fully aware of their roles. Privacy and confidentiality were maintained.
2.	The philosophical differences of perspective in research areas were explored. The social processes and phenomenon were explained to the participants to measure the effect of folk media on the growth and development.	Semi-structured interviews, deductive research logic. Documents used were emails.	The consent was taken before the interview process, and no deception was there at any stage of the research process.

Source: researchers' own analysis

Table 10.4 Gamification Strategies

Sl. No	Gamification Strategies	Remarks
1.	Contests and Challenges	Start-ups often run brand-related content contests. We may design a logo, write original subtitles, or show new product uses. Social media user-generated content engages participants and promotes the brand.
2.	Rewards and Loyalty Programs	Gamified loyalty programs are widespread among start-ups. Purchases, content sharing, referrals, and other brand engagements earn points or incentives. These prizes keep consumers engaged and promote the brand for more benefits.
3.	Interactive Quizzes and Polls	Quick tests and polls boost participation. To test consumers' knowledge and publicize results, start-ups offer industry, product, or belief quizzes. Brand support and value may increase via polls that include people.
4.	Achievement Badges and Milestones	Start-up achievement systems provide digital badges, awards, or titles for tasks or accomplishments. These badges allow users to display their achievements and promote the brand.
5.	User-Generated Content Campaigns	Helping users develop and share brand-related content, start-ups engage users. Sharing photos, videos, critical reviews, or personal suggestions is possible. UGC humanizes the brand and promotes customer interaction.

Source: researchers' own analysis

Table 10.5 Social Gratification of Gamified Communication Initiatives

Sl. No.	Social Gratification	Remarks
1.	Recognition and Achievement	Achievement badges and medals let users feel appreciated. Prizes and achievements increase self-esteem and brand recognition, enhancing social satisfaction.
2.	Belonging and Community	Gamified community-building firms let customers meet others with similar interests. Sharing experiences via collaborative activities or places boosts social happiness.
3.	Social Interaction	Contests, quizzes, and polls promote sociability. Engaging discussions, exchanging thoughts, and participating establish genuine connections. These events meet a person's social need and boosts their social happiness.
4.	Personal Expression	User-generated content lets users express themselves and share new brand experiences. Users' self-expression and social pleasure increase when the start-up appreciates and spreads their content.
5.	Social Validation	Gamification elements like user voting or peer recognition may validate communication endeavors via social validation. Validated views increase self-esteem and social satisfaction.

Source: researchers' own analysis

Case Story of BYJU

BYJU'S has revolutionized the Indian education system by leveraging technology and innovative pedagogical methods. Its success story showcases the potential for EdTech start-ups to address gaps in traditional education systems, improve learning outcomes, and make quality education accessible to a wider audience. As it continues to grow and evolve, BYJU'S remains a key player in shaping the future of education in India and beyond. As key innovative feature, BYJU'S used interactive quizzes and assessments to engage the customer. The interactive quizzes and assessments help students practice what they've learned and track their progress. Immediate feedback and explanations are provided to reinforce learning. As a gamification element to keep students motivated and engaged, BYJU'S incorporates points, rewards, and leaderboards. This encourages healthy competition and a sense of achievement.

Case Story of OYO Rooms

OYO Rooms, an Indian company, brought about a significant transformation in the cheap hotel sector via the implementation of standardization and digitalization processes for affordable lodgings. OYO has established partnerships with inexpensive hotels, resulting in their conversion into standardized establishments that are efficiently managed and equipped with advanced technology. The company offered a streamlined booking process through their mobile application and website. OYO's business strategy, characterized by innovation and a technology-driven approach, has significantly disrupted the conventional hotel booking procedure, hence enhancing the accessibility of economical and high-quality lodgings for visitors. The achievement of the company resulted in a rapid growth, both domestically inside India and on a global scale. OYO Rooms employs gamification as a strategy, whereby social media competitions and challenges are organized to incentivize the user engagement via the completion of certain tasks. These tasks include activities such as sharing personal travel experiences, uploading imaginative photographs, or solving travel and accommodation-related riddles. Participants were awarded points, badges, and awards as a result of their active involvement, so fostering a feeling of accomplishment and a competitive atmosphere. OYO Rooms has implemented a gamified loyalty program on social media, whereby users are able to accumulate virtual check-ins or points by actively participating with the brand's content, sharing posts, providing reviews, and recommending friends. Subsequently, these points may be exchanged for discounts, upgrades, or other privileged incentives.

Case Story of Swiggy

Swiggy, an Indian-based meal delivery firm, successfully introduced a disruptive innovation to the food delivery sector by providing a user-friendly and streamlined platform for customers to order food from a diverse selection of eateries. The company implemented a real-time order tracking system, expedited delivery services, and a user-friendly mobile application that facilitated meal ordering with little user input. Swiggy's strategic emphasis on logistics, technology, and customer experience has facilitated the acquisition of a substantial market share and the reconfiguration of food ordering practices, hence augmenting convenience and expanding choices for customers. Swiggy organizes social media challenges whereby people are motivated to engage in food-related chores or challenges. Participants are requested to replicate a well-recognized culinary preparation originating from a dining establishment that is accessible via the Swiggy platform and thereafter disseminate their own renditions by using a designated hashtag. Prizes or discounts are awarded to the submissions that demonstrate the highest level of creativity or aesthetic appeal. Swiggy offers customers the opportunity to participate in virtual gastronomic expeditions, showcasing various towns or areas renowned for their culinary traditions. Instagram Stories and Facebook Live are used as platforms to exhibit renowned culinary offerings from diverse eateries, providing consumers with a sensory experience of distinct flavors and fostering a desire to patronize these establishments.

Case Story of Paytm

Paytm was founded in 2010 as a firm specializing in financial technology and digital payments. Paytm, an Indian enterprise, is acknowledged for its role in introducing a transformative phase in financial transactions due to the development of a robust digital payment's infrastructure. Mobile wallet services were created, enabling individuals to conveniently pay bills and make online purchases without the need for physical currency. Paytm capitalized on the increasing prevalence of smartphones in India and successfully navigated the challenges related to establishing confidence in digital transactions. The accomplishments of the company enabled it to diversify its operations into sectors such as finance, insurance, and investments, so contributing to its emergence as one of the most prosperous fintech enterprises in India. Paytm organizes tournaments known as "refer-and-earn" with the aim of incentivizing consumers to invite their acquaintances and relatives to avail themselves of the service. One has the potential to get monetary incentives or other forms of rewards via the act of introducing new users. Paytm used its diverse range of social media channels to organize cashback challenges, whereby users are encouraged to engage in purchases and then employ hashtags to either accompany images of their receipts or their transaction identification numbers. Participants are eligible to be included in a randomized selection process, whereby they have the opportunity to potentially receive monetary reimbursement or other forms of incentives. Paytm customers engage in interactive polls on their financial and lifestyle preferences. Customers are provided with unique incentives in the form of exclusive discounts or rebates, regardless of whether they choose for cash transactions or use digital currencies.

Case Story of Zomato

Zomato, an Indian-based firm, first emerged as a platform for discovering restaurants and then transformed into a multifaceted food services enterprise. The platform furnished customers with comprehensive data pertaining to eateries, including details on menus, reviews, and ratings. Subsequently, Zomato extended its operations to include meal delivery services, capitalizing on its extensive network of restaurants. The app and website, known for their user-friendly interface, quickly gained popularity among users in search of dining suggestions and meal delivery services. Zomato's adept integration of technology into the food business has significantly contributed to its extensive appeal and worldwide reach. Zomato employs gamification strategies and incorporates game aspects in order to effectively captivate their target audience and enhance brand promotion. Zomato organizes gastronomic challenges on social media platforms, aimed at motivating people to try novel dining establishments, diverse culinary traditions, and unfamiliar gastronomic offerings. Individuals engage in the act of sharing their own experiences at dining establishments, visual depictions of food items, or evaluations of restaurants by using a designated hashtag. Individuals who successfully complete the challenges are eligible to get badges, incentives, or discounts. Zomato has included interactive games aimed at fostering user engagement and facilitating the exploration of novel culinary options. Participants engage in a gaming activity whereby they are required to correctly associate food descriptions with their respective dish titles or components. Accurate responses result in exclusive incentives or promotional vouchers.

Case Story of Cure.fit

Cure.fit is an Indian health and wellness company that was founded in 2016. The integration of exercise, nutrition, and mental well-being services into a holistic platform has attracted significant interest within the health and wellness industry. The major aim of the organization is to promote and enhance the overall well-being of people, while also striving to make the advantages of a healthy lifestyle accessible to a wide variety of persons from varied backgrounds. This is accomplished via a unique amalgamation of technical progress, educational content, and customized encounters. Cure.fit offers a diverse selection of live and on-demand fitness courses, including activities such as yoga, meditation, and training sessions. These programs may be conveniently accessed via the specialized Cure.fit application and website. Individuals are given the option to engage in virtual sessions led by seasoned teachers, being provided a convenient avenue for sustaining physical exercise inside the confines of their own houses. Cure.fit exemplifies how an Indian company has successfully used technology, information, and gamification tactics to develop a comprehensive health ecosystem. Cure.fit has effectively disrupted the traditional wellness market via the provision of a complete digital platform that encompasses a wide range of exercise, nutrition, and mental well-being services. The accessibility of this user-friendly platform has facilitated individuals in placing a higher emphasis on their comprehensive health and well-being in a holistic fashion. Cure.fit has included social gamification elements that allow users to form teams or groups with their contacts and engage collectively in challenges or events. Leaderboards have the capacity to display the hierarchical positions of several teams. The platform includes many mini-games and interactive tasks into its application. The study involves individuals participating in a cognitive activity focused on fitness, where they engage in a memory game and solve problems related to physical exercise, with the aim of earning rewards.

Finding and Results

Gamified communication may enhance start-up brand advocacy. Gamified communication boosts new firm social media brand marketing. Non-gaming environments gain challenges, rewards, competition, and engagement from gamification. Gamification increases start-up brand engagement, loyalty, and endorsement. Start-up content engagement increases with gamification. This relationship boosts brand advocacy by engaging users.

Gamification uses points, badges, and other incentives to complete tasks. These services may boost brand loyalty by making consumers feel valued. Gaming competitions build social proof. Social media users refer friends to the company after events or incentives.

Gaming boosts happiness and makes travel more fun. Company enthusiasts share their stories. Gamified communication promotes start-up products and ideas, educational games, and quizzes. Gamification helps start-up social media companies. User engagement and loyalty boost brand advocacy.

Innovation is shown in start-up contests. These events promote submissions and brands. Start-ups provide points, discounts, and incentives. Reward winners promote the brand for benefits. A startup's industry or product poll or quiz may be entertaining and educational, sparking interest and engagement. Discussion of indirect brand endorsement outcomes highlights how these activities subtly reinforce brand affinity. Users feel successful after gaining badges, trophies, and other digital incentives for milestones and tasks. Consumer success promotes the brand by creating a sense of achievement and loyalty, which in turn encourages further interaction and positive word-of-mouth, ultimately driving brand growth and customer retention.

Start-ups emphasize brand content generation and distribution. Sharing user experiences, reviews, and testimonials in UGC campaigns engages people and organically promotes the brand. Goal-oriented teamwork issues arise. Challenges engage brands and communities.

Gamification increases start-up social media loyalty, engagement, and brand endorsement. Enjoyable experiences help start-ups generate loyal advocates who promote the company to their networks. The researcher examines how companies create social media brand support with gamified communication.

Examining Social Gratification of Gamified Communication Initiatives for Brand Advocacy

Social pleasure comes from meeting social demands including recognition, connection, and belonging on social media. Gamified communication may improve start-up brand marketing social pleasure.

Challenges and Limitations

Gamified social media communication has helped firms boost brand support and customer satisfaction. These activities recognize, establish community, encourage social involvement, and enable personal expression, improving social experiences and brand–user interactions.

The study investigated the challenges and limitations given in Table 10.6 faced by start-ups when implementing gamified communication strategies on social media platforms for brand advocacy.

Table 10.6 Challenges and Limitations

Sl. No	Challenges and Limitations	Remarks
1	Resource Constraints	Start-ups generally lack funds, staff, and technology. Gamified communication solutions involve time, money, and trained workers, which may strain a startup's resources.
2	Design and Development Complexity	Gamified components need strategy, design, and development. Start-ups may struggle to adopt complicated gamification aspects, resulting in poor user experiences.
3	User Engagement and Participation	Gamification aims to engage users, but it doesn't ensure it. Gamified features may be neglected if they lack persuasiveness or immediate benefits, resulting in poor brand support.
4	Sustainability and Longevity	Gamified items must be refreshed to keep users interested. Start-ups may lose momentum and relevance, diminishing their effectiveness.
5	Integration with Brand Identity	Gamified elements must reflect start-up ideals and brand. Gamified methods that don't fit the company's messaging may confuse or alienate customers, undermining brand advocacy.
6	Measuring Impact and ROI	The brand advocacy effects of gamified communication tactics are hard to quantify. Start-ups may have trouble measuring ROI, making it hard to evaluate initiatives and justify their continuance.
7	User Fatigue and Overload	Gamification and warnings may tire and anger users. Start-ups must balance user engagement with consumer flood.
8	Competition and Distraction	Social networking is busy and competitive. Start-ups struggle to attract clients due to information and gamification.
9	Privacy and Data Concerns	Gamified approaches may compromise privacy if data is acquired improperly. Start-ups must comply with data privacy laws and build trust.
10	Changing Algorithms and Trends	Gamified material may be affected by social media algorithm and trend fluctuations. Changes in start-up brand advocacy are needed.
11	User Diversity	Start-up users may have varied interests and reasons. Gamified aspects that appeal to many users and demographics are difficult to design.

Source: researchers' own analysis

Conclusion

Gamified communication may help entrepreneurs' social media brands. Game design builds brand, engagement, and loyalty. Gamification and user involvement may help businesses generate dynamic, compelling content. Gamified communication includes competition, incentives, quizzes, badges, and user-generated content. These approaches satisfy people's desire for recognition, connection, and success. Start-ups may increase their reach and impact by building a network of brand advocates who share good experiences.

Gamifying communication may be tough. Start-ups must balance resources, design complexity, and dedication when implementing gamification strategies. Gamification's influence on start-up and brand advocacy can be profound, driving user engagement and loyalty. Despite limitations, the benefits are significant, as well-designed gamification elements can create a compelling user experience, foster community, and enhance customer retention, ultimately contributing to long-term business success.

Despite limitations, benefits are significant. Gamified communication solutions satisfy social pleasure demands with acknowledgment, community, engagement, and self-expression. Start-ups that solve these difficulties may win offline consumer loyalty and advocacy.

Gamifying brand communication helps organizations reach their target audience and generate social media brand advocates. In the ever-changing digital environment, creative, technical, and user-centric design must be harmonized to optimize gamified communication advantages. Brand advocacy and start-up success need this modification to effectively leverage gamification, ensuring that interactions are engaging, technologically feasible, and aligned with user needs, which in turn drives meaningful engagement and sustained growth.

Limitations of the Study

Temporal constraints may have limited the research's comprehension of start-up brand advocacy gamified communication. The study's small start-up and social media sample restrict its findings, potentially affecting the generalizability of the results and limiting the ability to draw broader conclusions about the effectiveness of gamification strategies across different contexts and industries. The study may have misrepresented user perceptions and experiences with gamified communication methods using interviews and secondary data. Subjective biases may affect user engagement, brand support, and social delight, impacting the research. Results are limited to select social media platforms and industries.

Future Scope of the Study

Start-up brand advocacy may be examined via gamified communication.

Gamifying brand advocacy contests may be better than awards. Understanding cultural variances in gamified communication through user engagement and social enjoyment may help global companies tailor their strategies to diverse audiences. Empirographies and focus groups may reveal complicated user experiences and gamified brand promotion, providing valuable insights into how different cultural contexts influence user interaction and engagement, thereby enabling more effective and culturally relevant gamification approaches. Researching social media user engagement and brand support may expand. Gamified communication may show how techniques effect user behavior and advocacy. Gamification's conversion from involvement to brand advocacy to sales may justify its value. Gamified AR or VR may uncover new user engagement and advocacy possibilities as technology improves. Despite limitations, gamified marketing enhances start-up social media brand support, according to study. Future research, technique improvements, and new factors to comprehend this dynamic area are possible.

References

Al-Zyoud, M. F. (2021). The impact of gamification on consumer loyalty, electronic word-of mouth sharing and purchase behavior. *Journal of Public Affairs, 21*(3), e2263.

AlSaad, F. M., & Durugbo, C. M. (2021). Gamification-as-innovation: A review. *International Journal of Innovation and Technology Management, 18*(05), 2130002.

Amelia, N. N. (2020). *The impact of gamification for attracting e-commerce customer loyalty* [Doctoral dissertation, President University].

Aparicio, A. F., Vela, F. L. G., Sánchez, J. L. G., & Montes, J. L. I. (2012, October). Analysis and application of gamification. In *Proceedings of the 13th international conference on interacción persona-ordenador* (pp. 1–2).

Armstrong, D. (2013). The new engagement game: The role of gamification in scholarly publishing. *Learned Publishing, 26*(4), 253–256.

Arroyo, M., & Wan, N. (2019). The effects of gamification on brand engagement and purchase intention in the context of social media. *Journal of Interactive Advertising, 19*(1), 74–85.

Basten, D. (2017). Gamification. *IEEE Software, 34*(05), 76–81.

Bilro, R. G., Loureiro, S. M. C., & Angelino, F. J. D. A. (2021). The role of creative communications and gamification in student engagement in higher education: A sentiment analysis approach. *Journal of Creative Communications, 17*(1), 7–21.

Cavalcanti, J., Valls, V., Contero, M., & Fonseca, D. (2021). Gamification and hazard communication in virtual reality: A qualitative study. *Sensors, 21*(14), 4663.

Chen, J., & Brown, T. (2022). Understanding consumer feedback in gamified communication: A content analysis of social media reviews. *Journal of Interactive Advertising, 25*(2), 152–167.

Conaway, R., & Garay, M. C. (2014). Gamification and service marketing. *SpringerPlus, 3*(1), 1–11.

De-Marcos, L., Garcia-Lopez, E., & Garcia-Cabot, A. (2016). On the effectiveness of game-like and social approaches in learning: Comparing educational gaming, gamification & social networking. *Computers & Education, 95*, 99–113.

Dymek, M., & Zackariasson, P. (Eds.). (2016). *The business of gamification: A critical analysis*. Taylor & Francis.

Fuchs, M., Fizek, S., Ruffino, P., & Schrape, N. (2014). *Rethinking gamification* (p. 344). Meson Press.

Garcia, J. E., Rodrigues, P., Simões, J., & da Fonseca, M. J. S. (2022). Gamification strategies for social media. In *Implementing automation initiatives in companies to create better-connected experiences* (pp. 137–159). IGI Global.

Gatautis, R., Banytė, J., Piligrimienė, Ž., Vitkauskaitė, E., & Tarutė, A. (2016). The impact of gamification on consumer brand engagement. *Transformations in Business & Economics, 15*, 173–191.

Groh, F. (2012). Gamification: State of the art definition and utilization. *Institute of Media Informatics Ulm University, 39*, 31.

Hamari, J., Koivisto, J., & Sarsa, H. (2014, January). Does gamification work?–A literature review of empirical studies on gamification. In *2014 47th Hawaii international conference on system sciences* (pp. 3025–3034). IEEE.

Hamari, J., Xi, N., Legaki, Z., & Morschheuser, B. (2023). Gamification. In *Hawaii international conference on system sciences* (p. 1105).

Hofacker, C. F., De Ruyter, K., Lurie, N. H., Manchanda, P., & Donaldson, J. (2016). Gamification and mobile marketing effectiveness. *Journal of Interactive Marketing, 34*(1), 25–36.

Hsu, C. L. (2023). Enhancing brand love, customer engagement, brand experience, and repurchase intention: Focusing on the role of gamification in mobile apps. *Decision Support Systems*, 114020.

Hsu, C. L., & Chen, M. C. (2018). How gamification marketing activities motivate desirable consumer behaviors: Focusing on the role of brand love. *Computers in Human Behavior, 88*, 121–133.

Huang, L., & Saravanakumar, M. (2018). Engaging consumers through gamification-based brand experience on social media. *Computers in Human Behavior, 79*, 59–73.

Huotari, K., & Hamari, J. (2012, October). Defining gamification: A service marketing perspective. In *Proceeding of the 16th international academic MindTrek conference* (pp. 17–22).

Huseynov, F. (2020). Gamification in E-commerce: Enhancing digital customer engagement through game elements. In *Digital innovations for customer engagement, management, and organizational improvement* (pp. 144–161). IGI Global.

Jakubowski, M. (2014, March). Gamification in business and education–project of gamified course for university students. In *Developments in business simulation and experiential learning: Proceedings of the annual ABSEL conference* (Vol. 41).

Kapp, K. M. (2012). What is gamification. In *The gamification of learning and instruction: Game-based methods and strategies for training and education* (pp. 1–23). John Wiley & Sons.

Kim, H. W., Chan, H. C., & Gupta, S. (2019). Effective design of brand community gamification: A psychological ownership perspective. *Journal of Business Research, 94*, 300–310.

Kim, S. (2013). Fundamental strategic approach for gamification: How to start a gamification in your organization. *International Journal of Digital Content Technology and Its Applications, 7*(12), 48.

Lam, J., Robson, K., Kirk Plangger, J., Kietzmann, I. M., & Pitt, L. (2022). Play, games and gamification: Possibilities for customer loyalty. In *Handbook of research on customer loyalty* (p. 173). Edward Elgar Publishing.

Love, S. M., Sanders, M. R., Turner, K. M., Maurange, M., Knott, T., Prinz, R., Metzler, C., & Ainsworth, A. T. (2016). Social media and gamification: Engaging vulnerable parents in an online evidence-based parenting program. *Child Abuse & Neglect, 53*, 95–107.

Marcial, D. E., dela Peña, L., Montemayor, J., & Dy, J. (2021, March). The design of a gamified responsible use of social media. In *Frontiers in education* (Vol. 6, p. 635278). Frontiers Media SA.

Marczewski, A. (2013). *Gamification: A simple introduction.* Andrzej Marczewski.

Mesko, B., Drobni, Z., Bényei, É., Gergely, B., & Győrffy, Z. (2015). Digital health is a cultural transformation of traditional healthcare. *Journal of Clinical and Translational Research, 1*(3), 109–116.

Mitchell, R., Schuster, L., & Drennan, J. (2017). Understanding how gamification influences behaviour in social marketing. *Australasian Marketing Journal, 25*(1), 12–19.

Mustikasari, A., Fista, T. F. F., Wijaya, T., & Wardana, W. (2022). The influence of gamification and rewards on customer loyalty in Z generation with moderating role of gender (case study on the Shopee marketplace). *Management Analysis Journal, 11*(2).

Nicholson, S. (2015). A recipe for meaningful gamification. In *Gamification in education and business* (pp. 1–20). Springer.

Nobre, H., & Ferreira, A. (2017). Gamification as a platform for brand co-creation experiences. *Journal of Brand Management, 24,* 349–361.

Noorbehbahani, F., Salehi, F., & Zadeh, R. J. (2019). A systematic mapping study on gamification applied to E-marketing. *Journal of Research in Interactive Marketing, 13*(3), 392–410.

Papamichael, I., Pappas, G., Siegel, J. E., & Zorpas, A. A. (2022). Unified waste metrics: A gamified tool in next-generation strategic planning. *Science of the Total Environment, 833,* 154835.

Paruthi, M., Nagina, R., & Gupta, G. (2023, March). Measuring the effect of consumer brand engagement on brand-related outcomes in gamified mobile apps: A solicitation of technology acceptance model. In *Proceedings* (Vol. 85, No. 1, p. 10). MDPI.

Permana, F. H., Handayani, P. W., & Pinem, A. A. (2021, October). The influence of gamification on brand engagement and brand awareness in online marketplaces. In *2021 International conference on advanced computer science and information systems (ICACSIS)* (pp. 01–06). IEEE.

Prince, J. D. (2013). Gamification. *Journal of Electronic Resources in Medical Libraries, 10*(3), 162–169.

Raj, B., & Gupta, D. (2018, September). Factors influencing consumer responses to marketing gamification. In *2018 International conference on advances in computing, communications and informatics (ICACCI)* (pp. 1538–1542). IEEE.

Richter, G., Raban, D. R., & Rafaeli, S. (2015). *Studying gamification: The effect of rewards and incentives on motivation* (pp. 21–46). Springer International Publishing.

Robson, K., Plangger, K., Kietzmann, J. H., McCarthy, I., & Pitt, L. (2015). Is it all a game? Understanding the principles of gamification. *Business Horizons, 58*(4), 411–420.

Sailer, M., Hense, J. U., Mayr, S. K., & Mandl, H. (2017). How gamification motivates: An experimental study of the effects of specific game design elements on psychological need satisfaction. *Computers in Human Behavior, 69,* 371–380.

Seaborn, K., & Fels, D. I. (2015). Gamification in theory and action: A survey. *International Journal of Human-Computer Studies, 74,* 14–31.

Sgueo, G. (2018, November). *A discussion on gamified digital advocacy.* Humboldt University Berlin, International Workshop on the Future of Law: Technology, Innovation and Access to Justice. https://papers.ssrn.com/sol3/papers.cfm?abstract_id=3311209

Singla, V., & Gupta, G. (2019, August 2). Emotional branding scale and its role in formation of brand trust. *Paradigm, 23*(2), 148–163. https://doi.org/10.1177/0971890719859668

Spais, G., Behl, A., Jain, K., Jain, V., & Singh, G. (2022). Promotion and branding from the lens of gamification in challenging times. *Journal of Promotion Management, 28*(4), 413–419.

Stieglitz, S., Lattemann, C., Robra-Bissantz, S., Zarnekow, R., & Brockmann, T. (2017). *Gamification* (pp. 1–164). Springer.

Streukens, S., van Riel, A., Novikova, D., & Leroi-Werelds, S. (2019). Boosting customer engagement through gamification: A customer engagement marketing approach. In *Handbook of research on customer engagement* (pp. 35–54). Edward Elgar Publishing.

Sultan, Y. H., & Suhail, K. S. (2019). The impact of significant factors of digital leadership on gamification marketing strategy. *International Journal for Advance Research and Development, 4*(5), 29–33.

Thompson, A., Chen, J., & Lee, K. (2021). Emotional involvement in gamified communication: A qualitative analysis of social media interactions. *Journal of Interactive Marketing, 45*, 67–82.

Thorpe, A. S., & Roper, S. (2019). The ethics of gamification in a marketing context. *Journal of Business Ethics, 155*, 597–609.

Volkova, I. I. (2013). Four pillars of gamification. *Middle-East Journal of Scientific Research, 13*, 149–152.

Wood, L. C., & Reiners, T. (2015). Gamification. In *Encyclopedia of information science and technology* (3rd ed.) (pp. 3039–3047). IGI Global.

Zatwarnicka-Madura, B. (2015). Gamification as a tool for influencing customers' behaviour. *International Journal of Economics and Management Engineering, 9*(5), 1461–1464.

Chapter 11

Gamification Strategies for Enhancing Sustainability Marketing

Engaging Consumers in Eco-Friendly Behaviors

Faiz Ahmad, Mohd Danish Kirmani and Asadul Haque

Introduction

In the present era, organizations are facing environmental sustainability issues along with the challenges of addressing global climate crises. Organizations are seeking innovation and feasible strategic moves to address these problems by inducing positive change in behavior among the consumers (Escudeiro & Campos, 2023). To mitigate, techniques used for gamification are one of such innovative approaches which has gained substantial consideration (Zhang & Anwar, 2023). In this chapter, the authors emphasize how gaming and sustainability can be linked, to encourage and engage consumers to adopt and advocate sustainable practices.

Gamification is a technique that uses game-like technology and artifacts to motivate and encourage people to make better environmental decisions. Its basic concepts, such as competition (Behl, Pereira et al., 2023), rewards (Xu & Hamari, 2022), success, and achievement (Hallifax et al., 2023), tap into the natural drives of people. This chapter explains gamification from its theoretical foundation, it looks at psychological impact, and analyzes how it can be applied to sustainability marketing.

At its core, this chapter seeks to identify the key factors that contribute to successful gaming concepts and environmentally friendly practices. Consumer behavior has never been more important as the world is facing resource scarcity (Chu, 2023), climate change (Boncu et al., 2022; Brannon et al., 2022), and pollution (Ourdas & Ponis, 2023; Hayes et al., 2022). Thus, understanding exactly how gamification can be incorporated into sustainable business specifically in marketing practices can unlock significant and sustainable impacts.

The present chapter is structured to provide a comprehensive analysis of gamification-sustainable marketing collaboration. It begins with an introduction of the core ideas and design mechanics underpinning the tactics of gamification, elucidating the importance of such mechanisms that may be utilized to inculcate pro-environmental behaviors. The successive sections explain the psychological theories changing the individual behaviors in gamified

DOI: 10.4324/9781032694238-15

perspective, highlighting the chemistry between intrinsic and extrinsic motivation. The chapter next scrutinizes the connection between gamification and sustainability marketing, emphasizing the potential benefits, and emanating issues of this synergy.

As the discussion proceeds, a critical assessment of probable stumbling blocks and concerns related to ethical issues is presented, yielding with advice on feasible implementation of these mechanisms to the practitioners and policymakers. Further, the implication of gamified customization which accommodates different consumers helps to increase the efficacy. The chapter then delves to get into the practical aspect as to how the gamification strategies including key success factors are investigated, followed by discussing the growing current trends and future recommendations.

At last, the chapter provides a useful insight to the stakeholders with a comprehensive understanding as to how innovative gamification strategies may be utilized to enhance the sustainability initiatives specifically in marketing. Gamification possesses the competence to catalyze mass adoption of environmentally friendly behaviors by engaging consumers in profound and impactful approaches, thus helping to contribute to an eco-friendlier conscious society.

Background and Rationale for the Study

The ominous concerns of ecological degradation and change in climate in present world call for effective solutions involving individuals in adopting as well as practicing sustainable behavior. The literature explicates that "traditional approaches to promoting environmental stewardship, which are frequently oriented on information dissemination and moral duty appeals, have demonstrated lackness in their capacity to generate long-term behavioural change" (Thomas Muñoz, 2022). As the global community works collectively to address these difficulties, new strategies for motivating consumers to indulge in eco-friendly activities need to be implemented.

The fusion of gamification with sustainability marketing poses a promising avenue to tie this gap. Gamification is defined as "the use of game components and mechanics in non-game contexts, has been shown to be effective in encouraging behavioral change in a variety of fields" (Hamari et al., 2014). It has the potential to transform individual attitudes and actions toward environmental sustainability by exploiting the intrinsic human desire for accomplishment, competition, and rewards (Dikcius et al., 2021).

The worldwide gamification market is exponentially increasing yearly, which is evident from one of the reports by precedence research (2023) that records *US$* 10 billion in 2022. The report forecasted that the global gamification market will be *US$* 116.68 billion by 2032 with a calculated annual growth rate (CAGR) of 27.9% from 2023 to 2032, which is shown in Figure 11.1.

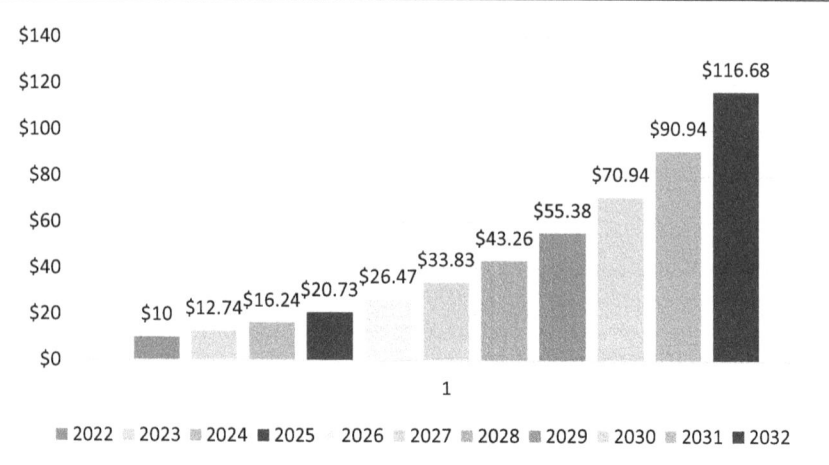

Figure 11.1 Global gamification market size (in US$ billion)
Source: Gamification Market (n.d.), https://www.precedenceresearch.com/gamification-market

The combined focus with respect to engagement and change in behavior between gamification and sustainability marketing crafts a synergy. There are various examples of consumer sustainable behaviors such as reusing, consuming responsibly, and conservation of energy practices which demand a change in habits and mindsets. It provides distinctive platform that holds and grabs the attention with the help of interactive experiences encouraging such transitions (Deterding, 2011, 2015; Deterding, Dixon et al., 2011; Deterding, Sicart et al., 2011).

The purpose of this chapter is to investigate the convergence of gamification and sustainability marketing as a strategic method to encouraging eco-friendly behaviors. This study aims to contribute to the expanding body of knowledge on effective techniques for addressing environmental concerns by studying the conceptual framework, psychological underpinnings, and practical applications of gamification in the context of sustainability. This chapter provides insights for practitioners, policymakers, and researchers interested in harnessing the potential of gamification to promote a more environmentally conscious society by analyzing the benefits, challenges, and ethical considerations associated with gamified sustainability marketing.

Definition of Key Terms

Gamification

Gamification is the inclusion of game-like features into nongame contexts, such as challenges, prizes, competition, and feedback, to inspire and engage participants in desired behaviors. Gamification capitalizes on the human need for achievement, recognition, and fulfillment by exploiting the psychological principles that underpin game experiences.

Gamification is considered to be a multifaceted concept as various scholars explained, keeping distinct context in their exploration. It is defined by Deterding, Sicart et al. (2011) as "combining the game like features into nongame conditions to provide gamified experience with an emphasis in terms of engagement and motivational game features". In another way, Hamari et al. (2014) have defined it as "usage of game mechanism in different field in order to fuel engagement of users and change in their behaviour". In terms of user motivation and objectives, Zichermann and Cunningham (2011) have defined it as "a procedure to keep users engaged and motivated to accomplish anticipated objectives by utilizing rationality and mechanics of game".

Gamification in terms of benefits for the user is defined by Werbach and Hunter (2012) as "utilizing the features of game in non-game activities to foster consumer engagement that leads to incentivize desired behaviour". In one of the studies conducted by Kapp (2012) focused on the utilization of different components, methods, and notions into various nongame elements in stressing the role of gamification in building the engagement, helps in motivating and learning outcomes of the consumer.

To summarize, gamification is the purposeful incorporation of game design concepts and mechanics into nongame contexts with the goal of engaging and motivating people through a sense of achievement, competitiveness, and enjoyment. These definitions highlight the transformative power of gamification in generating behavioral change and increasing engagement across multiple domains.

Sustainability Marketing

According to Sheth and Parvatiyar (2021), sustainability marketing, also known as sustainable marketing, "is a strategic approach to promoting products or services that emphasizes their positive environmental, social, and economic impacts". As depicted in Figure 11.2, Sheth and Parvatiyar (2021) conformed to the aggregate marketing system (AGMS) proposed by Wilkie and Moore (1999), which emphasizes the primary involvement of stakeholders such as marketers, consumers, and governments and that marketing requires two-dimensional focus which shifts from consumption to sustainability, and from a free-market orientation to a guided market orientation of active engagement of policymakers. It involves incorporating principles of environmental and social responsibility into all stages of a product's life cycle, from production to consumption and disposal.

Sustainability marketing is the strategic planning and execution of marketing initiatives that promote products, services, or behaviors that are compatible with environmental sustainability goals. This method aims to strike a

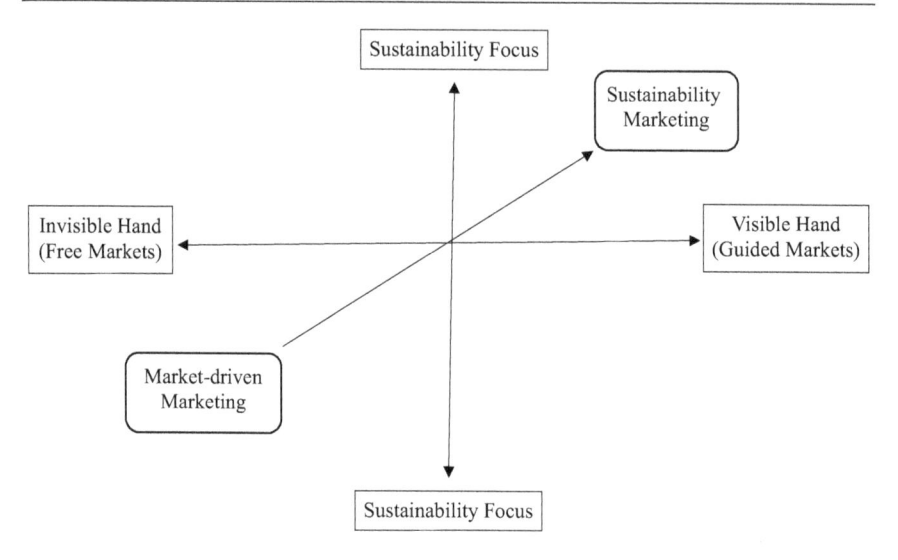

Figure 11.2 From market-driven to sustainable marketing – two-dimensional shift
Source: adopted from Sheth and Parvatiyar (2021, p. 151)

balance between economic goals and social and environmental responsibilities, establishing a harmonious relationship between enterprises, consumers, and the environment.

Marketing as sustainability has been at the forefront of business and environmental responsibility, studied from various differential viewpoints by numerous researchers. Polonsky (2008) defined it as "inclusion of social and ecological considerations into strategic marketing activities, with a focus on equilibrium when it comes to the organizational objectives keeping in mind the environmental and societal welfare". Peattie and Peattie (2003) studied sustainability marketing underlining its impact on providing value to the various stakeholders as well as incorporating with organizational sustainable goals.

Sustainability marketing, as per the father of modern marketing Phil Kotler and researchers, is defined as "the methods of creation, exploration, conveying and delivering customer value at the same time addressing environmental and societal challenges" (Kotler et al., 2019). Their research is surrounded with three major aspects, viz. planet, people, and profitability. The study conducted by Belz and Peattie (2012) emphasizing the implication of sustainable marketing strategies that helps to make a shift toward green methods of production as well as sustainable consumption vis-à-vis holistic approach with stakeholders.

In essence, marketing approaches with sustainability result in merging ecological and social factors to serve value to customers and also helping to promote to achieve sustainability goals. These various studies provide an insightful and multifaceted disposition of sustainability marketing which plays a crucial role in bridging the gap linked with organizational objectives with societal and ecological obligations.

Significance of Integrating Gamification and Sustainability

The synergy between gamification and marketing specifies a distinctive avenue to tackle the challenges of engaging and motivating ecological friendly behavior among the stakeholders. Conventional maneuvers, mostly relying on the transmission of information and asserting ethical obligation, can have a constraint effect. It prevails over these constraints by banking upon individual's innate needs and wants for accomplishment and incentives which ultimately improves engagement and motivation of consumer. The chapter deals with the theoretical, conceptual, and practical underpinnings with issues related to ethical and environmental concerns.

The synergy between gamification and sustainability marketing lays a foundational stone that has the potential to tackle ecological issues and at the same time inculcating change in behavior of consumers in a progressive manner. The ability to connect and motivate consumers coined with sustainability goals and objectives provides room for efficient interaction and activity on ecological bottlenecks. It may help the organization to create connections among individuals and develop a sense of pro-environmental behavior resulting from satisfied experience by incorporating various elements of games such as gifts, coupons, and contests while designing the sustainable games for individuals.

The synergy of sustainable marketing signifies its impact. In order to promote pro-ecological behavior, gamified programs help to remove psychological barriers, engage and motivate users by adopting ecological behavior (Dong et al., 2023). The study done by Koivisto and Hamari (2019) explains how an individual can exhibit environmental behavior with the help of gamification practices by linking the intention–conduct difference via motivational engagement. Such practice not only pushes individualistic sustainability conducts but also broadens ethnic transformation in the direction of eco-friendly conscious culture.

As sustainable practices are growing pivotally, the synergy of gamification and sustainability provides a novel way to link individual interests with the larger good. The synergy provides a feasible mechanism to initiate progressive behavioral shift while raising ecological awareness coupled with the utilization of recent scientific and technological advancements.

Theoretical Foundations

The theoretical foundation of gamification specifically in sustainability marketing is developed on considering the various game elements' design, social psychology, and behavioral economics. This segment tries to underpin the theoretical perspective to highlight the factors which boost the efficiency of gamification techniques in exemplifying ecological user behavior.

Overview of Gamification Principles and Mechanics

Gamification principles and mechanics refer to a combination of features established on game dynamics aiming to exponentiate user engagement, motivation, and transformation of behavior in nongame setting. These mechanics convert boring tasks into entertaining and pleasing experiences with the help of users' inherent motivations, encouraging a sense of achievement. In the next paragraphs, essential principles and mechanics are discussed.

Gamification concepts and mechanics refer to a set of design features based on game dynamics that aim to improve engagement, motivation, and behavior change in nongame environments. These components turn mundane tasks into enjoyable experiences by appealing to users' innate motivations and instilling a sense of accomplishment. Given in the following sections are some key principles and mechanics.

Challenges and Goals

Gamifications bring challenges and add goals which match with expected behavior (pro-environmental behaviour) and excite players to exhibit desired pursuit. These difficult challenges and goals point toward a purposeful direction encouraging involvement in games (Seaborn & Fels, 2015).

Awards and Recognition

Gamification employs points, badges, or even virtual cash to identify participants' accomplishments. These tactics of incentives offer immediate responses, strengthening a positive change in behavior and supporting more involvement (Hamari et al., 2014).

Levels and Progression

The notion of advancement necessitates splitting of various tasks into minor levels or phases, letting users to know their progression. This tactic nurtures a feeling of victory and concomitantly makes participants interested over a period of time (Kapp, 2012).

Leaderboards and Competition

Leaderboards are meant for comparing the players' performances with that of their counterparts, keeping competition stiff and shoving players to try hard to get the higher position. This mechanics of social endeavor enhances engagement and uplifts motivation (Deterding, 2011, 2015).

Feedback and Feedback Loops

The mechanism of real-time comment and feedback informs participants about their progress and assists players to identify the effect of their actions. The roundabout comment and feedback loops foster a constructive move in the game while focusing players en route for expected outcomes (Jahn et al., 2021).

Immersion and Narrative

To build emotional connections, inclusive gamification tactics such as narratives and immersive experience enhance involvement. With the help of storytelling, interest of the participants can also be created which also blossoms engagement (Anderson & Dill, 2000).

Present-day research by Krath et al. (2022) highlighted blending a number of gamification features so as to enhance involvement and change in behavior, which were found to be fruitful. The study also examines the combination of competitive challenges, incentivization, and interacting socially, disclosing how these tactics help to efficiently stimulate participants. These findings necessitate to tailor gamification mechanism to potential users and set of circumstances, as well as the likelihood for in-progress modernization in utilizing dynamics of game to generate optimistic results.

Psychological Theories Supporting Gamified Behavior Change

Gamification exploits psychological theories to make reforms in behavior by spouting implicit thinking, molding perceptions, and boosting participation. There are numerous worthy psychological theories available to reinforce the efficiency of gamified interferences' result in behavioral change covering several fields. The underlying theories help to understand the mechanisms which facilitate gamification to prompt a prolonged change in behavior.

Self-Determination Theory (SDT)

As per Deci and Ryan (1985), users exhibit innate motivation which is navigated by major three psychological needs, viz autonomy, competence and relatedness. Gamification is congenial with SDT as it provides choices, authorizes participants to oversee their performances, and promotes sense of autonomy. The perceived competence of players helps them to cope up with challenges and keep an eye on their progress, and parallelly social involvement in gamified settings fulfills their urge for relatedness. Thus, gamification fosters intrinsic motivation, which leads to a long-term behavior change (Ryan & Deci, 2000b).

Goal-Setting Theory (GST)

Locke and Latham (1990) pioneered goal-setting theory, emphasizing the need of defining clear, demanding, and attainable goals to improve motivation and performance. Gamification applies this notion by framing work as challenges or quests, with clear goals for users to achieve. As participants achieve these objectives, they feel a sense of satisfaction and inspiration to take on new tasks.

Flow Theory (FT)

According to Csikszentmihalyi (1975), flow theory explains the optimal psychological state that occurs when individuals are totally absorbed in an activity, feeling a balance of competence and difficulty. Gamification features such as progressive advancement and adjusted difficulty levels foster a flow-friendly environment. Users are drawn into the task, increasing motivation and engagement (Koivisto & Hamari, 2019; Krath et al., 2021).

Operant Conditioning and Behavioral Reinforcement (OCBR)

Gamification uses positive reinforcement mechanisms to encourage desired actions based on operant conditioning principles. Reinforcers like as rewards, badges, and points increase the link between conduct and positive results (Skinner, 1953). As per Hamari et al. (2014), gamification provides rewards in varied proportions and reserves and promotes unforeseeable which helps in engagement and motivation. It utilizes mechanism of comments and feedback for example monitoring of progress and prompt gifts and prizes, which is in accordance with psychological theories viz. operant conditioning (Skinner, 1938). The sustainable behaviors are enhanced with the help of optimistic implementation using incentives, improving the probability that similar action will be recurrent (Anderson & Dill, 2000).

Social Cognitive Theory (SCT)

The social cognitive theory that was proposed by Bandura (1977) underlines the role of observational learning, imitation, and exhibiting in the behavioral development. The strategies of gamification incorporate social components, for example leaderboards and sharing in community, letting the players to view the achievements of their fellow players and contest with them in a friendly manner. With the help of explicit strengthening, social mechanism fuels competition and persuades change in behavior (Cugelman, 2013).

Theory of Planned Behavior (TPB)

It is one of the mostly used psychological theories employed to portray and prophesize the behavior of human beings – specifically gamified involvement behavior. According to TPB, behavioral intention is the chief carter of real conduct which is supervised by three key factors, viz. attitude toward the action, subjective norms, and perceived behavioral control.

In gamified behavioral modification framework, attitude toward the behavior is defined as the participants' optimistic or pessimistic engagement in a particular activity, for example, contributing to sustainability concerns, which is supported by technology (Ajzen, 1991). The participants' personal attitude may possibly be affected by gamification initiatives for example competition, tracking of progress, and incentives which may be enjoyable and rewarding when engaged in such sustainable activities. Gamification may effectively mold behavioral intentions and, therefore, perceived behavior in support of sustainability aims by experiencing sustainable conduct enjoyable, building a sense of belongingness, and enhancing an individual's perceived control over their etiquettes (Abou Kamar et al., 2024).

The study carried out by Ntoumanis et al. (2021) demonstrated that the combination of various psychological theories to build gamification strategy is found to be valuable. The study explicates as to how SDT, GST, and FT help to improvise the users' engagement and change in behavior in a healthcare environment. These theories with a holistic approach take care of all the possible motivation and support a well-rooted basis for building efficient and smooth gamification practices.

Definitely the integration of various psychological theories helps to carve out better tactics of gamification which ultimately mold individual behavior. It captures the elementary mechanisms which impact human behavior positioned with individuals' inherent incentives, assisting in engagement and offering a sense of achievement.

Role of Intrinsic and Extrinsic Motivation in Sustainability Marketing

Understanding and utilizing both extrinsic and intrinsic motivation are critical in sustainability marketing for fostering a long-term change in terms of eco-friendly behaviors. Intrinsic motivation is caused by internal elements such as personal values, beliefs, and a sense of success, whereas extrinsic motivation is caused by external incentives or recognition.

Intrinsic Motivation

It is critical in sustainability marketing because it creates a true commitment toward environmentally responsible habits. The inclination toward the sustainability is more apt from individuals who have inborn intrinsic value which compels them to engage in behaviors, viz. reducing waste or conservation of energy, etc. This engagement is consistent and out of one's own will. These kinds of sustainable acts exhibited due to an individual's own fundamental beliefs create a sense of persistence and subjective fulfillment (Vallerand, 1997). To aid innate motivation, it is important to put an emphasis on ecological pros of action, develop a sense of obligation, and cultivate a formidable connection to achieve sustainability goals.

Extrinsic Motivation

This kind of motivation is for a shorter period of time as it is powered by some temporal or contextual benefits in terms of incentives, which do not end up with longer commitment toward sustainability activities (Deci et al., 1999). These benefits, for example, honor, social status, recognition, coupons, and discounts are temporal which may grab initial involvement and motivation, and over a period of time they lose their credibility when such kind of rewards are taken away (Ryan & Deci, 2000a, 2000b). Marketing with sustainability approach must be aligned in such a manner so that individual motivational activities shift toward the intrinsic involvement. The mechanism to narrow this gap between extrinsic and intrinsic motivation needs to be built so that individuals feel a sense of belongingness and achievement in terms of sustainable goals.

Wang and Udall (2023) and Kaushal and Prashar (2022) discovered that both internal and external motivations play a pivotal role in sustainable consumption. These studies highlighted the importance of amalgamating external and internal benefits in such a way that individual beliefs must be mapped with extrinsic motivation, and the components which force an individual to act in a responsible manner must be mapped with intrinsic motivation. This amalgamation may create a synergy between underlying motivations and helps to boost participation in sustainable consumption behavior. Figure 11.3 integrates the various theories applicable in terms of motivation, involvement, and attitude which lead to sustainable behavior.

The synergy between external and internal motivation may help to develop long-lasting behavioral change in individuals. This may also drive the external stimuli to associate themselves with sustainable activities, and at the same time internal stimuli may urge them to develop a commitment toward eco-friendly behavior.

Gamification in Sustainability Marketing

Gamification is found to be an excellent mechanism in terms of sustainable marketing due to its innovative game mechanics and for providing entertainment experiences that help to foster ecology-responsible conduct. Since its mechanism incorporates various game challenges, rewards, and healthy contests, it increases users' inherent drive to develop and boost ecologically friendly behavior. With various investigations, it is evident that this mechanism encourages conservative habits via engagement (Hsu, 2022; Hsu & Chen, 2021).

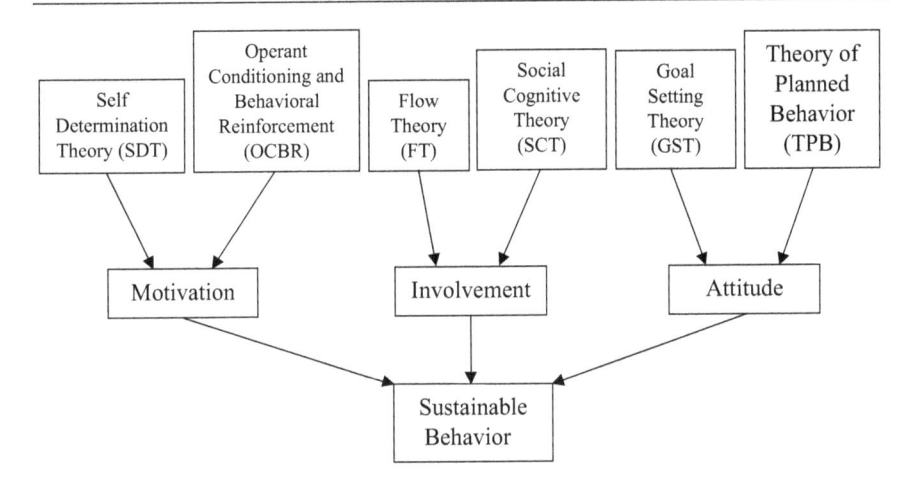

Figure 11.3 Integration of theories
Source: authors' compilation of theories

The examination undertakes as to how interactional mechanism accelerates engagement and assists in a change in behavior, emphasizing the potentiality of sustainable marketing initiatives helping to build a better environmental determined society.

Exploring the Synergy between Gamification and Sustainability

The synergy between gamification and sustainability marketing has the possible capabilities to transform behavioral aspect resulting in positive environmental behaviors. With its transformative, appealing mechanism and stimulating subtleties, sustainability objectives are achieved through gamification by effectively capitalizing into human cognitive motivation and through changes in attitudes and manners concerning environmental affability.

The study conducted by Jami Pour et al. (2021) shows the kinship between sustainability and gamification, pointing out their mutually bolstering nature. The study exhibits that if gamification strategies are linked with sustainable development objectives, they result in increasing engagement toward eco-friendly behaviors. It nurtures an environment in which users are motivated to adopt sustainable habits through various awards, competitions, and challenges. Such studies show how this synergy uplifts the performance of sustainable initiatives renovating monotonous actions into interesting chores with gaugeable benefits.

Moreover, due to its engaging and fascinating nature, gamification is specifically effective at bridging intention–behaviour gaps, which usually prevent to adopt eco-friendly practices. The current research in the concerned field explores this, revealing as to how gamification helps to bridge the gap between the objectives of individuals to be inclined toward sustainability and their innate behaviors (Boncu et al., 2022, 2023; Ng & Cheung, 2022). As per the study, intrinsic motivation is enhanced due to gamified interventions, encouraging individuals to transfer their intentions into practical, prolonged environmental activities. This practice of individuals brings about forming a sustainable culture. However, this synergy faces a handful of challenges, in terms of executing ethically and evasion of unpredicted pessimistic consequences. It is inspected by assessing and focusing the necessity for gamified sustainable effort that perpetuates authenticity and security (Sharif & Ameen, 2020; Scholefield & Shepherd, 2019). It is utmost important to shield the integrity of like methods to ensure that this mechanism align with actual environmental aims, lessen overconsumption, highlight issues regarding greenwashing so as to encourage pro-ecofriendly awareness, attitudes, and actions.

Finally, the fusion of gamification and sustainability brings forth a zestful platform enhancing awareness about the environment and subtle change in behavior. It not only enhances the efficacy of sustainable marketing by banking upon innate motivations but also cultivates a paradigm shift with respect to eco-friendly attitudes and actions.

Benefits of Gamification for Promoting Eco-friendly Behaviors

Gamification has a number of advantages that make it an effective tool for promoting environmentally friendly habits and driving sustainable actions. Its ability to engage, motivate, and persuade people contributes to its success in raising environmental awareness.

Increased Engagement

Gamification captivates people by transforming sustainable behaviors into interactive and enjoyable experiences. Behl, Jayawardena et al. (2023) and Whittaker et al. (2021) emphasized that gamified elements such as challenges, rewards, and competition create an engaging environment, sustaining people's interest and commitment to environmentally friendly practices. This increased involvement leads to longer engagement with sustainability initiatives.

Behavioral Shaping

Gamification helps to shape positive behavior by cutting eco-friendly tasks down into achievable steps. Krath et al. (2022) observed that individuals are guided toward adopting new habits over time through progressive growth and achievable challenges. This behavioral shaping strategy encourages participants to internalize sustainable actions and promotes long-term behavior change.

Incentivized Participation

Gamification uses rewards and recognition as incentives to reinforce environmentally responsible behaviors. Extrinsic rewards, according to Doğan-Südaş et al. (2023), stimulate participation and provide tangible benefits that motivate a continuous engagement. Such rewards can stimulate behavioral change, especially for those who require an external encouragement to establish long-term behaviors.

Promoting Intrinsic Motivation

The interactive and goal-oriented nature of gamification aligns with intrinsic motivation. According to Jones et al. (2022) and Chan et al. (2018), gamified experiences tap into users' desires for autonomy, mastery, and relatedness, fostering a sense of personal accomplishment and fulfillment. This innate desire sustains environmentally favorable behavior in the absence of extrinsic rewards (Mekler et al., 2017).

Overcoming Obstacles

Gamification targets psychological hurdles that impede environmentally beneficial behavior. According to Ouariachi et al. (2020), gamification reduces feelings of isolation and develops a sense of community, enhancing individuals' willingness to participate in common sustainability initiatives.

Data Collection and Insights

Gamification platforms allow for the collection of data on user behavior, preferences, and challenges. According to Ayastuy et al. (2021) and Rodrigues et al. (2021), analyzing this data yields valuable insights that allow for the fine-tuning of gamification strategies and the customization of interventions to cater to specific audiences.

To summarize, gamification offers a number of advantages along with promoting environmentally responsible habits. It is a compelling way to driving long-term behavioral change toward sustainability by increasing engagement, influencing habits, encouraging participation, fostering intrinsic motivation, overcoming barriers, and offering data-driven insights.

Designing Effective Gamification Strategies

Designing effective gamification techniques is an important component of using gamification's potential to induce behavior change and advance sustainability goals. As corporations and organizations acknowledge the value of engaging consumers in environmentally responsible activities, the artful incorporation of gaming mechanics becomes increasingly important. It has progressed beyond being simply a source of amusement to become a deliberate technique to inspiring and motivating individuals to embrace sustainable behaviors.

Krath et al. (2022) investigated the complexities of gamification design, along with investigating the impact of various game aspects on user engagement and behavior change. This study emphasizes the importance of adapting gamification tactics to appeal to a wide range of target audiences and desired behaviors. Organizations may create gamification experiences that effectively develop eco-conscious behaviors by addressing the interplay of challenges, incentives, social dynamics, and narrative immersion.

This section discusses the fundamental features of a successful gamification for sustainability, emphasizing the relevance of personalization, psychological theories, and ethical issues. Practitioners can construct powerful interventions that can empower consumers to make eco-friendly choices by knowing the subtleties of gamification design.

Elements of Successful Gamification for Sustainability

Gamification for sustainability is successful when important components that resonate with users are strategically integrated, boosting engagement and creating positive behavioral change. When these elements are thoroughly implemented, they produce a holistic and inspiring experience that encourages users to adopt and advocate environmentally beneficial behavior.

Specific Goals and Challenges

Setting clear objectives and challenges is critical to the effectiveness of gamification. Douglas and Brauer's (2021) research highlighted the necessity of creating attainable goals that are matched with sustainability objectives. Well-defined challenges provide participants with a feeling of purpose and direction, motivating them to take action.

Meaningful Rewards

Rewards act as strong motivators, reinforcing desired actions. However, meaningful rewards, whether intrinsic or extrinsic, must align with the values of participants. Alsawaier (2018) emphasized the need of aligning rewards with a person's environmental attitudes in order to increase the perceived value of sustainable actions.

Advancement and Feedback

It is critical to incorporate advancement and real-time feedback. Krath et al. (2022) emphasized the importance of progression in retaining engagement by breaking down tasks into manageable segments. Regular feedback informs users of their progress, boosting their sense of accomplishment and encouraging them to participate in the future.

Social Interaction

Social interactions foster a sense of community and a sense of common purpose. The studies demonstrate the potential of social sharing and collaboration in gamification for sustainability. Engaging with others, whether through competition or collaboration, boosts motivation and increases the overall impact of sustainable behaviors (Dikcius et al., 2021; Liu & Tanaka, 2020)

Narrative Immersion

Incorporating sustainable actions into fascinating narratives enhances the gamification experience. Douglas and Brauer (2021) investigated narrative-driven gamification in sustainability education, demonstrating how storytelling boosts engagement and comprehension, making sustainable practices more relatable and meaningful.

Personalization and Flexibility

Creating gamification tactics that are tailored to individual tastes increases engagement. Hsu (2022) emphasized the efficacy of individualized challenges and experiences that adapt to users' interests, increasing motivation and connection to sustainability goals.

Finally, incorporating above features into gamification approaches has the transformative potential to drive eco-friendly behavior. Organizations can design compelling and powerful interventions that inspire individuals to embrace sustainability by matching challenges, rewards, progression, social interactions, narratives, and personalization.

Tailoring Gamification to Target Audiences and Behaviors

A key component of successful sustainability marketing is effectively customizing gamification tactics to specific target groups and desired behaviors. Knowing that different individuals have different motivations, interests, and barriers, personalization guarantees that gamified interventions resonate with users, resulting in meaningful engagement and behavior change.

Audience Segmentation

Koivisto and Hamari (2019) stressed the significance of audience segmentation based on demographics, preferences, and motives. Tailoring gamification to distinct segments provides for more personalized experiences, boosting the intervention's relevance and efficacy.

Behavior Alignment

It is critical to create gamification experiences that align with the targeted behaviors. Krath et al. (2022) underline the need of mapping out the behavioral journey and developing game features that guide players toward adopting and maintaining environmentally friendly behaviors.

Motivational Triggers

Identifying and incorporating motivational triggers that resonate with the target audience increase engagement. Altmeyer et al. (2021) discussed the importance of aligning gamification elements with users' intrinsic motivations, such as altruism or personal achievement, to drive behavior change.

Cultural Sensitivity

Cultural nuances influence user's perceptions and responses. Deterding (2011) emphasized the importance of considering cultural factors when designing gamification, ensuring that elements are culturally relevant and respectful, thereby increasing their impact on behavior change.

Accessibility and User Experience

It is vital to create inclusive gamification experiences that cater to consumers of varied abilities and technological familiarity. Deterding, Sicart et al. (2011) accentuated the need of building intuitive and accessible interfaces in order to increase engagement among a wider audience.

The literature demonstrates the effectiveness of targeted gamification in encouraging sustainable transportation choices (Christian et al., 2022; Anagnostopoulou et al., 2018). According to these studies, personalized gamification components such as location-based challenges and tailored prizes greatly improve participant engagement and pro-environmental behavior.

Thus, the ability of gamification in sustainability marketing to adapt to the individual demands and motivations of target audiences is critical to its success. Organizations can develop gamification interventions that motivate individuals to embrace and promote eco-friendly actions by segmenting audiences, aligning with desired behaviors, tapping into internal incentives, being culturally sensitive, and optimizing user experience.

Incorporating Social Dynamics and Competition

Gamified sustainability efforts might benefit from social interactions and competition. Leaderboards, team challenges, and collaborative activities build a sense of community and a common goal. Healthy competition enables people to push themselves beyond their comfort zones while also inspiring others to join in. Gamification can establish a supportive community that jointly pushes eco-friendly actions by tapping into an individual's social nature.

Challenges and Ethical Considerations

While gamification has great avenues in terms of motivating sustainable behaviors, it also poses obstacles and ethical concerns that must be properly addressed in order to assure its positive influence and integrity.

Potential Overemphasis on Rewards

An overemphasis on rewards might shift the focus away from internal motivation and toward external incentives. Dikcius et al. (2021) argued that when rewards are eliminated, people may prefer rewards over true commitment to sustainability, potentially leading to a drop in eco-friendly activities.

Behavioral Addiction

Hawi and Samaha (2017) explored the risk of gamification creating behavioral addiction in which people engage in environmentally friendly activities purely for the satisfaction of achieving in-game rewards. To avoid negative outcomes, it is critical to balance participation with an avoidance of obsessive behavior.

Unintended Consequences

The competitive elements of gamification may inadvertently foster unethical behaviors. Degirmenci (2023) stated that participants may resort to cheating or unethical practices to outperform others, undermining gamification's positive impact on sustainability goals.

Greenwashing

There is a risk that organizations will use gamification to project an environmentally friendly image without making significant changes. Boncu et al. (2022) warned against such greenwashing, emphasizing the importance of open communication and a genuine commitment to sustainability.

Equity and Access

To prevent further disparities, gamification experiences must be inclusive and accessible to diverse populations. Deterding, Sicart et al. (2011) emphasized the importance of ensuring that gamification strategies do not inadvertently exclude individuals with disabilities or limited technological access.

Addressing above issues requires a thorough understanding of gamification's ethical aspects. Kriz et al.'s (2022) research emphasized the significance of ethical game design that respects user autonomy, promotes positive social values, and avoids deceptive strategies. This method protects the user experience while also ensuring that gamification remains a tool for positive behavior modification.

To summarize, while gamification provides creative techniques to enhance sustainability, it must be used with caution to prevent problems. It is vital to strike a balance between rewards and intrinsic motivation, to prevent addictive behavior, to anticipate unexpected consequences, to counteract greenwashing, and to ensure fair access. Following ethical principles in gamification design protects its potential as a catalyst for significant and long-term eco-friendly behaviors.

Potential Pitfalls of Gamified Sustainability Marketing

While gamified sustainability marketing has the potential to influence positive behavior change, it is critical to recognize and address possible flaws that could jeopardize its effectiveness and ethical integrity.

Shallow Engagement

An overemphasis on game components may result in shallow engagement. Deterding, Dixon et al. (2011) and Deterding, Sicart et al. (2011) warned that focusing primarily on prizes and competition may deflect attention away from the true relevance of sustainability, resulting in short-term engagement with no long-term behavior change.

Short-Term Focus

Gamification can inadvertently encourage short-term actions at the expense of long-term sustainability. Krath et al. (2021) highlighted that participants may prioritize immediate rewards while overlooking the broader context and environmental implications of their actions.

Psychological Burnout

Excessive competition or challenges can lead to psychological burnout. Hamari et al. (2014) warned that persistent pressure to accomplish gamification goals may induce stress and tiredness, leading to disengagement and poor perceptions of the intervention.

Manipulative Techniques

Gamification tactics must avoid manipulation and undue influence. Kriz et al. (2022) emphasized the significance of preserving users' autonomy and dignity by avoiding manipulative strategies that impair users' ability to make informed choices.

Perceived Inauthenticity

If users view gamification to be fake or opportunistic, they may become distrustful of the organization's commitment to sustainability. To avoid a sense of greenwashing, Boncu et al. (2022) underline the necessity of matching gamified initiatives with actual environmental goals.

To avoid above-mentioned issues, gamification design must be approached holistically. Xi and Hamari (2019) provided ethical principles that emphasize user well-being, intrinsic motivation, and meaningful interaction. Organizations make sure that gamification must be a positive factor for fostering sustainable behaviors by adhering to the above principles.

To sum up, gamified sustainability marketing requires a balanced and ethical strategy to optimize its positive impact. The awareness of difficulties such as superficial involvement, short-term focus, psychological exhaustion, manipulative approaches, and perceived inauthenticity leads to the design of such interfaces that truly motivate individuals to embrace environmentally friendly behavior.

Ensuring Transparency, Fairness, and User Autonomy

Maintaining openness, fairness, and user agency is crucial for ethically implementing long-term gamification tactics. Organizations must follow ethical standards to generate trust and promote real engagement as gamification interventions try to inspire eco-friendly habits.

Transparency

Deterding, Sicart et al. (2011) emphasized the need of transparency in conveying gamification's aim, rules, and consequences. Clarifying how users' behaviors contribute to long-term sustainability goals develops trust and avoids misconceptions.

Fairness

Fairness is essential to user engagement and motivation. Xi and Hamari (2019) emphasized the need of ensuring that gamification mechanics do not discriminate or favor specific users, hence minimizing the feelings of unfairness that may impede participation.

User Autonomy

It is pivotal to maintain user autonomy. Kriz et al. (2022) emphasized the need of allowing users to make informed choices and opt out if they do not wish to participate in gamified activities. This protects user's freedom to engage in environmentally beneficial practices voluntarily.

Avoid Manipulation

Gamification should avoid manipulative practices that take advantage of consumers' psychological vulnerabilities. Deterding (2015) warn against tactics that push or pressure users into specific actions, assuring authentic and ethical participation.

Christian et al. (2022) investigated a gamification intervention that encourages sustainable transportation choices to demonstrate these concepts. The study reveals how ethical gamification may empower users to make sustainable decisions by describing the incentives system publicly, assuring fairness in reward distribution, allowing users to opt out, and avoiding manipulative features.

It is utmost to preserve openness, fairness, and user liberty in gamified sustainability interventions to ensure ethical implementation. Organizations that follow these principles can foster true participation, increase trust, and contribute to a culture of responsible and purposeful eco-friendly activities.

Addressing Concerns Related to Overconsumption and Greenwashing

Gamification should be utilized carefully to avoid overconsumption or over involvement, which might have negative environmental consequences. To avoid allegations of greenwashing, it is critical that gamification activities connect with true environmental objectives. Authenticity is vital for credibility and long-term influence when promoting environmentally responsible habits through gamification.

Addressing overconsumption and greenwashing concerns in the context of gamified sustainability marketing is critical to maintaining the integrity of the efforts employed by the organizations. Organizations may navigate these concerns by focusing on some of the important aspects as explained in the next sections.

Encourage Genuine Sustainability

Make sure that the activities promoted through gamification truly contribute to sustainability and environmental protection. It is utmost to avoid rewarding practices that may lead to excessive consumption or provide insignificant environmental benefits.

Educational Aspects

Include educational aspects in gamification experience. To avoid tokenistic behavior, assist users in understanding the greater environmental context and the meaning of their activities.

Transparency in Communication

Transparently communicate the environmental consequences of various acts. Avoid unclear or misleading wording and provide explicit information about how each activity contributes to sustainability goals.

Third-Party Verification

Collaborate with credible environmental organizations or specialists to validate the authenticity of gamification activities' sustainability claims. This increases credibility and prevents potential greenwashing.

Measurable Impact

Construct the gamification system in such a way that users can see the measurable impact of their actions. Provide data and figures on how their actions help to achieve favorable environmental outcomes.

Long-Term Perspective

Encourage users to embrace long-term sustainable behaviors rather than short-term activities that may result in overconsumption. Emphasize conservation and efficiency-promoting activities.

Holistic Approach

Promote a holistic knowledge of sustainability that extends beyond individual activities. Encourage users to participate in systemic changes and to push for larger environmental benefits.

Avoid Excessive Rewards

Be cautious of the gamification process' rewards and incentives. Avoid lavish gifts that may encourage overconsumption or a singular emphasis on material gain.

Transparent Progress Tracking

Allow users to follow their progress and comprehend the long-term consequences of their activities. This openness can discourage token gestures while encouraging continuous interaction.

Overconsumption and greenwashing must be addressed with care and ethics. The above explained aspects provide insights on behavioral psychology, ethical consumerism, and sustainable behaviors that can help to guide the efforts of the organization.

Conclusions and Future Directions

Emerging Trends in Gamification and Sustainability

New prospects for gamified sustainability efforts are emerging as technology improves. Virtual reality, augmented reality, and wearable technologies provide unique ways for people to participate in immersive experiences. Data analytics integration can enable more personalized and successful gamification methods. Collaboration platforms and collaborations between enterprises, nongovernmental organizations, and governments could accelerate the adoption of gamification for sustainability.

Recommendations for Practitioners and Policymakers

As gamification is increasingly being included into sustainability marketing tactics, practitioners and policymakers can play a critical role in optimizing its impact while adhering to ethical norms. The recommendations below outline the effective adoption and responsible use of gamification for promoting environmentally friendly behaviors.

Align with Genuine Environmental Goals

Organizations should ensure that their gamification activities are connected with genuine sustainability goals rather than being driven primarily by marketing aims. This authenticity increases users' trust and dedication to the cause.

Prioritize User Experience

According to Hsu and Chen (2018), user-centric design is critical in gamification and sustainability synergy. Gamification practitioners should concentrate on developing entertaining, intuitive, and accessible gamification experiences for a wide range of audiences. Deterding, Sicart et al.'s (2011) research emphasizes the importance of user-centered design in order to maximize engagement.

Integrate Ethical Principles

Gamification design should be guided by ethical issues. Transparency, justice, and user liberty must be ensured by practitioners, and deceptive approaches must be avoided. Kriz et al. (2022) provide insights on ethical game design ideas that can protect the well-being and autonomy of users.

Consider Audience Preferences

Customization is critical. To properly design gamification techniques, organizations should understand audience preferences, incentives, and barriers. For a successful implementation, Koivisto and Hamari (2019) underline the necessity of identifying user types.

Long-Term Impact Assessment

It is critical to assess the long-term impact of gamification activities. Longitudinal research that follows maintained eco-friendly behavior after the first engagement period should be funded by policymakers and practitioners. The impact assessment practices must be incorporated for the long-term sustainability and growth of the organization (Hsu, 2022).

Collaboration and Knowledge Sharing

In order to exchange knowledge and ideas, practitioners should collaborate with academics, designers, and policymakers. Open communication can foster innovation, assure best practices, and prevent mistakes from being repeated (Dikcius et al., 2021; Liu & Tanaka, 2020; Sailer & Homner, 2020).

By following these principles, practitioners and policymakers can effectively promote sustainable habits while preserving ethical standards and guaranteeing meaningful and long-term consequences.

Concluding Remarks on the Potential Impact of Gamification on Sustainability Marketing

Gamification has the potential to have a deep and far-reaching impact on sustainable marketing. Gamification, through the deliberate integration of game mechanics and design components, provides a dynamic approach to inspiring individuals to adopt and support environmentally beneficial behavior. Gamification has the potential to address complex environmental concerns and achieve long-term change by encouraging engagement, tapping into inherent motivations, and giving concrete incentives.

However, when firms begin to include gamification into their sustainable marketing strategy, it is critical that they manage difficulties and ethical concerns. The success of gamification strategies can be hampered by flaws such as shallow engagement, short-term focus, manipulation, and perceived inauthenticity. Maintaining the integrity and authenticity of gamified sustainability activities requires ensuring openness, fairness, and user agency.

Looking ahead, the relationship between gamification and sustainable marketing will continue to expand. The discipline is primed for unique innovations, such as the incorporation of emerging technology and the discovery of novel tactics that appeal to a wide range of users. Practitioners and academicians can exploit gamification's revolutionary potential for establishing an environmentally conscious society by adhering to ethical values, working across disciplines, and embracing user-centered designs.

The potential influence of gamification should not be underestimated in a constantly changing world where environmental concerns are becoming increasingly pressing. It provides a unique opportunity for individuals to become active participants in shaping a more sustainable future, influencing good behavioral change, and contributing to a more environmentally conscious society.

References

Abou Kamar, M., Maher, A., Salem, I. E., & Elbaz, A. M. (2024). Gamification impact on tourists' pro-sustainability intentions: Integration of technology acceptance model (TAM) and the theory of planned behaviour (TPB). *Tourism Review*, 79(2), 487–504.

Ajzen, I. (1991). The theory of planned behaviour. *Organizational Behaviour and Human Decision Processes*, 50(2), 179–211.

Alsawaier, R. S. (2018). The effect of gamification on motivation and engagement. *International Journal of Information and Learning Technology*, 35(1), 56–79. https://doi.org/10.1108/IJILT-02-2017-0009

Altmeyer, M., Lessel, P., & Jantwal, S. (2021). Potential and effects of personalizing gameful fitness applications using behaviour change intentions and Hexad user types. *User Modeling and User-Adapted Interaction*, 31, 675–712. https://doi.org/10.1007/s11257-021-09288-6

Anagnostopoulou, E., Bothos, E., Magoutas, B., Schrammel, J., & Mentzas, G. (2018). Persuasive technologies for sustainable mobility: State of the art and emerging trends. *Sustainability*, 10(7). https://doi.org/10.3390/su10072128

Anderson, C. A., & Dill, K. E. (2000). Video games and aggressive thoughts, feelings, and behaviour in the laboratory and in life. *Journal of Personality and Social Psychology*, 78(4), 772–790. https://doi.org/10.1037/0022-3514.78.4.772

Ayastuy, M. D., Torres, D., & Fernández, A. (2021). Adaptive gamification in collaborative systems, a systematic mapping study. *Computer Science Review*, 39, 100333. https://doi.org/10.1016/j.cosrev.2020.100333

Bandura, A. (1977). *Social learning theory*. Prentice-Hall.

Behl, A., Jayawardena, N., Pereira, V., Jabeen, F., Jain, K., & Gupta, M. (2023). Engaging and motivating crowd-workers in gamified crowdsourcing mobile apps in the context of logistics and sustainable supply chain management. *Annals of Operations Research*. https://doi.org/10.1007/s10479-023-05557-2

Behl, A., Pereira, V., Jayawardena, N., Nigam, A., & Mangla, S. (2023). Gamification as an innovation: A tool to improve organizational marketing performance and sustainability of international firms. *International Marketing Review*, Vol. ahead-of-print (No. ahead-of-print). https://doi.org/10.1108/IMR-05-2022-0113

Belz, F. M., & Peattie, S. (2012). *Sustainability marketing: A global perspective*. John Wiley & Sons.

Boncu, S., Candel, O.-S., & Popa, N. L. (2022). Gameful green: A systematic review on the use of serious computer games and gamified mobile apps to foster pro-environmental information, attitudes and behaviours. *Sustainability*, *14*(16), 10400. https://doi.org/10.3390/su141610400

Boncu, Ș., Candel, O.-S., Prundeanu, O., & Popa, N. L. (2023). Growing a digital iceberg for a polar bear: Effects of a gamified mobile app on university students' pro-environmental behaviours. *International Journal of Sustainability in Higher Education*, Vol. ahead-of-print(No. ahead-of-print). https://doi.org/10.1108/IJSHE-03-2023-0092

Brannon, L., Gold, L., Magee, J., & Walton, G. (2022). The potential of interactivity and gamification within immersive journalism & interactive documentary (I-docs) to explore climate change literacy and inoculate against misinformation. *Journalism Practice*, *16*(2–3), 334–364.

Chan, E., Nah, F. F. H., Liu, Q., & Lu, Z. (2018). Effect of gamification on intrinsic motivation. In F. H. Nah & B. Xiao (Eds.), *HCI in business, government, and organizations. HCIBGO 2018. Lecture notes in computer science* (Vol. 10923). Springer. https://doi.org/10.1007/978-3-319-91716-0_35

Christian, A., Katharina, E., & Stefan, S. (2022). Free ride in rush-hour traffic – designing gamified smart mobility systems for sustainable use. *ICIS 2022 Proceedings*, 6. https://aisel.aisnet.org/icis2022/user_behaivor/user_behaivor/6

Chu, C. H. (2023). Deep resource allocation for a massively multiplayer online finance of tourism gamification in metaverse. *Information Technology & Tourism*, 1–19. https://doi.org/10.1007/s40558-023-00267-8

Csikszentmihalyi, M. (1975). *Beyond boredom and anxiety*. Jossey-Bass.

Cugelman, B. (2013). Gamification: What it is and why it matters to digital health behaviour change developers. *JMIR Serious Games*, *1*(1), e3. https://doi.org/10.2196/games.3139

Deci, E. L., Koestner, R., & Ryan, R. M. (1999). A meta-analytic review of experiments examining the effects of extrinsic rewards on intrinsic motivation. *Psychological Bulletin*, *125*(6), 627–668. https://doi.org/10.1037/0033-2909.125.6.627

Deci, E. L., & Ryan, R. M. (1985). *Intrinsic motivation and self-determination in human behaviour*. Springer.

Degirmenci, K. (2023). The role of serious games in shaping pro-environmental behaviours: Changing attitudes toward renewable energy. In *Handbook of research on decision-making capabilities improvement with serious games* (pp. 364–381). IGI Global. https://doi.org/10.4018/978-1-6684-9166-9.ch015

Deterding, S. (2011). Situated motivational affordances of game elements: A conceptual model. In *The workshop at CHI*. Retrieved from http://www.quilageo.com/wp-content/uploads/2013/07/09-Deterding.pdf

Deterding, S. (2015). The lens of intrinsic skill atoms: A method for gameful design. *Human-Computer Interaction*, *30*(3–4), 294–335. https://doi.org/10.1080/07370024.2014.993471

Deterding, S., Dixon, D., Khaled, R., & Nacke, L. (2011). From game design elements to gamefulness: Defining "gamification". In *Proceedings of the 15th international academic MindTrek conference: Envisioning future media environments* (pp. 9–15). https://doi.org/10.1145/2181037.2181040

Deterding, S., Sicart, M., Nacke, L., O'Hara, K., & Dixon, D. (2011). Gamification using game-design elements in non-gaming contexts. In *Proceedings of the CHI on factors in computing systems* (pp. 2425–2428). https://doi.org/10.1145/1979742.1979575

Dikcius, V., Urbonavicius, S., Adomaviciute, K., Degutis, M., & Zimaitis, I. (2021). Learning marketing online: The role of social interactions and gamification rewards. *Journal of Marketing Education*, *43*(2), 159–173. https://doi.org/ 10.1177/0273475320968252

Doğan-Südaş, H., Kara, A., & Karaca, E. (2023). Effects of gamified mobile apps on purchase intentions and word-of-mouth engagement: Implications for sustainability behaviour. *Sustainability*, *15*(13), 10506. https://doi.org/10.3390/su 151310506

Dong, X., Chang, Y., Liao, J., Hao, X., & Yu, X. (2023). The impact of virtual interaction on consumers' pro-environmental behaviours: The mediating role of platform intimacy and love for nature. *Information Technology & People*, Vol. ahead-of-print(No. ahead-of-print). https://doi.org/10.1108/ITP-02-2021-0164

Douglas, B. D., & Brauer, M. (2021). Gamification to prevent climate change: A review of games and apps for sustainability. *Current Opinion in Psychology*, *42*, 89–94. https://doi.org/10.1016/j.copsyc.2021.04.008

Escudeiro, P. S., & Campos, M. G. (2023). A gamified approach to enhance environmental sustainability awareness and responsibility. In *Handbook of research on decision-making capabilities improvement with serious games* (pp. 343–363). IGI Global.

Gamification Market. (n.d.). *Gamification market report*. Retrieved March 3, 2024, from https://www.precedenceresearch.com/gamification-market

Hallifax, S., Altmeyer, M., Kölln, K., Rauschenberger, M., & Nacke, L. E. (2023). From points to progression: A scoping review of game elements in gamification research with a content analysis of 280 research papers. *Proceedings of the ACM on Human-Computer Interaction*, *7*(CHI PLAY), 748–768.

Hamari, J., Koivisto, J., & Sarsa, H. (2014). Does gamification work? A literature review of empirical studies on gamification. In *2014 47th Hawaii international conference on system sciences* (pp. 3025–3034). IEEE. https://doi.org/10.1109/ HICSS.2014.377

Hawi, N. S., & Samaha, M. (2017). The relations among social media addiction, self-esteem, and life satisfaction in university students. *Social Science Computer Review*, *35*, 576–586. https://doi.org/10.1177/0894439316660340

Hayes, D., Symonds, J. E., & Harwell, T. A. (2022). Preventing pollution: A scoping review of immersive learning environments and gamified systems for children and young people. *Journal of Research on Technology in Education*, 1–19. https://doi. org/10.1080/15391523.2022.2107589

Hsu, C. L. (2022). Applying cognitive evaluation theory to analyze the impact of gamification mechanics on user engagement in resource recycling. *Information Management*, *59*, 103602. https://doi.org/10.1016/j.im.2022.103602.

Hsu, C. L., & Chen, M. C. (2018). How does gamification improve user experience? An empirical investigation on the antecedences and consequences of user experience and its mediating role. *Technological Forecasting and Social Change*, *132*, 118–129. https://doi.org/10.1016/j.techfore.2018.01.023

Hsu, C. L., & Chen, M. C. (2021). Advocating recycling and encouraging environmentally friendly habits through gamification: An empirical investigation. *Technology in Society*, *66*, 101621. https://doi.org/10.1016/j.techsoc.2021.101621

Jahn, K., Kordyaka, B., Machulska, A., Eiler, T. J., Gruenewald, A., Klucken, T., Brueck, R., Gethmann, C. C., & Niehaves, B. (2021). Individualized gamification elements: The impact of avatar and feedback design on reuse intention. *Computers in Human Behaviour*, *119*, 106702. https://doi.org/10.1016/j.chb.2021. 106702

Jami Pour, M., Rafiei, K., Khani, M., & Sabrirazm, A. (2021). Gamification and customer experience: The mediating role of brand engagement in online grocery

retailing. *Nankai Business Review International, 12*(3), 340–357. https://doi.
org/10.1108/NBRI-07-2020-0041

Jones, M., Blanton, J. E., & Williams, R. E. (2022). Science to practice: Does gamification enhance intrinsic motivation? *Active Learning in Higher Education, 0*(0).
https://doi.org/10.1177/14697874211066882

Kapp, K. M. (2012). *The gamification of learning and instruction: Game-based methods and strategies for training and education.* John Wiley & Sons.

Kaushal, L. A., & Prashar, A. (2022). Determinants of service consumer's attitudes
and behavioural intentions towards sharing economy for sustainable consumption:
An emerging market perspective. *Journal of Global Information Technology Management, 25*(2), 137–158. https://doi.org/10.1080/1097198X.2022.2062993

Koivisto, J., & Hamari, J. (2019). The rise of motivational information systems:
A review of gamification research. *International Journal of Information Management, 45,* 191–210. https://doi.org/10.1016/j.ijinfomgt.2018.10.013

Kotler, P., Kartajaya, H., & Setiawan, I. (2019). *Marketing 3.0: From products to
customers to the human spirit.* John Wiley & Sons.

Krath, J., Morschheuser, B., & von Korflesch, H. F. O. (2022). Designing gamification
for sustainable employee behaviour: Insights on employee motivations, design features and gamification elements. In *55th Hawaii international conference on system
sciences (HICSS)* (pp. 1594–1603). http://hdl.handle.net/10125/79530

Krath, J., Schürmann, L., & von Korflesch, H. F. O. (2021). Revealing the theoretical basis of gamification: A systematic review and analysis of theory in research
on gamification, serious games and game-based learning. *Computers in Human
Behaviour, 125,* 106963. https://doi.org/10.1016/j.chb.2021.106963

Kriz, W. C., Kikkawa, T., & Sugiura, J. (2022). Manipulation through gamification
and gaming. In T. Kikkawa, W. C. Kriz, & J. Sugiura (Eds.), *Gaming as a cultural
commons. Translational systems sciences* (Vol. 28). Springer. https://doi.org/10.10
07/978-981-19-0348-9_11

Liu, B., & Tanaka, J. (2020). Integrating gamification and social interaction into an
AR-based gamified point system. *Multimodal Technologies and Interaction, 4*(3),
51. https://doi.org/10.3390/mti4030051

Locke, E. A., & Latham, G. P. (1990). *A theory of goal setting & task performance.*
Prentice-Hall.

Mekler, E. D., Bruhlmann, F., Tch, A. N., & Opwis, K. (2017). Towards understanding the effects of individual gamification elements on intrinsic motivation
and performance. *Computers in Human Behaviour, 71,* 525–534. https://doi.
org/10.1016/j.chb.2015.08.048

Ng, P. M. L., & Cheung, C. T. Y. (2022). Why do young people do things for the environment? The effect of perceived values on pro-environmental behaviour. *Young
Consumers, 23*(4), 539–554. https://doi.org/10.1108/YC-11-2021-1411

Ntoumanis, N., Ng, J. Y. Y., Prestwich, A., Quested, E., Hancox, J. E.,
Thøgersen-Ntoumani, C., Deci, E. L., Ryan, R. M., Lonsdale, C., & Williams,
G. C. (2021). A meta-analysis of self-determination theory-informed intervention
studies in the health domain: Effects on motivation, health behaviour, physical, and
psychological health. *Health Psychology Review, 15*(2), 214–244. https://doi.org/1
0.1080/17437199.2020.1718529

Ouariachi, T., Li, C.-Y., & Elving, W. J. L. (2020). Gamification approaches for
education and engagement on pro-environmental behaviours: Searching for best
practices. *Sustainability, 12*(11), 4565. https://doi.org/10.3390/su12114565

Ourdas, C., & Ponis, S. (2023). Evaluating the effects of gamification in behavioural
change: A proposed SEM-based approach. *Sustainability, 15*(6), 5442. https://doi.
org/10.3390/su15065442

Peattie, S., & Peattie, K. (2003). Ready to fly solo? Reducing social marketing's dependence on commercial marketing theory. *Marketing Theory, 1*(3), 365–385. https://doi.org/10.1177/147059310333006

Polonsky, M. J. (2008). An introduction to green marketing. *Global Environment: Problems and Policies, 2*(1), 1–10.

Rodrigues, L., Palomino, P. T., Toda, A. M., Klock, A. C., Oliveira, W., Avila-Santos, A. P., & Isotani, S. (2021). Personalization improves gamification: Evidence from a mixed-methods study. *Proceedings of the ACM on Human-Computer Interaction, 5*, 1–25. https://doi.org/10.1145/3474714

Ryan, R. M., & Deci, E. L. (2000a). Intrinsic and extrinsic motivations: Classic definitions and new directions. *Contemporary Educational Psychology, 25*(1), 54–67. https://doi.org/10.1006/ceps.1999.1020

Ryan, R. M., & Deci, E. L. (2000b). Self-determination theory and the facilitation of intrinsic motivation, social development, and well-being. *American Psychologist, 55*(1), 68–78. https://doi.org/10.1037/0003-066X.55.1.68

Sailer, M., & Homner, L. (2020). The gamification of learning: A meta-analysis. *Educational Psychology Review, 32*, 77–112. https://doi.org/10.1007/s10648-019-09498-w

Scholefield, S., & Shepherd, L. A. (2019). Gamification techniques for raising cyber security awareness. In A. Moallem (Ed.), *HCI for cybersecurity, privacy and trust. HCII 2019. Lecture notes in computer science* (Vol. 11594). Springer. https://doi.org/10.1007/978-3-030-22351-9_13

Seaborn, K., & Fels, D. I. (2015). Gamification in theory and action: A survey. *International Journal of Human-Computer Studies, 74*, 14–31. https://doi.org/10.1016/j.ijhcs.2014.09.006

Sharif, K. H., & Ameen, S. Y. (2020). *A review of security awareness approaches with special emphasis on gamification.* 2020 International Conference on Advanced Science and Engineering (ICOASE), Iraq, 151–156. https://doi.org/10.1109/ICOASE51841.2020.9436595

Sheth, J. N., & Parvatiyar, A. (2021). Sustainable marketing: Market-driving, not market-driven. *Journal of Macromarketing, 41*(1), 150–165. https://doi.org/10.1177/0276146720961836

Skinner, B. F. (1938). *The behaviour of organisms.* D. Appleton-Century Company.

Skinner, B. F. (1953). *Science and human behaviour.* Pearson Education.

Thomas Muñoz, R. (2022). Environmental education networks for social empowerment and global citizenship: A case of non-formal education from Mexico. In M. Öztürk (Ed.), *Educational response, inclusion and empowerment for SDGs in emerging economies. Sustainable development goals series.* Springer. https://doi.org/10.1007/978-3-030-98962-0_12

Vallerand, R. J. (1997). Toward a hierarchical model of intrinsic and extrinsic motivation. *Advances in Experimental Social Psychology, 29*, 271–360. https://doi.org/10.1016/S0065-2601(08)60019-2

Wang, B., & Udall, A. M. (2023). Sustainable consumer behaviours: The effects of identity, environment value and marketing promotion. *Sustainability, 15*(2), 1129. https://doi.org/10.3390/su15021129

Werbach, K., & Hunter, D. (2012). *For the win: How game thinking can revolutionize your business.* Wharton Digital Press.

Whittaker, L., Mulcahy, R., & Bennett, R. R. (2021). Go with the flow' for gamification and sustainability marketing. *International Journal of Information Management, 61*, 102305. https://doi.org/10.1016/j.ijinfomgt.2020.102305

Wilkie, W. L., & Moore, E. S. (1999). Marketing's contributions to society. *Journal of Marketing, 63*(4), 198–218.

Xi, N., & Hamari, J. (2019). Does gamification satisfy needs? A study on the relationship between gamification features and intrinsic need satisfaction. *International Journal of Information Management*, *46*, 210–221.

Xu, H., & Hamari, J. (2022). How to improve creativity: A study of gamification, money, and punishment. *Behaviour & Information Technology*. https://doi.org/10.1080/0144929X.2022.2133634

Zhang, Q., & Anwar, M. A. (2023). Leveraging gamification technology to motivate environmentally responsible behaviour: An empirical examination of ant forest. *Decision Sciences*. https://doi.org/10.1111/deci.12618

Zichermann, G., & Cunningham, C. (2011). *Gamification by design: Implementing game mechanics in web and mobile apps*. O'Reilly Media, Inc.

Chapter 12

Ethical Dilemmas in Gamified Marketing Approaches

Lipsa Das, T.S. Poornachandrika and Deepshikha Bhargava

Introduction

'Gamification' is the process of incorporating components of game design into non-gaming situations with the primary goal of improving performance and motivation in a variety of tasks, including learning, rehabilitation, well-being, and productivity at work (Deterding et al., 2011). A good example is provided by Hamari et al. (2014), who show how gamification can effectively increase motivation for tasks that would otherwise be considered difficult and boring. Even with the best of intentions, designers, developers, and funders trying to improve players' lives may unintentionally create outcomes that are morally dubious or even unethical as a result of the trend toward gamified solutions. This moral conundrum is similar to the opinion ascribed to Albert Einstein, who stated that he would rather be a watchmaker than a scientist after considering the unintended effects of atomic power. This emphasizes how gamified systems must be developed and implemented with careful ethical concerns in mind to ensure that the path to better outcomes is morally sound.

Given that gamification appeals to the basic playful elements of human nature, those who create gamified solutions bear a great deal of responsibility. These producers may unintentionally or intentionally create goods and services that endanger or worsen conditions for users, the environment, or society at large. Though it could be difficult to educate people who have bad intentions, it is crucial for good-hearted engineers to understand the moral dilemmas that arise from their methods. Beyond their personal goals, which should ideally coincide with the welfare of stakeholders, developers need to put justice first when building applications and make sure that the results have a good effect on customers, users, and the intended recipients of the systems that are being developed (Moor, 1999). Even though many developers think of themselves as morally pure, in order for them to constantly behave morally, they must deliberately cultivate virtues connected to their line of work. This emphasizes how important ethical considerations are to the thoughtful creation of gamified solutions.

DOI: 10.4324/9781032694238-16

Applied ethics is based on theoretical ethical principles and focuses on particular domains. Recently, gamification-related ethical questions have gained attention due to the work of many researchers (Bui et al., 2015; Hyrynsalmi, Kimppa et al., 2017; Hyrynsalmi, Smed et al., 2017; Kim & Werbach, 2016). There are an increasing number of new research works exploring these ethical issues, despite the fact that the topic is still relatively unexplored. This summary attempts to provide a general overview of the ethical problems that arise from gamification, while acknowledging that it is not a comprehensive list of all the possible problems. It is anticipated that as the field and its methods advance, new ethical dilemmas may surface, making some more traditional subjects outdated when new systems are implemented. This entry provides an overview of the ethical dilemmas that are inherent in gamification. The following sections will group these ethical issues into three primary categories: those related to gamification design, those related to the technology that powers gamified systems, and those concerning the morality of the data that gamified systems use (Sicart, 2015).

Gamification is becoming increasingly famous in industry, especially as a marketing tool. Research on gamification falls behind practical aspects however, though some frameworks are beginning to emerge (Maican et al., 2016). Till date, the ethics of gamification in a marketing context have largely missed deep insights despite some resemblances with other techniques that industry closely supervises such as subliminal advertising. Marketing ethics is a well-stabilized and emerging area of interest, and it is this revelation we join overall. In particular, we aim to encourage further proceedings and possible outcome on the ethics, and potential regulation, of gamification (Ferrell et al., 2015) (Gaski, 1999) (Schauster et al., 2017).

The aim of gamification in marketing is to get consumers to indulge in purchasing behavior contrary to other gamified contexts that intend to change people's behavior in other predetermined ways (Raftopoulos et al., 2014). An organization designs an engaging and interesting experience, which then motivates an audience, or 'users', to make a purchase. Gamification includes components of design that subliminally convince engagement. In digital game design – a common touch point for designers of gamified systems – and more importantly within advergaming, designing deceptively the speed of the game experience and the level of similarity between the game and the product, for example, can both influence brand recall and purchase behavior (Vashisht & Royne, 2019). The nature of how such manipulative design features work at a cognitive and subliminal level raises ethical concerns over potential manipulations. These concerns are likely to become very important as research shows the triggers of effective gamified systems and gives green signals to the firms to create more advanced and more trendy designs that become stealthier in their persuasion. To encourage the responsible growth and development of gamification, it is advised that both industry practitioners and researchers concentrate more on ethics. Till now it has not been done, and not doing so potentially puts consumers at risk. Till now, research has focused on examining the effectiveness of gamification in different situations.

Ethics of Gamification as an Overall System

Strategically, and from the dimension of the organization, 'good' gamification is 'successful' gamification. The organization designs an engaging gaming experience to bring about definite behavioral outcome. In marketing discipline, best final result typically relates to profits for the organization – for example, targeted users buy an increased proportion of the firm's products or services. Although users are aware of their involvement, the gamification process still involves substantial covert activity. Users might be unaware that attributes of the experience are designed to target a special behavior, for example. Indeed, these marketing gimmicks work most effectively when they are as subtle and subliminal as possible. In addition to this, firms may conceal the possible outcome from the potential users. The ethics of the entire system depend on the comparative number of target audience between varied groups – users and others who are influenced by the possible outcome (shareholders, employees, communities, etc.). Increase in sales or purchases for example could produce positive effects such as profit sharing, increased value of stocks, or individual career progression. While such benefits might not cause the 'loss' to consumers, the principle of the greatest good for the greatest number remains applicable. Therefore, if the amount of 'good' for stakeholders is more than that for users, covert persuasion and an aim are not only justified but also show the most ethical course of action: deceiving a comparative few to benefit the majority is more ethical. Currently, there is no proof that says designers intentionally create addictive games, or that organizations plan to create addictive gamified experiences. Hyper-engagement is intentionally or unintentionally present, its possibility raises the concern of harm. Using principles such as the 'golden rule' and the 'disclosure rule', virtue ethics might suggest that each one involved in the design process must take accountability on deciding an acceptable level of user engagement, whether they would be choosing to describe their personal role in the design process to others, without feeling guilt or embarrassment. From a deontological perspective, hyper-engagement is particularly problematic, and the prospect of entertainment cannot offset the risk. Conversely, intentionally designing for hyper-engagement not only might be justified for consequentialists but may also represent the most ethical course of action. If an organization can visualize that only a tiny portion of users would be adversely affected, this is offset by major enjoyment for the majority.

Gamification Mechanics

By influencing behaviors and inspiring users to complete activities, gamification is used as a marketing and commercial approach to increase consumer engagement and loyalty. It is recommended that retailers looking to incorporate gamified mechanisms into their mobile retailing applications use challenge levels, which are similar to those seen in video games, for maximum efficacy. Notably, WeChat and other platforms have effectively implemented this tactic, becoming China's first multifunctional application, with users spending more than 360 minutes a day on it. According to Shevchuk et al. (2019), gamification – which involves incorporating reward-based game elements – proves to be effective in improving consumers' knowledge, attitudes, and behaviors for long-term results. Thoughtful game design is necessary to accomplish the desired behavioral consequences, as researchers emphasize, as the technology has the capacity to mold desired behavior by creating eco-friendly mindsets and loyalty awareness. Effective gamification projects place a high priority on interaction because they understand how important it is to achieve the intended outcomes. Gamification platforms play a major role in creating customer value in the retail industry. Gamified motivators have a beneficial impact on hedonic value, which in turn changes consumer behavior (Gatautis et al., 2021). Hedonic value is more satisfying than rewards; therefore, it encourages longer-term involvement. Gamification's ongoing engagement is positively connected with brand engagement (Högberg et al., 2019).

Utilizing Gamified Data: Applications and Scope

The ethical considerations surrounding gamification are greatly influenced by the particular circumstances in which these solutions are implemented. Gamified solutions naturally produce personal data by tapping into players' unique interests, behaviors, and habits. In order to explore the complex ethical terrain, we have distinguished five domains: healthcare, work life, government, education, and leisure systems. These domains represent points of divergence between the goals to gamify and the related ethical concerns. A customized ethical framework that takes into account the complex dynamics at play at the nexus between gamification and these various domains is vital, since each of these contexts present distinct considerations and obstacles.

Role of Gamification in Marketing

Gamification can be used in the form of playable ads as a mechanism of combining the individual ad units and ad campaigns with an interactive game or incorporating gaming elements in a non-gaming context. Providing an all-time immersive, engaging, involving, and fun experience with the product/brand/service will help customers to remember the name, and this is the greatest advantage of a gamified campaign.

Gamification has time and again proved to be a reliable and consistent marketing tool by dwelling into people's basic habit to play. The gamification of products and services in the virtual world provides an affirmative, personalized digital experience while building and strengthening brand awareness and building on customer loyalty and patronage. By creating attractive, enticing, entertaining, and informative content, gaming influencers can show the organizations' brands/products/services in a way that not only triggers sales but also builds brand loyalty and patronage. Gaming influencer marketing provides a great opportunity for brands to get the noticing and identity and create top of the mind awareness. The retail industry in particular is using gamification to increase brand awareness, generate top of the mind awareness, build a long-lasting relation with customers, and trigger sales. Game mechanics can be used in different ways to solve issues and challenges. One great example of gaming in marketing is customer loyalty programs. In the modern day's hyper competitive gaming industry, effective game marketing plays an important role in the success of any mobile game or video game. Game marketing includes various strategies and creative techniques intended to promote and increase the visibility of mobile games and video games to reach the audience.

Gamification in Healthcare Sector

The healthcare industry is always looking for new technology, and gamification is one technique that looks having potential for improving people's health-related behaviors. Positive impact can be achieved by imagining a gamified healthcare system inside public health programs that attempt to modify people's lifestyles by reducing alcohol use, increasing physical exercise, or adopting a generally medically appropriate living. It is important to highlight the inherent hazards associated with gamification, even as we acknowledge its potential benefits in reaching these health goals. One of the main issues is the vulnerability of health, since people's options for healthcare services are frequently restricted by geographic or financial limitations. Given how sensitive personal health records are, secondary worries center on the privacy of the data created by such gamified health solutions. Ethical concerns are raised by the possibility of consumers losing control over data gathered by gamified systems, particularly if that data is used for more extensive medical research or other objectives. There have been cases where genetic data from entire nations was turned into a commodity that could be traded, causing people to lose control over their own data. These cases emphasize the importance of carefully navigating privacy problems when gamifying healthcare.

It is important to understand that human experiences of health go beyond biological features to existential dimensions, which are commonly described as a 'homelike-being-in-the-world' (Svenaeus, 2001), despite healthcare gamification's tendency to promote a biomedically desirable lifestyle. This suggests that everyone's definition of good health is arbitrary and depends on their own aspirations and life goals. It is critical to recognize this variation as the healthcare industry works to integrate gamification while maintaining sensitivity to the complex and unique nature of health experiences in the pursuit of biological health goals.

Work-Life Enhancement through Gamification Strategies

With job automation, financial instability, and intense rivalry for jobs, many people find it more and more difficult to change companies in today's work-life environment. This leads to an increased sense of commitment to present work environments, and gamification of the workplace has a risk of putting employees in constant rivalry with one another. Such gamified work environments run the risk of turning workers into a corporate resource that can be exploited, thereby undermining important facets of personal autonomy and jeopardizing the legitimacy of an individual's self-owned existence in the workplace (Heidegger, 1977). In spite of these reservations, some employers implement new technologies in the workplace with the goal of enabling staff members. Enhancing the work experience is the goal of solutions connected to job happiness, feedback, or development suggestions inside data-driven gamified frameworks. But it is important to proceed with caution when putting these solutions into practice, particularly when it comes to protecting people's privacy by hiding distinctive traits that might be used to identify them. This delicate balance protects employee autonomy and privacy while ensuring that the great potential of gamified work settings is fully realized.

Government Applications of Gamification

Governmental information systems are a vital component of society communication, significantly influencing how governments and individuals communicate. The possibility that citizens will be forced to use government systems raises questions regarding individual autonomy and should be taken into consideration while thinking about the gamification of these systems. Gamification's transformative power to influence behavior through data collection runs the risk of undermining individuality by forcing persons to fit into government frameworks by conforming to an 'average' identity. The fundamental value of each person's unique aspirations, dreams, and concerns could be undermined by the possible loss of individual life goals, which would reduce people to nothing more than numbers in government schemes. Moreover, privacy issues are heightened by gamified government systems' lack of transparency and control over the use of individuals' information, underscoring the necessity of strong protections to maintain democratic foundations (Blanco et al., 2022).

The use of gamification in the classroom poses concerns about the power relationships between students and teachers, especially for the younger population. Because they don't have the authority to select the educational resources they utilize, students' privacy and related rights must be respected (Purwandari et al., 2019). The incorporation of gamification into the classroom has the potential to highlight student divisions and exacerbate inequity. Since youth do not have the same rights and obligations as adults, it is the duty of society to protect youth rights, protect their privacy, and guarantee that they are treated equally in the larger social structure. As these people grow up and become adults, they ought to be able to decide how their personally identifiable information is used, including whether it should be deleted or used.

Gamification in the workplace presents ethical questions, especially in light of the possible exploitation of jobless individuals. Although the idea of gamifying benefits to reactivate jobless people may be well-intentioned, it does not produce new jobs and could burden those who are already vulnerable. The danger that gamification poses for the most disadvantaged members of society emphasizes how crucial it is to take into account the power dynamics at work and make sure that these kinds of systems actually empower people, as opposed to just emphasizing how helpless the unemployed are. Therefore, in order to avoid compromising the tenets and foundations of a democratic society, ethical issues become crucial when introducing gamification into governmental institutions.

Leisure and Entertainment: The Role of Gamification

The domain of gamified leisure presents unique considerations in which the influence of gamified systems on our leisure pursuits becomes an individual decision. When it comes to leisure gamification, people have the freedom to choose not to participate, unlike in other sectors like healthcare or government, unless there is an oligopoly or monopoly of systems. But even in this space, it is still important to retain some control over personal information. Sports applications, such as heart rate monitors, for instance, gamify exercise by utilizing user and other users' data. These devices also come with a variety of other capabilities, such as *GPS* tracking and sleep monitoring. Although consumers are free to stop using these apps, the ability to have their data removed from the system they have interacted with is a crucial control necessity. In the context of gamified leisure, maintaining an individual's privacy and autonomy requires this minimal amount of control.

Making sure people still have control over their data when they stop using gamified leisure systems is still an issue. Users are frequently left vulnerable to possible exploitation by application developers since the existing landscape frequently lacks tools for users to exert influence over the data that has already been acquired. With the gamification of leisure becoming more and more integrated into our daily lives, there is an increasing need for ethical considerations and regulatory frameworks that provide people the power to not only opt out of these systems but also exercise control over their personal data, protecting their privacy and autonomy in the rapidly changing gamified leisure landscape.

Revolutionizing Retail with Gamified Experiences

According to researchers (Hofacker et al., 2016), there is a considerable chance that the incorporation of gamification in online retail would affect different parts of service companies during the consumer selection process. Gamification is becoming a crucial tool among the many cutting-edge technologies that retail companies are implementing as they strive to remain competitive in the face of constant technology breakthroughs. It can be difficult to get customers to participate in data disclosure procedures, especially for businesses who are grappling with poor customer trust. Good gamification design increases hedonic and meaningful engagement in addition to amplifying positive effects through the use of game components and an emphasis on relevance (Jayasooriya et al., 2020). An effective implementation of gamified marketing initiatives has the potential to enhance consumer brand stickiness, as enjoyment plays a pivotal role in grabbing customers' initial interest and promoting sustained engagement (Bidler et al., 2020) (Lu & Ho, 2020).

Gamification is acknowledged as an effective technique to increase user engagement through emotional engagement and goal-oriented inspiration. Understanding and utilizing human motivation – which can be divided into intrinsic and extrinsic motivation – are essential to the success of gamification. Gamification alone can reduce the effectiveness of extrinsic rewards, even when intrinsic motivation is driven by internal incentives such as enjoyment. However, when used intelligently, gamification and social media marketing can show promise for increasing user engagement and changing behavior (Gajanova & Radišić, 2021). Interest is piqued by the current trend of gamification implementation in business-to-consumer contexts, particularly in online retail, since it fits in with important game mechanics that have been shown to increase customer engagement, such as challenges, prizes, and feedback. Notably, the access platform and gaming device selected for gamification are important factors that impact consumer attitudes and memories about the brand. The requirement for strategic alignment in the deployment of gamified systems is further highlighted by the mediation of customer involvement and flow experience (Sreejesh et al., 2021).

The relationship between gamification and online buying is changing, and studies show how important it is to use consumers' innate motivations to understand their preferences. Successful marketing initiatives that clarify the online buying process can improve consumers' understanding of the online channel, increasing their participation and improving their online shopping experiences. Gamified mobile apps are positioned as being more dynamic, engaging, and versatile, which increase platform–user engagement. Nonetheless, the platform must consistently provide social and gamified cues for gamification to be used successfully; this could have an impact on changes to marketing strategies (De Canio et al., 2021). Additional evidence supports the beneficial effects of gamification on behavior modification, highlighting the potential advantages of this strategy in shaping consumer behavior (Zain et al., 2021).

Beyond retail, gamification is gaining traction in a variety of industries, including online education. In order to comprehend the effects of gamified activities, it is essential to grasp the notion of user engagement, which has two components: deep involvement and meaningful engagement. According to studies, playing casual games can greatly improve students' motivation to use online learning platforms. This leads to a favorable link between gamified activities and higher percentages of correctly answered questions and participation. Gamification also contributes to the knowledge of retail and customer viewpoints in the context of dynamic pricing, especially as retail outlets modify their supply chains to account for the adjustments brought about by dynamic pricing. Previous studies on the subject of services highlight how well gamification works to boost client loyalty, promote good word-of-mouth, and increase engagement. According to researchers, providing hedonic values within gamified experiences is a good strategy for attracting clients and encouraging repeat purchase intentions. Customers use gamified applications for a variety of reasons, including rewards, competitiveness, achievement, challenges, and knowledge development. These factors eventually affect users' attitudinal commitment toward the core service (Shi et al., 2022) (Kunkel et al., 2021).

Challenges and Compromises in the Underlying Technology of Gamification

The protection of players' private information must come first in gamification technology, and players should have the ability to decide how their data is used (Lahtiranta et al., 2017). It should also make sure that everyone has an equal opportunity to compete, preventing any possible attempts at cheating. These characteristics are susceptible to a variety of attacks originating from technological or societal vulnerabilities. Passwords can be compromised, for example, via a technical attack known as cracking or by using social engineering techniques like assuming the identity of an administrator and convincing participants to divulge their passwords.

Clients, servers, or the network that connects them can all be the subject of technical attacks (Smed and Hakonen, 2017). These attacks can happen within the client (e.g., changing code in the memory), under (e.g., hacking a driver), or over (e.g., reading pixel values from the user interface). Network attacks such as denial-of-service attacks and IP spoofing can affect servers, while packet tampering, which involves copying, intercepting, or forging payload data, can undermine network communication.

Attacks using social engineering techniques include blackmail, taking advantage of people's gullibility, getting unauthorized access by impersonating a superuser, and bribery – either by paying less for bigger rewards or by cooperating to obtain unfair advantages (Mitnick and Simon, 2003). These attacks on games can have a variety of motivations, but they generally fall into three categories (Consalvo, 2007):

- Improving Gameplay: players aim to improve their gameplay experience due to many reasons like inexperience, lack of time, or boredom.
- Playing with the Game System: participants interact with the gamified system in creative ways, motivated by a desire to explore, experiment, prolong the game's life cycle, or develop new gameplay strategies.
- Extra-gaming Elements: These are elements that can pose dangers outside of the gaming environment, such as money gains, celebrity, vandalism, or nonconformity.

Even though any information security breach can have serious effects for players, determining the possible ethical ramifications requires an understanding of the motive behind their activities. Gamers who want to improve their experience could unintentionally make more people unequal. While not intending to harm others, even users of the gamified system can have comparable effects. The group driven by non-gaming considerations poses the most threat, treating other players like disposable tools. It becomes imperative to take these incentive variables into account while developing ethical standards and handling possible fallout in the field of gamification.

Critical Issues in Gamification Design

Activities carried out both before and during the installation of a gamified system are included in the design phase of gamification. Although the main objective of gamification is to increase players' involvement with moral problems and activities, there are cases where it has been used maliciously, like when CCTV cameras are stolen or damaged, or even when players are forced to take their own lives (Hyrynsalmi, Smed et al., 2017). Leaving aside these extreme instances, there are situations when legal remedies create ethical dilemmas or where well-meaning solutions have unethical by-products. To give a simple example, gamifying a service for medical personnel like firefighters, paramedics, or nurses could potentially increase their level of job satisfaction. But in high-stress situations where every moment matters, spending time on unimportant goals, like gaining points in a game, might endanger someone's life or property. The primary question in design that should always come before implementation is: is gamification appropriate for this particular context? Two broad categories can be distinguished from the standpoint of gamification design, each with consequences for the welfare of the person and the larger community. These factors must be carefully considered to make sure that gamification is implemented in a way that respects ethics and doesn't have unexpected effects (Alhammad and Moreno, 2020).

Personal Implications of Gamification

It is common for design conversations to ignore the problem of gamification overload. To alleviate the cognitive strain of balancing several tasks, narratives, and game mechanics, the average player usually plays only a few games at a time. Gamified solutions are also subject to this cognitive constraint (Trang and Weiger, 2021). The question that needs to be answered is this: can the average gamification player successfully engage in gamified physical activity, education, and energy conservation at the same time? As a result, designers need to determine if gamification in a given environment adds long-term value or runs the risk of compromising its goals because of possible overload. It is essential to understand that individual players are not a homogeneous bunch. Let us examine the situation of a game junkie. Should their place of employment introduce them to a gamified system? If not, would they be in a different, potentially more precarious situation than their colleagues? Another demographic to which this thought experiment could be applied includes young students (think of educational gamification), the elderly, or people with cognitive disabilities. In order to promote inclusion and prevent unintended outcomes, it becomes imperative to adjust gamification tactics to the varied requirements and susceptibilities within the player base.

Societal Implications of Gamification

Workers may purposefully fabricate accomplishments to improve their position on leaderboards while negotiating salaries, or they may actively manipulate data in gamified systems. The integrity of the gamification approach may be compromised by the possibility of widespread cheating in gamified systems that offer real-world rewards. Furthermore, taking advantage of players' competitive drive in a gamified setting could influence real-world competition and possibly create disruptive dynamics at work. Participants who are younger and more tech-savvy may have an edge when navigating gamification because they are accustomed to the gaming mechanics seen in entertainment games (Zainuddin et al., 2020). It is difficult to guarantee that each player starts from the same place – a challenge that game designers attempt to solve with methods like game balance (Adams, 2014). With challenges that are suited for each player's skill level in the work at hand, a fair and balanced game gives everyone an equal chance of success right from the start. The player's performance in the task should be the primary determinant of their success, not the gamification layer that is added on top of it.

Furthermore, a gamified system's structure or storyline may unintentionally favor the majority while ignoring the values or interests of minority groups due to gender, race, or other considerations (Vanduhe et al., 2020). This bias might, in a professional setting, amplify preexisting attitudes and prejudices that may be hidden. Furthermore, participants may not be aware of the intentions underlying gamification, which poses hazards and raises ethical questions. For example, gamified systems created for political objectives may end up being instruments for monitoring and disinformation. This presents moral difficulties, such as the possible upholding of traditional values and privacy risks. The necessity of carefully weighing the ethical implications of gamification when used for political or surveillance goals is highlighted by comparisons to historical precedents, such as the Stasi or similar groups gamifying citizen surveillance.

Gamification and Ethics

The introduction and use of persuasive technology, which aims to change behavior and attitude, can have a variety of effects on the user, both good and bad. The blending of the lighthearted world of games with the somber world of business, or 'gamification', raises ethical questions that have not been thoroughly investigated and lead to normative tension points (Thorpe and Roper, 2019). Even though gamification is one of the behavioral techniques in business that is spreading quickly, there hasn't been much research done on its ethical implications, which suggests that its potential negative effects and moral validity are not fully understood (Goethe, 2019).

When gamification is used to maintain high levels of motivation, it depends on extrinsic rewards, which raise ethical questions. According to research, people who are originally motivated by intrinsic factors may lose motivation as a result of gamification, believing they are being used as test subjects and being forced to react in certain ways. A gamification practice's ethical status mostly, but not solely, depends on how much it is seen to be exploitative, manipulative, detrimental to participants – intentionally or unintentionally – and how much it crosses the line into socially unacceptable behavior. Comprehending these ethical aspects is crucial, given that gamification persists in exerting a substantial influence on user conduct in diverse commercial environments (Kim & Werbach, 2016).

Ethical Considerations in Gamification

In the context of gamification ethics, manipulation is defined as any action that violates users' autonomy and includes essential components like self-reflection, transparency, and permission. This unethical practice is demonstrated in situations where brands or organizations purposefully conceal information about the goals and content of a gamified system, effectively manipulating consumers by depriving them of knowledge in an effort to increase engagement. There are additional situations in which consumers might not give their informed consent for data collecting, especially if internet service providers don't sufficiently disclose privacy policies. Additionally, gamified systems have the potential to take advantage of players' compulsive or addictive inclinations by posing obstacles that make it impossible for users to stop playing, which constitutes manipulation (Kim & Werbach, 2016).

According to gamification ethics, manipulation includes hiding gamification features and processes from people who are impacted by these systems. Instances where gamification strategies purposefully obscure the components of the game encounter and impede logical introspection are undesirable because they compromise autonomy (Vashisht & Sreejesh, 2015; Arora and Razavian, 2021). Because it impairs users' autonomy and makes it more difficult for them to make educated judgments, this type of manipulation poses ethical questions. This highlights the necessity of taking ethics into account while developing and implementing gamified systems (Kriz et al., 2022).

There has been a lot of discussion sparked by the ongoing debate among researchers about the moral implications and corporate ethics in marketing gamification. The complicated issues within gamification are reflected in ethics, which is defined here as a 'collection of beliefs and rules that assist us in judging whether behavior helps or damages sentient creatures' (Paul and Elder, 2003). Andrzej Marczewski recognizes the subjectivity in determining damage and applies ethics to gamification designers, emphasizing the significance of creating systems that help users rather than harm them (Marczewski, 2017). In the literature that is currently available, this ethical investigation of gamification has primarily used a practice-based approach to persuasion. Choosing a normative approach is essential for directing organizations toward moral behavior since it is ideal for examining ethics in action (Michalos, 1995). As a subfield of applied ethics, which applies theories, norms, and concepts from ethics to particular technical questions, gamification ethics may be philosophically located within the larger lineage of technology ethics. Users who are exposed to environments that involve deceiving consumers for maximum profit instead of convincing them will notice the subsequent coercion. This is an example of unethical gamification. Users may actively try to delete gamified aspects and publicly express their unhappiness upon identifying offensive design and misleading behaviors (Lowry et al., 2013). In order to approach gamification ethically, designers must emphasize user intelligence throughout the design process and see themselves as users. Promoting brand loyalty through user-generated content about the design highlights the importance of ethical issues in the creation and application of gamification (Goethe, 2019).

Understanding Manipulation in Gamification

According to gamification ethics, manipulation includes hiding gamification features and processes from people who are impacted by these systems.

Instances where gamification strategies purposefully obscure the components of the game encounter and impede logical introspection are undesirable because they compromise autonomy. Because it impairs users' autonomy and makes it more difficult for them to make educated judgments, this type of manipulation poses ethical questions. This highlights the necessity of taking ethics into account while developing and implementing gamified systems (Kim & Werbach, 2016).

Exploitation and Its Role in Gamified Systems

The use of gamified elements to force people to go above and beyond the call of duty is known as 'exploitation' in the context of gamification ethics. This creates situations where businesses take advantage of the social environment to extract more work from users without offering them tangible rewards (Kriz et al., 2022). Business ethicists have begun to debate the ethics of gamifying labor, raising concerns about the viability of employing gamified methods to encourage greater productivity without providing equal rewards for the workers. According to author Vdov, the Octalysis framework classifies exploitation as 'black hat', which refers to the manipulation of consumers. Scarcity, avoidance, and unpredictability are listed as the variables that contribute to discontent and unpleasant customer experiences (Vdov, 2020). Gamification's intrinsic danger is caused by badly built systems that serve as powerful demotivators, increasing user unhappiness and, ultimately, weakening the practice's ethical justifications.

Beyond just being unhappy, the ethical ramifications of exploitation in gamification raise questions about justice, openness, and how people are treated fairly in gamified environments. In order to allay these worries, gamification tactics must be carefully designed and put into practice to make sure that they adhere to moral standards and strike a balance between fairness and motivation in the quest for higher productivity. Furthermore, encouraging honest communication and cooperation between designers, companies, and users can aid in the creation of moral gamification strategies that put the autonomy and well-being of those using gamified environments first (Kazhamiakin et al., 2021).

Harms in Gamification: Physical and Psychological Aspects

Researchers make a distinction between physical and psychological injury in the context of gamification. The physical dimension might appear in situations where users are unintentionally pushed to their limits by gamification, especially in apps related to fitness or the job. For example, well-meaning design elements such as push alerts, social media integration, or contests in fitness or diet apps may ignore users' health issues, which could result in eating disorders or injuries from activity. Regarding gamification in the workplace, such as contact centers, there may be worries regarding overworked personnel. Psychological injury is linked to the feeling of being continuously monitored and assessed in an information system, similar to Jeremy Bentham's Panopticon, a jail layout that permits a single guard to monitor inmates without their knowledge. This psychological component presents ethical questions because gamification designs could unintentionally serve as instruments of suppression, putting administrative objectives ahead of the welfare of employees. These concerns are similar to those found in socio-technical systems and China's social credit system (Fitzpatrick et al., 2022).

A Disney gamification system for cleaning staff at an Oregon Disneyland hotel serves as an excellent illustration of the ethical subject of harm. Employees were given points for accomplishing several cleaning-related duties as part of the gamified design, and these points were tallied and shown on a leaderboard that was conspicuously placed in the staff lunchroom (Kim & Werbach, 2016). However, because of the fierce competitiveness this gamification created, workers avoided taking lunch breaks and using the restroom out of concern that their jobs would be threatened if they failed to regularly move up the scoreboard. Employees who participated in interviews called this gamification application the 'electronic whip,' emphasizing the negative psychological and physical effects of it, such as stress from continual monitoring and injuries from overworking (Kim & Werbach, 2016). These incidents highlight the possible harm that might result from gamification techniques that disregard the dignity and well-being of those using these systems.

In order to address the ethical subject of harm in gamification, design principles must be reevaluated with a focus on user awareness, permission, and well-being (Nyström, 2021). The possible psychological and physical effects must be taken into account by designers to make sure that gamification improves rather than degrades users' quality of life. In order to create ethical gamification practices that put the health and dignity of people participating in gamified activities first, designers, organizations, and users can work together.

Character in Gamification

A research investigation of the moral and essential human values delves into the ethical aspects of gamification. It highlights how gamification can lead users to make decisions that could be viewed as immoral, particularly when it comes to human rights. Gamification has been used in civilian settings as well as in military training simulations, as demonstrated by the use of gamification in the Israel Defense Force and the U.S. Army, which raises ethical questions. Through a gamified blog where readers may earn badges for finding material on the site and sharing it on social media, the Israel Defense

Force used gamification in civil society. The idea was to blur the boundaries between military propaganda and public involvement by developing a viral platform to support military operations carried out by the Israeli Defense Force (Kim & Werbach, 2016).

Likewise, gamification was integrated by the U.S. Army into a counterterrorism training simulation. For completing objectives like intercepting coworkers' emails or locating contraband, participants received points and milestones. The possibility for citizens to unintentionally distribute military propaganda while playing this gamified training simulation raises ethical concerns about privacy rights. The question of how to characterize gamified systems – whether they are seen as games or as a representation of reality – centers the ethical conundrum. Studies on gamification in higher education indicate that, even in critical situations, users of gamified learning management systems could see them in a lighter manner. This change in perspective blurs the lines between important societal issues and amusement, raising questions about how people interact with gamified systems that may have real-world consequences (Martin and Tyler, 2017).

A critical analysis of the potential for manipulating users for ideological or strategic ends is prompted by examining the ethical implications of gamification in these military contexts. It emphasizes the necessity of striking a careful balance between using gamification to increase user engagement and taking into account the moral ramifications of influencing users' decisions and actions, particularly where human rights and more general societal issues are involved.

Positioning Diversity in Gamification

Gamification's complex nature reveals both positive opportunities to improve life's little pleasures and possible hazards that can have detrimental effects on communities. Widely used in modern society, gamified systems have a significant impact because they include feedback, progress tracking, and rewards for accomplishments – all of which are powerful levers for encouraging learning, changing behavior, and promoting personal development (Deterding et al., 2011). Gamification's dual nature denotes its dual function as a societal problem source and a catalyst for good change.

In order to understand the complex relationship between gamification and diversity, this chapter will acknowledge that it is a two-edged sword that needs to be carefully considered (Patrício et al., 2021). Three essential components comprise the lens with which diversity is analyzed: culture, gender, and age. The goal is to gain a deeper understanding of how gamification can either unintentionally perpetuate prejudices and exclusions or encourage inclusivity and fairness by exploring these elements. The complex interaction that exists between gamification and various diversity characteristics is depicted in Figure 12.1, which highlights the need for a thorough

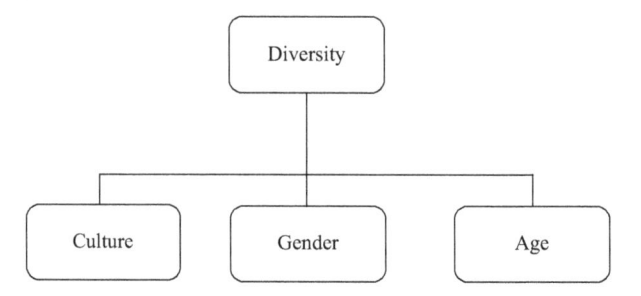

Figure 12.1 Positioning diversity in gamification
Source: authors' work

investigation that goes beyond the obvious advantages to identify any potential sociocultural ramifications.

Cultural Dynamics in Gamification

A deep understanding of the complex interactions between behavioral design
and cultural quirks is necessary for effective gamification in a variety of settings, including business, education, and health. The importance of taking
the cultural context and surroundings into account in gamification research
and practice is emphasized. Gamification experts and academics need to look
beyond a one-size-fits-all strategy and explore the various cultural expressions that influence people's lifestyles in order to promote meaningful engagement. Researchers (Deterding et al., 2011) emphasize how important cultural
models are to understanding involvement in gamification. Although the significance of culture in gamification has been recognized, there is still a dearth
of research in this area, which has prompted a request for interdisciplinary
investigation (Breuer et al., 2020).

According to researchers, culture includes all the various aspects of a
person's life, such as language, work habits, dress rules, marital customs,
and leisure activities. It is crucial for scholars and professionals working
in the field of gamification to comprehend the cultural context, especially
when creating worldwide efforts (Marques et al., 2023). For example, while
designing a gamified onboarding program for a global manufacturing corpo-
ration, several cultural domains such as country conventions, work culture,
and family traditions need to be taken into account. Through its insights
into group characteristics, emotional attachments, communication norms,
and decision-making within a particular culture, cultural psychology proves
to be a useful ally in this investigation. Gamification designers may avoid
common mistakes like stereotyping and effectively negotiate the complex
web of cultural impacts on behavior change by utilizing ideas from cultural

psychology. When working with cultures that place a high importance on self-improvement or self-enhancement, the integration of cultural psychology becomes even more important (Khan et al., 2020). Cultural norms and unwritten conventions play a crucial role in shaping responses to gamification designs, as actions that impact behavioral change are intricately linked to social and cultural settings. Therefore, a comprehensive understanding of these factors is essential. The 'law of Jante' in Scandinavian societies serves as an example of an unwritten ethic that discourages overt personal ambition. This highlights the necessity for gamification specialists to be sensitive to cultural nuances and draw on anthropological knowledge in order to traverse the complexities of engagement. The subtle dance between culture and user involvement is highlighted by the use of cultural semiotics, metaphors, and tropes, which further add complexity to the cultural dimension of gamification design. Through acknowledging the complex interplay between culture and gamification, scholars and practitioners can facilitate the development of inclusive and culturally aware design methodologies.

Navigating Age Diversity in Gamification

In the context of gamification, age stands out as a crucial aspect of diversity, bringing with it complex issues and difficulties. The idea of an age-based 'digital divide' has long been debated in the digital space, and gamification is no different. Since young adults are more likely to connect with gamified products, they are typically designed with them in mind. Nevertheless, research delving into the perceived utility of gamification presents a more nuanced picture, casting doubt on the notion that gamification's allure wanes with age (Bennani et al., 2020). A more complex picture emerges from other research, suggesting that age may not have a significant effect on motivation in gamified exercise software, despite other study suggesting that people over 40 find gamification less appealing. According to this, the way gamified products strategically use game elements may be more important than age itself. A younger audience may be drawn to the visually appealing and design features because of their 'gam-y' appearance and feel, which could influence the age-related dynamics of gamification's success.

Examining the similarities with the serious gaming industry, which has studied aspects like perceived utility, usability, and enjoyment, offers important insights into developing gamification tactics that appeal to a variety of age group. It is imperative to acknowledge that consumer perceptions of gamified products may transcend beyond the realm of gamification per se, mirroring more general concerns about the digital divide between younger and older demographics. Comprehending the range of ages in society is not only essential for creating captivating gamification experiences, but it also has wider consequences for inclusive design methodologies in other fields. Determining the target audience is essential to creating not only engaging gamification but also successful design overall. Adopting an escape perspective and including environmental psychology viewpoints to examine the nuances of how and why gamification functions, especially with regard to age dynamics, are potential directions for future research (Koivisto et al., 2021).

In summary, the relationship between age and gamification is complex, and assumptions may not match actual results. For researchers and designers hoping to fully utilize gamification across a range of age groups, a thorough grasp of age-related subtleties is essential.

Navigating Gender Diversity in Gamification

The relationship between gamification and gender reveals complex aspects that go beyond simple interaction. In the game creation industry, where both digital and analog games are frequently geared toward particular gender expectations, acknowledging gender disparities has long been a standard practice. Gender differences also appear in the field of game-based learning, where research indicates that female college students are less likely than their male counterparts to enjoy the competitive elements of games. However, younger generations show a wider acceptance of video games without attaching strict gender norms to the gaming experience, suggesting that this gender coding of gaming attitudes correlates with age. However, guys seem to have more positive opinions toward video games in educational contexts than girls do, even among younger persons (Dele-Ajayi et al., 2018).

The gender–gamification relationship is further complicated by the use of gamification in education. Although opinions regarding gamification are not greatly impacted by the gender of teachers in higher education settings, there are differences in the elementary school setting. It is found that differential effects on boys and girls in a gamification campaign targeted at increasing good behavior. The gamified design had a stronger positive effect on males (Goethe and Palmquist, 2020). Beyond classrooms, research on corporate training indicates that gender diversity influences how engagement is impacted by gamified competition. In competitive gamification environments, men are more likely than females to demonstrate higher levels of engagement and better learning outcomes. A study conducted on university undergraduates delves deeper into the topic of playfulness perceptions and finds that different game mechanics may be more enticing to men and women. Men tend to favor points, while women seem to appreciate badges more (Ortega Sánchez and Gómez Trigueros, 2019).

Gender diversity adds a degree of complexity to gamification design, which affects how people react to different game mechanics in both business and educational settings. Comprehending these subtleties is crucial for efficacious and comprehensive gamification tactics, underscoring the substantial influence of variables like gender on the acceptance of gamified applications. Understanding these nuances enables more sophisticated and customized methods of gamification design that take into account the various gender-related expectations and preferences.

Beyond gender, gamification explores diversity in a variety of contexts, including cultural, age, socioeconomic, and personal interests. Although this conversation sheds light on the complex interactions between gender and gamification, it should be viewed as a springboard for additional research and the formulation of hypotheses rather than a definitive test of them. In order to create gamification experiences that appeal to a wide range of user demographics, designers must have a comprehensive understanding of factors such as gender, age, and cultural orientations (Denden et al., 2021).

Conclusion

Finally, gamification includes using fun and game elements to motivate individuals and drive desired and responsible behaviors which are action oriented. In the arena of digital marketing, it provides an innovative way to get and hold the attention of the target audience, facilitating brand loyalty and driving desired outcomes.

Use of gamification might have unfavorable effects if it is done without a thorough knowledge of its ethical implications. When decision-makers give priority to flimsy incentives like points, badges, and leaderboards, they may be engaging in unethical behavior by neglecting the deeper motivations behind behaviors that are beneficial. Because users may become less motivated to interact with a system due to this move toward extrinsic motivators, there is a possible ethical risk. In order to prevent unintentionally undermining users' sincere interest in the system, the essay highlights the necessity for experts to refrain from placing an excessive amount of emphasis on accomplishments. The chapter highlights the need for a more comprehensive, experience-centered approach to gamification, acknowledging the possible risks associated with concentrating just on little or unnecessary tasks. In order to produce meaningful and morally responsible user experiences, it recommends that gamification specialists go beyond standard game features and use a more extensive toolkit. The entry urges designers and developers to appropriately handle these issues by providing a critical study of the ethical dimensions inherent in gamification tools and methodologies. Although it draws attention to possible dangers, it supports the ongoing use of gamification strategies as long as they are used sensibly and morally to advance humankind.

References

Adams, E. (2014). *Fundamentals of game design* (3rd ed.). New Riders.

Alhammad, M. M., & Moreno, A. M. (2020). Challenges of gamification in software process improvement. *Journal of Software: Evolution and Process, 32*(6), e2231.

Arora, C., & Razavian, M. (2021). Ethics of gamification in health and fitness tracking. *International Journal of Environmental Research and Public Health*, *18*(21), 11052.

Bennani, S., Maalel, A., & Ghezala, H. B. (2020). AGE-learn: Ontology-based representation of personalized gamification in E-learning. *Procedia Computer Science*, *176*, 1005–1014.

Bidler, M., Zimmermann, J., Schumann, J. H., & Widjaja, T. (2020). Increasing consumers' willingness to engage in data disclosure processes through relevance-illustrating game elements. *Journal of Retailing*, *96*(4), 507–523.

Blanco, I., Lowndes, V., & Salazar, Y. (2022). Understanding institutional dynamics in participatory governance: How rules, practices and narratives combine to produce stability or diverge to create conditions for change. *Critical Policy Studies*, *16*(2), 204–223.

Breuer, H., & Ivanov, K. (2020). Gamification to address cultural challenges and to facilitate values-based innovation. In *ISPIM conference proceedings* (pp. 1–18). The International Society for Professional Innovation Management (ISPIM).

Bui, A., Veit, D., & Webster, J. (2015). Gamification – a novel phenomenon or a new wrapping for existing concepts? In T. Carte, A. Heinzl, & C. Urquhart (Eds.), *Proceedings of the international conference on information systems – exploring the information Frontier, ICIS 2015*. Association for Information Systems. http://aisel.aisnet.org/icis2015/proceedings/ITimplementation/23

Consalvo, M. (2007). *Cheating: Gaining advantage in video-games*. The MIT Press.

De Canio, F., Fuentes-Blasco, M., & Martinelli, E. (2021). Engaging shoppers through mobile apps: The role of gamification. *International Journal of Retail and Distribution Management*. https://doi.org/10.1108/IJRDM-09–2020–0360

Dele-Ajayi, O., Strachan, R., Pickard, A., & Sanderson, J. (2018, October). Designing for all: Exploring gender diversity and engagement with digital educational games by young people. In *2018 IEEE Frontiers in education conference (FIE)* (pp. 1–9). IEEE.

Denden, M., Tlili, A., Essalmi, F., Jemni, M., Chen, N. S., & Burgos, D. (2021). Effects of gender and personality differences on students' perception of game design elements in educational gamification. *International Journal of Human-Computer Studies*, *154*, 102674.

Deterding, S., Dixon, D., Khaled, R., & Nacke, L. (2011, September). From game design elements to gamefulness: defining "gamification". In *Proceedings of the 15th international academic MindTrek conference: Envisioning future media environments* (pp. 9–15). ACM. https://doi.org/10.1145/2181037. 2181040

Ferrell, O. C., Ferrell, L., & Sawayda, J. (2015). A review of ethical decision making models in marketing. In A. Nill (Ed.), *Handbook on ethics & marketing* (pp. 38–60). Edward Elgar Publishing.

Fitzpatrick, S., & Marsh, T. (2022). The dehumanising consequences of gamification: Recognising coercion and exploitation in gamified systems. In *Handbook of research on cross-disciplinary uses of gamification in organizations* (pp. 398–417). IGI Global.

Gajanova, L., & Radišić, M. (2021). Self-determination theory as mediator in the nexus of gamification and customer purchasing behaviour. In *SHS web of conferences* (Vol. 90, p. 01005). EDP Sciences.

Gaski, J. F. (1999). Does marketing ethics really have anything to say? A critical inventory of the literature. *Journal of Business Ethics*, *18*(3), 315–334.

Gatautis, R., Banytė, J., Kuvykaitė, R., Virvilaitė, R., Dovalienė, A., Piligrimienė, Ž., Gadeikienė, A., Vitkauskaitė, E., & Tarutė, A. (2021). The conceptual model of gamification-based consumer engagement in value creation. In *Gamification and consumer engagement*. Springer. https://doi.org/10.1007/978-3-030-54205-4_5

Goethe, O. (2019). *Gamification mindset*. Springer International Publishing.

Goethe, O., & Palmquist, A. (2020, July 19–24). Broader understanding of gamification by addressing ethics and diversity. In *HCI international 2020–late breaking papers: Cognition, learning and games: Proceedings of the 22nd HCI international conference, HCII 2020, 22* (pp. 688–699). Springer International Publishing.

Hamari, J., Koivisto, J., & Sarsa, H. (2014). Does gamification work? – A literature review of empirical studies on gamification. In *47th Hawaii international conference on system sciences* (pp. 3025–3034). IEEE. https://doi.org/10.1109/HICSS.2014.377

Heidegger, M. (1977). *The question concerning technology and other essays*. Harper & Row, translated by W. Lovitt.

Hofacker, C. F., De Ruyter, K., Lurie, N. H., Manchanda, P., & Donaldson, J. (2016). Gamification and mobile marketing effectiveness. *Journal of Interactive Marketing, 34*, 25–36.

Högberg, J., Ramberg, M. O., Gustafsson, A., & Wästlund, E. (2019). Creating brand engagement through in-store gamified customer experiences. *Journal of Retailing and Consumer Services, 50*, 122–130. https://doi.org/10.1016/j.jretconser.2019.05.006

Hyrynsalmi, S., Kimppa, K. K., Koskinen, J., Smed, J., & Hyrynsalmi, S. (2017). The shades of grey: Datenherrschaft in data-driven gamification. In M. Meder, A. Rapp, T. Plumbaum, & F. Hopfgartner (Eds.), *Proceedings of the data-driven gamification design workshop, CEUR-WS, CEUR workshop proceedings* (Vol. 1978, pp. 4–11). http://ceur-ws.org/Vol-1978/paper1.pdf

Hyrynsalmi, S., Smed, J., & Kimppa, K. K. (2017). The dark side of gamification: How we should stop worrying and study also the negative impacts of bringing game design elements to everywhere. In P. Tuomi & A. Perttula (Eds.), *Proceedings of the 1st international GamiFIN conference, CEURWS, CEUR workshop proceedings* (Vol. 1857, pp. 96–109). http://ceur-ws.org/Vol-1857/gamifin17_p13.pdf

Jayasooriya, S., Alles, T., & Thelijjagoda, S. (2020). Demystifying the concept of IoT enabled gamification in retail marketing: An exploratory study. In *2020 International research conference on smart computing and systems engineering (SCSE)* (pp. 234–241). IEEE.

Kazhamiakin, R., Loria, E., Marconi, A., & Scanagatta, M. (2021). A gamification platform to analyze and influence citizens' daily transportation choices. *IEEE Transactions on Intelligent Transportation Systems, 22*(4), 2153–2167.

Khan, I., Melro, A., Amaro, A. C., & Oliveira, L. (2020). Systematic review on gamification and cultural heritage dissemination. *Journal of Digital Media & Interaction, 3*(8), 19–41.

Kim, T. W., & Werbach, K. (2016). More than just a game: Ethical issues in gamification. *Ethics and Information Technology, 18*(2), 157–173. https://doi.org/10.1007/s10676-016-9401-5

Koivisto, J., & Malik, A. (2021). Gamification for older adults: A systematic literature review. *The Gerontologist, 61*(7), e360–e372.

Kriz, W. C., Kikkawa, T., & Sugiura, J. (2022). Manipulation through gamification and gaming. In *Gaming as a cultural commons* (pp. 185–199). Springer.

Kunkel, T., Lock, D., & Doyle, J. P. (2021). Gamification via mobile applications: A longitudinal examination of its impact on attitudinal loyalty and behavior toward a core service. *Psychology & Marketing, 38*(6), 948–964.

Lahtiranta, J., Hyrynsalmi, S., & Koskinen, J. (2017). The false Prometheus: Customer choice, smart devices, and trust. *SIGCAS Computers and Society, 47*(3), 86–97. https://doi.org/10.1145/3144592.3144601

Lowry, P. B., Gaskin, J., Twyman, N. W., Hammer, B., & Roberts, T. L. (2013). Taking 'fun and games' seriously: Proposing the hedonic-motivation system adoption model (HMSAM). *Journal of the Association for Information Systems*, 14(11), 617–671.

Lu, H. P., & Ho, H. C. (2020). Exploring the impact of gamification on users' engagement for sustainable development: A case study in brand applications. *Sustainability*, 12(10), 4169.

Maican, C., Lixandroiu, R., & Constantin, C. (2016). Interactivia. Ro–a study of a gamification framework using zero-cost tools. *Computers in Human Behavior*, 61, 186–197.

Marczewski, A. (2017). The ethics of gamification. *ACM Interactions IX, Fall*, 24(1), 56.

Marques, C. G., Pedro, J. P., & Araújo, I. (2023). A systematic literature review of gamification in/for cultural heritage: Leveling up, going beyond. *Heritage*, 6(8), 5935–5951.

Martin, C., & Tyler, B. (2017). Character creation: Gamification and identity. *Teaching Media Quarterly*, 5(2).

Michalos, A. C. (1995). *A pragmatic approach to business ethics*. Sage.

Mitnick, K. D., & Simon, W. L. (2003). *The art of deception: Con-trolling the human element of security*. Wiley.

Moor, J. H. (1999). Just consequentialism and computing. *Ethics and Information Technology*, 1(1), 61–65. https://doi.org/10. 1023/A:1010078828842

Nyström, T. (2021). Exploring the darkness of gamification: You want it darker?. In *Intelligent computing: Proceedings of the 2021 computing conference* (Vol. 3, pp. 491–506). Springer International Publishing.

Ortega Sánchez, D., & Gómez Trigueros, I. M. (2019). Gamification, social problems, and gender in the teaching of social sciences: Representations and discourse of trainee teachers. *PLoS ONE*, 14(6), e0218869.

Patrício, R., Moreira, A. C., & Zurlo, F. (2021). Enhancing design thinking approaches to innovation through gamification. *European Journal of Innovation Management*, 24(5), 1569–1594.

Paul, B. R., & Elder, L. (2003). *Miniature guide to ethical reasoning*. Foundation for Critical Thinking. https://www.criticalthinking.org/files/Concepts&Tools.pdf

Purwandari, B., Sutoyo, M. A. H., Mishbah, M., & Dzulfikar, M. F. (2019, October). Gamification in E-government: A systematic literature review. In *2019 Fourth international conference on informatics and computing (ICIC)* (pp. 1–5). IEEE.

Raftopoulos, M. (2014). Towards gamification transparency: A conceptual framework for the development of responsible gamified enterprise systems. *Journal of Gaming & Virtual Worlds*, 6(2), 159–178.

Schauster, E., & Neill, M. (2017). Have the ethics changed? An examination of ethics in advertising and public relations agencies. *Journal of Media Ethics*, 32, 45–60.

Shevchuk, N., Degirmenci, K., & Oinas-Kukkonen, H. (2019). Adoption of gamified persuasive systems to encourage sustainable behaviours: Interplay between perceived persuasiveness and cognitive absorption. In *Proceedings of the 40th international conference on information systems, ICIS 2019* (pp. 1–17). Association for Information Systems.

Shi, S., Leung, W. K., & Munelli, F. (2022). Gamification in OTA platforms: A mixed-methods research involving online shopping carnival. *Tourism Management*, 88, 104426.

Sicart, M. (2015). Playing the good life: Gamification and ethics. In S. P. Walz & S. Deterding (Eds.), *Gameful world: Approaches, issues, applications* (pp. 225–244). The MIT Press.

Smed, J., & Hakonen, H. (2017). *Algorithms and networking for computer games* (2nd ed.). Wiley.

Sreejesh, S., Ghosh, T., & Dwivedi, Y. K. (2021). Moving beyond the content: The role of contextual cues in the effectiveness of gamification of advertising. *Journal of Business Research*, *132*, 88–101.

Svenaeus, F. (2001). *The hermeneutics of medicine and the phenomenology of health: Steps towards a philosophy of medical practice* (2nd ed.). Kluwer.

Thorpe, A. S., & Roper, S. (2019). The ethics of gamification in a marketing context. *Journal of Business Ethics*, *155*(2), 597–609. http://www.jstor.org/stable/45023079

Trang, S., & Weiger, W. H. (2021). The perils of gamification: Does engaging with gamified services increase users' willingness to disclose personal information?. *Computers in Human Behavior*, *116*, 106644.

Vanduhe, V. Z., Nat, M., & Hasan, H. F. (2020). Continuance intentions to use gamification for training in higher education: Integrating the technology acceptance model (TAM), social motivation, and task technology fit (TTF). *IEEE Access*, *8*, 21473–21484.

Vashisht, D., & Royne, M. B. (2019). What we know and need to know about the gamification of advertising: A review and synthesis of the advergame studies. *European Journal of Marketing*, *53*(4), 607–634.

Vashisht, D., & Sreejesh, S. (2015). Effects of brand placement strength, prior game playing experience and game involvement on brand recall in advergames. *Journal of Indian Business Research*, *7*(3), 292–312.

Vdov, K. (2020). The effect of gamification on customer experience in the digital environment (Bachelor's thesis, Jyväskylä University of Applied Sciences). Theseus. https://urn.fi/URN:NBN:fi:amk-2020051912403.

Zain, N. H. M., Johari, S. N., Aziz, S. R. A., Teo, N. H. I., Ishak, N. H., & Othman, Z. (2021). Winning the needs of the Gen Z: Gamified health awareness campaign in defeating COVID-19 pandemic. *Procedia Computer Science*, *179*, 974–981.

Zainuddin, Z., Chu, S. K. W., Shujahat, M., & Perera, C. J. (2020). The impact of gamification on learning and instruction: A systematic review of empirical evidence. *Educational Research Review*, *30*, 100326.

Index

accomplishment 7
achievement 145, 148, 152
advertise 132
age differences 110
attitude 160–165
automation 126
autonomy 7, 25, 26

badges 48, 122–124, 130, 131
behaviour(al) 121, 124–126, 128–131, 133; change 193
bibliometric 82, 84, 94
brand 170–188; advocacy 170–177, 179, 181, 183, 184–188; experience 111; interaction 66; love 103, 104, 105, 110–114; loyalty 61, 82, 89, 90, 93, 94; perception 73, 74; satisfaction 73, 74
business 122, 123, 125, 127–129, 131–133
buying 122, 125, 127–130, 133

challenges 143, 145–148, 151
challenge-skill balance 27
chat room 8
clear feedback 27
co-creation 87, 92–94
cognitive 143, 145, 148
Cognitive Evaluation Theory (CET) 43
collaboration 32, 34, 35
communication 7, 124, 128, 170–177, 179, 181, 183–188
conceptual framework 108, 109
consumer 121, 124–128, 130–133; behaviour 111; perception 58; preference 58
content analysis 42

correlation 110, 113
crowdsourcing 25–35
cultural 143, 238, 238, 239, 241, 241
customer 121, 122, 125–133, 170, 171, 173–175, 178–183, 185, 186; engagement 103, 104, 106, 107, 109, 110, 112, 114
cybertext 8

demographic 112
descriptive 84, 86
digital 121–130, 132, 133
digital innovation 4
digitalization 122
discount 121, 122, 126, 128, 130
discriminant validity 113
diversity 237, 238, 239, 240, 241
Dual Systems Theory 29
dynamics 148

eco-friendly 192–194, 197, 201–204, 206, 208–212, 215
ecosystems 144
education 144, 147, 152
efficacy 144, 146, 149, 150
emotional 106–108, 110, 111, 114, 115
endorsement 185
engagement 143–147, 150, 152, 170–176, 179, 180, 182, 184–188
engaging 143, 145, 146, 149, 151
enhance 122, 123, 125–128
enjoyment 121, 123, 124, 126
environment 145–149
equilibrium 147
Ethical Decision-Making Framework 30
ethics 223, 224, 232–235
evidence 150

experiences 108, 109, 111, 112, 114, 115
exploitation 228, 235

fascination 126
fatigue 32, 143–153
feasibility 148
First Cry 64
focus group 112, 188

game design 81, 88
game elements 123, 124, 130, 133
gameful 49
game mechanics 125, 130, 131
gamification 6, 7, 49
gamification strategies 59, 60
gamified marketing 109, 112, 113
goal-setting theory 28
government 225, 227, 228

Hamleys 65
healthcare 144, 147
hedonic 157, 160, 161, 163–165
hypotheses development 109, 110
hypothetical 150–152

immersive 143–145, 147–153
implementation 143, 150, 152, 153
implications 114, 146–148, 150–153, 232–234, 237, 241
influencer 160–163, 165–167
intention 167
internet 126, 128, 129

latent variables 112, 113
leaderboards 48, 124
loyalty 170, 171, 173, 174, 178–180, 182, 184, 185, 187

marketing 103–107, 109, 110, 112, 157–159, 165–167, 170–172, 174, 176, 184, 185, 222–226, 228–230, 232, 234, 236, 238, 240, 241
message board 8
minimizing 150
mitigate 145, 146, 148
motivation 24, 31, 32, 35, 81, 91–94, 143, 144, 150

narratology 8
non-gaming 143, 145

online 124, 126, 127, 129–133; platforms 103, 104; travel agencies 103, 104
organizations 123, 125, 127

perceived 123, 125
performance 146
personalization 27
perspective 145, 147
player agency 9
playfulness 123, 125–128, 130, 131
pleasure 122–128, 130
points 121–124, 130–132
policymakers 144, 146, 151, 152
population 112
price 126–128
promotion 170, 171, 178, 179, 183, 184, 188
psychology 144, 146, 151–153
purchases 126, 128, 129

questionnaire 112

relatedness 25, 26, 31
reliability 112, 113
research 144, 147–153
research design 111
research methodology 111
rewards 121, 122, 127, 131, 132
rhetoric 5

satisfaction 125, 131, 143–145, 147, 149, 152
scoreboards 48
Self-Determination Theory (SDT) 6, 25, 26, 31, 44
shopping 104, 107, 121, 126, 127, 129, 133, 134
skill development 32–34
social gratification 172, 174–176, 181, 185
Social Identity Theory 28
social media 170–180, 182–188
start-up 170–175, 177–188
strategy(ies) 121, 126, 131–133, 144, 147, 151, 174–177, 182, 186
stressful 149
structural model 113
sustainability marketing 192–197, 201–203, 207, 208, 210–212, 214, 215

techniques 124–127
technologies 143, 146, 148, 152
Technology Acceptance Model (TAM)
    29, 30
tourism 143–153
tourist experience 143–147,
    151, 153
tourists 144, 150–152
tourist satisfaction 144, 149
traditionally 146
transformation 1, 5, 145

unavailability 150
Until Dawn 5–21
user engagement 49, 60, 61, 170–172,
    175, 179, 182, 184–188
user experience 104
utilitarian 160, 161, 163, 165

validity 112, 113
variance 112, 113
virtual reality 143–145, 148
vulnerable 144

Milton Keynes UK
Ingram Content Group UK Ltd.
UKHW031329071224
451979UK00005B/87

9 781032 694177